First World War
and Army of Occupation
War Diary
France, Belgium and Germany

7 DIVISION
91 Infantry Brigade
Headquarters
1 January 1917 - 30 November 1917

WO95/1667

The Naval & Military Press Ltd
www.nmarchive.com
Published in association with The National Archives

Published by

The Naval & Military Press Ltd

Unit 10 Ridgewood Industrial Park,
Uckfield, East Sussex,
TN22 5QE England
Tel: +44 (0) 1825 749494

www.naval-military-press.com

www.nmarchive.com

This diary has been reprinted in facsimile from the original. Any imperfections are inevitably reproduced and the quality may fall short of modern type and cartographic standards.

© Crown Copyright
Images reproduced by permission of The National Archives, London, England, 2015.

Contents

Document type	Place/Title	Date From	Date To
Heading	7th Division. B.H.Q. 91st Infantry Brigade. January 1917		
War Diary	Beaussart	01/01/1917	10/01/1917
War Diary	Q 17 A 8. B	11/01/1917	12/01/1917
War Diary	Beaussart.	13/01/1917	21/01/1917
War Diary	Puchevillers	21/01/1917	31/01/1917
Operation(al) Order(s)	91st Infantry Brigade. Instructions For Forthcoming Operations-No. 3. Appendix 1	01/01/1917	01/01/1917
Operation(al) Order(s)	7th Division Order No. 120. Appendix 2	02/01/1917	02/01/1917
Operation(al) Order(s)	20th Infantry Brigade Order No. 109. Appendix 2 A	01/01/1917	01/01/1917
Operation(al) Order(s)	91st Infantry Brigade. Instructions For Forthcoming Operations-No. 4. Appendix 3	02/01/1917	02/01/1917
Operation(al) Order(s)	91st Infantry Brigade. Instructions For Forthcoming Operations-No. 5. Appendix 4	04/01/1917	04/01/1917
Operation(al) Order(s)	91st Infantry Brigade. Instructions For Forthcoming Operations-No. 6. Appendix 5	06/01/1917	06/01/1917
Miscellaneous	91st Infantry Brigade. Addendum To Instructions For Forthcoming Operations-No. 6.	06/01/1917	06/01/1917
Operation(al) Order(s)	22nd, Infantry Brigade Operation Order No. 106. By Lieut. Colonel A.G. Pritchard, C.M.G. Appendix 5 A	03/01/1917	03/01/1917
Miscellaneous	March Table		
Operation(al) Order(s)	20th Infantry Brigade Order No. 110. Appendix 5 B	03/01/1917	03/01/1917
Miscellaneous	Relief Table		
Operation(al) Order(s)	91st Infantry Brigade. Instructions For Forthcoming Operations No.7. Appendix 6	09/01/1917	09/01/1917
Miscellaneous	Relief Table		
Miscellaneous	91st Infantry Brigade. Amendments To Instructions For Forthcoming Operations. Appendix 6 A	09/01/1917	09/01/1917
Miscellaneous	Narrative Of Attack On Union Trench. Appendix 7		
Miscellaneous	Headquarters, 22nd Infantry Brigade.		
Map			
Map	Redan		
Map	Attack On Munich Trench By 91st Infantry Brigade Jan. 11th 1917.		
Operation(al) Order(s)	91st Infantry Brigade Operation Order No. 58. Appendix 8	12/01/1917	12/01/1917
Miscellaneous	Relief Table		
Operation(al) Order(s)	Amendment To 91st Infantry Brigade Operation Order No. 59.	20/01/1917	20/01/1917
Miscellaneous	Weekly Programme Of Training. 91st Infantry Brigade.		
Miscellaneous	Instructions In The Event Of The 7Th Division Being Orders To Reinforce The Vth Corps Front. Appendix 11		
Miscellaneous			
Miscellaneous	March Table To Accompany 91st Infantry Brigade No. B.M. /1056.		
Heading	Headquarters. 91st Infantry Brigade February 1917		
War Diary	Puchevillers	01/02/1917	20/02/1917
War Diary	Bertrancourt	20/02/1917	20/02/1917
War Diary	Mailly Maillet	21/02/1917	26/02/1917

Type	Description	Start	End
War Diary	Beaussart	26/02/1917	28/02/1917
Miscellaneous	91st Infantry Brigade. Programme Of Training For Week Ending 10th February. 1917. Appendix 1		
Miscellaneous	91st Infantry Brigade. Programme Of Training For Week Ending 17th February, 1917. Appendix 2		
Miscellaneous	B.M./1082/1.		
Operation(al) Order(s)	7th Division Order No. 130. Appendix 4	19/02/1917	19/02/1917
Miscellaneous	March Table To Accompany 7th Division Order No. 130		
Operation(al) Order(s)	91st Infantry Brigade Operation Order No. 60. Appendix 4 A.	19/02/1917	19/02/1917
Miscellaneous	March Table		
Operation(al) Order(s)	91st Infantry Brigade Operation Order No. 61. Appendix 5	20/02/1917	20/02/1917
Miscellaneous	Relief Table.		
Miscellaneous			
Operation(al) Order(s)	91st Infantry Brigade. Summary Of Operation-No. 17. Appendix 6	21/02/1917	22/02/1917
Operation(al) Order(s)	91st Infantry Brigade. Summary Of Operations-No. 18 Appendix 7	22/02/1917	23/02/1917
Operation(al) Order(s)	91st Infantry Brigade. Summary Of Operations-No. 19. Appendix 8	23/02/1917	24/02/1917
Operation(al) Order(s)	91st Infantry Brigade Operation Order No. 63 Appendix 9	24/02/1917	24/02/1917
Miscellaneous	Messages		
Miscellaneous	Report on Operations Against Serre.	03/03/1917	03/03/1917
Miscellaneous	On His Majesty's Service.		
Heading	Headquarters 91st Infantry Brigade March 1917		
War Diary	Beaussart	01/03/1917	11/03/1917
War Diary	Appletrees (Q 2 B)	12/03/1917	14/03/1917
War Diary	Beaussart	15/03/1917	18/03/1917
War Diary	Appletrees (Q 2 B)	18/03/1917	23/03/1917
War Diary	Ablainzevelle	23/03/1917	24/03/1917
War Diary	Courcelles Le Comte	25/03/1917	26/03/1917
War Diary	Ervillers.	27/03/1917	31/03/1917
Operation(al) Order(s)	91st Infantry Brigade Operation Order No. 64. Appendix 1	12/03/1917	12/03/1917
Miscellaneous	91st Infantry Brigade. Summary Of Intelligence-No. 22. Appendix 2		
Operation(al) Order(s)	91st Infantry Brigade Operation Order No. 65. Appendix 3	12/03/1917	12/03/1917
Miscellaneous	B.M./1140. Scheme For Attack On Bucquoy To Be Carried Out By 7th Division.		
Miscellaneous	A Form. Messages And Signals.		
Miscellaneous	Narrative Of Attack On Bucquoy carried Out By 91st Infantry Brigade On Night 13/14th March, 1917.		
Miscellaneous	War Diary,		
Operation(al) Order(s)	91st Infantry Brigade Operation Order No. 66. Appendix 4	14/03/1917	14/03/1917
Operation(al) Order(s)	91st Infantry Brigade Operation Order No. 67.	24/03/1917	24/03/1917
Miscellaneous			
Operation(al) Order(s)	91st Infantry Brigade Operation Order No. 68.	26/03/1917	26/03/1917
Miscellaneous	Amendments And Additions To 91st Infantry Brigade Operation Order No. 68.	27/03/1917	27/03/1917
Miscellaneous	On His Majesty's Service.		
Heading	Headquarters 91st Infantry Brigade April 1917		

War Diary	Ervillers	01/04/1917	02/04/1917
War Diary	Bucquoy	03/04/1917	11/04/1917
War Diary	Ablainzevelle	11/04/1917	12/04/1917
War Diary	Bucquoy	12/04/1917	18/04/1917
War Diary	L'Homme Mort	18/04/1917	21/04/1917
War Diary	Ablainzevelle	21/04/1917	30/04/1917
War Diary	L'Homme Mort	30/04/1917	30/04/1917
Miscellaneous	Narrative Of Attack On Croisilles Carried Out By 91st Infantry Brigade On 28th March. 1917.		
Operation(al) Order(s)	91st Infantry Brigade Operation Order No. 69.	31/03/1917	31/03/1917
Miscellaneous	Additions And Amendments To 91st Infantry Brigade Operation Order No. 69.	01/04/1917	01/04/1917
Miscellaneous	91st Infantry Brigade. Administrative Instructions (Issued In Connection With 91st Infantry Brigade Operation Order No. 69.	01/04/1917	01/04/1917
Operation(al) Order(s)	91st Infantry Brigade Operation Order No. 70.	02/04/1917	02/04/1917
Miscellaneous	Appendix 3 A		
Miscellaneous	Narrative of attack on Croisilles Carried Out By 91st Infantry Brigade on 2nd April, 1917	13/04/1917	13/04/1917
Miscellaneous	Appendix "A".		
Miscellaneous	Copy Appendix 3 C		
Operation(al) Order(s)	7th Division Order No. 144.	03/04/1917	03/04/1917
Operation(al) Order(s)	91st Infantry Brigade Operation Order No. 71.	14/04/1917	14/04/1917
Miscellaneous	March Table. (Issued With 91st Infantry Brigade Operation Order No. 71.)		
Miscellaneous	91st Infantry Brigade. Summary Of Intelligence-No. 1.		
Miscellaneous	91st Infantry Brigade. Summary Of Intelligence-No. 2.	20/04/1917	20/04/1917
Miscellaneous	91st Infantry Brigade. Summary Of Intelligence-No. 3.	21/04/1917	21/04/1917
Operation(al) Order(s)	7th Division Order No. 149.	20/04/1917	20/04/1917
Operation(al) Order(s)	91st Infantry Brigade Operation Order No. 72.	20/04/1917	20/04/1917
Miscellaneous	S. C / 1823 / 11.	20/04/1917	20/04/1917
Operation(al) Order(s)	7th Division Order No. 150.	27/04/1917	27/04/1917
Operation(al) Order(s)	91st Infantry Brigade Operation Order No. 75.	27/04/1917	27/04/1917
Miscellaneous			
Miscellaneous	91st Infantry Brigade. Summary Of Intelligence-No. 4.	30/04/1917	30/04/1917
Heading	B.H.Q. 91st Infantry Brigade. May 1917.		
War Diary	L'Homme Mort	01/05/1917	01/05/1917
War Diary	Gomiecourt	02/05/1917	03/05/1917
War Diary	Courcelles	04/05/1917	05/05/1917
War Diary	Gomiecourt	06/05/1917	10/05/1917
War Diary	L'Hommemort	10/05/1917	10/05/1917
War Diary	L'Hommemort Ecoust	11/05/1917	11/05/1917
War Diary	Ecoust	12/05/1917	15/05/1917
War Diary	Achiet Le Petit	16/05/1917	28/05/1917
War Diary	Courcelles	29/05/1917	31/05/1917
Operation(al) Order(s)	B.M./494. To All Recipients Of O. O. 74.	01/05/1917	01/05/1917
Miscellaneous	91st Infantry Brigade Operation Order No. 74.	30/04/1917	30/04/1917
Miscellaneous	91st Infantry Brigade. Summary Of Intelligence-No. 5.	01/05/1917	01/05/1917
Operation(al) Order(s)	91st Infantry Brigade Operation Order No. 75.	09/05/1917	09/05/1917
Operation(al) Order(s)	91st Infantry Brigade Operation Order No. 76. Appendix 3	10/05/1917	10/05/1917
Operation(al) Order(s)	Administrative Instructions With Reference To Operation Order No. 76.	10/05/1917	10/05/1917
Operation(al) Order(s)	91st Infantry Brigade Operation Order No. 77. Appendix 4	12/05/1917	12/05/1917

Operation(al) Order(s)	91st Infantry Brigade Operation Order No. 78. Appendix 5	12/05/1917	12/05/1917
Miscellaneous			
Operation(al) Order(s)	91st Infantry Brigade Operation Order No. 79. Appendix 6	13/05/1917	13/05/1917
Miscellaneous	Instructions For Capture Of Red Patch.	13/05/1917	13/05/1917
Operation(al) Order(s)	91st Infantry Brigade Operation Order No. 80. Appendix 8	13/05/1917	13/05/1917
Operation(al) Order(s)	91st Infantry Brigade Operation Order No. 81. Appendix 9	14/05/1917	14/05/1917
Miscellaneous	Relief Table. (Reference Operation Order No. 81.)		
Operation(al) Order(s)	91st Infantry Brigade Operation Order No. 82. Appendix 10	15/05/1917	15/05/1917
Miscellaneous	Relief Table		
Miscellaneous	Casualties For Period 11th May To 15th May 1917. Appendix II		
Miscellaneous	91st Infantry Brigade. Narrative Of Operations Against Bullecourt-11th To 15th May, 1917.	27/05/1917	27/05/1917
Operation(al) Order(s)	91st Infantry Brigade Operation Order No. 83. Appendix 13	27/05/1917	27/05/1917
Miscellaneous	March Table (Issued With Operation Order No. 83)		
Operation(al) Order(s)	91st Infantry Brigade Operation Order No. 84. Appendix 14	29/05/1917	29/05/1917
Miscellaneous	C Form Messages And Signals.		
Heading	7th Division B.H.Q. 91st Infantry Brigade. June 1917		
War Diary	Courcelles	01/06/1917	23/06/1917
War Diary	Mort Homme	24/06/1917	30/06/1917
Miscellaneous	Programme Of Training-91st Infantry Brigade.		
Operation(al) Order(s)	91st Infantry Brigade Order No. 2. Appendix 2	05/06/1917	05/06/1917
Miscellaneous			
Operation(al) Order(s)	91st Infantry Brigade Order No. 1. Appendix 3	04/06/1917	04/06/1917
Operation(al) Order(s)	91st Infantry Brigade Order No. 3. Appendix 4	12/06/1917	12/06/1917
Miscellaneous			
Operation(al) Order(s)	91st Infantry Brigade Order No. 4. Appendix 5	18/06/1917	18/06/1917
Operation(al) Order(s)	91st Infantry Brigade Order No. 5.	20/06/1917	20/06/1917
Miscellaneous	Table Issued With 91st Infantry Brigade Order No.5.		
Operation(al) Order(s)	91st Infantry Brigade Order No. 6.	26/06/1917	26/06/1917
Operation(al) Order(s)	21st Battalion The Manchester Regiment. Operation Order No. 65	26/06/1917	26/06/1917
Operation(al) Order(s)	Addendum To Operation Order No. ?	27/06/1917	27/06/1917
Miscellaneous	Operation Orders By Lieut.-Colonel. A.B. Beauman. D.S.O. Commanding,-Bn. South Staffordshire Regiment.	27/06/1917	27/06/1917
Operation(al) Order(s)	Wave Operation Orders. No. 48		
Miscellaneous	Operation Orders	27/06/1917	27/06/1917
Miscellaneous	Brigade H. Q		
Miscellaneous	Warning Order.	18/06/1917	18/06/1917
Operation(al) Order(s)	7th Division Order No. 161.	18/06/1917	18/06/1917
Miscellaneous			
Operation(al) Order(s)	Amendments To 7th Division Order No. 161.	20/06/1917	20/06/1917
Heading	7th Division B.H.Q. 91st Infantry Brigade. July 1917		
War Diary	L'Homme Mort	01/07/1917	31/07/1917
Operation(al) Order(s)	91st Infantry Brigade Order No. 7.	02/07/1917	02/07/1917
Miscellaneous	Appen "A"		
Operation(al) Order(s)	91st Infantry Brigade Order No. 8.	06/07/1917	06/07/1917
Miscellaneous			

Type	Description	Date From	Date To
Map			
Operation(al) Order(s)	Amendment To 91st Infantry Brigade Order No. 8.	08/07/1917	08/07/1917
Operation(al) Order(s)	91st Infantry Brigade Order No. 9.	08/07/1917	08/07/1917
Operation(al) Order(s)	91st Infantry Brigade Order No. 10.	11/07/1917	11/07/1917
Operation(al) Order(s)	Amendments And Additions To 91st Infantry Brigade Order No. 8.	13/07/1917	13/07/1917
Miscellaneous	Report On Raid Carried Out By 1st Bn. South Staffordshire Regt., Night 14/15th July, 1917.	15/07/1917	15/07/1917
Operation(al) Order(s)	91st Infantry Brigade Order No. 11.	19/07/1917	19/07/1917
Miscellaneous	91st Infantry Brigade. Defence Scheme.		
Map	Croisilles		
Map			
Operation(al) Order(s)	91st Infantry Brigade Order No. 12.	27/07/1917	27/07/1917
Miscellaneous	7th Division No. G. 938	07/07/1917	07/07/1917
Operation(al) Order(s)	20th Infantry Brigade Order No. 148	09/07/1917	09/07/1917
Operation(al) Order(s)	Lake Operation Order No. 71	15/07/1917	15/07/1917
Heading	7th Division. B.H.Q. 91st Infantry Brigade. August 1917.		
War Diary	L'Homme Mort	01/08/1917	07/08/1917
War Diary	Pommier	08/08/1917	10/08/1917
Miscellaneous			
War Diary	Pommier	11/08/1917	27/08/1917
War Diary	Grenas	28/08/1917	28/08/1917
War Diary	Ouderdom	29/08/1917	31/08/1917
Operation(al) Order(s)	91st Infantry Brigade Order No. 13	05/08/1917	05/08/1917
Operation(al) Order(s)	Amendments To 91st Infantry Brigade Order No. 13.	07/08/1917	07/08/1917
Miscellaneous	March Table (To Accompany Brigade Order No. 13.)		
Map	Secret.		
Map	Fifth Army		
Miscellaneous	General Idea		
Operation(al) Order(s)	91st Infantry Brigade Order No. 500 (A).	20/08/1917	20/08/1917
Miscellaneous	Notes.		
Map			
Operation(al) Order(s)	91st Infantry Brigade Order No. 14.	27/08/1917	27/08/1917
Miscellaneous	March Table (To Accompany 91st Inf. Order No. 14)		
Operation(al) Order(s)	91st Infantry Brigade Order No. 15.	27/08/1917	27/08/1917
Miscellaneous	Entrainment Table (to Accompany 91st Inf. Bde. Order No. 15)		
Heading	7th Division. B.H.Q. 91st Infantry Brigade. September 1917.		
War Diary	Ouderdom	01/09/1917	01/09/1917
War Diary	Steenvoorde	02/09/1917	02/09/1917
War Diary	Le Nieppe	03/09/1917	12/09/1917
War Diary	Arques	13/09/1917	14/09/1917
War Diary	Boisdinghem	15/09/1917	27/09/1917
War Diary	Elnes	28/09/1917	28/09/1917
War Diary	St Hubeqiushoek	29/09/1917	30/09/1917
Operation(al) Order(s)	91st Infantry Brigade Order No. 16.	01/09/1917	01/09/1917
Operation(al) Order(s)	91st Infantry Brigade Order No. 17.	02/09/1917	02/09/1917
Miscellaneous	March Table (to Accompany 91st Inf. Order No. 17)		
Operation(al) Order(s)	91st Infantry Brigade Order No. 18.	12/09/1917	12/09/1917
Miscellaneous	March Table For September 13th, 1917 Issued With 91st Infantry Brigade Order No. 18.		
Miscellaneous	March Table For September 15th, 1917 Issued With 91st Infantry Brigade Order No 18.		
Miscellaneous	Brigade Scheme No. 1. Appx 4		

Type	Description	Date 1	Date 2
Miscellaneous	Brigade Scheme No. 2. Appx 5		
Miscellaneous Diagram etc			
Operation(al) Order(s)	91st Infantry Brigade Order No. P1.	21/09/1917	21/09/1917
Map			
Operation(al) Order(s)	Appendix 1 To 91st Infantry Brigade Order No. 21.	22/09/1917	22/09/1917
Operation(al) Order(s)	Appendix 3 To 91st Infantry Brigade Order No. P1	23/09/1917	23/09/1917
Miscellaneous	Schedule "A".		
Operation(al) Order(s)	Additions And Amendments To 91st Infantry Brigade Order No. P. 1.	23/09/1917	23/09/1917
Operation(al) Order(s)	91st Infantry Brigade Order No. P.2.	25/09/1917	25/09/1917
Operation(al) Order(s)	Appendix 1. To 91st Infantry Brigade Order No. P. 2.	26/09/1917	26/09/1917
Operation(al) Order(s)	Administrative Instructions In Connection With 91st Infantry Brigade Order No. P. 2.	25/09/1917	25/09/1917
Operation(al) Order(s)	91st Infantry Brigade Order No. 19.	27/09/1917	27/09/1917
Miscellaneous	March Table (Issued With 91st Infantry Brigade Order No. 19).		
Miscellaneous	3. C. / 915. Reference 91st Infantry Brigade Order No. 19.	27/09/1917	27/09/1917
Operation(al) Order(s)	1st Infantry Brigade Order No. 20.	28/09/1917	28/09/1917
Miscellaneous	Entraining Table		
Miscellaneous	March Table-Personnel.		
Miscellaneous	March Table-Transport.		
Heading	7th Division B.H.Q. 91st Infantry Brigade October 1917		
War Diary	St Hubertushoek	01/10/1917	02/10/1917
War Diary	Hooge	03/10/1917	06/10/1917
War Diary	Chateau Segard	07/10/1917	10/10/1917
War Diary	St Hubertushoek	11/10/1917	11/10/1917
War Diary	Thieushouk	12/10/1917	21/10/1917
War Diary	Carnarvon Camp	22/10/1917	22/10/1917
War Diary	Fairy House	23/10/1917	24/10/1917
War Diary	Canada Street	25/10/1917	26/10/1917
War Diary	Reninghelst	27/10/1917	28/10/1917
War Diary	Ebblinghem	29/10/1917	31/10/1917
Operation(al) Order(s)	91st Infantry Brigade Order No. 21.	02/10/1917	02/10/1917
Operation(al) Order(s)	91st Infantry Brigade Order No. 22.	02/10/1917	02/10/1917
Operation(al) Order(s)	Appendix 1. To 91st Infantry Brigade Order No. 22.	02/10/1917	02/10/1917
Miscellaneous	Time Table Of Assembly March To Accompany Appendix 1.		
Operation(al) Order(s)	Appendix 2. To 91st Infantry Brigade Order No. 22.	02/10/1917	02/10/1917
Miscellaneous	B. M/22/1 To All Recipients Of BO 22.		
Operation(al) Order(s)	Administrative Instructions In Connection With 91st Infantry Bde. Order No. 22	01/10/1917	01/10/1917
Miscellaneous	Schedule A.		
Map			
Miscellaneous	App 2		
Operation(al) Order(s)	91st Infantry Brigade Order No. 23.	09/10/1917	09/10/1917
Operation(al) Order(s)	91st Infantry Brigade Order No. 24.	12/10/1917	12/10/1917
Miscellaneous	To All Recipients Of B. O. 24.	12/10/1917	12/10/1917
Miscellaneous	Narrative Of Operation Of 91st Infantry Brigade October 4th-6th, 1917.	14/10/1917	14/10/1917
Operation(al) Order(s)	91st Infantry Brigade Order No. 26.	21/10/1917	21/10/1917
Miscellaneous			
Miscellaneous	Amendment To 91st Infantry Brigade Order No. 26.	22/10/1917	22/10/1917
Operation(al) Order(s)	91st Infantry Brigade Order No. 28.	22/10/1917	22/10/1917

Miscellaneous	March Table. (To Accompany Brigade Order No. 28.)		
Operation(al) Order(s)	91st Infantry Brigade Order No. 29.	28/10/1917	28/10/1917
Miscellaneous	Reference 91st Infantry Brigade Order No. 29.	28/10/1917	28/10/1917
Operation(al) Order(s)	91st Infantry Brigade Order No. 27.	22/10/1917	22/10/1917
Operation(al) Order(s)	Appendix 3 To 91st Infantry Brigade Order No. 27.	23/10/1917	23/10/1917
Operation(al) Order(s)	Appendix 4 To 91st Infantry Brigade Order No. 27.	25/10/1917	25/10/1917
Operation(al) Order(s)	Administrative Instructions In Connection With 91st Infantry Brigade Order No. 27	21/10/1917	21/10/1917
Operation(al) Order(s)	Amendments And Additions To Administrative Instructions In Connection With 91st Infantry Brigade Order No. 27.	23/10/1917	23/10/1917
Miscellaneous	Further Amendments And Additions To Administrative Instructions In Connection With 91st Infantry Brigade Order No. 27.	24/10/1917	24/10/1917
Operation(al) Order(s)	91st Infantry Brigade Order No. 28.	22/10/1917	22/10/1917
Miscellaneous	March Table. (To Accompany Brigade Order No. 28.)		
Operation(al) Order(s)	Appendix 2 To 91st Infantry Brigade Order No. 27.	23/10/1917	23/10/1917
Operation(al) Order(s)	Appendix No.1. To 91st Infantry Brigade Order No. 27.	23/10/1917	23/10/1917
Heading	7th Division B.H.Q. 91st Infantry Brigade November 1917		
War Diary	Ebblinghem	01/11/1917	10/11/1917
War Diary	Blequin	11/11/1917	11/11/1917
War Diary	Campagne	12/11/1917	12/11/1917
War Diary	Fruges	13/11/1917	13/11/1917
War Diary	Tangry	14/11/1917	16/11/1917
War Diary	Tangry And Train	17/11/1917	17/11/1917
War Diary	Train	18/11/1917	23/11/1917
War Diary	Roveredo	24/11/1917	26/11/1917
War Diary	Agucliaro	27/11/1917	27/11/1917
War Diary	Ponte Di Barbarano	28/11/1917	29/11/1917
War Diary	Crisic Nana	30/11/1917	30/11/1917
Operation(al) Order(s)	91st Infantry Brigade Order No. 30.	07/11/1917	07/11/1917
Miscellaneous	March Table. (Issued With 91st Infantry Brigade Order No. 30.)		
Miscellaneous	Addendum to 91st Infantry Brigade Order No. 30.	07/11/1917	07/11/1917
Operation(al) Order(s)	91st Infantry Brigade Order No. 31.	09/11/1917	09/11/1917
Miscellaneous	Marche Table. (Issued With 91st Infantry Brigade Order No. 31.)		
Operation(al) Order(s)	Amendments And Additions To 91st Infantry Brigade Order No. 31.	09/11/1917	09/11/1917
Miscellaneous	March Table. (Issued With Amendments Additions To 91st Inf. Bde. Order No. 31.)		
Operation(al) Order(s)	91st Infantry Brigade Order No. 32.	11/11/1917	11/11/1917
Miscellaneous	March Table (Issued With 91st Infantry Brigade Order No. 32.)		
Operation(al) Order(s)	91st Infantry Brigade Order No. 33.	12/11/1917	12/11/1917
Miscellaneous	March Table. (Issued With 91st Infantry Brigade Order No. 33.)		
Operation(al) Order(s)	91st Infantry Brigade Order No. 34.	13/11/1917	13/11/1917
Miscellaneous	March Table (Issued With 91st Infantry Brigade Order No. 34.)		
Miscellaneous	Narrative Of Operations Of 91st Infantry Brigade. 26th October, 1917.	14/11/1917	14/11/1917
Operation(al) Order(s)	91st Infantry Brigade Order No. 35.	15/11/1917	15/11/1917
Miscellaneous	Instructions For Entraining Of 91st Infantry Brigade Commencing 17th November, 1917.	15/11/1917	15/11/1917

Miscellaneous
Operation(al) Order(s)   91st Infantry Brigade Order No. 36.   27/11/1917   27/11/1917
Operation(al) Order(s)   91st Infantry Brigade Order No. 37.   29/11/1917   29/11/1917

7th DIVISION.

B. H. Q.

91st INFANTRY BRIGADE.

JANUARY 1917.

Army Form C. 2118.

WAR DIARY or INTELLIGENCE SUMMARY

(Erase heading not required.)

91st Infantry Brigade   January 1917

Place	Date	Hour	Summary of Events and Information	Remarks and references to Appendices
BEAUSSART	1-1-17		Showery – Casualties NIL. Reinforcements NIL.	Appendix 1 MB
"	2-1-17		Showery – 2nd Bn Queens Regt relieved 9th Bn Devon Regt in R & Sector. Remaining under "orders" of 20th Infy Bde. Casualties NIL. Reinforcements 1/5th S.Staffs Regt 2 O.R. 21st Manchester Regt 5 O.R.	Appendix 2. 2A MB
"	3-1-17		Showery. Casualties 2nd Bn Queens Regt 1 O.R. killed, 2 O.R. wounded. Reinforcements 2nd Bn Queens 6 O.R. 1st S.Staffs Regt 2 O.R. 21st Manchester Regt 3 officers. 22nd Manchester Regt 2 officers. 9th MGC 6 O.R.	Appendix 3 MB
"	4-1-17		Heavy rain in morning. Remainder of day fine. Casualties 2nd Bn Queens Regt 4 O.R. wounded. Reinforcements 2nd Bn Queens Regt 1 officer & 100 O.R. 1/5 S.Staffs Regt 1 officer & 100 O.R.	MB
"	5-1-17		Fine but cold – Casualties 2nd Queens Regt 1 officer wounded. Reinforcements 1/5 S.Staffs Regt 7 O.R. Post K 35 & 17 recaptured and Post K 35 & 88 captured.	Appendix 4. MB
"	6-1-17		Hot night. Fine during day. 2nd Rifle Queens Regt relieved in R & Sector by 2nd Bn Manchester Regt. 2nd Queens Regt went on billets in Mailly Maillet from 22nd Manchester Regt. 22nd Manchester Regt went into Y Camp BERTRANCOURT. Casualties 2nd Queens Regt 3 O.R. killed, 5 wounded. 1st S.Staffs 1 O.R. killed 1 O.R. wounded. 21st Manchester Regt 1 O.R. wounded. Reinforcements 7 O.R. 22nd Manchester Regt	Appendix 5. 5A + B MB
"	7-1-17.		Frosty and fine. Casualties 2nd Queens 2 officers 1 O.R. missing. Reinforcements 1 O.R. 1st S.Staffs Regt.	MB
"	8-1-17		Showery. Casualties 2nd Queens Regt 1 O.R. missing. Reinforcements 1/5 S.Staffs Regt 5 O.R. 22nd Manchester Regt 1 officer. 2nd Queens Regt 4-3 O.R.	MB MB
"	9-1-17		Fine. Casualties NIL. Reinforcements 2nd Queens Regt 2 officers. 22nd Manchester Regt 4 officers & 6 O.R.	MB MB

Army Form C. 2118.

WAR DIARY
or
INTELLIGENCE SUMMARY

(Erase heading not required.)

9th Infantry Brigade

Place	Date	Hour	Summary of Events and Information	Remarks and references to Appendices
BEAUCOURT	10.1.17		The Bde moved up to support at Q.17.a.3.8. - 2nd Queens Regt. moved Beaumont Hamel. 1st South Staffs Regt 2nd & 23rd Manchester Regt moved to dug outs in BEAUMONT HAMEL.	MR
Q.17.a.3.8.	11.1.17		Misty morning. Clearing up later. Some guns. 2nd Manchester on right, 1st South Staff centre, 21st Manchester on left. Brigade attacked MUNICH TRENCH at 6.am from Q.6.c.6.5. to K.36.c.15 and LAGER ALLEY from K.36.c.15 to K.35.d.58. Captured and consolidated. Ground extremely bad making consolidation very difficult.	MR Appendix 7
Q.17.a.28	12.1.17		Some rain. Brigade relieved by 22nd Infantry Brigade during night 12/13. Casualties 10th to 13th	MR Appendix 8 MR

	Killed		Wounded		Missing	
	Officers	O.R.	Officers	O.R.	Officers	O.R.
2nd Bn. Queens Regt.	-	-	-	3	-	-
1st Bn. S. Staffs Regt.	-	8	4	81	1	9
21st Bn. Manchester Regt.	2	17	2	66	-	3
22nd Bn. Manchester Regt.	1	15	-	54	1	8
Total	3	40	6	204	2	20

Reinforcement 16th b. 73rd N/L

Army Form C. 2118.

WAR DIARY
or
INTELLIGENCE SUMMARY

(Erase heading not required.)

9th Infantry Brigade

Place	Date	Hour	Summary of Events and Information	Remarks and references to Appendices
BEAUSSART	13.1.17		Brigade HQrs moved back to BEAUSSART. 2nd Bn. Queens to BERTRANCOURT. 1st Bn. Lincoln Regt to MAILLY WOOD. 2/1st Manchester Regt to Camp P.17.a. 22nd Bn Manchester Regt to MAILLY.	MB
"	14.1.17		Cold with some snow. Very cold day with snow and sleet. Casualties NIL. Reinforcements NIL.	MB
"	15.1.17		HQrs. Casualties NIL. Reinforcements 2nd Bn Queens Regt 1 Officer 110 O.R. 2nd Bn Queens Regt moved from BERTRANCOURT to MAILLY MAILLET.	MB
"	16.1.17		HQrs. Casualties 1st Bn L. Staffs Regt 1 O.R. killed 2 O.R. wounded. Reinforcements 1st Bn S. Staffs Regt 3 O.R. 2/1st Bn Manchester Regt 4 Officers 104 O.R. 22nd Bn Manchester Regt 2 Offrs 80 O.R.	MB
"	17.1.17		About 3 inches of snow fell in night. Casualties NIL. Reinforcement 1st Bn South Staffs Regt 1 Officer 2 O.R.	MB
"	18.1.17		Snow. BEAUSSART shelled between 9 a.m. and 10 a.m. mostly in Transport lines. No casualties and little damage. Casualties NIL. Reinforcements 1st L. Staffs Regt 10 O.R. 22nd Bn Manchester Regt moved from MAILLY MAILLET to BERTRANCOURT. Lt.Col. A.R. BEAUMAN D.S.O. 1st Bn L. Staffs Regt assumed command of Brigade vice Brigadier CUMMING on leave.	MB
"	19.1.17		HQrs. Casualties 2/1st Bn Manchester Regt 3 O.R. wounded. Reinforcements 2nd Queens Regt 4 O.R. 2/1st Bn Manchester Regt 1 Officer.	MB
"	20.1.17		HQrs. Casualties NIL. Reinforcements NIL.	MB
PUCHEVILLERS	21.1.17		HQrs. Brigade moved back to training to PUCHEVILLERS Area. Brigade HQrs, 2nd Bn Queens Regt, 22nd Bn Manchester Regt, French Hunts Battery & French Engr Section from VERT in PUCHEVILLERS, 1st Bn South Staffs Regt at RAINCHEVAL, 2/1st Bn Manchester Regt at BEAUQUESNE, 2/1st Bn Manchester Regt 3 Officers. Reinforcements NIL.	Appendix 7 MB

Army Form C. 2118.

WAR DIARY
or
INTELLIGENCE SUMMARY.

(Erase heading not required.)

91st Infantry Brigade.

Instructions regarding War Diaries and Intelligence Summaries are contained in F.S. Regs., Part II and the Staff Manual respectively. Title pages will be prepared in manuscript.

Place	Hour, Date	Summary of Events and Information	Remarks and references to Appendices
PUCHEVILLERS	22.1.17	Trained. Casualties NIL. Reinforcements 2nd/5th Queens Regt 67 O.R. 22nd/Bn Manchester Regt 2 Officers.	Training carried out as per Appendix 10.
"	23.1.17	Trained. Casualties NIL. Reinforcements 21st/Bn Manchester Regt 1 O.R.	
"	24.1.17	Trained. Casualties NIL. Reinforcements 1st Bn North Staff Regt 2 Officers. 22nd Bn Manchester Regt 38 O.R. 1 Officer.	
"	25.1.17	Trained. Casualties NIL. Reinforcements 21st Bn Manchester Regt 1 O.R.	
"	26.1.17	Trained. Casualties NIL. Reinforcements 2nd/5th Queens Regt 2 O.R.	
"	27.1.17	Trained. Casualties NIL. Reinforcements 21st Bn Manchester Regt 1 O.R. Colonel W.W. NORMAN D.S.O 22nd/Bn Manchester Regt. assumed command of Brigade.	
"	28.1.17	Trained. Casualties NIL. Reinforcements 2nd/5th Queens Regt 2 O.R. 1st Bn South Staffs Regt 6 O.R.	
"	29.1.17	Trained. Casualties NIL. Reinforcements NIL.	
"	30.1.17	Trained with some snow. Casualties NIL. Reinforcements 1st Bn South Staffs Regt 2 O.R.	Appendix 11.
"	31.1.17	Trained with some snow. Casualties NIL. Reinforcements NIL.	

A. L. Spencer Colonel
Comdg 91st Infantry Brigade.

SECRET.

Appendix 1.

Copy No. 17

91st Infantry Brigade.

INSTRUCTIONS FOR FORTHCOMING OPERATIONS - NO.3.

Monday, 1st January, 1917.

Reference REDAN Sheet. 1/5,000.

1. **DRESS.**

    (a) **ATTACKING TROOPS AND RESERVE.**

    1st Wave.   Fighting Order.
                 Cardigan jackets in waterproof sheet.
                 Leather jerkins.
                 120 rounds S.A.A. per man.
                 2 Mills Grenades per man.
                 4 Sandbags per man.
                 2 Flares per Officer and N.C.O.
                 1 Flare each Other Rank.

    2nd Wave.   As for above, but 1 shovel per man will be
                 carried in addition.

    (b) **CARRYING AND DIGGING PARTIES.**

                 Fighting Order.
                 Cardigan jackets rolled in waterproof sheet.
                 Leather jerkins.
                 120 rounds S.A.A. per man.
                 4 Sandbags per man.

2. **TRAFFIC.**

    Communication Trenches will be allotted for the use of Battalions as follows:-

WALKER AVENUE.	22nd Bn. Manchester Regt.
CRATER LANE.	1st Bn. South Staffordshire Regt.
CAKE TRENCH.	21st Bn. Manchester Regt.

    Battalions will not use other trenches than those allotted to them, except in cases of emergency.

3. **ACKNOWLEDGE.**

                                                    R N O'[illegible] Captain,

                                          Brigade Major, 91st Infantry Brigade.

    Copy No. 1 7th Division.   Copy No. 10 1st S.Staffs.R
             2 Bde.Major.   11 21st Manch.R
             3 Staff Captain.   12 22nd Manch.R
             4 20th Inf.Bde.   13 Sig.Off.91st Inf.Bde.
             5 22nd Inf.Bde.   14 91st T.M.Battery.
             6 8th Inf.Bde.   15 91st Bde.Gren.Coy.
             7 C.R.E., 7th Divn.   16 Capt.F.W.Petrie-Hay.
             8 C.R.A., 7th Divn.   20th M.G.Coy.
             9 2nd Queen's R   17 War Diary.
                                                 18 War Diary.

Appendix 2

S E C R E T.   Copy No. 9

7th DIVISION ORDER No. 120.

2nd January, 1917.

Reference:-
REDAN Sheet
1/5,000.

1. On 2nd and night 2nd/3rd January, the Battalion 91st Infantry Brigade now in BEAUMONT HAMEL, will relieve the Battalion 20th Infantry Brigade in R.2.

2. The 22nd Infantry Brigade will take over the Divisional front from the 20th Infantry Brigade on the 5th inst, night 5th/6th and 6th inst. as under :-

   (i) On 5th inst and night 5th/6th inst. 3 Battalions 22nd Infantry Brigade will relieve the 3 Battalions 20th Infantry Brigade, which are in the line and in BEAUMONT HAMEL.

   (ii) On the 5th inst, the Battalion of 22nd Infantry Brigade at LOUVENCOURT will move into billets at BERTRANCOURT.

   (iii) On the 6th inst and night 6th/7th inst,
   (a) The Battalion 91st Infantry Brigade in R.2 will be relieved by a Battalion of 22nd Infantry Brigade.

   (b) The Battalion of 22nd Infantry Brigade in BERTRANCOURT will move into the front area.

   (iv) By the evening of the 6th inst, the 22nd Infantry Brigade will be distributed as follows :-

   2 Battalions holding the line each with 2 Companies in front and 2 Companies in immediate support.
   $1\frac{1}{2}$ Battalions in BEAUMONT HAMEL.
   $\frac{1}{2}$ Battalion in vicinity of Q.17.a.8.8.

3. (i) The 91st Infantry Brigade on 6th inst, will move one Battalion from MAILLY MAILLET into billets in BERTRANCOURT.

   (ii) The Battalion 91st Infantry Brigade in R.2, will, on relief, move into MAILLY MAILLET.

   (iii) By the evening of the 6th inst, the 91st Infantry Brigade will be situated as follows :-

   1 Battalion in MAILLY MAILLET.
   1   ,,   ,, MAILLY WOOD.
   1   ,,   ,, Huts in P.17.a.
   1   ,,   ,, BERTRANCOURT.

4/

2.

4. On relief the 20th Infantry Brigade will be distributed as follows :-

   1 Battalion MAILLY MAILLET.
   2 Battalions BERTRANCOURT.
   1 Battalion LOUVENCOURT.

5. Arrangements for all moves necessitated by above reliefs will be made by the Brigade Commanders concerned.

6. Working parties for the C.R.E. will be found from one of the support Battalions of 22nd Infantry Brigade, and also from the Battalion 91st Infantry Brigade in MAILLY MAILLET, after the latter has had 3 clear days out of the line.

7. Brigade Headquarters will be as follows :-

   20th Infantry Brigade - BERTRANCOURT.
   22nd ,, ,, - APPLE TREE.
   91st ,, ,, - BEAUSSART.

8. Machine guns will continue to be relieved in accordanse with Orders issued by the Divisional Machine Gun Officer.

9. The utmost care will be exercised in handing and taking over the various posts.
  The 20th Infantry Brigade will arrange to leave a proportion of Lewis Gunners in the line for 24 hours after relief.

10. The Command will pass to 22nd Infantry Brigade on completion of the relief of the 3 Battalions of 20th Infantry Brigade on night 5th/6th.

11. ACKNOWLEDGE.

         G. W. Howard.

           Lieut-Colonel.
         General Staff, 7th Division.

Issued at 6 a.m. to :-

   A.D.C. (for G.O.C.) Copy No. 1
   Office.   2 & 3
   "Q".   4
   7th Div. R. A.   5
   C. R. E.   6
   20th Infy. Brigade. 7
   22nd Infy. Brigade. 8
   91st Infantry Brigade. 9
   Div. Pioneer Battalion. 10
   7th Signal Company. 11
   A. D. M. S.   12
   Divisional Train.   13
   D. A. D. O. S.   14
   Div. Gas Officer.   15
   3rd Division.   16.
   11th Division.   17.
   War Diary.   18.

SECRET   Appendix 2A

Copy No. 21

20th INFANTRY BRIGADE ORDER No 109.

Ref: TRENCH MAP.   1st Jan, 1917.

1. The 2nd QUEENS REGIMENT, 91st Infantry Brigade, will relieve the 9th DEVON REGIMENT in R.2 Sector on 2nd instant and night of 2nd/3rd Jan, 1917.

2. All details of relief will be arranged between Commanding Officers concerned.

3. The greatest care will be observed in the taking over of Advanced Posts and Lewis Gun Positions.

4. All stores, etc., will be taken over and the usual certificates forwarded to Brigade Headquarters by 9 p.m. 4th Jan, 1917.

5. On completion of relief the 9th DEVON REGIMENT will come into Brigade Reserve and will occupy the dugouts vacated by 2nd QUEENS REGIMENT.

6. Completion of relief to be reported by wire to Brigade Headquarters by the code word 'OWL'.

7. ACKNOWLEDGE.

G. N. Croland
Captain.
Brigade Major.
20th Infantry Brigade.

Issued at 8'45 p.m.

Copies to all recipients of 20th Inf Bde Orders.
and

95th Fd Coy R.E.	23rd Field Ambulance.
7th Division 'G'	S.C.20th Inf Bde.
22nd Inf Bde.	No 2 Coy, A.S.C.
32nd Inf Bde.	7th Div'l Artillery.
91st Inf Bde.	14th Bde R.H.A.
2nd Queens Regt.	22nd Bde R.F.A.
Major Petrie Hay,	35th Bde R.F.A.
20th M.G.Corps.	

SECRET.

Appendix 3.
Copy No. 20.

91st Infantry Brigade.

INSTRUCTIONS FOR FORTHCOMING OPERATIONS - NO.4.

Tuesday, 2nd January, 1917.

Reference REDAN Sheet, 1/5,000.

1. In order to assist in the capture of the re-entrant at K.36.c.1.5., The Officer Commanding, 91st Brigade Grenade Company, will arrange to have two parties of rifle grenadiers so disposed as to bring an effective cross-fire to bear on this re-entrant, should the enemy attempt to offer any resistance after the lift of the Artillery barrage.

1st Party.

Will move with the attacking waves to vicinity of K.36.c.1.2.
It will then:-
(a) Deal with any resistance up to and to the EAST of WAGON ROAD.
(b) Knock out any enemy attempting escape across the open North-eastwards.
(c) Assist the bombing parties working towards K.36.c.4.6.

After the capture of the re-entrant, this party will move to POINT 15 and report to The Officer Commanding, "D" Company, 21st Bn. Manchester Regt., for duty during the remainder of the day.

2nd Party.

Will move to vicinity of K.35.d.5.6.
It will then:-
(a) Deal with any hostile resistance to the WEST of and including WAGON ROAD.
(b) Knock out any enemy attempting to escape across the open Northwards.
(c) Assist the bombing parties working up MUNICH TRENCH towards SALFORD TRENCH.

After the capture of the re-entrant, this party will return to WALKER QUARRY, Q.5.b.7.2.

2. ACKNOWLEDGE.

R.O'C...
Captain,
Brigade Major, 91st Infantry Brigade.

Copy No. 1 7th Division.	Copy No. 12 22nd Manch.R
2 Bde. Major.	13 Sig.Off.91st Inf.Bde.
3 Staff Captain.	14 91st T.M.Battery.
4 20th Inf.Bde.	15 91st Bde.Gren.Coy.
5 22nd Inf.Bde.	16 Capt.F.W.Petrie-Hay.
6 8th Inf.Bde.	20th M.G.Coy.
7 C.R.E., 7th Divn.	17 22nd Bde.R.F.A.
8 C.R.A., 7th Divn.	18 35th Bde.R.F.A.
9 2nd Queen's R	19 14th Bde.R.H.A.
10 1st S.Staffs.R	20 War Diary.
11 21st Manch.R	21 War Diary.

Appendix 4
Copy No. 21

SECRET.

91st Infantry Brigade.

INSTRUCTIONS FOR FORTHCOMING OPERATIONS - NO.5.

Thursday, 4th January, 1917.

Reference REDAN Sheet.1/5,000.

1. Dug-out accommodation, as shown below, will be allotted to Units from the evening of "Y" day throughout the forthcoming operations:-

    (a) 22nd Bn.Manchester Regt.

    Dug-outs.

    (1) Off the WAGON ROAD between Q.5.d.1.5. - Q.5.c.8.1.
    (2) In vicinity of Battalion Headquarters near Q.5.c.7.1.
    (3) In vicinity of Q.5.d.6.6.

    (b) 1st Bn.South Staffordshire Regt.

    Dug-outs.

    (1) In vicinity of Q.5.c.8.8.
    (2) Between Q.5.c.15.20. (POINT 12.) and Q.5.c.25.45.
    (3) At Q.5.c.35.55.

    (c) 21st Bn.Manchester Regt.

    HARPER'S WORK.

    (d) 2nd Bn.Queen's Regt.

    Headquarters SOUTH of Church Q.11.a.55.80.

    Dug-outs.

    (1) Between Q.11.a.3.6. and Q.11.a.25.80.
    (2) At Q.11.a.0.6. and Q.10.b.8.5.
    (3) At Q.11.a.6.1.
    (4) At Q.4.d.9.3.

    (e) Two Companies Pioneers and Two Sections, R.E.

    Dug-outs in "Y" RAVINE.

2. Units are responsible for reconnoitering beforehand, the area allotted to them.

3. The Units detailed in Para.1 (e) will find one Common Headquarters to which messages will be sent. The location will be reported to Brigade Headquarters as soon as possible.

4. Attached diagram shows allotment of dug-out accommodation in WALKER QUARRY (issued to 1st Bn.South Staffordshire Regt., and 21st Bn.Manchester Regt., only).

5. ACKNOWLEDGE.

R.R.O'Connor Major,

Brigade Major, 91st Infantry Brigade.

SECRET.

Copy No 1 7th Division.   Copy No 12 22nd Manch.R
       2 Bde Major.   13 Sig.Off.91st Inf.Bde.
       3 Staff Captain.   14 91st T.M.Battery.
       4 20th Inf.Bde.   15 91st Bde.Gren.Coy.
       5 22nd Inf.Bde.   16 Capt.F.W.Petrie-Esy.
       6 8th Inf.Bde.   20th M.G.Coy.
       7 C.R.E.,7th Divn.   17 22nd Bde.R.F.A.
       8 C.R.A.,7th Divn.   18 35th Bde.R.F.A.
       9 2nd Queen's R   19 14th Bde.R.H.A.
      10 1st S.Staffs.R   20 War Diary.
      11 21st Manch.R   21 War Diary.

SECRET.   Copy No. 21.

                           Appendix 5

                    91st Infantry Brigade.

           INSTRUCTIONS FOR FORTHCOMING OPERATIONS - NO.6.

                                     Saturday, 6th January, 1917.
Reference REDAN Sheet, 1/5,000.

1.   COMMUNICATIONS.

     (1) Between Battalion and Brigade Headquarters.

         (a) Telephonic Communication to the four Battalions.
         (b) Visual (back) to Brigade Headquarters.
         (c) Wireless. One set at Battalion Headquarters at the
             QUARRY (Q.5.b.7.2.) and one in vicinity of Brigade
             Headquarters at Q.17.a.8.8.
         (d) Runners.
         (e) Carrier Pigeons.

     (2) Between Battalion Headquarters and present Front Line
         prior to the assault.

         (a) Combined Telephone and Visual Posts.

             (i)   22nd Bn. Manchester Regt.
                   Combined Posts at junction of:-
                       CLIVE AVENUE and NEW MUNICH TRENCH (Q.6.c.3.5.)
                       WALKER AVENUE and NEW MUNICH TRENCH.

             (ii) 1st Bn. South Staffordshire Regt.
                   Combined Post at junction of CRATER LANE and
                   NEW MUNICH TRENCH. (Q.5.b.9.7.)

             (iii) 21st Bn. Manchester Regt.
                   Combined Post at junction of C.X.3 TRENCH and
                   NEW MUNICH TRENCH (K.35.d.6.2.)

         (b) Battalion Runners.

     (3) Between Battalion Headquarters and Company Headquarters in
         MUNICH TRENCH after the assault.

         (a) Telephone lines will be run out by Battalion Signallers
             with the second wave of the attack from the following
             posts in NEW MUNICH TRENCH to proposed Company
             Headquarters in MUNICH TRENCH:-

             (i)   22nd Bn. Manchester Regt.
                       Q.6.c.3.5. to Q.6.c.7.8.
                       Q.6.a.0.2. to Q.6.a.6.2.

             (ii) 1st Bn. South Staffordshire Regt.
                       Two lines (by different routes)
                       Q.5.b.9.7. to Q.6.a.3.9.

             (iii) 21st Bn. Manchester Regt.
                       K.35.d.6.2. to K.36.c.1.2. and K.36.c.1.5.

         (b) Visual.

             If practicable Visual Stations will be established
             by Battalions as under:-
             (i)   22nd Bn. Manchester Regt.   at Q.6.c.7.8.
             (ii) 1st Bn. South Staffordshire Regt.   at Q.6.a.3.9.
             (iii) 21st Bn. Manchester Regt.   at K.36.c.1.5.

             Existing Stations will be kept manned in NEW MUNICH
             TRENCH until orders are received to close down.

                                                  (continued).

-2-

    (c) Battalion Runners.

    (d) <u>Carrier Pigeons.</u>

         Two men with four pigeons will move to the following Company Headquarters with the second wave of the attack.

        (i)   22nd Bn.Manchester Regt.   - Q.6.a.6.2.
        (ii) 1st Bn.South Staffordshire Regt. - Q.6.a.3.9.
        (iii) 21st Bn.Manchester Regt.   -- K.36.c.1.5.

    (e)   It is hoped to obtain the use of an "Induction Buzzer Set". These will be established in dug-outs near Company Headquarters at K.36.c.1.5., Q.6.a.3.9., and Q.6.a.6.2.

    (f)   A contact patrol aeroplane will be in the air throughout the operations.
        One ground sheet, and one ground signalling panel will be laid out at Headquarters, 22nd Bn.Manchester Regt., and the Combined Headquarters of the 1st Bn. South Staffordshire Regt., and 21st Bn.Manchester Regt., respectively.
        The Company Headquarters at Q.6.a.6.2., Q.6.a.3.9., and K.36.c.1.5., will endeavour to keep touch with the contact patrol aeroplane with the lamp.

(4)   The following O.Ps.will be connected up to the Battalion Headquarters at the QUARRY.

    (a) Q.6.a.1.1.
    (b) Q.5.a.5.7.

(5)   Artillery communications are being arranged by R.A. Brigades concerned.

3. ACKNOWLEDGE.

                                        R.M.O'Connor Major,

                      Brigade Major, 91st Infantry Brigade.

Copy No		Copy No	
1	7th Division.	12	22nd Manch.R
2	Bde.Major.	13	91st Bde.Sig.Off.
3	Staff Captain.	14	91st T.M.Battery.
4	20th Inf.Bde.	15	91st Bde.Gren.Coy.
5	22nd Inf.Bde.	16	Maj.F.W.Petrie-Hay, 20th M.G.Coy.
6	8th Inf.Bde.		
7	C.R.E.,7th Divn.	17	22nd Bde.R.F.A.
8	C.R.A.,7th Divn.	18	35th Bde.R.F.A.
9	2nd Queen's R	19	14th Bde.R.H.A.
10	1st S.Staffs.R	20	15th Squadron,R.F.C.
11	21st Manch.R	21	War Diary.
		22	War Diary.

SECRET.

Copy No. 21

91st Infantry Brigade.

ADDENDUM TO INSTRUCTIONS FOR FORTHCOMING OPERATIONS – NO.6.

Saturday, 6th January, 1917.

1. The following are the Battalion and Company Code Calls which will be used for all means of communication:-
    Brigade Headquarters.   TR
    1st Bn. South Staffordshire Regt.   CF.
    21st Bn. Manchester Regt.   LK
    22nd Bn. Manchester Regt.   LR
    2nd Bn. Queen's Regt.   OV

2. Company Code Calls will be as above, with the addition of the letter of the Company. i.e. CFA. CFB. etc.

3. The Combined Headquarters of the 1st Bn. South Staffordshire Regt., and 21st Bn. Manchester Regt., in the QUARRY will be CF.

4. ACKNOWLEDGE.

R N O'Connor
Major,
Brigade Major, 91st Infantry Brigade.

Copies to all recipients of I.F.O. No.6.

Appendix 5A

SECRET.

Copy No. 11

22nd. Infantry Brigade Operation Order No. 106.

by Lieut. Colonel A.G. PRITCHARD, C.M.G.

1. The 22nd. Infantry Brigade, less 20th. Manchester Regt. will relieve the 20th. Infantry Brigade less 1 Battalion on the 5th. inst. and the night 5th./6th. 20th. Manchester Regt. on the 5th., will occupy the Camp vacated by 2/H.A.C.
On the 6th. inst., 20th. Manchester Regt. will relieve 2nd. Queens, 91st. Infantry Brigade, in R.2.

2. Arrangements for relief will be made by Commanding Officers concerned, in accordance with attached March Table.

3. Maps and Defence Schemes will be taken over from relieved Units.

4. The utmost care will be exercised in taking over the various Posts. The 20th. Infantry Brigade have arranged to leave a proportion of Lewis Gunners in the Line for 24 hours after relief.

5. Completion of reliefs will be reported to Brigade Headquarters by the word, "MANCHESTER".

6. On completion of relief of 20th. Infantry Brigade, G.O.C. 22nd. Infantry Brigade will assume command of the Sector.

7. Brigade Headquarters will close at BERTRANCOURT at 3 p.m., and open at the same hour at the APPLE TREE.

8. ACKNOWLEDGE.

3rd. January 1917.

E.V. Lawton, Lieutenant,
A/Brigade Major 22nd. Infantry Brigade.

Issued to Signals at 4 p.m.

Copy No. 1 and 2. War Diary.
3. 2nd. R. War. Regt.
4. 1st. R.W.FUS.
5. 20th. Man. Regt.
6. 2/H.A.C.
7. Signals.
8. 22nd. T.M.Battery.
9. Grenade Coy.
10. 20th. Inf. Bde.
11. 91st. Inf. Bde.
12. 8th. Inf. Bde.
13. 34th. Inf. Bde.
14. 20th. Bde. M.G.Cy.
15. 14th. Bde. R.H.A.
16. 22nd. Bde. R.F.A.
17. 35th. Bde. R.F.A.
18. 54th. Fd. Coy. R.E
19. Supplies.
20. 7th. Division.
21. Staff Captain.

MARCH TABLE.

Unit of 22nd. Inf. Bde.	Destination.	Unit of 20th. Bde. to be relieved.	REMARKS.
2nd. R. Warwickshire Rgt.	BEAUMONT HAMEL Defences.	8th. Devons.	Platoon guides from 8th. Devons will be at Junction of OLD & NEW BEAUMONT Roads at 11.30 a.m.
1st. R.W.Fusiliers.	RIGHT SUB-SECTOR. R.1.	2nd. Gordons.	Platoon guides from 2nd.Gordons will be at AUCHONVILLERS STATION at 2 p.m.
2/H.A.C.	Dug-outs in Q.5.c.	8th. Devons.	Platoon guides from 9th. Devons will be at junction of OLD & NEW BEAUMONT RDS. at 9.30 a.m.
20th. Manchester Rgt.	LEFT SUB-SECTOR. R.2.	2nd. Queens.	Platoon guides from 2nd. Queens will be at junction of OLD & NEW BEAUMONT ROADS at 2 p.m., the 6th. inst. Arrangements have been made for Commanding Officer, Company Commanders, and Lewis Gun Officer to visit H.qrs. 2nd. Queens at 11 a.m., 4th. inst.
22nd.T.M.Battery. 22nd. Grenade Company. }	Will remain in their present positions.		

ALL MOVEMENTS TO BE BY PLATOONS WITH 50 yards INTERVAL BETWEEN EACH.

SECRET   Inf O/o   Appendix 5 B.

Copy No. 24

20th INFANTRY BRIGADE ORDER No 110.

Ref: BEAUMONT & HEBUTERNE Maps
1/10,000 and Sheet 57.d.1/40,000.   3rd January, 1917.

1.   (a)   The 22nd Infantry Brigade will relieve the 20th INFANTRY BRIGADE and one battalion 91st Infantry Brigade (2nd QUEENS REGIMENT) on the Divisional front on the 5th instant, the night of 5th/6th, and the 6th January, 1917.

     (b)   The relief will be carried out under arrangements to be made by Commanding Officers concerned subject to the instructions contained in the attached RELIEF TABLE.

     (c)   On completion of relief 20th INFANTRY BRIGADE Headquarters will be established in BERTRANCOURT near 7th Division H.Q. Hutment.

     (d)   Completion of relief will be reported to 20th INFANTRY BRIGADE Headquarters at APPLE TREES (Q.2.b.4.6.) by wire by the code word "THRUSH".

     (e)   Commands will pass on completion of reliefs.

2.   The greatest care is to be exercised in handing over Advanced Posts and Lewis Gun Posts.

3.   Maps, Defence Schemes and Aeroplane photographs will be handed over on relief.

4.   All stores, drying rooms, soup kitchens etc., will be carefully handed over, and the usual certificates, in duplicate, signed by the Commanding Officers concerned, forwarded to Brigade Headquarters by 9 p.m. 7th instant.

5.   A proportion of Lewis Gunners will remain in the line for 24 hours after relief. These will be returned to their respective units under arrangements to be made by 22nd Infantry Brigade by the evening of 7th instant.

6.   The Commanding Officer, Company Commanders and Lewis Gun Officer, 20th MANCHESTER REGIMENT will visit H.Q. 2nd QUEENS REGIMENT at 11 a.m. 4th instant.

7.   ACKNOWLEDGE.

Captain.
Brigade Major.
20th Infantry Brigade.

Issued at 3 p.m.

Copies to all recipients of 20th Inf Bde Orders.
and

95th Fd. Coy R.E.	7th Division G.
S.O. 20th Inf Bde.	7th Division Q.
No 2 Coy, 7th Divl Train.	22nd Inf Bde.
23rd Field Ambulance.	91st Inf Bde.
Major F.W. Petrie Hay 20th M.G. Coy.	34th Inf Bde.
7th Div'l Artillery.	8th Infantry Bde.
14th Brigade R.H.A.	22nd Brigade R.F.A.
35th Brigade R.F.A.	

RELIEF TABLE.

Unit.	From.	To.	Relieving.	Platoon guides will be at	Remarks.
8th DEVON REGT.	Immediate Support BEAUMONT HAMEL.	LOUVENCOURT.	2nd R.WARWICK REGT.	Junction of Old & New BEAUMONT Roads at 11.30 a.m. 5th instant.	Take over billets from 20th MANCHESTER Regiment.
9th DEVON REGT.	Brigade Reserve. BH.Qrs & 2 Coys Dugouts in Q.5.c. 2 Companies in Dugouts in Q.17.a. 8.8.	BERTRANCOURT.	2nd H.A.C.	(1) Junction of New & Old BEAUMONT Roads at 9.30 a.m. 5th instant.	Take over billets from 1st R.Welsh Fusiliers.
2nd BORDER RGT.	TO	REMAIN	IN	PRESENT	BILLETS.
2nd GORDON HRS.	Right Sector. R.1.	BERTRANCOURT.	1st R.WELSH FUSILIERS.	AUCHONVILLERS STATION at 2 p.m. 5th instant.	Take over huts from 2nd R.Warwick Regt.
2nd QUEENS RGT.	Left Sector. 4.2.	MAILLY MAILLET	20th MANCHESTER Regt.	Junction of Old & New BEAUMONT Roads at 2 p.m. 6th instant.	
20th T.M.Bty.	TO	REMAIN	IN	PRESENT	BILLETS.

X (2) Point where Duckboards leave AUCHONVILLERS - HAMEL Road at 10 a.m. 5th instant.

S E C R E T.

Appendix 6.

Copy No. 22

91st Infantry Brigade.

INSTRUCTIONS FOR FORTHCOMING OPERATIONS - NO.7.

Tuesday, 9th January, 1917.

Reference REDAN Sheet 1/5,000.

1. (a) Three Battalions, 91st Infantry Brigade will relieve the 20th Bn. Manchester Regt., of the 22nd Infantry Brigade in R.2. Sub-sector, on the night 10th/11th instant. Relief to be completed by 2-0.a.m., 11th instant.
    Frontage of each Battalion will be as follows:-
    (i) 22nd Bn. Manchester Regt.
    Junction of GRAVE AVENUE and NEW MUNICH TRENCH Q.6.c.24.54.(inclusive) - junction of WALKER AVENUE and NEW MUNICH TRENCH Q.6.a.01.19.(inclusive).

    (ii) 1st Bn. South Staffordshire Regt.
    Junction of WALKER AVENUE and NEW MUNICH TRENCH Q.6.a.01.19.(exclusive) - junction of CRATER LANE and NEW MUNICH TRENCH Q.5.b.9.7. (inclusive).

    (iii) 21st Bn. Manchester Regt.
    Junction of CRATER LANE and NEW MUNICH TRENCH Q.5.b.9.7. (exclusive) - junction of LAGER ALLEY and NEW MUNICH TRENCH K.35.d.2.5. (inclusive), thence to K.35.d.5.6. (inclusive).

    Posts No.12. - DESPAIR - and HOPE will continue to be held by the 22nd Infantry Brigade.

    (b) 2nd Bn. Queen's Regt., will relieve 2nd Bn. Royal Warwick.Regt., and 2nd/1st H.A.C., in the dug-outs shown in Instructions for Forthcoming Operations No.5., para.1.(d), on afternoon of 10th instant.

2. Details of relief to be arranged between Battalion Commanders concerned, subject to the times laid down in Relief Table attached.

3. G.O.C., 91st Infantry Brigade will assume Command of R.2. Sub-sector on completion of relief.
    R.1. Sub-sector will continue to be held by 22nd Infantry Brigade.

4. Brigade Headquarters will close at BEAUSSART at an hour to be notified later, and will open at the same hour at Q.17.a.8.8.

5. Completion of relief to be reported to Brigade Headquarters by the Code Word "LUSITANIA".

6. ZERO day will be January, 11th. ZERO hour will be 6-40.a.m.

7. Watches will be synchronised by the Staff Captain at the Bomb Store, AUCHONVILLERS, Q.9.a.4.3., whilst the issue of bombs is proceeding.

8. Heavy Artillery bombardment commenced at 8-0.a.m., 9th instant, and will continue for 48 hours with the following exceptions:-

    (a) There will be complete pauses on 9th instant, between:-

    11-20.a.m. to 11-50.a.m.
    4-30.p.m. to 4-45.p.m.
    5-40.p.m. to 9-40.p.m.

(continued).

-2-

on 10th instant, between:-

        1-0.p.m. to 1-20.p.m.
        5-0.p.m. to 5-20.p.m.
        5-40.p.m. to 9-40.p.m.

    (b) The 9.2"s, will lift off MUNICH TRENCH opposite the point of attack after 10-30.p.m., on 10th instant.
    (c) The 6"s, will continue to fire on junction of WALKER AVENUE and MUNICH TRENCH, junction of CRATER LANE and MUNICH TRENCH and K.36.c.1.5., until ZERO hour.

9.   An alteration in the barrage Scheme of 7th Divisional Artillery will be forwarded as soon as received.

10.   The new trench mentioned in Instructions for Forthcoming Operations No.1., para.13, sub-para.4, will not be dug, and the work on PRITCHARD TRENCH (Instructions for Forthcoming Operations No.1., para.13, sub-para.5) will not be carried out.

11.   The troops will therefore form up on a tape line (a tracing of which is attached to the copies of the I.F.O's for 7th Division, 7th Div.R.A., 3 Battalions of 91st Infantry Brigade taking part in operations, and 1/3rd Durham Field Coy.,R.E.).
    Troops will not form up on this line before 1.am 11th instant.

12.   Between 9-30.p.m., and 2-0.a.m., night 10th/11th instant, NO MAN'S LAND will be kept continually patrolled by the 22nd Infantry Brigade. These patrols will come in at 2-0.a.m., Each Battalion is responsible for keeping its whole front patrolled from that hour.
    The pass word for all patrols will be "MAMETZ".

ACKNOWLEDGE.

                            R M O'Brien   Major,

                      Brigade Major, 91st Infantry Brigade.

Copies to:-

    Copy No 1. 7th Divn.   Copy No.12. 22nd Manch.R
           2. Bde.Major.   13. Sig.Off.91st Inf.Bde.
           3. Staff Captain.   14. 91st T.M.Battery.
           4. 20th Inf.Bde.   15. 91st Bde.Gren.Coy.
           5. 22nd Inf.Bde.   16. Maj.F.J.Petrie-Hay.
           6. 8th Inf.Bde.   20th M.G.Coy.
           7. C.R.E.,7th Divn.   17. 22nd Bde.R.F.A.
           8. C.R.A.,7th Divn.   18. 35th Bde.R.F.A.
           9. 2nd Queen's R   19. 14th Bde.R.H.A.
          10. 1st S.Staffs.R   20. 15th Squadron,R.F.C.
          11. 21st Manch.R   21. War Diary.
                                                     22. War Diary.

Reference para.4., Brigade Headquarters will close at 5-0.p.m., at BEAUSSART, and open at the same hour at Q.17.a.8.8.

RELIEF TABLE.

(Issued with 91st Infantry Brigade Instructions for Forthcoming Operations - No.7.)

UNIT.	From.	To.	ROUTE.	REMARKS.
2nd Bn.Queen's Rgt.	MAILLY MAILLET.	BEAUMONT HAMEL.	Leading Platoon will pass junction of OLD, and NEW BEAUMONT Road U.4.c.8.3., at 3-30.p.m.	Platoons at 200 yards interval.
21st Bn.Lanch.Rgt.	LYTHAM CAMP.	R.2.Sub-sector.	Leading Platoon will pass AUCHONVILLERS STATION at 9-30.p.m.	Platoons at 50 yards interval.
1st Bn.S.Staffs.Rgt.	MAILLY MAILLET.	-do-	Leading Platoon will pass AUCHONVILLERS STATION at 10-15.p.m.	-do-
2nd Bn.Manch.Rgt.	BERTRANCOURT.	-do-	Leading Platoon will pass AUCHONVILLERS STATION at 11-0.p.m.	-do-

The Officer Commanding,1st Bn.S.Staffs.Regt.,will be prepared to accommodate about 150 of 2nd Bn. Royal Warwick.Rgt.,who will be relieved by the 2nd Bn.Queen's Regt.,in the afternoon. (vide I.F.O. No.7.,para.1(b).

SECRET.   Appendix 6 A   Copy No. 21

91st Infantry Brigade.

AMENDMENTS TO INSTRUCTIONS FOR FORTHCOMING OPERATIONS.

Reference BEDAN Sheet, 1/5,000.   Tuesday, 9th January, 1917.

Reference Instructions for Forthcoming Operations – No.1.

Para.3 (d) (3). For K.36.c.4.6. read K.36.c.3.5.

Para.13, add:-
From the point in CAKE TRENCH where the U frames end, a duckboard track runs alongside of the trench to the front line, with a branch off to POINT 95.

Para.15, add:-
Prisoners will be escorted from the front to the QUARRY in BEAUMONT HAMEL, where the 2nd Bn. Queen's Regt., will arrange to take them over from the escort of the forward Battalions, who will at once be despatched to rejoin their units in the firing line. An escort will then be provided to march the prisoners to the cage opposite CAFE JOURDAIN, MAILLY MAILLET, at P.12.d.7.4., where they will be handed over to the A.P.M.

Para.17, line 4, add:-
This dug-out will be cleared by the 22nd Infantry Brigade by 4-0.p.m., 10th instant.

Reference Instructions for Forthcoming Operations – No.2.

Para.1.(a) add:-
Platoons will be issued with grenades on passing the Grenade Store at Q.9.a.4.3. No change of formation is required.

Reference Instructions for Forthcoming Operations – No.3.

Para.1. add:-
(1) All troops will carry the long rifle cover.
(2) Long Covers for Lewis Guns will be taken.

Reference Instructions for Forthcoming Operations – No.4.

Under instructions for 1st Party, para.(c). – For K.36.c.4.6. read K.36.c.3.5.

Reference Instructions for Forthcoming Operations – No.5.

Cancel para.1 (e) and substitute:-
(e) Two Companies Pioneers and Two Sections, R.E., will be at MAILLY MAILLET.
The Officer Commanding, 1/3rd Durham Field Coy., R.E., will remain throughout the operations at Brigade Headquarters.

Cancel para.3.

Reference Instructions for Forthcoming Operations – No.6.

Para.3.(f) add:-
Flares will be lit on demand by the aeroplane; this demand will probably be made $\frac{3}{4}$ of an hour after ZERO.

                                                     Major,
                              Brigade Major, 91st Infantry Brigade.

Issued to all recipients of I.F.Os.

Appendix 7.

NARRATIVE OF ATTACK ON MUNICH TRENCH.

1. OPERATION.

Acting under orders received from 7th Division, the 91st Infantry Brigade attacked MUNICH TRENCH and LAGER ALLEY at dawn on January 11th, 1917.

2. METHOD OF ATTACK.

The assault was carried out by 3 battalions as under, the remaining battalion, the 2nd Bn. Queen's Regt., remaining in reserve in BEAUMONT HAMEL.
(a) <u>22nd Bn. Manchester Regt.</u>, on the right - objective - MUNICH TRENCH from Q.6.c.65.60., to its junction with WALKER AVENUE at Q.6.a.60.20. (inclusive). WALKER AVENUE was allotted to this Battalion.
(b) <u>1st Bn. South Staffordshire Regt.</u>, in the centre, objective - MUNICH TRENCH at Q.6.a.60.20. (exclusive) to its junction with CRATER LANE at Q.6.a.3.9. (inclusive) CRATER LANE was allotted to this Battalion.
(c) <u>21st Bn. Manchester Regt.</u>, on left, - objective -
(1) MUNICH TRENCH from Q.6.a.3.9. (exclusive) to its junction with LAGER ALLEY K.36.c.1.5. (inclusive)
(2) LAGER ALLEY from K.36.c.1.5. to K.35.d.5.6. LAGER ALLEY to be formed into a defensive flank. OAKS TRENCH was allotted to this Battalion.

To assist in the capture of POINT 15, two sections of Rifle Grenadiers of the Brigade Grenade Company under 2nd Lieut. PULLEN Brigade Bombing Officer were ordered to proceed direct to a point in LAGER ALLEY and MUNICH TRENCH respectively whence cross fire could be brought to bear on the re-entrant.

3. SYSTEM OF DEFENCE.

The objective when captured was to be held by means of a series of posts.

For this purpose arrangements had been made for the construction of blocks and strong points at the following places:-
(a) Blocks at -
Q. 6.a.7.5. (RYCROFT AVENUE).
Q. 6.a.4.9. (CRATER LANE).
K.36.c.4.6. (LAGER ALLEY).
K.36.c.2.7. (SALFORD TRENCH).
K.36.c.1.6. (WAGON ROAD).

(b) Posts at -
Q. 6.c. 7. 8.
Q.6.a. 6. 2. (junction WALKER AVENUE - MUNICH TRENCH)
Q. 6.a. 6. 5. (junction RYCROFT AVENUE - MUNICH TRENCH)
Q. 6.a. 3. 9. (junction CRATER LANE - MUNICH TRENCH).
K.36.c. 1. 2.
K.36.c. 1. 5.
K.35.d.90.45.
K.35.d.70.50.
K.35.d.50.60.

4. ARTILLERY PROGRAMME.

Apart from a very heavy bombardment which had been continuing for several days and nights previous to the operation no special preparation for the assault had been ordered.

At 5 minutes before ZERO the Divisional Artillery opened an intensive bombardment on a line 100 yards in front of a tape-line on which the assaulting troops had been formed up. This barrage advanced at the rate of 50 yards in 5 minutes, the re-entrant at K.36.c.1.5., being subjected to special treatment with Howitzers in addition to a further 5 minutes barrage from field batteries.

This slow rate of advance was rendered necessary by the state of the ground which was very bad and waterlogged as the result of continuous bad weather.

5. **PREVIOUS OPERATIONS.**

The success of the enterprise was to a great extent dependent on the capture of certain trenches to the South of the objective. At 2-0.a.m.,on January 10th,the 20th Infantry Brigade attacked LEAVE AVENUE between Q.6.d.2.4. and Q.6.c.6.3. with complete success,establishing a line from Q.6.d.2.4. - Q.6.c.6.5. - Q.6.c.5.3.

6. **THE ASSAULT.**

ZERO hour had been fixed for 5-45.a.m.,at which hour a heavy mist lay on the ground making observation impossible. The troops who had filed into the trenches at 2-0.a.m. were lined up on the tape which had been laid in front of NEW MUNICH TRENCH earlier in the evening. The assembly and forming up was carried out without incident and with no casualties from the hostile artillery.

MUNICH TRENCH was found to be almost entirely obliterated, the ground on either side being practically impassable. On the right the 2nd Bn.Manchester Regt.,crossed the trench without realising it,and subsequently withdrew to a line of posts in MUNICH TRENCH. The right Company of the 1st Bn.South Staffordshire Regt.,similarly crossed the trench and swinging left handed established themselves some 80 yards in front. The left Company dug in 80 yards short of MUNICH TRENCH,finding the ground in front impassable.

On the left the 21st Bn.Manchester Regt.,gained their objective at once with the exception of the re-entrant at POINT 15,which was reported (by pigeon) as taken at 8-30.a.m.

All battalions had thus reached their objective and were in touch on their flanks with the exception of the extreme right flank. Touch between 2nd Bn.Manchester Regt.,and 1st Bn.Royal Welsh Fusiliers was not established until that night.

7. **SUBSEQUENT PERIOD.**

At 10-0.a.m.,I decided,owing to the thick mist to order up the 1/3rd Durham Field Coy.,R.E. and the Pioneers,whom I had intended to keep back in MAILLY MAILLET during the day, to the front line to assist in the consolidation. Unfortunately the mist rose shortly after their arrival in BEAUMONT HAMEL, and except in two cases where they had already gone forward no use could be made of them.

Considerable hostile shelling took place during the latter part of the morning and the afternoon,BEAUMONT HAMEL, the WAGON ROAD,STUARTS' WORK,LEAVE AVENUE and WALKER AVENUE, receiving special attention. At dusk the hostile artillery became quieter and consolidation continued. A new line of 8 posts was established by the 1st Bn.South Staffordshire Regt., in the centre,running some 50 yards WEST of MUNICH TRENCH. This line was occupied by the reserve Company,the two assaulting companies being withdrawn into support.

During the night duck-board tracks were laid as under:-
(a) in continuation of CARD TRENCH,from NEW MUNICH TRENCH to LAGER ALLEY.
(b) up WAGON ROAD to within 50 yards of K.36.c.1.5.
(c) along CRATER LANE to MUNICH TRENCH.
(d) along WALKER AVENUE to MUNICH TRENCH.

Existing posts were strengthened and firesteps made. Wire was laid out along LAGER ALLEY from POINT 15 to the left of the line,and for 150 yards South of WALKER AVENUE in front of the left post of the 2nd Bn.Manchester Regt. The remainder of the night was quiet and nothing of importance occurred. Snow fell at intervals during the night,which was bitterly cold with a northerly wind.

-3-

Next day, January 12th, was uneventful. Hostile artillery shewed considerable activity throughout the day, especially during the afternoon when LAGER ALLEY and POINT 15 were heavily shelled. Towards 5-0 p.m., a S.O.S. signal was sent up on the right flank of the 32nd Division and a counter-attack was expected. No attack however materialised and subsequent intercepted messages proved that the barrage was intended for defensive purposes only.

The Brigade was relieved during the night of January 12th/13th by the 22nd Infantry Brigade, posts being handed over to relieving units in accordance with the attached map.

Prior to the relief some 1,500 yards of tape line had been laid out, linking up posts, gaining touch with the flanks, and indicating routes for relieving parties.

The night was comparatively quiet and the relief was effected without incident.

6. REMARKS.

The artillery barrage was all that could be desired and the rate at which it moved (50 yards in 10 minutes) proved to be correct under the difficult circumstances of the ground encountered.

The communication between aeroplanes and the advanced line was satisfactory, flares being called for at different times on both days. In each case these were answered and seen by the contact aeroplanes.

It is estimated that 175 prisoners were taken during the operation in addition to 30 captured on the night of January 10th/11th during the hours of assembly.

The total casualties were as under:-

	Officers.	Other Ranks.
Killed.	3	40
Wounded.	6	204
	(1 still at duty)	(10 still at duty)
Wounded and missing.	1	-
Missing.	1	20
T O T A L.	11	264

I wish to bring to notice the names of the following Officers, who proved themselves of the greatest assistance during the operations, and contributed largely to their success:-

Staff.
    Bt.Major R.N.O'Connor,M.C.   Brigade Major.
    Captain O.W.Morshead,M.C.   Staff Captain.

2nd Bn.Queen's Regt.   Major W.Hayes.
1st Bn.S.Staffs Regt.   Lieut-Col.A.B.Beauman,D.S.O.
21st Bn.Manchester Regt.   Major F.W.Woodward,D.S.O.
1st Bn.S.Staffs Regt.   2nd Lieut.R.S.Pullen,
    (Brigade Grenade Officer).

To this list I would add the name of Major F.S.Watkins, R.E., Commanding 1/3rd Durham Field Coy., R.E. who was most unfortunately wounded at 2-0 a.m., on the night of relief. During the short time he had been working with this Brigade I had formed a very high idea of his capabilities and I regard his loss as a great misfortune to the Brigade.

Brigadier General.

Bde.Hd.Qtrs.

16th January, 1917.   Commanding 91st Infantry Brigade.

SECRET.  B.M./1023.

Headquarters,

22nd Infantry Brigade.

I herewith enclose map of front handed over to you on night 12th/13th instant.

If you approve ~~same~~, will you please counter-sign same and return, in order that it may be forwarded to Divisional Headquarters, in accordance with 7th Division No.G.216 of the 4th instant.

Cummings

Bde.Hd.Qtrs.   Brigadier General,
14th January, 1917.   Commanding, 91st Infantry Brigade.

Headquarters
   91st Inf Bde

Map returned herewith duly signed.

15 January 1917   A.G. Pritchard   Lieut Colonel
                                  Commanding 22 Inf Bde

Cumming Lt. Col.
Comdg. 51. I.B.
Handing over.

A.J. Pritchard Lt Colonel
Commd. 22nd Inf Brigade
Taking over

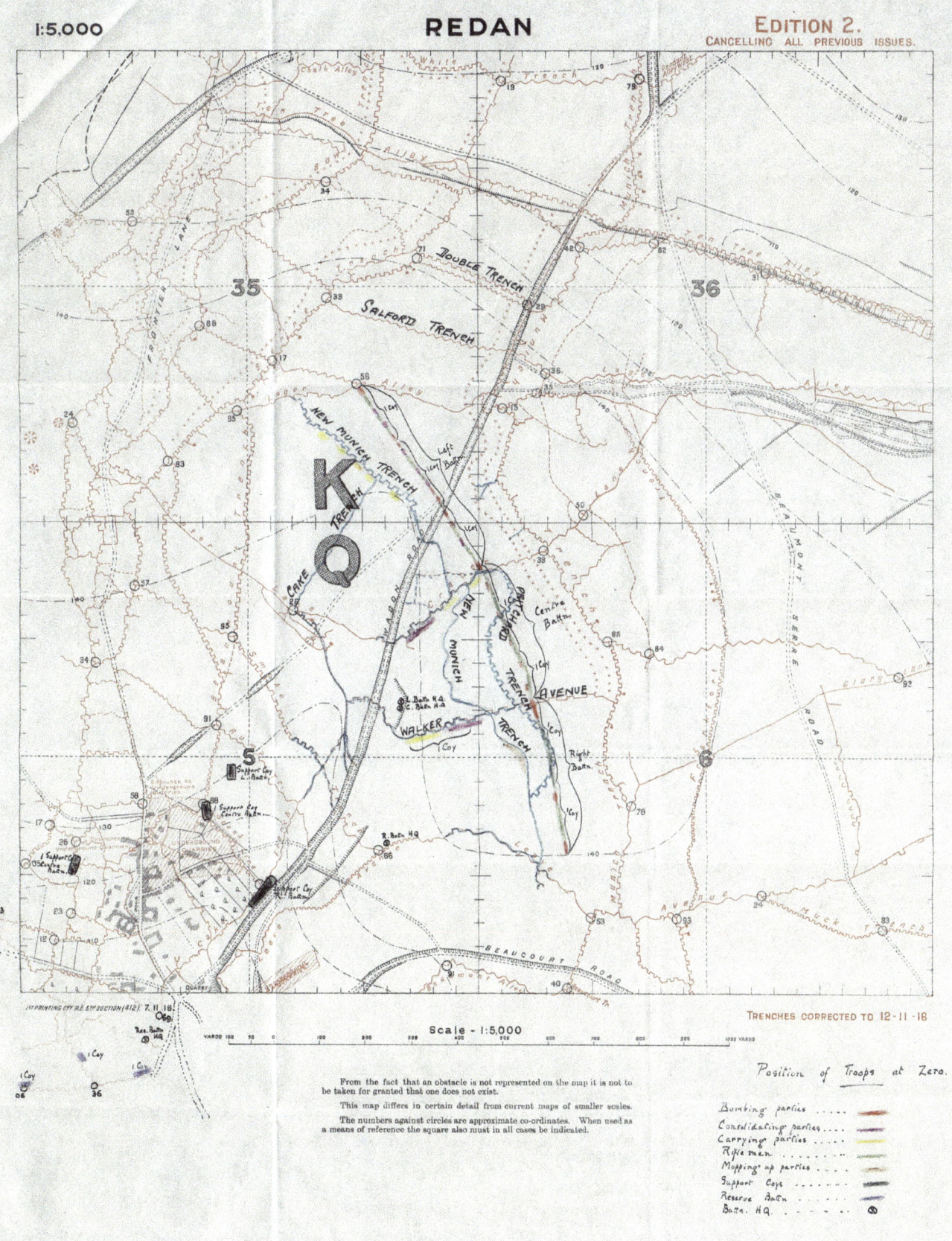

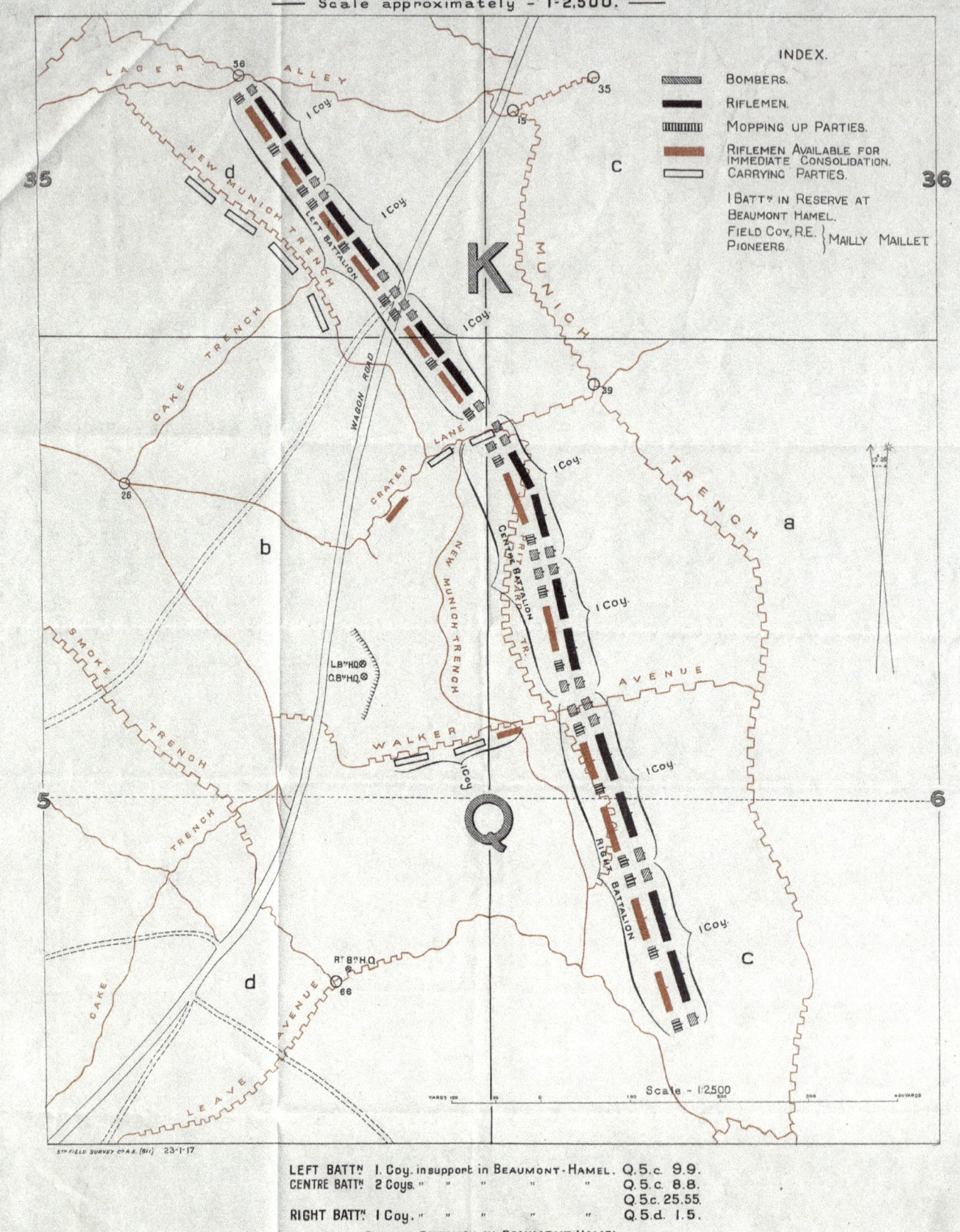

SECRET.

Appendix 8.   Copy No. 23

91st Infantry Brigade Operation Order No.58.

Friday, 12th January, 1917.

Reference REDAN Sheet 1/5,000.

-:-:-:-:-:-:-:-:-:-:-:-:-:-

1. The 91st Infantry Brigade will be relieved by the 22nd Infantry Brigade in MUNICH TRENCH and LAGER ALLEY to-night, in accordance with relief table and map attached.

2. The command of the Divisional Front will pass to 22nd Infantry Brigade on completion of the relief.

3. The Divisional front will be divided into 2 Sectors:-
   (a) R.1., from present right (R.1.c.3.1.) to Q.6.c.7.8. (junction of GLORY LANE and MUNICH TRENCH) inclusive.

   (b) R.2., from above point exclusive to HOPE POST, K.35.d.1.7.

4. (a) For the next few days both Sectors will be held by 3 Companies holding posts along the front, and 1 Company in immediate support.

   (b) Two battalions will be kept in reserve:-

      (i) 1 in vicinity of POINT 88.
      (ii) 1 in BEAUMONT HAMEL.

   (c) The 91st Infantry Brigade will remain in MAILLY MAILLET and its vicinity in support.
   The 20th Infantry Brigade will remain in its present billets.

5. The 2nd Bn. Queen's Regt., will remain in Brigade Reserve, until completion of relief of the three battalions in the front line, which will be notified to them by Brigade Headquarters. Parties of this Battalion whose dug-outs are taken over by units of relieving Brigade will march back independently; Such relieving troops coming under the orders of the G.O.C., 91st Infantry Brigade, until completion of relief.

6. The greatest care will be taken in handing over all posts and positions, and no post or position will be evacuated until properly relieved.

7. Completion of relief of the Battalions in the front line, will be reported to Brigade Headquarters by the Code Word "DEVONPORT".

8. ACKNOWLEDGE.

                                              Major,
                              Brigade Major, 91st Infantry Brigade.

Issued at .... p.m.

Copy No 1 7th Division.   11 & 12 1st S.Staffs.R
        2 Bde.Major.   13 & 14 21st Manch.R
        3 Staff Captain.   15 & 16 22nd Manch.R
        4 20th Inf.Bde.   17 91st T.M.Battery.
        5 22nd Inf.Bde.   18 91st Bde.Gren.Coy.
        6 14th Inf.Bde.   19 Div.M.G.Off.
        7 C.R.E., 7th Divn.   20 Sig.Off.91st Inf.Bde.
        8 C.R.A., 7th Divn.   21 File
        9 2nd Queen's R   22 & 23 War Diary.
       10   -do-   24 Supply Officer.

RELIEF TABLE.

(Issued with 91st Infantry Brigade Operation Order No.58).

UNIT.	Posts to be relieved.	Units to whom handed over.	Guides for each post at.		Destination.
22nd Manch.Regt.	W. X. & 78.	2/1st H.A.C.	Junction of OLD and NEW BEAUMONT Road.	8.p.m.	MAILLY MAILLET.
—do—	Y. Z.	2nd R.Warwick.R	—do—	9.p.m.	
1st S.Staffs.Regt.	1 to 8 (inclusive) NEW LUNICH TRENCH S.of WAGON Road.	2nd R.Warwick R 2 platoons, 2nd R.Warwick R	—do— —do—	9.p.m. 10-25.pm.	MAILLY WOOD EAST.
21st Manch.Regt.	E. 12,15,35 & A.	2nd R.Warwick R	—do—	9-30.P.m.	LYTHAM CAMP.
—do—	1. 2. 56.	—do—	—do—	10.0.P.M.	
—do—	NEW MUNICH TRENCH N.of WAGON Road.	2 platoons, R.W.Warwick R	—do—	10-15.pm.	
2nd Queen's Regt.	BEAUMONT HAMEL.	—	—		BERTRANCOURT.

SECRET.

Copy No. 20

AMENDMENT
to
91st Infantry Brigade Operation Order No.59.

Reference Map FRANCE 57D - 1/40,000.

Saturday, 20th January, 1917.

1. The 21st Bn.Manchester Regt., will be billetted in BEAUQUESNE instead of RAINCHEVAL.

2. The 54th Field Coy., R.E., will be billetted in PUCHEVILLERS instead of 21st Field Ambulance. A billeting party should be sent on in advance to report to the Town Major.

3. The 21st Field Ambulance will be billetted in VAL DE MAISON, and should send a billeting party on in advance to report to the Town Major, who has been warned.

4. From 22nd January, inclusive, Railhead will be at BELLE EGLISE, Refilling Point on the PUCHEVILLERS - MARIEUX Road due W. of RAINCHEVAL, and Ordnance Refilling Point at 6 RUE BREAUX, BEAUQUESNE.

Column 5 of March Table issued with Operation Order No.59, will be amended in accordance with paras.1 and 2 above. Times of starting etc., remain unchanged.

ACKNOWLEDGE.

[signature]
Captain
for Brigade Major, 91st Infantry Brigade.

Issued at 7/15 p.m.

Copies to all recipients of O.O.59, and to 54th Field Coy., R.E.

Appendix 10.

WEEKLY PROGRAMME OF TRAINING.

91st Infantry Brigade.

Date.	Unit.	Time.	Place.	Form of Training.
1917. Monday, Jan.29th.	2nd Bn.Queen's R'	8-30.a.m. to 12-30.p.m.	PUCHEVILLERS.	Physical Training – Trench Routine,Posting and duties of Sentries – Section Training – Musketry – Consolidation of captured positions – Close Order Drill.
	1st Bn.S.Staffs.R'	-do-	RAINNEVAL.	Close order drill – Physical Training – Section Training – Wiring Practices – Musketry.
		6.p.m. to 7.p.m.		Wiring by night.
	21st Bn.Manch.R'	8-30.a.m. to 12-30.p.m.	BEAUQUESNE.	Physical Drill – Musketry – Out-Posts (Elementary) – Company Drill.
	22nd Bn.Manch.R'	-do-	PUCHEVILLERS.	Physical Training – Musketry – General Training – Bombing – Lewis Gun Instruction.
		6.p.m.		Scouts under Scouting Officer.
	91st Machine Gun Coy.	8-30.a.m. to 12-30.p.m.	-do-	Rifle Drill – Machine Gun Training.
	91st T.M.Battery.	-do-	-do-	Physical Drill – Squad Drill – Gun Drill.
	91st Bde.Gren.Coy.	-do-	-do-	Physical Drill – Musketry and Arm Drill – Bomb Throwing.
Tuesday, Jan.30th.	2nd Bn.Queen's R'	8-30.a.m. to 12-30.p.m.	PUCHEVILLERS.	Close Order Drill – Company in Attack – Bayonet Fighting and Box Respirator Drill – Physical Training – Section Training.
		6.p.m. to 8.p.m.		Night Out-posts.
	1st Bn.S.Staffs.R'	8-30.a.m. to 12-30.p.m.	RAINNEVAL.	Close Order Drill – Physical Training – Section Training – Company Trench Attack.

Date.	Unit.	Time.	Place.	Form of Training.
Tuesday Jan.30th. (contd.)	21st Bn.Manch.Regt.	8-30.a.m. to 12-30.p.m.	BEAUQUESNE.	Physical Training – Bayonet Fighting – Advance & b Guards – Saluting Drill – Night Operations.
	22nd Bn.Manch.Regt.	–do–	PUCHEVILLERS.	Physical Training – Musketry – General Training – Lewis Gun Instruction – Bombing.
	91st Machine Gun Coy.	–do–	–do–	Physical Training – Machine Gun Training – Night Operations.
	91st T.M.Battery.	–do–	–do–	Physical Training – Route March.
	91st Bde.Grenade Coy.	–do–	–do–	Physical Training – Grenade Throwing.
Wednesday, Jan.31st.	2nd Bn.Queen's Regt.	8-30.a.m. to 12-30.p.m.	Brigade Training Area.	Battalion Attack.
	1st Bn.S.Staffs.Regt.	–do–	RAINCHEVAL.	Close Order Drill – Physical Training – Section Training – Bayonet Fighting – Musketry.
	21st Bn.Manch.Regt.	–do–	BEAUQUESNE.	Physical Training – Musketry – Attack Practice – Company Drill.
	22nd Bn.Manch.Regt.	–do–	PUCHEVILLERS.	Physical Training – Musketry – General Training and Lewis Gun Instruction – Bombing – Night Operations.
	91st Machine Gun Coy.	–do–	–do–	Rifle Drill – Machine Gun Training.
	91st T.M.Battery.	–do–	–do–	Physical Training – Saluting – Musketry – Lecture on Stokes Bombs.
	91st Bde.Grenade Coy.	–do–	–do–	Physical Training – Company Drill and Bayonet Fighting – Tests.

Date.	Unit.	Time.	Place.	Form of Training.
Thursday, Feb.1st.	2nd Bn.Queen's Regt.	8-30.a.m. to 12-30.p.m.	PUCHEVILLERS.	— Saluting — Physical Training — Section Training — Bayonet Fighting — Outpost drill — Close Order Drill.
	1st Bn.S.Staffs.Regt.	—do—	RAINCHEVAL.	Close Order Drill — Physical Training — Section Training — Company Attack, consolidation &c. — Entrenching by night.
	21st Bn.Manch.Regt.	—do—	Brigade Training Area.	Battalion Attack.
	22nd Bn.Manch.Regt.	—do—	PUCHEVILLERS.	Physical Training — Musketry — General Training and Lewis Gun Instruction — Bombing.
	91st Machine Gun Coy.	—do—	—do—	Physical Training — Machine Gun Training.
	91st T.M.Battery.	—do—	—do—	Physical Training — Gas Helmet Drill — Gun Drill — Digging and Ammunition carrying.
	91st Bde.Grenade Coy.	—do—	—do—	Physical Training — Musketry and Arm Drill.
Friday, Feb.2nd.	2nd Bn.Queen's Regt.	8-30.a.m. to 12-30.p.m.	PUCHEVILLERS.	Physical Training — Section Training — Musketry — Close Order Drill — Extended Order Drill — Artillery Formations — Inter Communication.
	1st Bn.S.Staffs.Regt.	—do—	RAINCHEVAL.	Close Order Drill — Physical Training — Section Training — Company Attack.
	21st Bn.Manch.Regt.	—do—	BEAUQUESNE.	Physical Training — Bayonet Fighting — Attack Scheme — Night Operations.
	22nd Bn.Manch.Regt.	—do—	Brigade Training Area.	Battalion Attack.
	91st Machine Gun Coy.	—do—	PUCHEVILLERS.	Rifle Drill — Machine Gun Training — Night Operations.
	91st T.M.Battery.	—do—	—do—	Physical Training — Judging Distance — Lecture on construction of Emplacements.
	91st Bde.Grenade Coy.	—do—	—do—	Physical Training — Company Drill and Bayonet Exercise — Instruction in Grenade Throwing.

Date.	Unit	Time.	Place.	Form of Training.
Tuesday, Jan.30th. (contd.)	21st Bn.Manch.Regt.	8-30.a.m. to 12-30.p.m.	BEAUQUESNE.	Physical Training - Bayonet Fighting - Advance &b Guards - Saluting Drill - Night Operations.
	22nd Bn.Manch.Regt.	--do--	PUCHEVILLERS.	Physical Training - Musketry - General Training - Lewis Gun Instruction - Bombing.
	91st Machine Gun Coy.	--do--	--do--	Physical Training - Machine Gun Training - Night Operations.
	91st T.M.Battery.	--do--	--do--	Physical Training - Route March.
	91st Bde.Grenade Coy.	--do--	--do--	Physical Training - Grenade Throwing.
Wednesday, Jan.31st.	2nd Bn.Queen's Regt.	8-30.a.m. to 12-30.p.m.	Brigade Training Area.	Battalion Attack.
	1st Bn.S.Staff's.Regt.	--do--	RAINCHEVAL.	Close Order Drill - Physical Training - Section Training - Bayonet Fighting - Musketry.
	21st Bn.Manch.Regt.	--do--	BEAUQUESNE.	Physical Training - Musketry - Attack Practice - Company Drill.
	22nd Bn.Manch.Regt.	--do--	PUCHEVILLERS.	Physical Training - Musketry - General Training and Lewis Gun Instruction - Bombing - Night Operations.
	91st Machine Gun Coy.	--do--	--do--	Rifle Drill - Machine Gun Training.
	91st T.M.Battery.	--do--	--do--	Physical Training - Saluting - Musketry - Lecture on Stokes Bombs.
	91st Bde.Grenade Coy.	--do--	--do--	Physical Training - Company Drill and Bayonet Fighting - Tests.

Date.	Unit.	Time.	Place.	Form of Training.
Thursday, Feb.1st.	2nd Bn.Queen's Regt.	8-30.a.m. to 12-30.p.m.	PUCHEVILLERS	Physical Training - Section Training - Bayonet Fighting - Outpost drill - Close Order Drill.
	1st Bn.S.Staffs.Regt.	--do--	RAINCHEVAL.	Close Order Drill - Physical Training - Section Training - Company Attack, consolidation &c. Entrenching by night.
	21st Bn.Manch.Regt.	--do--	Brigade Training Area.	Battalion Attack.
	22nd Bn.Manch.Regt.	--do--	PUCHEVILLERS	Physical Training - Musketry - General Training and Lewis Gun Instruction - Bombing.
	91st Machine Gun Coy.	--do--	--do--	Physical Training - Machine Gun Training.
	91st T.M.Battery.	--do--	--do--	Physical Training - Gas Helmet Drill - Gun Drill - Digging and Ammunition carrying.
	91st Bde.Grenade Coy.	--do--	--do--	Physical Training - Musketry and Arm Drill.
Friday, Feb. 2nd.	2nd Bn.Queen's Regt.	8-30.a.m. to 12-30.p.m.	PUCHEVILLERS	Physical Training - Section Training - Musketry - Close Order Drill - Extended Order Drill - Artillery Formations - Inter Communication.
	1st Bn.S.Staffs.Regt.	--do--	RAINCHEVAL.	Close Order Drill - Physical Training - Section Training - Company Attack.
	21st Bn.Manch.Regt.	--do--	BEAUQUESNE.	Physical Training - Bayonet Fighting - Attack Scheme - Night Operations.
	22nd Bn.Manch.Regt.	--do--	Brigade Training Area.	Battalion Attack.
	91st Machine Gun Coy.	--do--	PUCHEVILLERS	Rifle Drill - Machine Gun Training - Night Operations.
	91st T.M.Battery.	--do--	--do--	Physical Training - Judging Distance - Lecture on construction of Emplacements.
	91st Bde.Grenade Coy.	--do--	--do--	Physical Training - Company Drill and Bayonet Exercise - Instruction in Grenade Throwing.

Date.	Unit.	Time.	Place.	Form of Training.
Saturday, Feb. 3rd.	2nd Bn.Queen's Regt. 1st Bn.S.Staffs.Regt. 21st Bn.Manch.Regt. 22nd Bn.Manch.Regt.	8-30.a.m. to 12-30.p.m.	OPUCHEVILLERS.	Brigade Ceremonial.
	91st Machine Gun Coy.	—do—	—do—	Route March.
	91st T.M.Battery.	—do—	—do—	Physical Training – Bayonet Fighting – Squad Drill – Arm Drill – Gun Drill.
	91st Bde.Grenade Coy.	—do—	—do—	Physical Training – Musketry and Arm Drill – Grenade Throwing.

SECRET.   Appendix 11.   Copy No. 17

91st Inf. Bde.
No. B.M./1056.

INSTRUCTIONS IN THE EVENT OF THE 7TH DIVISION BEING ORDERED TO REINFORCE THE VTH CORPS FRONT.

Reference LENS Sheet – 1/100,000.

1. (a) If ordered to reinforce the Vth Corps the 7th Division (less Artillery) will, in the first instance, move in accordance with the attached table, and will be prepared afterwards to move thence to any part of the YELLOW or BLUE Line (as shown on the attached map) in the Vth Corps area.

    (b) The 7th Divisional Artillery, after arrival in back areas, will move, in the first instance, via AUTHIE to the Western outskirts of BUS.
    It may be ordered either to reinforce the Artillery of the Vth Corps holding the line or to take up a position covering any part of the YELLOW or BLUE Line.
    The necessary reconnaissances will be carried out.

2. 1st Line Transport will accompany units, but O.R.D. will send any vehicles not likely to be required (such as pontoon wagons) to SARTON.

3. It is improbable that any extra transport will be available for Light Trench Mortar Batteries.

4. No kits may be taken on baggage wagons, except those laid down in Field Service Manual. Arrangements will be made for storage of all surplus kits in village now occupied by unit. A guard of 1 N.C.O. and 3 men being left incharge. (Suitable accommodation should be reconnoitred beforehand and earmarked for the purpose).

5. Blankets will be rolled in bundles of 20 and stacked near the surplus kit store. Arrangements will be made by Divisional Headquarters to deliver these to units if circumstances permit.

6. If supplies for the next day have not yet been delivered to units, supply wagons will refill at the present refilling points, and join their Train Company without delivering to units.

7. On receipt of orders to move Baggage wagons will at once be sent to units, will load up and join their Train Companies.

8. Mounted Military Police at present attached to Brigades will at once be sent to rejoin A.P.M. at Divisional Headquarters.

9. Field Ambulances will despatch Bearer Sub-divisions to join Brigade Groups; Tent sub-divisions of the three Ambulances concentrating at SARTON.

10. ZERO hour will be notified to all units.

11. The 7th Division may be required to reinforce the IInd Corps Front, in which case a second march table will be forwarded to all concerned.

12. ACKNOWLEDGE.

Major,
1917. Brigade Major, 91st Infantry Brigade.

Copy No 1 7th Division.
" 2 Brigade Major.
" 3 Staff Captain.
" 4 2nd Queen's R.
" 5 1st S.Staffs.R
" 6 21st Manch.R
" 7 22nd Munch.R
" 8 91st M.G.Coy.
" 9 91st T.M.Battery.
" 10 91st Bde.Gren.Coy.
" 11 91st Bde.Sig.Off.
" 12 21st Field Amb.
" 13 No.3 Coy.Div.Train.
" 14 Supply Officer, 91st Inf.Bde.
" 15 Bde.Transport Officer
" 16 Files
" 17 War Diary.
" 18 War Diary.

March Table to accompany 91st Infantry Brigade No.B.M./1656.

Unit. (In order of march).	From.	To.	Route.	Hour of starting.
1st Infy.Staff.?	RAINNEVAL.	BUS.	ARQUEVES - LOUVENCOURT.	Will move off at ZERO hour.
Brigade Headquarters. Signal Section. Grenade Coy. Trench Mortar Bty.	PUCHEVILLERS.	BUS.	RAINNEVAL - ARQUEVES - LOUVENCOURT.	ZERO Hour.
91st Machine Gun Coy.	PUCHEVILLERS.	BUS.	-do-	ZERO plus 10 minutes.
2nd Bn.Queen's Regt.	PUCHEVILLERS.	BUS.	-do-	ZERO plus 20 minutes.
2nd Bn.Monck.Regt.	PUCHEVILLERS.	BUS.	-do-	ZERO plus 45 minutes.
21st Bn.Manch.Regt.	BEAUQUESNE.	BUS.	-do-	ZERO plus 70 minutes.
21st Field Ambulance Bearer Sub-division.	VAL DE MAISON.	BUS.	-do-	ZERO plus 35 minutes.

NOTE. - Intervals of 200 yards between Companies and 500 yards between Battalions will be observed.

Vol. 16.

Headquarters,

91st Infantry Brigade

February 1919.

Army Form C. 2118.

Vol/6

WAR DIARY
or
INTELLIGENCE SUMMARY.

(Erase heading not required.)

91st Infantry Brigade   February 1917

Instructions regarding War Diaries and Intelligence Summaries are contained in F.S. Regs., Part II. and the Staff Manual respectively. Title pages will be prepared in manuscript.

Hour, Date, Place	Summary of Events and Information	Remarks and references to Appendices
PUCHEVILLERS. 1.2.17	Frosty with a little snow. Casualties Nil. Reinforcements 19th Welsh Regt. 1/1 off. 1/1 & O.R. 21st Manchester Regt. 1.O.R.	HA
2.2.17	Very frosty, with cold wind. Casualties Nil.	RR?
3.2.17	Very frosty. Casualties Nil. Reinforcements 2nd Queens Regt. 2 O.R.	RR?
4.2.17	Very frosty. Casualties Nil. Reinforcements	
5.2.17	Frosty. Casualties Nil. 1/Queens 2 officers, 21st Manchesters, 2 officers 7 O.R. 22nd Manchesters 8 officers. 91st M.G. Coy. 1 officer.	Appendix 1. RR?
6.2.17	Frosty. Casualties Nil.	RR?
7.2.17	Frosty. Reinforcements. 1.O.R. 21st Manchesters. RR?	
8.2.17	Frosty. Reinforcements 1 cavalier Nil. RR?	
9.2.17	Frosty. 21st Mch. Reg. 1.O.R.	RR?
10.2.17	Frosty. Casualties Nil. Reinforcements 1/5 Staffords 3 officers 80 O.R. 21st Manchesters	RR?
11.2.17	Frosty. 17 O.R.	
12.2.17	Frosty. Reinforcements 21st Mch. Regt. 1. O.R. 2/Queens 3 O.R. 1/5.Staffds 1.O.R. RR? Appendix 2	

Army Form C. 2118.

WAR DIARY
or
INTELLIGENCE SUMMARY.
(Erase heading not required.)

Instructions regarding War Diaries and Intelligence Summaries are contained in F.S. Regs., Part II and the Staff Manual respectively. Title pages will be prepared in manuscript.

Place	Hour, Date	Summary of Events and Information	Remarks and references to Appendices
PUCHEVILLERS	13.2.17	Rain – Casualties NIL. Reinforcements NIL.	M/S
"	14.2.17	Train started – Casualties NIL. Reinforcements 1st R. Lanc. Regt. 1 O.R.	M/S
"	15.2.17	Heavy snow all day. Casualties & reinforcements NIL	M/S
"	16.2.17	Snow turning to rain in afternoon. Casualties NIL. Reinforcements 1/5 Manch Regt 1 Officer + 3 O.R. Brigade Football Competition. 1/8 Manch Regt won final.	M/S
"	17.2.17	Snow – some rain in evening. General NIVELLE, accompanied by F.M. Sir D. HAIG inspected the 3rd Division on parade in the French Reviewing ground and presented Commanding Officers at Bde. HQrs to discuss future operations in evening. Conference of Commanding Officers in evening. Casualties & reinforcements NIL.	M/S
"	18.2.17	Fair and windy. 1st Bn South Staffs Regt moved from RAINNEVAL to BEAUQUESNE and 21st Bn Manchester left DUDS & Camp BERTRANCOURT. Both battalions travelled in R. Royal buses. Trainers sent into Boise Ref. working parties. 1st Col. W.W. NORMAN D.S.O 21st Bn Manchester Regt 5 O.R. 1/5 Staffs Regt 1 Officer Casualties NIL. Reinforcements 2/Manch Regt 6 O.R. 2/1 Manchester Regt 5 O.R.	M/S Appendix 3.
"	19.2.17	Both cold and windy. 1st Bn South Staffs Regt moved to BERTRANCOURT. Casualties NIL. Reinforcements 2/7 Manchester Regt 1 Officer 1st Bn South Staffs Regt 1 Officer in 21 O.R. 2/1 Manchester Regt 8 O.R.	M/S

(7399) W4141–463. 400,000. 9/14. H.&J., Ltd. Forms/C. 2118/10.

Army Form C. 2118.

WAR DIARY
or
INTELLIGENCE SUMMARY.
(Erase heading not required.)

Instructions regarding War Diaries and Intelligence Summaries are contained in F.S. Regs., Part II. and the Staff Manual respectively. Title pages will be prepared in manuscript.

Hour, Date, Place	Summary of Events and Information	Remarks and references to Appendices
PUCHEVILLERS } 20.2.17 BERTRANCOURT. }	Heavy rain all day. Brigade moved in motor Bus H/qrs and 9th Kensis Coy and 9th T.M.B. to BERTRANCOURT. 2nd Bn Queens Regt to ALBERT when they came under orders of 2nd Division 22nd Bn Manchester Regt to THIEPVAL and ST. PIERRE DIVION when they came under orders of 18th Division. 1st Bn TyneSide Scott. 20th Bn Manchester Regt came under orders 1st 9th Bde also 2 1st Bn R. Irish Fusiliers and 20th Bn Border Regt 9th Infantry Coys came under orders of 62nd Division. Casualties and Reinforcements NIL.	Appendices 4, 4·A. N.V.S.
MAILLY MAILLET 21.2.17	Dull and wintry. Brigade H/qrs moved to left section MAILLY MAILLET – 21st Bn Manchester Regt moved from BERTRANCOURT to C.2 Section with Headquarters temporarily at WHITE CITY (Q4.c.5-8) relieving 2 Battalion 186th Infantry Brigade. 1st Bn R. Irish Fusiliers moved from BERTRANCOURT to BEAUMONT HAMEL with headquarters at BURN WORK and found Brigade Support. 9th Bde found Coy moved to MAILLY MAILLET. Casualties and Reinforcements NIL.	Appendix 5. N.V.S.
22.2.17.	Dull and mainly with some rain in morning. 1st Bn Irish Rifles Left BERTRANCOURT to C.1 Section with Headquarters at WALKER QUARRY (Q.5. b.7-3) relieving one Battalion and one Company of 187th Infantry Bde. 22nd Bn Manchester Regt moved from BERTRANCOURT to MAILLY MAILLET and formed Brigade Reserve, Relief by 21st Bn Manchester Left in C.2 Section completed at 8 am. H/qrs 1st Bn R Irish Fusiliers moved to R.35.c.3.2 and 1st Bn R Irish Fusiliers to WHITE CITY. Casualties 1st Bn R. Rifles Two. 1 O.R. Wounded. Reinforcements. 21st Bn Manchester Regt. 1 Officer.	Appendix 6. N.V.S.

Army Form C. 2118.

WAR DIARY
or
INTELLIGENCE SUMMARY.
(Erase heading not required.)

Instructions regarding War Diaries and Intelligence Summaries are contained in F.S. Regs., Part II. and the Staff Manual respectively. Title pages will be prepared in manuscript.

Hour, Date, Place		Summary of Events and Information	Remarks and references to Appendices
MAILLY MAILLET	23.2.17	Dull and misty. Casualties - 1st Staffs Regt. 1 O.R. wounded. Reinforcements. 91st M.G.C. 2 ORs.	Appendix 7.
"	24.2.17	Misty at first clearing up in the afternoon. Patrols went out as far as SERRE from left battalion and PENDANT COPSE from right battalion without encountering any enemy. Right Battalion front pushed forward about 300 yds. North of TEN TREE ALLEY. Casualties. 22nd Manchester Regt 2 OR wounded. Reinforcements. 7 men 1 OR 1/5th Staffs 21 OR Manchester 1 OR 91st MGC 2 OR.	Appendix 8.
"	25.2.17	Very foggy. Sharp patrol supported by 2 companies each from 1st Staffs Battn Regt on right and 21st Bn Manchester Regt on left pushed forward at 5 am and occupied SERRE establishing a line from K 30 b 6.8 to L 25 b 6.0 (France Sheet 57D). 1st Bn Royal Welch Fusiliers took on whole front relieving 1st Bn 1 Staffs Regt and 21st Bn Manchester Regt who returned to billets in MAILLY MAILLET. 2nd Bn Green Regt and 22nd Bn Manchester Regt rejoined Brigade Group also billets at BERTRANCOURT and P.1.d.- 9.1 respectively. Casualties 1st Bn 1/Staff Regt 1 OR missing 21st Bn Manchester Regt 1 OR killed 8 ORs wounded.	Appendix 9. " 9A. " 9B
BEAUSSART	26.2.17	Fine. P.O.C. 2nd Suffolks took over command of sector at 8 am. Brigade HQ moved to BEAUSSART. 1st Staffs Regt. and 21st Bn Manchester Regt moved to BERTRANCOURT. Casualties nil. Reinforcements 21st Bn Manchester Regt 24 OR. 22nd Bn Manchester Regt 1 OR. 91st MGC 1 OR.	

Army Form C. 2118.

WAR DIARY
or
INTELLIGENCE SUMMARY.
(Erase heading not required.)

Instructions regarding War Diaries and Intelligence Summaries are contained in F.S. Regs., Part II. and the Staff Manual respectively. Title pages will be prepared in manuscript.

Hour, Date, Place	Summary of Events and Information	Remarks and references to Appendices
BEAUSSART 27.2.17.	Fire - Casualties 1/S. Staff 2 O.R. wounded. 21/Manchesters 1 O.R. wounded. Reinforcements 2/Sp[ea]rs 7 Officers 5 O.R. 1/S. Staffs 6 O.R. 21/Manchester 10 O.R. 22/Manchester 4 O.R.	
" 28.2.17	Still. Casualties Nil. Reinforcements 2/Sp[ea]rs 8 O.R. 21/Manchester 1 Officer.	

Ri[char]d[so]n? [signature]
Brigadier General
Commanding 91st Infantry Brigade

Appendix 1

91st Infantry Brigade.

Programme of Training for week ending 10th February, 1917.

Date.	Unit.	Time.	Place.	Form of Training.
1917.				
Monday. Feb.5th.	2nd Bn.Queen's R¹	9-0.a.m.to 12.30.p.m. 6-0.p.m.-5p 8-0.p.m.	PUCHEVILLERS.	Physical Training - Musketry - Sectional Training - Advanced and Flank Guards - Ceremonial Drill. Forming up and assault - Re-organisation - Consolidating.
	1st Bn.S.Staffs.R¹	9-0.a.m.to 12-30.p.m.	RAINNEVAL.	Inspections - Close Order Drill - Physical Training - Sectional Training - Bayonet Fighting - Musketry.
	21st Bn.Manch.R¹	9-0.a.m.to 12-30.p.m.	BEAUQUESNE.	Physical Training - Ceremonial - Bayonet Fighting - Artillery Formation ending in Attack.
	22nd Bn.Manch.R¹st.	9-0.a.m.to 12-30.p.m. 6.p.m.	PUCHEVILLERS.	Battalion Exercise including Battalion Attack. Night Operations
	91st Machine Gun C.	9-0.a.m.to 12-30.p.m.	-do-	Close Order Drill. Rifle Training. Machine Gun Training (including Stoppages,Mechanism etc).
	91st T.M.Battery.	9-0.a.m.to 12-30.p.m.	-do-	Physical Drill - Squad Drill - Judging Distance - Gun Drill.
	91st Bde.Gren.Coy.	9-0.a.m.to 12-30.p.m.	-do-	Physical Drill - Bayonet Exercises - Bomb Throwing in open and along trench - Assembling and dissembling Mills No.5.Hand Grenades. Lecture on Rifle Grenades and method of firing.
Tuesday, Feb.6th.	2nd Bn.Queen's R¹	9-0.a.m.to 12-30.p.m.	PUCHEVILLERS.	Physical Training - Sectional Training - Bayonet Fighting - Battalion Advance Guard - Ceremonial Drill.
	1st Bn.S.Staffs.R¹	-do-	Brigade Training Area.	Battalion Exercise including Battalion Attack.
	21st Bn.Manch.R¹	-do- 6-15.p.m.- 8.p.m.	BEAUQUESNE. -do-	Physical Drill - Ceremonial - Extended Order Drill. Advance,Rear and Flank Guards. Outposts.

Date.	Unit.	Time.	Place.	Form of Training.
1917.				
Tuesday. Feb.6th. (contd.)	22nd Bn.Manch.R.	9-0.a.m. to 12-30.p.m. 5-30.p.m.	PUCHEVILLERS.	Musketry - Company Training - Lecture.
	91st Machine Gun C.	-do- 6-0.p.m. to 8-0.p.m.	-do-	Physical Training - Machine Gun Training (including stoppages,mechanism,Gun Drill etc.) Night Operations.
	91st T.M.Battery.	9-0.a.m. to 12-30.p.m.	-do-	Physical Drill - Gun Drill - Firing.
	91st Bde.Gren.Coy.	-do-	-do-	Physical Drill - Company Drill -, Throwing of Bombs into and along a trench - Formation of Grenadiers Parties - Lecture on Grenades and Detonating.
Wednesday, Feb.7th.	2nd Bn.Queen's R.	9-0.a.m. to 12-30.p.m.	Brigade Training Area.	Battalion Exercise and Battalion Attack.
	1st Bn.S.Staffs.R.	-do- 6-p.m. to 7.p.m.	RAINCHEVAL.	Inspections - Close Order Drill - Physical Training - Bayonet Fighting - Musketry - Company Attack across open - Lecture.
	21st Bn.Manch.R.	9-0.a.m. to 12-30.p.m.	BEAUQUESNE.	Physical Training - Ceremonial - Musketry - Company Defence Practice.
	22nd Bn.Manch.Regt.	-do- 5-30.p.m.	PUCHEVILLERS.	Musketry - Company Training -, Lecture.
	91st Machine Gun C	9-0.a.m. to 12-30.p.m.	-do-	Rifle Drill + Machine Gun Training (including Stoppages etc.)
	91st T.M.Battery.	-do-	-do-	Physical Training - Squad and Arm Drill - Digging and Ammunition Carrying - Bayonet Fighting - Lecture.
	91st Bde.Gren.Coy.	9-0.a.m. to 12-30.p.m.	-do-	Physical Training - Company Drill - Throwing Grenades - Test - Lecture on Grenade Tactics.

Date.	Unit.	Time.	PLACE.	Form of Training.
1917.				
Thursday, Feb.8th.	2nd Bn.Queen's R 1st Bn.S.Staffs.R 21st Bn.Manch.R 22nd Manch.R	9-0.a.m. to 12-30.p.m.	Brigade Training Area.	B R I G A D E D A Y.
	91st Machine Gun Coy.	—do—	PUCHEVILLERS.	Physical Training - Machine Gun Training -
	91st T.M.Battery.	—do—	—do—	Physical Training - Gun Drill and Firing.
	91st Bde.Gren.Coy.	—do—	—do—	Physical Training - Bayonet Exercises - Throwing Grenades - Firing Dummy Rifle Grenades - Lecture on Rifle Grenades.
Friday, Feb.9th.	2nd Bn.Queen's R	9-0.a.m. to 12-30.p.m. 6.p.m.- 8.p.m.	PUCHEVILLERS. —do—	Physical Training - Sectional Training - Ceremonial - Battalion Flank and Rear Guards - Battalion Outpost Scheme.
	1st Bn.S.Staffs.R	9-0.a.m. to 12-30.p.m.	RAINNEVAL.	Battalion Drill - Musketry - Company Training - Outposts.
	21st Bn.Manch.R	—do—	BEAUQUESNE & Bde.Tng.Area.	Physical Drill - Ceremonial Drill - Bayonet Fighting - Arm Drill - Battalion Attack.
	22nd Bn.Manch.R	—do— 5-30.p.m.	PUCHEVILLERS. —do—	Musketry - Company Training. Lecture.
	91st Machine Gun Coy.	9.a.m. to 12-30.p.m. 6.p.m.- 8.p.m.	—do— —do—	Rifle Drill - Machine Gun Training. Night Operations.
	91st T.M.Battery.	9-0.a.m. to 12-30.p.m.	—do—	Physical Training - Squad and Arm Drill - Ranging with Guns.
	91st Bde.Gren.Coy.	—do—	—do—	Physical Training - Bayonet Exercises - Firing live Grenades and Rifle Grenades - Final Lecture on Grenades.

Date.	Unit.	Time.	Place.	Form of Training.
1917.				
Saturday. Feb.10th.	2nd Bn.Queen's R 1st G.Guards.R 21st Bn.Manch.R 22nd Bn.Manch.R	9-0.a.m. to 12-30.p.m.	Brigade Training Area.	BRIGADE CEREMONIAL.
	91st Machine Gun Coy.	—do—	PUCHEVILLERS— VAL DE MAISON— RUBEMPRÉ— TOUTENCOURT.	Route March.
	91st T.M.Battery.	—do—	PUCHEVILLERS.	Physical Training – Gun Drill – Digging and Ammunition Carrying.
	91st Bde. Xen.Coy.	—do—	—do—	Physical Training – Company Drill – Tests.

Brigade Headquarters.
2nd February,1917.

Brigadier General.
Commanding,91st Infantry Brigade.

Appendix 2

91st Infantry Brigade.

Programme of Training for week ending 17th February, 1917.

Date.	Unit.	Place.	Form of Training.
1917. Monday, Feb.12th.	2nd Bn.The Queen's Regt.	PUCHEVILLERS.	Physical Training. Sections under their Commanders. Company Drill.
	1st Bn.S.Staffs Regt.	RAINCHEVAL.	Battalion Drill. Entrenching a position in the face of the enemy. Posts to be pushed out.
	21st Bn.Manchester Regt.	BEHUQUESNE.	Battalion Drill and Ceremonial. Assault on trenches, rallying, consolidation, exploiting success &c. Rapid wiring. Lewis Gun Practice. Bombing exercises. Lecture to Officers and N.C.Os on attack in Open Warfare. _Advanced Guards & Halt Outposts_
	22nd Bn.Manchester Regt.	PUCHEVILLERS.	1 Company on Range. 3 Companies Company Training. Bayonet fighting. Lecture.
	91st Machine Gun Co.	-do.-	Cleaning up generally. Physical Drill. Limber Drill. Recreational training.
	91st Trench Mortar Battery.	-do.-	Physical training. Squad Drill. Judging distance. Gun drill. Squad and Arm Drill.
	91st Bde.Grenade Co.	-do.-	Cleaning up generally. Bombers special physical drill. Bayonet exercises. Practice in throwing all existing types of grenades in the open, and along a trench, also working up a trench. Recreational training.
Tuesday, Feb.13th.	2nd Bn.The Queen's Regt.	Bde.Training Area.	Battalion Exercise.
	1st Bn.S.Staffs Regt.	Bde.Training Area.	Battalion attack practice.
	21st Bn.Manchester Regt.	BEHUQUESNE.	Battalion drill. Ceremonial. Advanced Guard and Halt outposts. Rapid wiring. Consolidation. Lewis Gun Practice. Bombing exercises. Lecture to Officers and N.C.Os on Attack in Open Warfare.

Date.	Unit.	Place.	Form of Training.
1917. Tuesday, Feb.13th.	22nd Bn.Manchester Regt.	PUCHEVILLERS.	Battalion Trench Attack,and Company training. Recreational training. Night Operations.
	91st Machine Gun Co.	-do.-	Cleaning up generally. Rifle drill. Revolver practice and Limber drill. Recreational training. Night operations
	91st Trench Mortar Battery.	-do.-	Physical Drill. Gun Drill. Firing.
	91st Bde.Grenade Co.	-do.-	Cleaning up generally. Bombers special physical drill. Musketry. Arm Drill. Throwing grenades (a) into (b) & (c) along a trench. Practice in dissembling and assembling the Mills (No.5.) Grenades. Recreational training.
Wednesday. Feb.14th.	2nd Bn.The Queen's Regt.	PUCHEVILLERS.	Physical Training. Sections under Section Commenders. Bayonet fighting. Ceremonial Drill.
	1st Bn.S.Staffs Regt.	RAINCHEVAL.	Battalion Drill. Musketry. Practice for all companies in Bombing and firing Lewis Guns. Consolidating and wiring by night, patrols and posts in front.
	21st Bn.Manchester Regt.	BEAUQUESNE.	Battalion Drill. Ceremonial. Attack in Open Warfare. Rapid, wiring. Consolidation. Lewis Gun Practice,and Bombing exercise. Lecture to Officers and N.C.Os. on Trench Assault.
	22nd Bn.Manchester Regt.	PUCHEVILLERS.	1 Company on Range. 3 Companies Route March,by Companies. Bayonet Fighting. Lecture.
	91st Machine Gun Co.	-do.-	Cleaning up generally. Firing practice. Recreational training.
	91st Trench Mortar Battery.	-do.-	Physical Drill. Squad and Arm Drill. Gun Drill. Firing.
	91st Bde.Grenade Co.	-do.-	Cleaning up generally. Bombers special physical drill. Bayonet exercises. Practising formation of Grenadier parties and working up a trench. Lecture. Practice in detonating grenades. Recreational training.

Date.	Unit.	Place.	Form of Training.
1917. Thursday, Feb.15th.	2nd Bn.The Queen's Regt.) 1st Bn.South Staffs Regt.) 21st Bn.Manchester Regt.) 22nd Bn.Manchester Regt.)	Brigade Training Area.	Brigade Day.
	91st Machine Gun Co.	PUCHEVILLERS.	Cleaning up generally. Physical Drill. Machine Gun training. Recreational training.
	91st Trench Mortar Battery.	-do.-	Physical Drill. Gun Drill and Firing.
	91st Bde.Grenade Co.	-do.-	Cleaning up generally. Bombers special physical drill. Company drill. Practice in throwing grenades out of a trench. Practice firing dummy rifle grenades. Lecture on Grenadier tactics. Recreation.
Friday, Feb.16th.	2nd Bn.The Queen's Regt.	PUCHEVILLERS.	Physical training. Sections under Section Commanders. Musketry and extended order drill. Night exercises - digging and wiring.
	1st Bn.S.Staffs Regt.	RAINCHEVAL.	Outposts by day and night.
	21st Bn.Manchester Regt.	BEAUQUESNE.	Battalion drill. Ceremonial. Attack on trench with variety of situation introduced. Rapid wiring Consolidation. Lewis Gun Practice and Bombing exercises. Lecture to Officers and N.C.Os on Lessons learnt during past week.
	22nd Bn.Manchester Regt.	PUCHEVILLERS.	1 Company on Range. 3 Companies Company Training. Bayonet fighting. Lecture.
	91st Machine Gun Co.	-do.-	Cleaning up generally. Rifle Drill. Machine Gun training. Recreational training. Night operations.
	91st Trench Mortar Battery.	-do.-	Physical Drill. Squad and Arm Drill. Ranging with Guns. Bayonet fighting.
	91st Bde.Grenade Co.	-do.-	Cleaning up generally. Bombers special physical drill. Bayonet exercises.M

Date.	Unit.	Place.	Form of training.
1917. Friday, Feb 16th.	91st Bde. Grenade Co. (continued).	PUCHEVILLERS.	Practice firing live Mills Hand Grenades. Lecture. Recreation.
Saturday, Feb.17th.	2nd Bn.The Queen's Regt. 1st Bn.S.Staffs Regt. 21st Bn.Manchester Regt. 22nd Bn.Manchester Regt.	PUCHEVILLERS Brigade Training Area.	Brigade Day.(Ceremonial).
	91st Machine Gun Co.	PUCHEVILLERS.	Cleaning up generally. Route March.
	91st Trench Mortar Battery.	-do.-	Physical Drill. Gun Drill. Firing. Digging practice.
	91st Bde. Grenade Co.	-do.-	Cleaning up generally. Bombers special physical drill. Musketry. Firing live Mills Rifle Grenades. Practice dissembling and assembling Mills Hand Grenade. Lecture. Recreational Training.

Bde. Hd. Qtrs.

[signature] Capt.

for Brigadier General.

Commanding 91st.Infantry Brigade.

9th February, 1917.

Appendix 3

SECRET

B.M/1082/1.

The Officer Commanding,
    2nd Queen's Regt.   1st S.Staffs Regt.
    21st Manch.Regt.   22nd Manch.Regt.
    91st M.Gun Co.   91st T.M.Battery.
    91st Bde.Gren.Co.   91st Bde.Signals.

---

1.   The following moves will take place to-morrow, 18th instant.,

    (a) 1st S.Staffs Regt. from RAINCHEVAL to BUS, via ARQUEVES and LOUVENCOURT. To be clear of RAINCHEVAL by 10 a.m.

    (b) 21st Manchester Regt from BEAUQUESNE to BERTRANCOURT, route as above. To be clear of RAINCHEVAL by 10-30 a.m.

2.   The usual interval of 200 yards between Companies and 500 yards between Battalions will be maintained.

3.   On arrival in the new area, both battalions, together with the 1st R.W.F. and 2nd Border Regt. will come under the Command of Bt.Colonel W.W.Norman, D.S.O., Commanding 21st Manchester Regt., until the 20th instant when Brigade Headquarters moves to BUS. They will be employed on working parties in back areas.

4.   Supply wagons of the train will accompany units, and will march full, delivering to units on arrival. They will then report to O.C., 62nd Divisional Train at BUS.

5.   2 lorries per battalion have been ordered to report at Battalion Headquarters at 7 a.m. It is possible that they may not arrive until the afternoon.

Bde.Hd.Qtrs.   (Sd.)O.F.MORSHEAD, Captain,
17th February, 1917.   a/Brigade Major, 91st Infantry Brigade.

Appendix 4

S E C R E T.
****

Copy No. 9

7th DIVISION ORDER No. 130.

Reference -   19th February, 1917.
BEAUMONT Sheet 57d S.E. 1 & 2 (parts of).
HEBUTERNE   "   57d N.E. 3 & 4 (parts of).

1.   The 7th Division (less Artillery) will relieve the 62nd Division on that portion of the latter's front between L.31.c. 2.6 (exclusive) and K.29.c. 3.1. (exclusive). Relief to be completed by morning of February 23rd.

2.   On relief :-

(a) The boundary between the 7th and 62nd Divisions will be a line running from L.31.c. 2.6. South of KYLE POST to Q.6.a. 5.0. thence North of LEAVE AVENUE to the cross-roads in BEAUMONT HAMEL; thence immediately South of the AUCHONVILLERS - BEAUMONT HAMEL Road.

(b) The boundary between the 7th and 19th Divisions will be a line from K.35.a. 8.8. due West as far as SACKVILLE STREET, thence immediately North of CHEEROH AVENUE.

(c) The 186th Infantry Brigade is the left Infantry Brigade of the 62nd Division, with Headquarters at BEAUSSART.
    The 57th Infantry Brigade is the right Infantry Brigade of the 19th Division, with Headquarters at COURCELLES.

(d) The 62nd Division will have the right to use the AUCHONVILLERS - BEAUMONT HAMEL Road.

3.   The 7th Division front will be divided into two Sectors - C.1 and C.2. The dividing line between the Sectors will be the WAGON ROAD (inclusive to C.2).

4.   The 91st Infantry Brigade will :-

(a) Take over C.1. from the 187th Infantry Brigade, and hold it with one battalion.
    The 187th Infantry Brigade Headquarters are at Point 88.

(b) Take over C.2.from the 186th Infantry Brigade, and hold it with one battalion.

(c) /

(c) Take over the dugout accommodation in BEAUMONT HAMEL and WHITE CITY from the 186th Infantry Brigade with one battalion 20th Infantry Brigade and one battalion 22nd Infantry Brigade, and use these two battalions to support the battalions holding the front.

(d) Make all arrangements for the above reliefs with the Brigade Commanders concerned.

5. The 62nd Division is going to arrange to leave a proportion of N.C.O's and Lewis gunners in the line for 24 hours after completion of the relief.

6. The C.R.E. will arrange with C.R.E. 62nd Division for the relief of Field Companies, and to take over all schemes of work on hand.

7. Orders for the move of the 7th Divisional Train and other administrative units will be issued by "Q".

8. The relief of Machine guns has already been carried out. Captain Stewart, Machine Gun Officer, 22nd Infantry Brigade, will forward to Divisional Headquarters, and to the 91st Infantry Brigade, a map showing the positions of all Machine guns taken over.

9. On completion of the relief the Division will be accommodated as follows :-

    (i) <u>20th Infantry Brigade</u> :-
        2 Battalions.   BERTRANCOURT.
        1 Battalion.   MAILLY MAILLET.
        1 Battalion.   BEAUMONT HAMEL.

    (ii) <u>22nd Infantry Brigade</u> :-
        2 Battalions.   BERTRANCOURT.
        1 Battalion.   MAILLY MAILLET.
        1 Battalion.   BEAUMONT HAMEL.

    (iii) <u>91st Infantry Brigade</u> :-
        2 Battalions.   In line.
        2 Battalions.   With IInd Corps.

    (iv) Pioneer Battn.   MAILLY MAILLET.
        (24th Manchester Regt).

    (v) 54th Field Coy, R.E.   LIVRE CAMP.
        95th Field Coy, R.E.   MAILLY MAILLET.
        528 (Durham)
          Field Coy, R.E.   MAILLY MAILLET.

3.

10. Headquarters will be as follows :-

    Divisional Headquarters. - BERTRANCOURT HUTS.
    20th Infantry Brigade. - BERTRANCOURT.
    22nd Infantry Brigade. - BEAUSSART.
    91st Infantry Brigade. - CAFÉ JOURDAIN.
    Battalion holding C.1. - WALKER QUARRY.
    Battalion holding C.2. - BURN WORK.
    2 Battalions in Support in BEAUMONT HAMEL.

11. All moves connected with the above reliefs will be made in accordance with attached March Table.

12. (a) The G.O.C. 91st Infantry Brigade will assume command of C.1 and C.2 Sectors on completion of the relief.

(b) The G.O.C. 7th Division will assume command of the Divisional front at 9 a.m. on 23rd February, at which hour the Divisional Headquarters closes at MARIEUX and opens at BERTRANCOURT.

13. ACKNOWLEDGE.

G W Howard.

Lieut-Colonel.

General Staff, 7th Division.

Issued at 5.30 p.m. to :-
  A.D.C.(for G.O.C)   Copy No. 1.
  Office.   "   2 & 3.
  "Q"   "   4.
  7th Divisional Artillery.   "   5.
  C.R.E.   "   6.
  20th Infantry Brigade.   "   7.
  22nd Infantry Brigade.   "   8.
  91st Infantry Brigade.   "   9.
  Div.Pioneer Battalion.   "   10.
  7th Signal Company.   "   11.
  A.D.M.S.   "   12.
  Divisional Train.   "   13.
  D.A.D.O.S.   "   14.
  Div. Gas Officer.   "   15.
  19th Division.   "   17.
  62nd Division.   "   18.
  War Diary.   "   19.

MARCH TABLE to accompany 7th Division Order No. 130.

Date.	Unit.	From.	To.	Route.	Remarks.
Feby 21st.	1 Battalion 20th Inf.Bde.	BEAUQUESNE.	BERTRANCOURT.	via RAINCHEVAL, ARQUEVES LOUVENCOURT.	
	1 Battalion 22nd Inf.Bde.	RUBEMPRE.	BERTRANCOURT.	via HERISSART, TOUTENCOURT, ACHEUX.	
Feby 22nd.	20th Infantry Brigade.	PUCHEVILLERS.	1 Battn.MAILLY MAILLET. 1 Battn.BERT- RANCOURT.	via RAINCHEVAL, ARQUEVES, thence - (Battn.for BERTRANCOURT via LOUVENCOURT) and (Battn.for MAILLY MAILLET via ACHEUX & FORCEVILLE).	To be clear of RAINCHEVAL 10 a.m
	528 (Durham) Fd.Coy.R.E. 24th Manchester Regiment(Pioneers)	PUCHEVILLERS. BEAUQUESNE.	MAILLY MAILLET. MAILLY MAILLET	via RAINCHEVAL, ARQUEVES, ACHEUX, FORCEVILLE.	To pass RAINCHEVAL between 10.15 a.m and 10.45 a.m.
	22nd Infantry Brigade.	LA VICOGNE. VAL DE MAISON.	1 Battn.MAILLY MAILLET. 1 Battn.BERT- RANCOURT.	Both Battalions via RAINCHEVAL, ARQUEVES. LOUVENCOURT, BERTRANCOURT.	To pass RAINCHEVAL between 11 a.m and 12 noon.
	21st Field Amb. 23rd " "	VAL DE MAISON RUBEMPRE.	VAUCHELLES. BERTRANCOURT.	via RAINCHEVAL, ARQUEVES, LOUVENCOURT.	Not to pass RAINCHEVAL before 12 noon.

NOTE. Usual intervals 200 yards between Companies, and 500 yards between Battalions will be kept.

Appendix 4. A
No. 13

91st Infantry Brigade Operation Order No.60.

Reference Sheet FRANCE 57D - 1/40,000.

Monday, 19th February, 1917.

-:-:-:-:-:-:-:-:-:-:-

1. The following moves will take place to-morrow, the 20th instant, in accordance with attached table.

2. First Line Transport will accompany Units.

3. Intervals of 200 yards will be maintained between Companies and 500 yards between larger formations. 200 yards will be kept between 1st Line Transport and rear of the Column.

4. Billeting Parties will report at 10 a.m. as follows:-

    Bde.Headqrs.detachment to Town Major, BERTRANCOURT.
    2nd Queen's Regt. to Town Major, ALBERT.
    22nd Manchester Regt. to Town Major, THIEPVAL.

5. Waggons have been allotted as follows:-

    4 waggons to 2nd Queen's Regt. at 8-0 a.m.
    4 " " 22nd Manchester Regt. at 8-0 a.m.
    1 waggon to Brigade Headquarters at 8-0 a.m.
    1 " " Brigade Grenade Co., at 8-0 a.m.
    1 " " 91st T.M.Battery at 8-0 a.m.

6. Brigade Headquarters will close at PUCHEVILLERS at 9-0 a.m. and will re-open at Divisional H.Q.Camp, BERTRANCOURT at 1 p.m.

7. On reaching their new areas the 2nd Queen's and 22nd Manchester Regts. will come under the orders of the 2nd and 18th Divisions respectively.

8. All surplus Lewis Gun Handcarts will be taken by Units.

9. ACKNOWLEDGE.

Issued at...... p.m.

                              Captain,
                     a/Brigade Major, 91st Infantry Brigade.

Copy No. 1. 7th Division.   8. 91st Machine Gun Co.
       2. Brigade Major.   9. 91st T.M.Battery.
       3. Staff Captain.   10. 91st Bde.Grenade Co.
       4. 2nd Queen's Regt. 11. 91st Bde.Signals.
       5. 1st S.Staffs Regt. 12. File.
       6. 21st Manchester Regt. 13. War Diary.
       7. 22nd Manchester Regt. 14. War Diary.

M A R C H   T A B L E.

(Issued with Operation Order No.60 dated 19th February, 1917.)

U N I T.	From.	To.	Route.	Remarks.
Bde. Hd. Qtrs.) 91st T.M.Battery.) 91st Bde.Gren.Co.)	PUCHEVILLERS.	BERTRANCOURT.	RAINCHEVAL - ARQUEVES LOUVENCOURT - BUS.	To be clear of PUCHEVILLERS by 9-15 a.m.
22nd Manchester Regt.	-do.-	THIEPVAL.	Via TOUTENCOURT, HARPONVILLE, etc.	To be clear of PUCHEVILLERS by 9-30 a.m.
2nd Queen's Regt.	-do.-	ALBERT.	Via TOUTENCOURT, VARICY - BAILLON, etc.	Not to clear PUCHEVILLERS before 9-50 a.m.

Appendix 5. No. 13

91st Infantry Brigade Operation Order No.61.

Reference Sheet France 57 D.
BEAUMONT
HEBUTERNE 1/10,000

Tuesday, 20th February, 1917.

1. The 91st Infantry Brigade will relieve the 186th Infantry Brigade and part of the 187th Infantry Brigade in the line from K.29.c.3.1. (exclusive) to L.31.c.2.6.(exclusive) in accordance with the attached relief table.

2. Details of relief will be arranged between Battalion Commanders concerned.

   A diagram showing posts taken over and disposition of troops will be forwarded to reach this office by 12 noon, 24th instant.

3. (a). The front will be divided into two sectors, C1 (right) and C2 (left), the dividing line between the sectors being the WAGON ROAD (inclusive to C2).

   (b) The boundary between the 91st Infantry Brigade and 187th Infantry Brigade on the right will be a line running from L.31.c.2.6. S. of KYLE POST to Q.6.a.5.0. Thence N. of LEAVE AVENUE to the Cross Roads in BEAUMONT HAMEL. Thence immediately S. of the AUCHONVILLERS - BEAUMONT HAMEL Road.

   (c) The boundary between the 91st Infantry Brigade and 57th Infantry Brigade on the left will be a line from K.35.a.8.8. due W. as far as SACKVILLE STREET, thence immediately N. of CHEEROH AVENUE.

4. (a) The 21st Manchesters will hold C2 sector with 1st Royal Welsh Fusiliers in support in BEAUMONT HAMEL.

   (b) The 1st South Staffords will hold C1 sector with 2nd Border Regt. in support in BEAUMONT HAMEL.

5. All diagrams, defence schemes, and aeroplane photographs will be taken over.

6. A proportion of Officers, N.C.Os. and Lewis Gunners will be left in the line for 24 hours after the relief by all outgoing Units.

   Completion of reliefs will be reported by the B.A.E. Code.

8. The G.O.C., 91st Infantry Brigade will assume Command of each Sector on completion of relief.

9. Brigade Headquarters will close at BERTRANCOURT at 11-0 a.m. on February 21st, and will open at Cafe Jourdain, MAILLY MAILLET at the same hour.

10. ACKNOWLEDGE.

Issued at 10 p.m.
Bde. Hd.Qtrs.
20th February, 1917.

Captain,
a/Brigade Major, 91st Infantry Brigade.

Copy No. 1 7th Divn.
2 Brigade Major.
3 Staff Captain
4 1st S.Staffs R.
5 21st Manch.R.
6. 1st R.W.F.
7. 2nd Border R.
8 91st M.G.Co.
9 186th Inf.Bde.
10 187th Inf.Bde.
11 57th Inf.Bde.
12 File
13 War Diary.
14 War Diary.
15 91st T.M.Battery.
16. 91st Bde.Gren.Co.
17. 91st Bde.Signals.

RELIEF TABLE.

Date.	Unit.	From	To	To relieve	Rendezvous for Guides. Pl.Co.	Time.	Remarks.
21st Feb.,1917.	21st March.Regt.	BERTRANCOURT	C2 Sector.	2/6th Duke of Wellington's Regt.(H.Q.: BURN JORN).	Junction of SERRE Road and DUCK-BOARD track.	6-30 p.m.	Battalion H.Q. WHITE CITY temporarily. Subsequently K.35.c.3.2.
				2/7th Duke of Wellington's Regt.(H.Q.: WHITE CITY.	BURN WORK.	6-50 p.m.	
-do.-	1st Royal Welsh Fusiliers.	BERTRANCOURT	BEAUMONT HAMEL.	—	—	—	To be clear of BERTRANCOURT by 12-30 p.m. Representatives to be at junction of New & Old BEAULENT Roads Q.4.c.8.3. at 10.30 a.m. to meet an officer of Bde.Hd.Qtrs.
-do.-	Bde.Hd.qtrs. 91st Bde.Gren.Co.	BERTRANCOURT	MAILLY MAILLET.	—	—	—	To be clear of BERTRANCOURT by 10 a.m. Billeting party of 91st Bde.Gren.Co. to report to Town Major,MAILLY MAILLET at 9-30 a.m.

Date.	Unit.	From	To	To relieve	Rendezvous for Guides.		Remarks.
					Place.	Time.	
22nd Feb.,1917.	1st S.Staffds R.	BERTRANCOURT	C1 Sector.	2/6th West Yorks Regt.	BEAUMONT HAMEL Church.	4-30 p.m.	Battalion H.Q. WALKER QUARRY.
-do.-	2nd Border Regt.	BERTRANCOURT	BEAUMONT HAMEL.	Left Coy. of 2/5th York and Lancs.Regt.	-do.-	4-30 p.m.	As for 1st R.W.Fusliers above.
23rd Feb.,1917.	91st T.M.Battery.	BERTRANCOURT.	MAILLY MAILLET.	186th T.M. Battery.	-	-	To be clear of BERTRANCOURT by 10 a.m. Billeting party to report to O.C. 186th T.M. Battery 10 a.m Feb.21st.

All movement forward of MAILLY MAILLET will be by platoons at 150 yards interval.

Copy No. 13

1. The 2nd Border Regt. will move from BERTRANCOURT to MAILLY MAILLET on February 22nd, 1917. To be clear of BERTRANCOURT by 12-30 p.m. ⚹

2. The 1st Royal Welsh Fusiliers will be in Brigade Support and the 2nd Border Regt. in Brigade Reserve.

3. The Northern boundary of the Brigade Sector will be FLAG AVENUE (inclusive to 57th Infantry Brigade).

    The necessary amendments will be made to O.O.61 paras 3 (c), 4, and relief table.

⚹ Billeting party will report to Town Major, MAILLY MAILLET at 9-30 a.m.

Bde. Hd. Qtrs.
21st February, 1917.

ofmorshead
Captain,
a/Brigade Major, 91st Infantry Brigade.

Addressed to all recipients of C.O.61.

Appendix 6.

91st Infantry Brigade.

Summary of Operations - No.17.

From 6 a.m., 21st February, 1917, to 6 a.m., 22nd February, 1917.

1. OPERATIONS - NIL.

2. INTELLIGENCE - NIL.

3. ENEMY MOVEMENT - None observed.

4. PATROLS.- Touch was obtained by means of patrols with CROW, PARROT, and PIGEON posts, and between DUN COW and BIRD.
   A patrol also obtained touch with the Battalion on the left.

5. GENERAL. - NIL.

6. ENEMY'S ATTITUDE.
   (a) Artillery - WHITE CITY was slightly shelled between 3 and 5 p.m. BEAUMONT HAMEL received the usual attention.
   (b) Infantry - Quiet.
   (c) Machine Gun fire - Slight, coming from the direction of SERRE.
   (d) General - Nil.

Bde.Hd.Qtrs.

22nd February, 1917.

Capt.
for Brigadier General.
Commanding 91st Infantry Brigade.

Appendix 7.

91st Infantry Brigade.

SUMMARY OF OPERATIONS - No.18.

From 6-0 a.m., 22nd February, 1917 to 6-0 a.m., 23rd February, 1917.

1. OPERATIONS - NIL.

2. INTELLIGENCE - A sniper's nest is reported at about K.36.a.4.6. Further observation is being kept to confirm this.

3. ENEMY MOVEMENT - None observed.

4. PATROLS - NIL.

5. GENERAL - NIL.

6. ENEMY'S ATTITUDE.

   (a) Artillery - Fairly active on whole front of left battalion between 12-15 and 1-30 p.m. with 4.2" and 5.9's. BLUE PIG was heavily shelled at 3 p.m. WALKER AVENUE was shelled about 7 p.m. Occasional shells fell in WAGON ROAD, and BEAUMONT HAMEL.

   (b) Infantry - General attitude - quiet. Sniper was active during the night from about K.36.d.2.8.

   (c) Machine Gun fire - Short bursts of fire during the night at irregular intervals from about K.36.d.2.8.

   (d) General - The enemy's general attitude is quiet. A good number of enemy shells are reported not to burst.

Bde.Hd.Qtrs.

23rd February, 1917.

Brigadier General.
Commanding 91st Infantry Brigade.

Appendix 8.

91st Infantry Brigade.

SUMMARY OF OPERATIONS - No.19.

From 6-0 p.m., 23rd February, 1917, to 6-0 p.m., 24th February, 1917.

1. **OPERATIONS.** - Left posts pushed forward distances between 50 and 70 yards and now form a semi-circle from L.31.c.25.55. to K.36.d.50.63. All close to edge of ridge overlooking valley before TEN TREE VALLEY.
The valley on right was wired to protect flank from L.31.c.20.40. to L.31.c.51.32.

2. **INTELLIGENCE.** - A sniper's post was located firing from behind TEN TREE ALLEY about K.36.b.4.15. Another post was located in the same vicinity about K.36.a.40.35.

3. **ENEMY MOVEMENT.** - Four men were seen in TEN TREE ALLEY about point K.36.b.30.35. at 7-30 a.m. 23rd instant.
Enemy reported to be busy on a trench about L.31.a.3.3. This is probably a M.G. emplacement.

4. **PATROLS.** - A patrol proceeded from PARROT POST at 12-30 a.m. towards the German front line. They passed through thick masses of wire at about K.29.c.9.0. but found no traces of the enemy.
Other patrol reports not yet received.

5. **GENERAL.** - Enemy quiet.

6. **ENEMY'S ATTITUDE** -

    (a) **Artillery** - A few heavy shells fell near the left battalion Headquarters (K.35.c.3.2.) between 7 and 11 p.m.
    Hostile artillery was active about K.36.d.50.30. about 10 p.m. 23rd instant. Also on L.31.c.10.18. Mainly Field pieces.
    A flash of a small gun perhaps a 6 pr. was seen at K.36.b.90.05.
    (b) **Infantry** - Quiet.
    (c) **Machine Gun Fire** - Nil.
    (d) **General.** - Our snipers have harassed the enemy and subdued his sniping considerably.

Bde.Hd.Qtrs.

24th February, 1917.

Capt.
Brigadier General.
Commanding 91st Infantry Brigade.

SECRET Appendix 9
No. 21

91st Infantry Brigade Operation Order No.63.

Reference Map SERRE 1/10,000.   Saturday, 24th February, 1917.

1. There is reason to believe that the enemy has retired from his line of posts in rear of TEN TREE ALLEY, and possibly evacuated the village of SERRE.

2. At 5 a.m. on February 25th, 1917, O.C., 21st Manchester Regt. will send forward strong patrols, supported by 2 companies (remainder in Reserve) with the following objectives.

    (1) JOHN ALLEY - MAXIM TRENCH.

    (2) Line from K.30.b.2.5. - POM POM ALLEY.

    (3) Line Q.30.b.6.8. - L.25.a.0.7. - L.25.a.7.5.

3. At the same hour O.C., 1st South Staffs Regt. will carry out a similar advance on a 2 company front from the line of TEN TREE ALLEY, with objectives as under.

    1. A line from Northern Corner of PENDANT COPSE - along track running N.W. through L.25.c.0.3. to junction MAXIM TRENCH - WAGON ROAD.

    2. PENDANT TRENCH.

    3. PENDANT ALLEY EAST.

    4. WING TRENCH - i.e. a line from L.25.b.5.2. - L.25.a.7.5.

4. The advance will not be continued beyond the objective as laid down above, on reaching which the line will be consolidated as far as possible.

5. Boundaries.

    (a) On South. A line from present Right boundary - PENDANT COPSE inclusive - L.25.b.5.2.

    (b) Between 1st South Staffs Regt. and 21st Manchester Regt. WAGON ROAD to point K.30.d.3.1. Thence along PENDANT ALLEY WEST - PENDANT TRENCH. (All inclusive to 1st South Staffs Regt)

    (c) On North. SERRE ROAD - WALTER TRENCH - FLAG ALLEY - K.30.b.2.5. - K.30.b.6.3.

    The closest touch will be maintained throughout the advance with units on either flank.

6. (a) O.C., 1st Royal Welsh Fusiliers will hold himself in readiness to move his battalion at short notice up the WAGON ROAD in support of 1st South Staffs Regt.

    (b) O.C., 2nd Border Regt. will similarly be prepared to move by the SERRE ROAD in support of 21st Manchester Regt.

7. The Divisional Machine Gun Officer will arrange for all Section Commanders in charge of detachments in the line to report for orders to the Battalion Commander in whose Sector they are situated. He will also hold his reserve detachments in readiness to move forward at short notice. He will take up his battle post at Brigade Headquarters.

(continued)

- 2 -

8. The Artillery are arranging to place a stationary protective barrage in advance of the final objective. Active counter-battery work will be carried out.

9. Battalion Commanders will arrange to take forward on the men as large a quantity of ammunition, grenades, tools, etc., as is practicable. Carrying parties will subsequently be organised from the reserve battalions.

10. Advanced Headquarters situated as under will be established at the discretion of Commanding Officers, due notice being previously given to all concerned.

    1st South Staffs Regt. Q.36.d.8.5.(present Right Company H.Q.)

    21st Manchester Regt MOUSE POST.

    Brigade Headquarters WALKER QUARRY.

    In each case orderlies will be left at the rear Headquarters to facilitate delivery of messages to Advanced Headquarters.

O. Thornhead

Bde.Hd.Qtrs.
24th February, 1917.

Captain,
a/Brigade Major, 91st Infantry Bde.

Copy No.
1	7th Divn.	12	C.R.E.
2	1st S.Staffs Regt.	13	20th Inf.Bde.
3	21st Manch.Regt.	14	22nd Inf.Bde.
4	1st R.W.Fusiliers.	15	187th Inf.Bde.
5	2nd Border Regt.	16	57th Inf.Bde.
6	91st T.M.Battery.	17	Supply Officer.
7	91st Bde.Gren.Co.	18	Brigade Major.
8	91st Bde.Signals.	19	Staff Captain.
9	Div.M.G.Officer.	20	File.
10	C.M.A.	21	War Diary.
11	O.C.Left Group R.A.	22	War Diary.

MESSAGE

	LAKE BURN SEA	
TO	LIGHT SLUSH FLAME	

Sender's Number: Bm. 640 Day of Month: 25th. AAA

In confirmation of conversations aaa BURN will relieve LAKE and SEA at dusk tonight in accordance with arrangements made between C.Os concerned aaa BURN will move to Brigade Support in locality of K.35.c. H.Q. at K.35.c.3.2. aaa SEA and LAKE will be withdrawn to billets in Mailly Maillet aaa LIGHT will move into Brigade Support in WHITE CITY and BURN WORK aaa FLAME will be in Brigade Reserve in MAILLY MAILLET.

From: WATER.
Place:
Time: 6-25 p.m.

(Sd.) C. I. Morshead / Capt

Appendix 9 B

Report on Operations against SERRE.
-:-:-:-:-:-:-:-:-:-:-

February 24th - 25th, 1917.
———————

Reference Map SERRE 1/10,000. Edition 1.

SECRET

-:-:-:-:-:-:-:-:-:-:-

1. **PRELIMINARY DISPOSITIONS.**

    On the nights of February 21/22 and 22/23, the 91st Infantry Brigade took over the portion of front allotted to the 7th Division for the intended operations against SERRE. This front extended from FLAG AVENUE on the North, where touch with posts of the 19th Division was made, across the SUCHERIE - SERRE Road at K.35.a.8.8., to the WAGON ROAD at K.36.a.50.35, thence through K.36.Central to K.31.c.1.7. whence the line was continued in a westerly direction by 62nd Division.

    This front was held by two battalions, the 21st Bn. The Manchester Regt., on the left, Headquarters at K.35.c.3.2., and the 1st Bn. South Staffordshire Regt., on the right, Headquarters at WALKER QUARRY, Q.5.b.6.4., the dividing line between the two sectors being the WAGON ROAD (inclusive to 1st Bn. South Staffordshire Regt.)

    The line consisted of a series of isolated posts, some on the site of German dugouts but for the most part in open shell holes. The condition of the ground was very bad, the heavy clay on the forward slopes of the hill being in an exceptionally adhesive state on account of the thaw and rain which had set in after the long spell of frost.

2. **PRELIMINARY EVENTS.**

    On February 24th, between 6-0.a.m., and 10-0.a.m., a patrol consisting of 3 Officers and 9 men of the 21st Bn. The Manchester Regt., established the fact that there were no enemy in the trenches to the S.W. of the village or even in the outskirts of SERRE itself. Moving by different routes under cover of the morning mist, these patrols advanced to within 15 yards of the trees on the outskirts of the village, and thence to a point on the SERRE - HEBUTERNE Road about point K.30.a.5.8. Throughout this reconnaissance no sign of the enemy was seen, nor was there any sniping.

    On the right of the sector also there were indications that the enemy was no longer holding his line on the slopes S. of SERRE and PENDANT COPSE. Our men were walking in the open in front of the strongly wired enemy post at K.36.d.7.9., and later in the morning a daylight patrol of the 1st Bn. South Staffordshire Regt., penetrated to within 200 yards of PENDANT COPSE without encountering any opposition. Posts were therefore established on the slopes of the SERRE ridge roughly on the 120 contour line.

3. **OPERATIONS.**

    In consequence of these facts I decided to advance my line, with the intention of occupying SERRE and establishing a line on the northern slopes of the SERRE RIDGE.

    Zero hour was fixed for 5-0.a.m., on February 25th at which hour both front line battalions were to advance under cover of strong patrols. A copy of operation orders is attached.

    Owing to the darkness and fog, and the difficulties of forming up and making the necessary preparations for an advance, the advance was not commenced until 6-0.a.m. Once launched, however, the advance continued steadily. The 1st Bn. South Staffordshire Regt. and the Right Company of the 21st Bn. The Manchester Regt., passed the line of PENDANT COPSE at 6-30.a.m., and PENDANT TRENCH at 7-45.a.m. Owing to the thick fog direction was lost to a great extent at this point, the front line bearing too far to the left. The left flank of this party met with considerable opposition from the ORCHARD at K.25.a.1.7., where a strong enemy post with machine guns was established. A determined attack was organised, and the enemy forced to retire. The final objective was reached at about 9-30.a.m., and the work of consolidation was put in progress.

(continued).

The left Company of the 21st Bn. The Manchester Regt., encountered an enemy post in SERRE and was held up for about an hour on the line JOHN TRENCH - MAXIM TRENCH. The enemy was eventually dislodged, and the final objective was reached at 10-30.a.m.

4. OPERATIONS ON THE FLANKS.

No trace of the troops of the 62nd Division having been found, at 3-15.p.m.,the reserve Company of the 1st Bn.South Staffordshire Regiment was ordered up to form a defensive flank on the right. By the time they had arrived in the front line the fog had lifted and patrols had succeeded in locating elements of the 62nd Division, about L.26.a.5.7. This Company therefore prolonged the Right down WING TRENCH and obtained touch with the battalion on the right.

On the left also, considerable difficulty was experienced in obtaining touch with the 2/8th Gloucestershire Regt., of the 19th Division. No sign was seen of them in spite of constant patrolling until 1-7.p.m., when a company was found and led up to MAXIM TRENCH, by an officer of the 21st Bn.The Manchester Regt. The Officer in charge however stated that his objective was the SERRE - PUISIEUX Road to which he shortly afterwards retired. Later in the evening a Battalion of the North Staffordshire Regt., came up, and touch was established on the left. Throughout the day the reserve Company of the 21st Bn.The Manchester Regt.,formed a defensive flank to the North,in the absence of any support from that quarter.

5. CONCLUSION.

The operation was thus accomplished with very little opposition. The total casualties only amounted to 1 killed and 8 wounded,and only 5 prisoners were taken. Such resistance as was offered was clearly that of a small party of the enemy holding on to a post till the last minute with the object of delaying our advance.

I had been anxious to press forward into PUISIEUX with the two Reserve Battalions,leaving the 1st Bn.South Staffordshire Regt., and the 21st Bn.The Manchester Regt.,to hold WING TRENCH as a support line. The fact that both my flanks were exposed however rendered any further advance extremely hazardous,and the orders for this operation were consequently suspended pending the arrival of the 19th Division.

At dusk on the 25th February,the 1st Bn.South Staffordshire Regt., and 21st Bn.Manchester Regt.,were relieved by the 1st Bn.Royal Welsh Fusiliers,the relief being complete by 9-30.p.m. The 2nd Bn.Border Regt.,were moved up into support in dugouts in vicinity of K.35.a. and c.,the 2/1st H.A.C.,moving into reserve in BEAUMONT HAMEL. The 2nd Bn.Royal Warwickshire Regt.,became Brigade Reserve in MAILLY MAILLET.

The Command of the Sector passed to G.O.C.,22nd Infantry Brigade at 11-01.a.m.,on 26th February.

In conclusion I should like to draw attention to the exceptionally good work done by the 1st Bn.South Staffordshire Regt., and the 21st Bn. The Manchester Regt. The exhaustion consequent upon the exposure and fatigue inseparable from a 4 days tour in the line needs no emphasis, and that these men should have carried out an operation of this nature (comparatively simple though it subsequently proved to be) calls for the highest praise,especially when the state of the ground is taken into consideration.

The names of the 3 young officers who carried out the patrol alluded to in para.2.,above have already been brought to notice.

Bde.Hd.Qtrs.

3rd March,1917.

Brigadier General,

Commanding,91st Infantry Brigade.

On His Majesty's Service.

Vol. 17.

March 1917

Headquarters,
91st Infantry Brigade

Army Form C. 2118.

WAR DIARY
or
INTELLIGENCE SUMMARY.
(Erase heading not required.)

91st Infantry Brigade. March 1917

Vol 7

Place	Hour, Date	Summary of Events and Information	Remarks and references to Appendices
BEAUSSART.	1.3.17.	Fine – Casualties NIL. Reinforcements NIL. Sec. finding & large working parties on roads & in front area.	MB.
"	2.3.17	Fine – Casualties NIL. Reinforcements 1/5.Staff 1 OR. 21st Manchester 1 OR. Working parties as on 1.3.17.	MB.
"	3.3.17.	Fine – Casualties NIL. Reinforcements 1/5.Staff 13 OR. BEAUSSART shelled at 11.30 p.m. by H.V. gun – No damage – working parties as on 1.3.17	MB.
"	4.3.17	Fine. Casualties 1/5.Staff 1 OR wounded. 91st MGC 1 OR killed. 1 OR wounded. Reinforcements 2/Queen 1 Officer – Working parties as above –	MB.
"	5.3.17.	Snow during night. fine rest of day. Casualties NIL. Reinforcements 2/Queen 14 OR – Working parties as above – 1/S.Staff Regt moved to ARQUEVES.	MB.
"	6.3.17	Fine – Working parties as above – Casualties NIL. Reinforcements 1/S.Staff 1 Officer.	MB.
"	7.3.17	Fine – Very strong wind all day. Working parties as above. Casualties 22nd Manchester 2 OR killed 5 OR wounded. Reinforcements 1/S.Staff 16 OR. 21st Manchester 8 OR. 22nd Manchester 5 OR.	MB.
"	8.3.17	Very strong wind with snow showers – Working parties as above – 22nd Manchester 2 Officers. Reinforcements NIL. Casualties NIL.	MB.

Army Form C. 2118.

WAR DIARY
or
INTELLIGENCE SUMMARY.
(Erase heading not required.)

Instructions regarding War Diaries and Intelligence Summaries are contained in F. S. Regs., Part II. and the Staff Manual respectively. Title pages will be prepared in manuscript.

Hour, Date, Place		Summary of Events and Information	Remarks and references to Appendices
BEAUSSART.	9-3-17	Quiet with some shell- looking parties as before - Casualties. 9/R. M.G.F. 1 OR missing. Reinforcements. 1/F Staff. 1 OR. 9th HLF. 1 OR	HMR
"	10.3.17.	Fine - looking parties as before. Casualties. NIL. 1/F Scamp. 1 OR. 22/Manchester. 1 Officer - Reinforcements.	HMR
"	11.3.17.	Fine - looking parties as before - Casualties. 21/Manchester. 4 OR Reinforcements. Killed 13 OR wounded 1 OR missing. 22/Manchester. 1 Officer.	HMR Appendix 1.
APPLETREES (Q.2.b)	12-3-17.	Some rain - Bonfire Rifle word (to APPLETREES (Q.2.b) relieving 94th Infantry Rifle - 22/Manchester with one company on the Divisional Moved to PUISIEUX and took front from - 22/Manchester 94th and 92nd Infantry Rifles. bar. 1 Corp. moved to MOUSE POST - Reinforcements 7/ Green 10 OR 22/Manchester 1 OR 22/Manchester 1 Officer	HMR Appendix 2
"	13.3.17.	Dull turning to rain in the evening- Information received from Bonmain that enemy had retired from LOUPART WOOD and others - received of patrols to push forward & get whether 'BUCQUOY was still held - Patrols reported that they were held up by machine gun fire + that how was not cut. Orders received that 9th Infantry Rifle was to attack BUCQUOY during night 13/14 March - 22/Manchester moved to PUISIEUX & took over right half of Divisional front. Reinforcements NIL.	HMR Appendix 3 + 3a
"	14.3.17.	Lieut Col. 1 am assault made against BUCQUOY. 22/Manchester on right 7/Green on left with 2/R Warwicks + 11 HAC in reserve in PUISIEUX.	Appendix 3 B.

Army Form C. 2118.

WAR DIARY
or
INTELLIGENCE SUMMARY.
(Erase heading not required.)

Hour, Date, Place	Summary of Events and Information	Remarks and references to Appendices

APPLETREES (Q.2.b.)

14.3.17 (cont.) Attacking troops held up by enemy wire - Right company again. 2/Manchesters entered enemy trenches but were bombed out again.
91" Inf Bde (less MGC & TMB) relieved by 22" Inf Bde during night 14/15 March. Bde HQrs moved back to BEAUSSART. 2/Sherwoods to BOLTON Camp MAILLY MAILLET, 2/Manchesters to MAILLY WOOD EAST - Reinforcement 2/Sherwoods 3 Officers.

MR

BEAUSSART 15.3.17. Fine. 91" M.G.C. relieved by 22" M.G.C. 91" TMB withdrawn without being relieved. Reinforcements NIL. Officers & 2/Manchesters arrived to BERTRANCOURT. 115 Staff from ARQUEVES to MAILLY.

Casualties 12/15 March.

Appendix 4.
MR

	Killed		Wounded		Missing	
	Officers	O.R.	Officers	O.R.	Officers	O.R.
2/Sherwoods	2	26	2	67	2	20
21/Manchester	-	-	-	1	-	-
22/Manchester	2	18	1	52	1	69
Total	4	44	3	120	3	89

16.3.17. Fine. Casualties NIL. Reinforcements 1/S.Staffs 80 O.R. 21/Manchesters 3 O.R.

MR

Army Form C. 2118.

WAR DIARY
or
INTELLIGENCE SUMMARY.
(Erase heading not required.)

Instructions regarding War Diaries and Intelligence Summaries are contained in F. S. Regs., Part II. and the Staff Manual respectively. Title pages will be prepared in manuscript.

Place	Hour, Date	Summary of Events and Information	Remarks and references to Appendices
BEAUSSART	17.3.17.	Fine. Casualties NIL. Reinforcements. 1/Green 5 O.R. 2/Manchester 9 O.R.	MB
"	18.3.17.	Fine. Bde HQrs moved to APPLETREES (Q&6). 1/Green + 2/Manchester moved from BERTRANCOURT to billets in MAILLY MAILLET. 2/Manchester Reinforcements from BERTRANCOURT to Camp at AUCHONVILLERS. Casualties NIL. 2/Manchester 21 O.R.	MB
APPLETREES (Q&6)	19.3.17	Fine with strong wind. Morning. Two battalions working on SERRE - PUISIEUX road - Casualties NIL. Reinforcements 91 MGC 6 O.R.	MB
"	20.3.17	Strong wind with some sleet. Three battalions working on roads. Casualties NIL. Reinforcements. 2/Manchester 10 O.R.	MB
"	21.3.17.	Bad with some sleet. Three battalions working on roads. Reinforcements NIL.	MB
"	22.3.17	Fine except for several snow storms. One battalion + half battalion Casualties NIL. Reinforcements. 1/5. Staff 1 Offr. 1/Green 7 O.R. 2/Manchester 2/Manchester 5 Offrs. 91 MGC 10 O.R. + 1/5. Cross moved from MAILLY MAILLET to PUISIEUX. 2/Green + 1/5.Cross	MB
ABLAINZEVELLE	23.3.17	Fine. Bde HQrs moved to ABLAINZEVELLE - 2/Green + ABLAINZEVELLE 1/5.Staffords + 2/Manchester to COURCELLES - LE - COMTE 2/Manchester to BUCQUOY - 91 MGC to PUISIEUX. Casualties + Reinforcements NIL.	MB

Army Form C. 2118.

WAR DIARY
or
INTELLIGENCE SUMMARY.
(Erase heading not required.)

Instructions regarding War Diaries and Intelligence Summaries are contained in F.S. Regs., Part II and the Staff Manual respectively. Title pages will be prepared in manuscript.

Place	Hour, Date	Summary of Events and Information	Remarks and references to Appendices
ABLAINZEVELLE	24. 3. 17	Fine. 91st MGC moved to HAMELINCOURT. 2/Manchester moved into its line at ST. LEGER being attached to 20th Infantry Bde. 3 Battalions worked on clearing villages and roads. Casualties & Reinforcements NIL.	MB
COURCELLES LE COMTE	25. 3. 17	Fine. Bde HQrs moved from ABLAINZEVELLE to Camp at COURCELLES LE COMTE. Temporarily working 2/Manchester moved from BUCQUOY to COURCELLES LE COMTE. Two Battalions working on roads to Casualties 2/Manchester — 3 OR Killed, 1 Officer & 7 OR wounded. 2 OR missing. Reinforcements NIL.	MB
"	26. 3. 17	Wet — Casualties. 1/Queen 1 Officer killed. Reinforcements 1/Queen 13 OR. 2/Manchester 1 OR. 2/Manchester 10 OR. 91 MGC 1 Officer.	MB
"	27. 3. 17	Strong wind with occasional hail storms — 1st Staff & 22/Manchester relieved 2/Manchester in the line. Bde HQrs moved to ERVILLERS. Casualties 2/Manchester 11 OR killed. 1 Officer 19 OR wounded. 8 OR missing. Reinforcements 10 OR.	MB
ERVILLERS	28. 3. 17	Showery — 1st Staff on left & 22/Manchester on right attacked CROISILLES at 5.45 a.m. Attack unsuccessful owing little strength of the line and enemy machine guns from 2/Manchester relieved 1st Staff, 17th & 22/Manchester in support. Casualties & Reinforcements NIL.	Appendix 5. MB
"	29. 3. 17	Wet. 1/R. Welsh Fus relieved 2/Manchester and 2/Manchester relieved 2/Manchester. 2/Manchester moved to BUCQUOY. 1/Queen & 2/Manchester to COURCELLES. Casualties 1/S. Staff 19R, 10 OR killed. 19 OR, 3 Officers, 57 OR wounded. 10 OR missing. 17 OR missing. 22/Manchester 1/Queen 1 OR. 22/Manchester 1 Officer 31 OR. 2/Manchester 1 Officer. Reinforcements 1/Queen 1 OR. 2/Manchester 1 Officer.	MB

Army Form C. 2118.

WAR DIARY
or
INTELLIGENCE SUMMARY.
(Erase heading not required.)

Instructions regarding War Diaries and Intelligence Summaries are contained in F. S. Regs., Part II. and the Staff Manual respectively. Title pages will be prepared in manuscript.

Hour, Date, Place		Summary of Events and Information	Remarks and references to Appendices
ERVILLERS	30.3.17	Usual work with heavy rain at intervals. G.O.C. 22nd Inf Bde came over. Command of the sector. Casualties. Manchesters 5 OR killed. 10 OR wounded. 6 OR missing. Reinforcements arrived NIL.	KMB
"	31.3.17	Usual work with heavy showers. Manchesters moved to COURCELLES. Casualties. Manchesters 1 OR missing. Reinforcements — 1 Officer. Queens 3 Officers.	KMB

Manning
Brigadier General
Commanding 91st Infantry Brigade.

SECRET.   Appendix 1
                                                    No. 23

            91st Infantry Brigade Operation Order No.64.

Reference Map FRANCE Sheet 57.D.N.E. - 1/20,000, Edition 4a.
                                         Monday, 12th March, 1917.

1.   The 91st Infantry Brigade will take over the Divisional
front from the Railway in L.10.a., and L.9.d., to FORK TRENCH
in L.8.b., inclusive on night 12/13th March, 1917.

2.   (a) The Brigade front will be held by 2nd Bn. The Queen's Regt.,
(Headquarters L.14.a.0.0.) with one Company 22nd Bn. Manchester
Regt., attached.
        (b) The 22nd Bn. Manchester Regt., less one Company, will be in
Support in the vicinity of LOUSE POST (Headquarters K.35.a.3.2.)
and will move in accordance with instructions already issued.

3.   BOUNDARIES:
        (a) Between 2nd Bn. The Queen's Regt., and 10th Bn. East Yorks.
Regt., on left. - A line from L.8.a.9.7., immediately SOUTH of the
SUNKEN ROAD and track in L.7.b.d and c. Thence to L.17.b.0.5.
        (b) Between 2nd Bn. The Queen's Regt., and 186th Infantry Brigade
on Right. - The line of the Railway from L.9.d.9.0. - L.15.b.8.2.
- L.21.d.5.0.

4.   All details of relief will be arranged by Officer Commanding
2nd Bn. The Queen's Regt., with Officer Commanding, 12th Bn. York
and Lancs. Regt. (holding from PUISIEUX - BUCQUOY Road to Right
Boundary) and with Officer Commanding, 10th Bn. East Yorks. Regt.,
(holding posts between above Road and FORK TRENCH). Headquarters,
10th Bn. East Yorks. Regt., are in BERG GRABEN at L.7.a.3.2.

5.   The 91st Machine Gun Company will relieve the 94th Machine
Gun Company in accordance with instructions already issued.

6.   Command of the Sector will pass on completion of relief.

7.   On relief the distribution of the Brigade will be as
follows:-

            2nd Bn. The Queen's Regt.   In forward Area.
            22nd Bn. Manchester Regt.   -do-
            21st Bn. Manchester Regt.   BERTRANCOURT.
            1st Bn. South Staffs. Regt.   ARQUEVES.

8.   91st Infantry Brigade Headquarters will close at BEAUSSART
at 3-0.p.m., and will open at the APPLE TREES at the same hour.

9.   ACKNOWLEDGE.
                                                    Captain,
                                    A/Brigade Major, 91st Infantry Brigade.

Issued at......a.m.

        Copy No. 1 7th Division.   14 22nd Inf. Bde.
                  2 2nd Queen's R'   15 92nd Inf. Bde.
                  3 1st S. Staffs. R'   16 94th Inf. Bde.
                  4 21st Manch. R'   17 186th Inf. Bde.
                  5 22nd Manch. R'   18 91st M.G. Coy.
                  6 91st Fld. Battery.   19 Supply Officer.
                  7 91st Bde. Gren. Coy.   20 Brigade Major.
                  8 91st Bde. Signals.   21 Staff Captain.
                  9 Div. M.G. Officer.   22 File.
                 10 C.R.A.   23 War Diary.
                 11 A.D.M.S.   24 War Diary.
                 12 C.R.E.
                 13 20th Inf. Bde.

91st Infantry Brigade.

Appendix 2

SUMMARY OF INTELLIGENCE - No.22.

From 6-0.a.m., 12th March, 1917 to 6-0.a.m., 13th March, 1917.

1. OPERATIONS. - N I L .

2. INTELLIGENCE. - NIL.

3. ENEMY'S MOVEMENTS. - N I L .

4. PATROLS. - Touch was established with the left post of the Brigade on the right. No other patrol reports have been received yet.

5. GENERAL. - The enemy sent up Very Lights at distance of 200/300 yards apart. His snipers appear to move out at night in front of his line and snipe our posts and the approaches to BUCQUOY.

6. ENEMY'S ATTITUDE. -
Artillery. - Between 5-0.p.m., and 7-30.p.m., PUISIEUX was fairly heavily shelled. The neighbourhood of Q.2.b., was shelled at 8-30.p.m., and 10-30.p.m., by a small H.V.Gun.
Infantry. - Quiet except for a few snipers.
Machine Gun Fire. - Active between 10-0.p.m., and 12.midnight.
General. - Slightly more active than usual.

Bde.Hd.Qtrs.

13th March, 1917.

Brigadier General,
Commanding, 91st Infantry Brigade.

SECRET.   Appendix 3   Copy No. 20.

91st Infantry Brigade Operation Order No. 65.

Monday, 12th March, 1917.

Reference Map - FRANCE, Sheet 57.d.N.E. - 1/20,000, Edition 4a.

-:-:-:-:-:-:-:-:-:-

1. The 91st Infantry Brigade will be held in Divisional Reserve for the forthcoming attack on BUCQUOY.

2. The attack will probably take place at dawn on March 15th, 1917. ZERO hour and day will be notified later.

3. The Brigade will be located as follows on ZERO day:-

Brigade Headquarters,	CAFE JOURDAIN.
22nd Bn. Manchester Regt.	In vicinity of ELLIS SQUARE. (K.33.b.)
2nd Bn. The Queen's Regt.	MAILLY MAILLET.
1st Bn. S. Staffs. Regt.	-do-
21st Bn. Manchester Regt.	-do-

Separate orders for these moves will be issued later.

4. All Battalions will be prepared to move at ½ hours notice from ZERO plus 2 hours.

5. The Officer Commanding, 91st Machine Gun Coy., will arrange to place eight guns in position so as to bring heavy fire to bear:-

(1) On BUCQUOY and ARMIN Trenches E. of L.10. Central until ZERO plus 15 minutes.
(2) On above trenches in L.11.c., and eastwards until ZERO plus 33 minutes.
(3) On RESURRECTION TRENCH until ZERO plus 60 minutes.

The remaining guns and teams will be held in readiness to move from MAILLY MAILLET at ½ hours notice after ZERO plus 2 hours.

He will remain at his present Headquarters, in MAILLY MAILLET.

6. The Officer Commanding, 91st Trench Mortar Battery will hold two guns and two limbers of ammunition in readiness in MAILLY MAILLET to move at ½ hours notice after ZERO plus 2 hours.

7. Administrative arrangements will be issued later.

8. ACKNOWLEDGE.

Moorshead
Captain.

A/Brigade Major, 91st Infantry Brigade.

Issued at.....

Copy No. 1 7th Division.	11 A.D.M.S.
2 2nd Queen's R.	12 C.R.E.
3 1st S. Staffs. R.	13 20th Inf. Bde.
4 21st Manch. R.	14 22nd Inf. Bde.
5 22nd Manch. R.	15 91st M.G. Coy.
6 91st T.M. Battery.	16 Supply Officer.
7 91st Bde. Gren. Coy.	17 Brigade Major.
8 91st Bde. Signals.	18 Staff Captain.
9 Div. M.G. Officer.	19 File.
10 C.R.A.	20 War Diary.
	21 War Diary.

SECRET.   Copy No. 20.
                                                  R.K./1140.

Scheme for Attack on BUCQUOY to be carried out by 7th Division.

Reference Map - FRANCE 57.d., N.E. - 1/20,000. Edition 4a.

-:-:-:-:-:-:-:-:-:-

1. (a) The 7th and 46th Divisions will attack BUCQUOY and Hill 155 respectively with objectives as under:-

    1. ARNIM and BUCQUOY Trenches from L.10.a.5.6. to L.2.d.4.7. Thence to L.2.b.8.9. - F.26.d.6.3. - F.26.a.3.2.

    2. A line from CRUCIFIX at L.4.a.4.6., along road to L.3.b.4.8. Thence to F.27.c.7.0. - F.27.c.4.4. Also from F.26.d.8.5., along trench running N. by W. E. to F.20.d.5.3.

    3. A line from F.28.d.3.7. - F.22.c.9.0. - F.22.c.0.5. - F.21.c.00.45. - F.20.c.8.0. - F.23.d.5.6.

    (b) No troops will be attacking on Right Flank of 7th Division nearer than an attack on LOUPART WOOD.

2. BOUNDARIES.

    (a) Between 7th and 46th Divisions on left. - F.21.d.55.60. - F.27.b.55.65. - L.2.b.55.75. - L.2.d.4.9. - S.E. Corner of ROSSIGNOL WOOD.

    (b) Between 7th and 62nd Divisions on Right. - The line of the Railway from L.9.d.9.0. to L.15.b.8.2. Thence to L.21.d.5.0.

3. The attack will be carried out from a tape by 20th Infantry Brigade on Left and 22nd Infantry Brigade on Right. The dividing line will be South along the main AYETTE - PUISIEUX Road, as far as L.3.d.0.4.(inclusive to 20th Infantry Brigade), thence the Railway to L.9.c.2.7. Thence a straight line to road junction at L.20.a.5.0.(inclusive to 20th Infantry Brigade).

4. The attack will be supported by the fire of about 150 guns and Howitzers.

5. Attack by 22nd Infantry Brigade. -
   (a) The attack on the first two objectives will be carried out by 2nd Bn. Royal Warwickshire Regt., on right (Headquarters L.15.c.3.4.) and 2/1st H.A.C., on left (Headquarters L.14.d.9.4.)
   2nd Bn. Royal Warwickshire Regt., will form a defensive right flank from the CRUCIFIX at L.4.a.5.5. to BUCQUOY Trench in the vicinity of L.10.a.5.2.

   (b) As soon as second objective has been gained, the 20th Bn. Manchester Regt., (Headquarters L.14.d.9.4.) will pass through and capture the final objective.
   Strong fighting patrols will then be pushed forward with the object of ascertaining whether the ABLAINZEVILLE line is held.

   (c) The 1st Bn. Royal Welsh Fusiliers will be held in Brigade Reserve and will be situated in ORCHARD ALLEY and GULGLON TRENCH.

   (d) Strong points will be established at:-

       (1) L.10.a.3.6.   (3) L.3.d.7.8.
       (2) L.4.c.7.8.
    (4)(3) L.4.a.1.6.   (6) F.28.a.8.4.
    (5)(4) F.28.c.8.5.

                                              (continued).

-2-

ARNIM and BUCQUOY Trenches will be blocked at L.10.a.6.4. and L.10.a.5.2.

Blocks will be made at L.4.a.8.0. and F.28.b.3.5.

(e) Brigade Headquarters will be established at L.20.b.8.9.

6. Attack by 20th Infantry Brigade.

(a) The attack on the first objective will be carried out by 8th Bn. Devon Regt. (Headquarters L.14.a.3.1.)

(b) As soon as the first objective has been taken, 2nd Bn. Gordon Highlanders will pass through and take the second and third objectives, pushing forward patrols as in 5(b) above.

(c) 9th Bn. Devon Regt., will be in Brigade Support in vicinity of ROSSIGNOL TRENCH (Headquarters L.19.d.8.8.)

(d) 2nd Bn. Border Regt., will be in Brigade Reserve in vicinity of MOUSE POST.

(e) Strong points will be established at:-

    (1) L. 3.a.0.6.
    (2) L. 3.a.6.9.
    (3) F.27.c.1.2.
    (4) F.27.b.6.2.
    (5) F.22.c.1.2.

(f) Brigade Headquarters will be established at L.20.c.3.9.

7. No.15.Squadron, R.F.C., will be having Contact Patrols working with 7th Division. Information obtained by these will be dropped at Brigade and Divisional Headquarters.
ACKNOWLEDGE.

[signature]

Bde. Hd. Qtrs.
                                                           Captain,

12th March, 1917.
                      A/Brigade Major, 91st Infantry Brigade.

Copy No.			
1	7th Division.	11	A.D.M.S.
2	2nd Queen's R	12	C.R.E.
3	1st S.Staffs.R	13	20th Inf. Bde.
4	21st Manch.R	14	22nd Inf. Bde.
5	22nd Manch.R	15	91st M.G.Coy.
6	91st T.M. Battery.	16	Supply Officer.
7	91st Bde. Gren. Coy.	17	Brigade Major.
8	91st Bde. Signals.	18	Staff Captain.
9	Div. M.G. Officer.	19	File.
10	C.R.A.	20 and 21	War Diary.

"A" Form. — MESSAGES AND SIGNALS. — Army Form C. 2121.

TO	WAVE	RIVER	BROOK	
	LIGHT	FLAME		

Sender's Number.	Day of Month	In reply to Number	
* B.M.817	13		AAA

WATER will attack BUCQUOY on 14 inst. Zero hour to be notified later aaa. WAVE on left RIVER on right aaa all boundaries as laid down in Divisional Scheme issued with OO.65 dated 12 instant WAVE representing 20 I.B. RIVER representing 22 I.B. aaa. RIVER will take over posts held by WAVE in right sector under arrangements to be made between Commanding Officers concerned aaa. LIGHT and FLAME will be in Brigade Support in PUISIEUX aaa.

"A" Form.
MESSAGES AND SIGNALS.
Army Form C. 2121.

Sender's Number.	Day of Month	In reply to Number	
B.M. 817	13		A A A

Headquarters will be established as follows WAVE L.19.b.9.5. aaa. RIVER L.20.b.8.9. aaa. FLAME L.15.c.3.4. aaa. LIGHT L.14.c.0.0. aaa. The attack will be carried out from a tape to be laid out by Battn. Commanders concerned, on a line from L.9.a.9.4. to L.8.b.0.9. aaa. First and second objectives as in Divisional scheme. aaa. Second objective to be consolidated and patrols sent forward to occupy DIERVILLE FARM. aaa. attack will be accompanied by creeping

"A" Form.   Army Form C. 2121.
MESSAGES AND SIGNALS.

Sender's Number.	Day of Month	In reply to Number	AAA
BM.817	13		

barrage. details later aaa. BROOK will assist Commanding Officers concerned with guns already in the line and will move his HQ and remaining guns to MOUSE POST aaa. Brigade HQ remains APPLE TREES with advanced Report Centre at L.20.c.5.8. aaa. Acknowledge

From: WATER.
Time: 6/50 pm.

Signed
O. F. Morshed. Capt.
a/Bde. Maj. 91st Inf. Bde.

SECRET.

Appendix 3B

Narrative of Attack on BUCQUOY carried out by 91st Infantry Brigade on night 13/14th March, 1917.

Reference Maps - LE SARS, ACHIET, FONQUEVILLERS and COULGEULES -
Scale 1/10,000.

-:-:-:-:-:-:-:-:-:-

On night March 12/13th, 1917, the 91st Infantry Brigade took over the front line posts opposite BUCQUOY (from Railway in L.10.c. and L.9.d. to FORK TRENCH in L.8.b. inclusive) from 9-th and 92nd Infantry Brigades. This front had been allotted to the 7th Division for the intended attack on BUCQUOY by 20th and 22nd Infantry Brigades on March 15th, 1917. The whole front was held by one Battalion (2nd Bn. Queen's Regt., with one Company 22nd Bn. Manchester Regt. attached), 22nd Bn. Manchester Regt., less one Company, being in support in MOUSE POST. Arrangements had been made for the right half of this sector to be taken over by two Battalions of 22nd Infantry Brigade on night 13/14th March, the left half being relieved by two Battalions 20th Infantry Brigade on the following night.

On the 13th March, however, there were indications that the enemy retirement would anticipate this attack and the following telegram was received from 7th Division:-

WATER. G.694. 13th AAA
GREVILLERS and LOUPART WOOD have been occupied by us AAA 5th Corps will advance and occupy general line GREVILLERS - ACHIET-LE-PETIT road thence road running through L.11.b. and L.4.c. and villages BUCQUOY and ESSARTS AAA WATER will send out strong patrols to get touch with enemy and push forward into BUCQUOY AAA acknowledge
SUN. 12-35.p.m.

WATER. G.698. 13th AAA
Situation GREVILLERS has been occupied by us AAA Unofficially reported ACHIET-LE-PETIT in our hands AAA Germans front line North of ESSARTS in our hands AAA If our patrols report BUCQUOY still held by enemy you will be prepared to attack this place under cover of barrage to-night AAA You will be supported by 2 battalions 22nd I.B. AAA Remaining 2 battalions 22nd I.B. will be prepared to move to MOUSE TRAP and ELLIS SQUARE to-night in reserve AAA DIERVILLE FARM will be occupied and touch obtained with 46th Division ordered to sieze Hill 135 AAA
7th Division. 1-15.p.m.

On receipt of the first message I ordered Officer Commanding 2nd Bn. Queen's Regt., to send forward strong patrols to endeavour to ascertain the situation in BUCQUOY TRENCH.

At 3-10.p.m., Officer Commanding 2nd Bn. Queen's Regt., reported that the right patrol was held up by heavy machine gun fire from strong point at L.10.c.1.7. (this was confirmed by Brigade on Right whose patrol had dug-in at L.10.c.2.6. in front of this post). The centre patrol proceeded up the railway in L.9.d. and a. and encountered heavy machine gun fire from BUCQUOY TRENCH in front and also cross-fire from both sides. On sighting this patrol the enemy sent up four sets of double red lights.

Another patrol reached the first row of wire at about L.9.b.4.6. where they were sighted by the enemy. Several groups of the enemy appeared and opened fire, standing knee-high in the trench. A machine gun opened fire from L.9.b.6.8. The patrol reported that BUCQUOY TRENCH appeared to be held by posts at about 50 yards interval.

A fourth patrol sent to work round the left flank of the position came under fire from two machine guns, one in BUCQUOY TRENCH at about L.3.c.2.1., the other firing from the outskirts of the village. The "triangle" - i.e. vicinity of Point L.2.b.4.2. - was also reported held by the enemy. All patrols reported that the wire was thick and apparently uncut.

(continued).

From those results it appeared that BUCQUOY TRENCH was still held by the enemy. I determined nevertheless to order up 22nd Bn. Manchester Regt. to a position of assembly behind PUISIEUX in case I was ordered to proceed with the attack.

At 5-0.p.m. the following messages were received:-

WATER. G.704. 13th. AAA
Continuation of G.698 aaa If attack necessary following are arrangements aaa Objective green and brown lines as in 7th Division Order No.135 dated 11th March aaa From brown line patrols will be pushed to DIERVILLE FARM aaa 46th Division will be attacking on left aaa Heavies will be bombarding BUCQUOY from 10-0.p.m. - 10-30.p.m. aaa At 11-45.p.m. Field Artillery barrage commences aaa 11-51 barrage lifts from German front line and barrage moves to brown line at rate of 100 yards in 2 minutes aaa Here becomes protective till 1.a.m. at which hour it will lift to enable patrols to go forward.
SUN. 4-20.p.m.

WATER. G.705. 13th. AAA
Continuation of G.698 aaa 62nd Division will be attacking simultaneously with objective road in L.11.a. and b. L.4.c. and d, as far as L.4.a.5.0.
7th Division. 4-20.p.m.

I thereupon issued orders for 22nd Bn.Manchester Regt., to relieve those posts of 2nd Bn.Queen's Regt.lying to the East of the Railway in L.9.d, and a., and for the attack to be carried out in accordance with the original 7th Division Scheme (details of which had already been issued to all Units),2nd Bn.Queen's Regt. representing 20th Infantry Brigade and 22nd Bn.Manchester Regt. 22nd Infantry Brigade. Each of the assaulting battalions was given one Company of the 2nd Bn. Royal Warwickshire Regt.,for carrying purposes.

The following message was subsequently received:-

WATER. G.717. 13th. AAA
Continuation of G.698 aaa Attack will take place to-night aaa artillery programme as arranged by you with modifications as in telephonic conversation with you aaa ZERO 1.a.m. instead of 11-45.p.m. aaa Other timings altered in proportion with exception heavy bombardment which remains 10-0. - 10-30.p.m. aaa Two battalions 22nd Bde.moving to MOUSE TRAP and LEWIS SQUARE at 6-0.a.m. to-morrow will be under your tactical control on reaching that place.
7th Division. 8-20.p.m.

The Artillery barrage was to be as follows:-

(a) ZERO. Barrage opens on BUCQUOY TRENCH.
(b) ZERO + 8 min. Barrage lifts allowing infantry to enter the trench. Barrage moves forward at the rate of 100 yards in 4 minutes until it reaches a position 200 yards beyond 2nd Objective,which it reaches at ZERO plus 48 minutes.
(c) ZERO + 75 min. Barrage lifts again and continues to advance at the same rate,allowing patrols to work forward. On reaching a semicircular line beyond the village it becomes a stationary protective barrage.

RESULT OF OPERATION.

At 1-0.a.m. the Infantry moved forward to the assault. The night was exceptionally dark,and the ground very heavy. The wire was found to be dense and impenetrable. The enemy's artillery fire was intense and his machine guns active throughout the operation. In one place only was an entrance effected,on the extreme right of the attack. Here the Right Company of the 22nd Bn.Manchester Regt.,got through the wire and established itself in the trench,forming a bombing block on either flank and holding out until the supply of bombs (both British and German) was exhausted. It was eventually driven out by a determined hostile counter-attack at about 6-30.a.m. Eight prisoners were captured by this Company.

(continued).

On perceiving that the operation had not met with success, I ordered such parties as could be withdrawn in daylight to fall back to the original line of posts. In the course of the day and the following night both battalions were relieved by 2/1st Bn.H.A.C. with 2nd Bn.Royal Warwickshire Regt. in support, the Command of the Sector passing to G.O.C., 22nd Infantry Brigade.

CASUALTIES.

UNIT.	Killed.		Wounded.		Missing.	
	Off.	O.R.	Off.	O.R.	Off.	O.R.
2nd Bn.Queen's Regt.	2	26	2x	67	2	20
22nd Bn.Manchester Regt.	2	18	1	52	1	69

x Includes 1 Still at Duty.

CAUSES OF FAILURE.

In my opinion the primary cause of failure was the state of the wire. No one who has seen the position by day, with its triple belt of wire scarcely damaged, can be surprised that it was able to withstand an impromptu attack in pitch darkness and pouring rain by men to whom the ground was entirely new.

As a result of the afternoon patrols, and in consequence of the Artillery Group Commander's report, I had made strong representations on this score. I had also urged that the assault should take place at daybreak this giving time for adequate preparations to be made and giving the attacking troops a chance of seeing the ground. In both of these matters my advise was overruled. ZERO hour was fixed for 11-45.p.m. (moonrise) and subsequently at my instigation postponed till 1.a.m.; the fact that there was no moon that night greatly added to the difficulty of the operation.

The decision that the heavy bombardment should remain from 10-. - 10-30.p.m., although Zero hour was put forward, was in my opinion a most unfortunate one. After the exceptional patrolling activity during the afternoon it only needed that to put the enemy on his guard, and allow him to bring more machine guns into play during the interval of 1½ hours before the assault, besides making all arrangements for a barrage of considerable intensity.

Finally I would again urge the paramount importance of giving sufficient time for the preparations for an assault on a position of this nature.

In this case Brigade Orders were received by Battalions at 6-10.p.m., the barrage details and change of ZERO hour being announced at 8-15.p.m. What did this entail on the part of Battalion Commanders?

(a) the summoning of Company Commanders to Battalion Headquarters. The state of the ground and the darkness made each journey at least an hour. Thus 3 hours were accounted for (Orderly's outward journey plus two journeys of Company Commander).
(b) Issuing of Battalion Orders.
(c) Company Commanders conference of Platoon Officers and N.C.Os, attended with similar delays.
(d) laying out of tape line.
(e) relief of right sector.
(f) issuing of stores, food and water and organising carrying parties.

At 10-30.p.m., I received a personal message from the Corps Commander that, in the event of my not being satisfied that the ground was sufficiently known to the troops taking part in the assault, I should consider the advisability of carrying out the attack by means of strong patrols adequately supported. I replied that I was satisfied that the two battalions would do their best; that in any case it was too late (2½ hours before ZERO hour) to take any action. Moreover the barrage was arranged for direct assault.

Brigadier General,
Commanding, 91st Infantry Brigade,

Bde.Hd.Qtrs.
21st March, 1917.

war diary

SECRET.   Appendix 4   Copy No. 23

91st Infantry Brigade Operation Order No.66.

Tuesday, 14th March, 1917.

Reference Map FRANCE Sheet 57.d.N.E. - 1/20,000, Edition 4a.

-:-:-:-:-:-:-:-:-:-

1. The 22nd Bn. Manchester Regt., and 2nd Bn. Queen's Regt., will be relieved on the Divisional Front to-night, by the 2/1st H.A.C.

2. The Officer Commanding, 2nd Bn. Royal Warwickshire Regt., will place one Company at the disposal of The Officer Commanding, 2/1st H.A.C.
   The remaining three Companies of 2nd Bn. Royal Warwickshire Regt., will be in Brigade Reserve at MOUSE POST.

3. All details of reliefs will be arranged between Commanding Officers concerned.

4. On relief 2nd Bn. Queen's Regt., and 22nd Bn. Manchester Regt., will march to BOLTON CAMP and No.2. Camp, MAILLY WOOD EAST respectively.

5. The 91st Machine Gun Coy., and 91st Trench Mortar Battery will be relieved on night of March 15/16, by 22nd Machine Gun Company, and 22nd Trench Mortar Battery respectively.
   Details of reliefs to be arranged between Commanding Officers concerned.

6. G.O.C., 22nd Infantry Brigade will assume Command of the Sector at 3-30.p.m., to-day, at which hour 91st Infantry Brigade Headquarters will close at APPLE TREES and open at BEAUSSART.
   22nd Infantry Brigade Headquarters will remain at APPLE TREES.

7. ACKNOWLEDGE.

                                                    Moorshead
                                                    Captain,
                                        A/Brigade Major, 91st Infantry Brigade.

Issued at ......

    Copy No 1 7th Division.   13 20th Inf. Bde.
           2 2nd Queen's R   14 22nd Inf. Bde.
           3 1st S.Staffs.R   15 187th Inf. Bde.
           4 21st Manch.R   16 137th Inf. Bde.
           5 22nd Manch.R   17 Supply Officer.
           6 91st T.M. Battery.   18 2/1st H.A.C.
           7 91st Bde.Gren.Coy.   19 2nd R.Warwick.R
           8 91st Bde.Signals.   20 Brigade Major.
           9 Div.M.G.Officer.   21 Staff Captain.
          10 C.R.A.   22 File.
          11 A.D.M.S.   23 War Diary.
          12 C.R.E.   24 War Diary.

SECRET.   Copy No. 19

91st Infantry Brigade Operation Order No. 67.

Saturday, 24th March, 1917.

Reference Maps - Sheets 51B S.W. and 57C N.W.

-:-:-:-:-:-:-:-:-:-

1. (a) The 7th Division will attack ECOUST - LONGATTE on the 26th instant.
    The 1st ANZAC Corps on the right will be co-operating by attacking simultaneously NOREUIL - LAGNICOURT.
   (b) Zero hour will be 4-30.a.m.
   (c) The 20th Infantry Brigade will carry out the attack with two battalions; keeping one battalion in reserve, and one battalion guarding its left flank, the attack being made from a southerly direction.
   (d) During the night 25th/26th instant, CROISILLES will be bombarded in order to simulate an attack on that place and gas shells will be thrown into the village. The 20th Infantry Brigade will arrange for strong patrols to exploit this bombardment and seize the village if practicable.
   (e) The attack will be made under an artillery barrage - a standing barrage being kept on the south and south-east outskirts of ECOUST - LONGATTE, gas shells being thrown into this village.
   (f) When ECOUST - LONGATTE is captured, this village will be cleared of enemy and a line of posts established on the north and north-east sides of the village from the north-eastern corner of the village - thence to the railway at U.26.d. - thence along the railway to U.25.b.4.3.
    The battalion guarding the left flank of the 20th Infantry Brigade will push forward its posts to conform to the above line.
    As soon as the village has been cleared of enemy, troops will be kept out of it.

2. The 91st Infantry Brigade, less 2nd Bn. Queen's Regt. and 21st Bn. Manchester Regt., will be in Divisional Support for above operation and will be prepared to take over the Divisional front after the attack.

3. On March 25th the 22nd Bn. Manchester Regt. will move to camp vacated by 21st Bn. Manchester Regt. COURCELLES, being clear of BUCQUOY by 9.a.m.

4. (a) The 22nd Bn. Manchester Regt. will be in support of the attack, and will be in a position of assembly at MORY by 5-30.a.m. on March 26th.
   (b) The 1st Bn. South Staffordshire Regt. will be in reserve, and will be in a position of assembly at ERVILLERS by the same hour.
    This battalion will be prepared to take over the right sector of the Divisional front after the attack.

5. Brigade Headquarters will close at ABLAINZEVILLE at 4.p.m. March 25th at which hour it will open at COURCELLES (adjacent to Divisional Headquarters).

6. ACKNOWLEDGE.

Captain,

A/Brigade Major, 91st Infantry Brigade.

Issued at.....p.m.

(Distribution overleaf).

Copy No 1 7th Division.
2 2nd Queen's R
3 1st S.Staffs.R
4 21st Manch.R
5 22nd Manch.R
6 91st T.M.Battery.
7 91st Bde.Gren.Coy.
8 91st Bde.Signals.
9 Div.M.G.Officer.
10 C.R.A.
11 A.D.M.S.
12 C.R.E.
13 20th Inf.Bde.
14 22nd Inf.Bde.
15 91st M.G.Coy.
16 Supply Officer.
17 Brigade Major.
18 Staff Captain.
19 File.
20 War Diary.
21 War Diary.

SECRET.   Appendix 5   Copy No..22

91st Infantry Brigade Operation Order No.68.

Monday, 26th March, 1917.

Reference Maps - Sheets 51B S.W.
              &   57C N.W.

-:-:-:-:-:-:-:-:-

1.   The 91st Infantry Brigade will attack CROISILLES at dawn on 28th March, 1917 with objectives as follows:-
T.24.b.1.2. - T.18.c.5.3. - T.17.d.6.8. - T.17.a.9.2. - T.16.b.9.5. with a defensive flank running through T.16.Central.

2.   (a) The attack will be carried out by 1st Bn. South Staffordshire Regt. on left (Headquarters - T.27.b.9.8.) and 22nd Bn. Manchester Regt. on right (Headquarters - B.3.b.4.9.), the dividing line being the FONTLINE LEZ CROISILLES to ST.LEGER Road from T.18.c.5.3. - T.23.d.2.7. - T.20.b.4.4.(all inclusive to 22nd Bn. Manchester Regt.)
(b)   The 2nd Bn. Queen's Regt. less one Company will be held in Brigade Support, and will be in a position of assembly in L.14.b. by ZERO hour.
Officer Commanding, 2nd Bn. Queen's Regt. will arrange to place one Company at the disposal of Officer Commanding, 1st Bn. South Staffordshire Regt. for the operation.
(c)   The 21st Bn. Manchester Regt. will be held in Brigade Reserve in COURCELLES.

3.   (a) The 2/6th London Regt. will be on the left, Headquarters T.25.a.7.4., Right hand post reported to be at T.15.b.7.1.
(b)   The 2nd Bn. Border Regt. will be on the right, Headquarters B.21.b.8.0., left hand post to be established in vicinity of Windmill, T.24.d.1.4.

4.   (a) The attack will be made under a barrage creeping forward at the rate of 100 yards in four minutes.
(b)   CROISILLES will be kept under a slow bombardment of howitzers until ZERO.
From ZERO, howitzers, firing ammunition with 106 fuzes, will continue shooting at the north-east end of the village as long as it is safe for them to do so.
(c)   Heavy Artillery will also bombard until ZERO plus 15, the reputed strong point at U.25.d.2.7. and the Sunken Road from T.17.c.9.0. to T.18.d.0.0. and the Sunken Road in T.17.a.
(d)   Gas shells will be fired into CROISILLES at intervals during to-night and to-morrow night, each discharge being followed by shrapnel fire searching the ground between our posts and the village, and also the ground immediately north-west of the village as far as the Sunken Road in T.17.a.

5.   The 1st Bn. South Staffordshire Regt. and 22nd Bn. Manchester Regt. will each advance on a two-company frontage, each company being preceded by a fighting patrol of strength not less than one platoon. One company will be in support, the remaining company holding the original line of posts.
Not more than two platoons of each assaulting Battalion will be detailed to work through the village, the remainder of the inner company working round the perimeter of the village to the final objective.
After capture, the village will be kept clear of troops as far as possible.

6.   Strong points will be formed in the vicinity of the following points. The exact site must be selected by the Officer on the spot.

T.24.b.1.2.
T.18.c.5.3.
T.17.d.9.2.
T.16.b.9.5.
T.16.b.4.1.
T.15.c.6.9.

(continued).

7. Officer Commanding, 91st Machine Gun Coy. will place two Machine Guns at the disposal of Officer Commanding, 1st Bn. South Staffordshire Regt., and two at the disposal of Officer Commanding, 22nd Bn. Manchester Regt.
He will hold one section complete with transport in readiness to move at half-an-hours notice in ERVILLERS.

8. (a) The 1st Bn. South Staffordshire Regt. and 22nd Bn. Manchester Regt. will take over the posts in their respective sectors from 21st Bn. Manchester Regt. on night 27/28th March under arrangements to be made between Commanding Officers concerned.
(b) The 21st Bn. Manchester Regt. will be withdrawn to billets vacated by 22nd Bn. Manchester Regt. in COURCELLES.
(c) The command of the CROISILLE Sector will pass to G.O.C. 91st Infantry Brigade on completion of this relief.

9. Administrative Instructions issued with Operation Order 67 dated 24th March, 1917, will apply to this operation.
A Brigade Store of S.A.A. and Grenades will be established at T.27.d.8.1., containing:-

2,300 Mills No.5 Grenades.
about 150 No.20 Rifle Grenades.
60,000 Rounds S.A.A.

Issues will be made on written demand signed by an Officer.

10. The following personnel will not accompany the Battalion into action. They will remain with the Battalion Transport:-

2nds in Command of Battalions.
2 Company Commanders per Battalion.
All Officers in excess of 20. (excluding Medical Officer).
2 Company Sergeant Majors.
3 N.C.O's and 12 men per Company.
25% of all Specialists.

11. ZERO hour and barrage details will be issued later.

12. Brigade Headquarters will close at COURCELLES at 2-30.p.m. at which hour it will open at D.13.b.3.4.

13. ACKNOWLEDGE.

Howrshead
Captain,
A/Brigade Major, 91st Infantry Brigade.

Issued at 11/6 p.m.

Copy No 1 7th Division.
2 2nd Queen's R
3 1st S.Staffs.R
4 21st Manch.R
5 22nd Manch.R
6 91st T.M.Battery.
7 91st Bde.Gren.Coy.
8 91st Bde.Signals.
9 91st M.G.Coy.
10 C.R.A.
11 A.D.M.S.
12 C.R.E.
13 20th Inf.Bde.
14 22nd Inf.Bde.
15 173rd Inf.Bde.
16 Supply Officer.
17 Bde.Transport Off.
18 Brigade Major.
19 Staff Captain.
20 File.
21 War Diary.
22 War Diary.

SECRET.

Copy No. 22.

Amendments and Additions to
91st Infantry Brigade Operation Order No.68.

Tuesday, 27th March, 1917.

1. ZERO hour will be 5-45.a.m.

2. Barrage programme is attached.

3. With reference to para.3.:-
(a) The 58th Division have no posts in T.15.b. and d. They hold the line of the track in T.14.b. and d. and T.15.c. Touch will be established with them, the defensive flank being prolonged for this purpose.
(b) The left post of the 2nd Bn. Border Regt. is at T.30.d.2.9. After the barrage has passed, this post will be advanced to the vicinity of the Windmill, T.24.d.1.4.

4. The C.R.E. is arranging to hold one Field Company in readiness to give assistance on night 28/29th March.

5. (a) After para.4(a) add "by jumps of 50 yards".
(b) In para.2(b), for L.14.b. read B.14.b.

6. ACKNOWLEDGE.

Morehead
Captain,
A/Brigade Major, 91st Infantry Brigade.

Issued at....p.m.

Copies to all recipients of O.O.68.

On His Majesty's Service.

Vol. 18.

April 1917

Headquarters,
91st Infantry Brigade.

Vol 18
Army Form
91st Infantry Brigade   April 1917

WAR DIARY
or
INTELLIGENCE SUMMARY
(Erase heading not required.)

Instructions regarding War Diaries and Intelligence Summaries are contained in F.S. Regs., Part II. and the Staff Manual respectively. Title pages will be prepared in manuscript.

Hour, Date, Place	Summary of Events and Information	Remarks and references to Appendices
ERVILLERS 1-4-17	Strong wind with rain in morning. 1st Battalion moved up to ST. LEGER in readiness for attack on morning 2/4/17. 1/S. Staffs 5.O.R. Casualties Nil. Reinforcements.	Appendix 1. (Narrative 2/4/17) Appendix 1A attack.
" 2.4.17	Fine morning. Snow in evening. Brigade attacked with brest of CROISILLES. 1/S.Staffs on right, 22/Manchesters in centre, 2/Queens on left, 21/Manchesters in Brigade reserve. All objectives gained into faubourg. 22/Manchesters then proceeded to clear CROISILLES – Brigade less 21/Manchesters relieved during night by 93rd April by 22nd Infantry Bde. 2/Queens went to billets in ERVILLERS. 1/S.Staffs + 22/Manchesters to COURCELLES. Casualties. (See Appendix 3). Reinforcements NIL	Appendix 2. Appendix 3. Appendix 3.A Appendix 3.R Appendix 3.C
BUCQUOY. 3.4.17	Dull turning to sleet in evening. Bde HQrs 2/Queens + 21/Manchesters went to camp at BUCQUOY. 1/S.Staffs to PUISIEUX. 91st MGC to ERVILLERS. Reinforcements NIL. Casualties. NIL.	
" 4.4.17	Wet morning. Bde remainder of 91st MG Coy moved to PUISIEUX. 22/Manchesters relieved by 2nd Bde + 22nd Inf Bde + moved to COURCELLES. Reinforcements NIL. Casualties NIL.	Appendix 4

WAR DIARY
or
INTELLIGENCE SUMMARY

Army Form C. 2118.

(Erase heading not required.)

Place	Date	Hour	Summary of Events and Information	Remarks and references to Appendices
BUCQUOY	5-4-17		Fine. Three battalions employed on working parties on the Railway at ACHIET LE PETIT. 2/Manchester hutted to BUCQUOY. Casualties Nil. Reinforcements - 1/Green 2 Officers 109 O.R. 1/S.Staff 2 Officers 2/Manchester 37 O.R.	Mt
"	6-4-17		Fine - Rain in the evening - Working parties as on 5-4-17. Casualties Nil. Reinforcements - 1/S.Staff 3 O.R. 2/Manchester 17 O.R.	Mt
"	7-4-17		Snow in the night. Fine day. Two battalions on working parties on railway - Casualties Nil. Reinforcements Nil.	Mt
"	8-4-17		Fine - Two battalions working on railway - Casualties Nil. Reinforcements 1/S.Staff 1 Officer 2/Manchester 1 O.R.	Mt
"	9-4-17		Rain and Snow in morning, clearing in afternoon. Strong wind. One battalion working on railway - Casualties Nil. Reinforcements 1/Green 9 O.R. 1/S.Staff 5 O.R. 2/Manchester 94 O.R. 9. M.G.C. 4 O.R.	Mt
"	10-4-17		Very windy with snow storms at intervals. Bde ease under 2 hours notice to move by 7 a.m. but this was cancelled at about 9-15 a.m. One battalion on working party. Casualties Nil. Reinforcements 1/S.Staff 10 O.R. 2/Manchester 1 O.R.	Mt

WAR DIARY or INTELLIGENCE SUMMARY

Army Form C. 2118.

Place	Date	Hour	Summary of Events and Information	Remarks and references to Appendices
BUCQUOY	11-4-17		Fine with very high winds. Brigade in reserve. Living to state in evening. At 11.30 a.m. orders received for Brigade to move to ABLAINZEVELLE. Rec MP, Pirate Cm, Trench Mortar Batty and 2/Manchester Regt. moved to billets in ABLAINZEVELLE. 1/Queen to camp at ABLAINZEVELLE, and 2/Manchester to camp in LOGEAST WOOD. 91 MGC to ABLAINZEVELLE. One Battalion working party on SERRE - PUISIEUX road. Casualties Nil. Reinforcements 1 Offr & Other Ranks. 91 MGC 4 OR. 127 LTM B. 1 Offr 2/Manchester 1 Offr.	MS
ABLAINZEVELLE	12-4-17		Fine morning. Rain later in evening. Brigade returned to BUCQUOY area. Rec MP, Pirate Corp, TMB, 2/Queen, 2/Manchester & 1/S Staff to PUISIEUX. 91 MGC to BUCQUOY. Reinforcements 1/S Staff 1 Offr. Casualties Nil. 2/Manchester 1 Offr.	MS
	13-4-17		Fine. Two battalions and two companies on road working parties. Reinforcements 1/S Staff 1 Offr 10 OR. Casualties Nil. 6 OR. 2/Manchester 1 Offr.	MS
	14-4-17		Fine. 2/Manchester moved to ERVILLERS to take over billets under order of 62nd Division. 2 Battns on road work. Reinforcements Nil. Casualties Nil.	MS
	15-4-17		Wet. Brigade stood by ready to move up to support 1st ANZAC Corps who were counter attacked near LAGNICOURT. Alm. Reinforcements. Three PoWs on road work. Casualties 2/Manchester 10 OR wounded. Reinforcements 1/Queen 1 Offr 50 OR. 2/Manchester 10 OR.	MS

2449 Wt. W14957/M90 750,000 1/16 J.B.C. & A. Forms/C.2118/12.

Army Form C. 2118.

WAR DIARY
or
INTELLIGENCE SUMMARY

(Erase heading not required.)

Instructions regarding War Diaries and Intelligence Summaries are contained in F. S. Regs., Part II. and the Staff Manual respectively. Title Pages will be prepared in manuscript.

Place	Date	Hour	Summary of Events and Information	Remarks and references to Appendices
BUCQUOY	16-4-17		Fine morning - Heavy rain in evening - 1/Manchesters moved to ERVILLERS and came under orders of 62nd Division - 2 Battalion on rodwork. Casualties NIL. Reinforcements 1/Manchesters 1 Officer 5 O.R.	N.B.
"	17-4-17		Snow and hail showers both night intervals - 1/S.Staffs and 21/Manchesters moved by motor lorry to GOMIECOURT and came under orders of 62nd Division - 21/Manchesters went into line at ECOUST. (right sector) 2 Coys 21/Manchesters in support at ECOUST. Casualties NIL. Reinforcements NIL.	N.B.
L'HOMME MORT	18-4-17	Aft.	Purple Hqrs. moved to L'HOMME MORT (57 D.c. B.17.a.7.9) and both men Commenced at 3 p.m. to take over of 62nd Division. 91st Bde moved to BUCQUOY. 1/S.Staff relieved 21/Manchesters in left sector 21/Manchesters in support at ST LEGER. Casualties NIL. Reinforcements NIL.	N.B.
"	19.4.17		Fine + Misty. Enemy intermittent shelling whole sector throughout day. Casualties 1/S.Staff 1 O.R. killed 2 O.R. wounded 21/Manchesters 1 O.R. killed 2 O.R. wounded 1 O.R. missing 21/Manchesters 1 O.R. wounded 1 Officer 2 O.R. Reinforcements 1/S.Staff 7 O.R. 21/Manchesters	Appendix 5. N.B.

2449 Wt. W14957/Mq0 750,000 1/16 J.B.C. & A. Forms/C.2118/12.

Army Form C. 2118.

WAR DIARY
or
INTELLIGENCE SUMMARY

(Erase heading not required.)

Instructions regarding War Diaries and Intelligence Summaries are contained in F. S. Regs., Part II. and the Staff Manual respectively. Title Pages will be prepared in manuscript.

Place	Date	Hour	Summary of Events and Information	Remarks and references to Appendices
L'HOMME MORT	20/4/17		Fine. White roots fairly heavily shelled. Casualties 2/Sherw 2 OR wounded. 1/S. Staff 1 OR killed 1 Officer & 6 OR wounded. 2/Manchester 1 OR wounded. 22/Manchester 1 OR wounded. Reinforcements. 2/Sherw 5 Officers 1 OR.	Appendix 6 MB
ARLAINZEVELLE	21/4/17		Fine. Brigade relieved by 20th Infantry Brigade during night 21/22 April. Relieving troops to ARLAINZEVELLE. 2/Manchester came to billets in ARLAINZEVELLE. Hqrs & 2 Coys 22/Manchester to Camp at ARLAINZEVELLE. 1/S. Staffs. 2/Sherwoods and 2 coys 22/Manchester to Camp near GOMIECOURT. Casualties 2/Sherw 1 OR wounded 1/S. Staffs 1 Officer 14 OR wounded 2/Manchester 1 Officer 10 OR wounded. 22/Manchester 2 Officers 8 OR.	Appendix 7 MB
"	22.4.17		Fine. 2/Sherw & 1/S. Staffs moved to LOGEAST WOOD. 2 Coys 22/Manchester to ARLAINZEVELLE. M.G.C. relieved in line by 20th M.G.C. and moved to Camp at GOMIECOURT. Casualties 2/Sherw 6 OR wounded 1/S. Staffs 5 OR wounded 1/S. Staffs 1 Officer 22/Manchester 2 Officers. Reinforcements NIL.	MB
"	23.4.17		Fine. Brigade resting and bathing. 91st M.G.C. moved to ARLAINZEVELLE. Casualties NIL. Reinforcements NIL.	MB
"	24.4.17		Fine. Training carried out. Casualties NIL. Reinforcements NIL.	MB

WAR DIARY or INTELLIGENCE SUMMARY

Army Form C. 2118.

Instructions regarding War Diaries and Intelligence Summaries are contained in F. S. Regs., Part II. and the Staff Manual respectively. Title Pages will be prepared in manuscript.

(Erase heading not required.)

Place	Date	Hour	Summary of Events and Information	Remarks and references to Appendices
ARLAINZEVELLE	25.4.17	—	Fine – Battalion training. Casualties Nil – Reinforcements Nil – Reinforcements 1/5.Staffs 1 Officer –	MB
"	26.4.17	—	Fine – Battalion training – Casualties Nil – Reinforcement 2/Manchester 1 O.R.	MB
"	27.4.17	—	Fine – Brigade field day. 2/Manchester Casualties Nil. Reinforcements 2/Manchester 5 O.R.	MB
"	28.4.17	—	Fine – Brigade field day – 2/Manchester & 1/5.Staffs attack practice on AYETTE - 2/Manchester & Capt 2/Queen went to Camp at GOMIECOURT. Casualties Nil. Reinforcements. 1/5.Staffs 3 O.R. 2/Manchester 1 Officer	MB
"	29.4.17	—	Fine – 2/Manchester took over left sector from 9th Devons. 2/Manchester both men right sector front line with 1/5.Staffs in support on left and 2/Queen in support on right – Casualties Nil Reinforcements Nil.	MA Appendix 9 " 9A
L'HOMME MORT	30.4.17	—	Fine – Brigade H.Q. went to L'HOMME MORT. G.O.C. took over Command Sector at 9.30 a.m. Enemy fairly quiet – & Advanced Posts 1/Manchester Rushed during night – Casualties 2/Manchester 8 O.R. missing 5 O.R. wounded. Reinforcements Nil.	Appendix 10

W Manning Lt Colonel
Commanding 91st Infantry Brigade

SECRET.

Appendix 1

Narrative of attack on CROISILLES carried out
by 91st Infantry Brigade on 28th March.1917.

Reference Maps - FRANCE 51B. S.W. and 57C. N.W. - Scale 1/20,000.

-:-:-:-:-:-:-:-:-:-:-

1. PRELIMINARY DISPOSITIONS.

   On March 26th the Brigade was disposed as under:-

   Brigade Headquarters.   )
   1st Bn.South Staffordshire Regt.) COURCELLES-LE-
   22nd Bn.Manchester Regt.   ) COMTE.

   2nd Bn.Queen's Regt.   ABLAINZEVILLE.

   21st Bn.Manchester Regt.   Holding the CROISILLES
                                    Sector under the
                                    Command of 20th
                                    Infantry Brigade
                                    (since night March
                                    24/25th).

   On March 27th Brigade Headquarters moved forward to
ERVILLERS (B.13.b.3.4.) and 2nd Bn.Queen's Regt. to COURCELLES-
LE-COMTE. That night (27/28th) the 1st Bn.South Staffordshire
Regt. and 22nd Bn.Manchester Regt. took over their respective
sectors from 21st Bn.Manchester Regt.,which was withdrawn to
COURCELLES-LE-COMTE. The 2nd Bn.Queen's Regt. moved to ERVILLERS
in the early morning of March 28th,being in support of the
attack,in a position of assembly in L.14.b. by ZERO hour.

2. SCHEME.

   The attack was to be carried out by two battalions,1st Bn.
South Staffordshire Regt. on the left,and 22nd Bn.Manchester
Regt. on right,dividing line being the FONTAINE-LEZ-CROISILLES -
ST.LEGER Road from T.18.c.5.3. - T.23.d.2.7. - T.28.b.4.4. (all
inclusive to 22nd Bn.Manchester Regt.) The task of the 1st Bn.
South Staffordshire Regt. was to make good the line of the
Sunken Road from T.18.c.5.3. - T.17.c.9.2. - T.16.b.7.6. and to
form a defensive flank on the North,along the spur running
North and South through T.16.Central,touch being maintained
with the 58th Division on the left whose right post remained at
T.22.a.2.7. In view of the wide front to be attacked by the
Officer Commanding 1st Bn.South Staffordshire Regt. (1500 yards
objective and 1200 yards defensive flank) I had placed one
Company 2nd Bn.Queen's Regt. and 4 Vickers Guns under his orders
for the operation.
   The objective of the 22nd Bn.Manchester Regt. was to
establish a line from the factory at T.24.b.1.2. across to
T.18.c.5.3.,touch being maintained with the 20th Infantry Brigade
on the right,whose posts were to advance under cover of the
barrage to the vicinity of the Windmill at T.24.d.1.4.
   The attack was to be made under a barrage creeping forward
at the rate of 50 yards in two minutes,the village of CROISILLES
and the sunken roads in the vicinity being kept under a
bombardment by heavy artillery up to the last moment compatible
with safety.
   The assaulting Battalions were to be formed up on a line
running parallel to and 200 yards beyond the N.E. edge of
ST.LEGER Wood by ZERO minus 30 minutes and to advance the line
300 yards so as to be close under the barrage by ZERO hour.

(continued).

Each Battalion had two companies in the front line (each in two waves, and each preceded by a strong patrol), one company in support following in extended order behind the attacking troops, and the remaining company holding the original line of posts N.E. of ST.LEGER.

Two platoons only of each Battalion were to enter the village, the remainder working round the outskirts. After capture, the village was to be kept as clear of troops as possible.

3. ATTACK.

The attack was launched at 5-45.a.m. on March 28th. Both companies of the right battalion were met with heavy machine gun fire, and failed to penetrate the wire, which was uncut excepting for a gap at about T.23.d.5.0. Only at one place was an entrance effected - at T.29.b.0.0, where Captain DUGUID with 12 men cut a passage through the wire and established himself within the defences where he remained for 36 hours until relieved.

The remainder of the 3 companies dug themselves in in front of the wire until nightfall when they were ordered to withdraw to the original line of posts.

At 8.a.m. I ordered Officer Commanding 22nd Bn. Manchester Regt. to move his reserve company in wide extensions down the valley running through T.30. Central, to endeavour to outflank the defences of the village and to effect an entrance between the Windmill at T.24.d.1.4. and Sunken Road through T.24.c.0.0. This company however came under direct observation, was heavily shelled, and failed to reach its objective.

One Company of 2nd Bn. Border Regt. was ordered up to ST.LEGER to replace this company as tactical reserve to 22nd Bn. Manchester Regt.

On the left, the right company of 1st Bn. South Staffordshire Regt. had immediately met with very heavy rifle and machine gun fire, but had nevertheless succeeded in advancing a considerable distance. The supporting company had been absorbed in the attack, and a mixed party worked close up to the enemy wire in T.23.c. Here they were heavily counter-attacked, but drove off the enemy with Lewis Gun and rifle fire inflicting considerable casualties on him.

Owing to their exposed position and the severity of the enemy's fire this party was eventually forced to withdraw to the Sunken Road in T.22.d., where they dug in and remained throughout the day.

Meanwhile the left company of the 1st Bn. South Staffordshire Regt. had advanced successfully over the road between T.22.a.2.7. and T.23.a.2.7., a considerable distance towards the Sunken Road in T.17.a. and c. They were here hung up by heavy enfilade and frontal machine gun and rifle fire. Owing to the failure of the right company to make headway a considerable gap had been formed between the two companies. The situation regarding the left company after 7.a.m. is very obscure. It appears probable however that after maintaining their isolated position under very heavy fire for two hours they were heavily counter-attacked from the road running from T.23.a.2.7. to T.17.c.7.5., and were thus completely enveloped. All except the left hand platoon, who were acting as a defensive flank, became casualties or were taken prisoners.

An attempt was made later in the morning (8.a.m.) to renew the attack with the reserve company and to push forward Vickers guns to relieve the pressure on the right company. Owing to the extremely exposed nature of the ground, however, any advance in the open was found to be impossible.

Orders having been received that the attack was to be renewed at dawn on the following day, 29th March, by a further two battalions, I relieved the 1st Bn. South Staffordshire Regt. (less 1 company) and 22nd Bn. Manchester Regt. by 21st Bn. Manchester Regt. and 2nd Bn. Queen's Regt. respectively.

The original line of posts, however, was to be held by a company of 1st Bn. South Staffordshire Regt. on the left and a company of 2nd Bn. Royal Warwickshire Regt. on right, in order that the four companies of the attacking battalions might remain intact.

(continued).

-3-

At 9.p.m. on 28th, however, this scheme was cancelled, the attack on the village being embraced in a larger attack four days later.

In the light of subsequent events there is little cause for surprise at the result of this attack. For one battalion to advance over a mile of exceedingly exposed country, and occupy an objective 1500 yards in extent is in itself an operation of considerable magnitude. When twelve hundred yards of this advance is exposed to a village heavily wired and (as was subsequently proved) strongly held, and when the left flank was also exposed to a depth of twelve hundred yards, the problem becomes harder.

Considered as a reconnaissance in force however, this attack established the fact that the enemy was not yet prepared to throw open the approaches to the HINDENBURG Line and so contributed to the success of the operations on April 2nd.

The total casualties are shewn below:-

	Killed.		Wounded.		Missing.	
	Off.	O.R.	Off.	O.R.	Off.	O.R.
1st Bn. S. Staffs. Regt.	1	18	4	54	1	57
22nd Bn. Manch. Regt.	1	28	3	61	-	-

Bde. Hd. Qtrs.
10th April, 1917.

Brigadier General,
Commanding, 91st Infantry Brigade.

SECRET.   Appendix 2.

Copy No. 23

91st Infantry Brigade Operation Order No.69.

Saturday, 31st March, 1917.

Reference Maps – Sheet 51B S.W.
& 57C N.W.

-:-:-:-:-:-:-:-:-:-:-:-:-:-:-

1. GENERAL SCHEME.

   (a) The Vth Corps has been ordered to take part in a general attack, on a date and at an hour to be notified later, with the object of capturing the villages of ECOUST-LONGATTE and CROISILLES, and the ground between them; and establishing a line of posts from which to attack the HINDENBURG LINE.
   (b) The task of the 7th Division is to attack on the whole front of the Vth Corps and to force its way through the village of ECOUST-LONGATTE and the ground between that village and CROISILLES with the object of establishing itself on the general line C.3.b.03 – U.27.a.0.4. – U.19.d.8.7. – T.18.b.5.3.
   CROISILLES itself will not be attacked in the first instance, the intention being to surround it first, and then send in troops in from the South to clear it.
   (c) The 21st Division will be attacking on the left, and the 4th Australian Division on the right of the 7th Division.

2. OBJECTIVES.

   The attack will be carried out by the 20th Infantry Brigade on the right, and the 91st Infantry Brigade on the left, with objectives as under:-
   (a) 20th Infantry Brigade.
       First Objective.
       From C.3.c.1.2., the North-eastern outskirts of LONGATTE as far as C.2.b.2.6. Thence along the Railway at C.2.b.2.6. to the bank (inclusive) U.25.b.4.3.
       This line will be consolidated.
       Second Objective.
       Establish a line of posts on a general line C.3.b.0.3. – U.27.c.0.4. – U.20.c.5.4.

   (b) 91st Infantry Brigade.
       First Objective.
       From the bank at U.25.b.4.3. (exclusive) along the railway to U.25.a.5.5. thence along the road to the Factory (inclusive) at T.24.b.0.4.
       Second Objective.
       Establish a line of posts on a general line U.20.c.4.4. – U.19.d.8.7. – T.18.b.5.3.

   The 22nd Infantry Brigade will remain in Divisional Reserve.

3. BOUNDARIES.

   (a) Between 7th and 4th Australian Divisions –
       C.9.a.7.7. – C.8.d.1.7. – B.30.Central.
   (b) Between 20th and 91st Infantry Brigades. –
       U.25.b.4.3. – B.6.d.3.5. – B.17.a.6.8.
   (c) Between 7th and 21st Divisions. –
       T.22.b.8.0. along the 100 metre contour to the railway at T.27.a.4.2.

4. ARTILLERY ARRANGEMENTS.

   (a) The Artillery programme is issued herewith.
       The barrage will be arranged so as to be thickest on the flanks and thinnest in the centre.
       At Zero, the creeping barrage will start on a line 200 yards in front of the assembly line; it will remain on this line for 3 minutes and then start creeping forward at the rate of 100 yards

(continued).

in three minutes - a stationary barrage being kept on the edges of ECOUST - LONGATTE and on the line of the Railway as far as T.24.d.4.7., also on the road from U.25.a.5.6. to Factory T.24.b.0.4.

The creeping barrage will pause for 30 minutes on a line 200 yards in front of the first objective. During this period the barrage will be slackened slightly. At the expiration of 30 minutes it will be intensified and commence creeping forward again to its final protective position on a line 200 yards in front of the outpost line to be taken up, where it will remain until consolidation is completed.

(b) CROISILLES will be kept bombarded by Heavy Artillery from Zero until the first objective is gained, special attention being directed to the outskirts of the village. ECOUST also is going to be bombarded by Heavy Artillery from Zero until Zero plus 12 minutes.

The roads leading from BULLECOURT to ECOUST and from FONTAINE to CROISILLES will be kept barraged by Heavy Artillery from Zero until consolidation is completed. Also the trenches on the South-west side of BULLECOURT, and the HINDENBURG LINE in U.20.b. and U.21.a. and d. as well as the trenches in U.19.b. and U.14.c. will be kept under fire until consolidation is completed.

5. METHOD OF ATTACK.

(a) The attack of the 91st Infantry Brigade will be carried out by three battalions, 2nd Bn. Queen's Regt. on left (Headquarters in Main Sunken Road in B.4.b.), 21st Bn. Manchester Regt. in centre (Headquarters as for 2nd Bn. Queen's Regt.), and 1st Bn. South Staffordshire Regt. on right (Headquarters B.10.b.0.4.)

Boundaries within the Brigade Sector will be as follows:-
Between 2nd Bn. Queen's Regt. and 21st Bn. Manchester Regt. -
U.13.c.4.3. - T.24.b.4.2. - T.24.c.9.1.
Between 21st Bn. Manchester Regt. and 1st Bn. South Staffordshire Regt. -
U.19.b.4.2. - U.25.a.3.9. - Bank at T.30.b.35.25.

The 22nd Bn. Manchester Regt. (Headquarters T.27.d.9.9.) will be in Brigade Reserve in the vicinity of the Railway in T.27.a. and will be prepared to clear the village of CROISILLES when the first objective has been gained. Should the 22nd Bn. Manchester Regt. have been drawn into the fight, this operation will be carried out by 2nd Bn. Royal Warwickshire Regt. (less one Company holding posts) 22nd Infantry Brigade which will be lent to this Brigade for the purpose.

(b) 2nd Bn. Queen's Regt. will advance to the attack on a one Company Front, supported by a second Company, both widely extended and organised in depth. The two remaining Companies will occupy the two Sunken Roads leading to strong point at T.23.b.9.3., when that point has been captured. On gaining the first objective a strong patrol will be pushed out to the road at T.18.c.5.3. to cut off the retreat of any enemy from CROISILLES, and to obtain touch with 21st Division who are pushing patrols towards this point from T.17.d.6.9.

Officer Commanding 2nd Bn. Queen's Regt. will arrange for a special party to be detached to deal with the enemy strong point at T.23.d.4.3. at Zero hour, under cover of a hurricane bombardment from the two Stokes Guns detailed in para. 8.

The battalion attacking on the left will be the 12th Bn. Northumberland Fusiliers, 62nd Brigade, Headquarters T.25.a.6.4. An officer will be detailed by Officer Commanding 2nd Bn. Queen's Regt. to act as Liaison officer with this Battalion.

(c) The 21st Bn. Manchester Regt. will advance on a two Company front. One company widely extended will follow in support of the assaulting companies, the remaining company being kept screened as far as possible in rear.

(d) 1st Bn. South Staffordshire Regt. will advance in a similar manner to 21st Bn. Manchester Regt. (above). A special party will be detailed to deal with the enemy strong point at U.25.Central.

The battalion attacking on the right will be 9th Bn. Devon Regt. (Headquarters L'HOMME MORT. T.17.a.8.5.)

(e) The clearing of the village will be carried out by two Companies each on a platoon frontage, one Company being responsible for the North-western, the other the South-western portion of the village.

A strong bombing party will work round the trench surrounding the village in a northerly direction, a small party being detailed to work eastwards towards T.29.b.7.9. This party will be met by a bombing party from the post of 2nd Bn. Queen's Regt. at T.23.d.9.3.

(continued).

6. STRONG POINTS will be constructed as under:-

    (a) U.25.Central.
    (b) U.25.a.5.6.
    (c) T.24.d.6.5.
    (d) T.24.b.0.3.
    (e) T.18.b.5.3.

The 1st Bn.South Staffordshire Regt. will be responsible for (a) and (b), the 21st Bn.Manchester Regt. for (c) and the 2nd Bn. Queen's Regt. for (d) and (e).

Each post will be constructed and garrisoned by a platoon of a supporting Company, previously detailed for the task and equipped accordingly.

A Lewis Gun will be placed in each post.

7. ACTION OF MACHINE GUN COMPANY.

Officer Commanding,91st Machine Gun Company will arrange:-
(a) To place three guns in the vicinity of the CEMETERY in T.28.a. sited so as to bring effective fire to bear on the South-eastern portion of the village of CROISILLES.

These guns will protect the left flank of the 2nd Bn.Queen's Regt. during the advance by barraging the outskirts of the village and enfilading the main street, from Zero hour till Zero plus 20 minutes.
(b) To place two guns in the vicinity of the CHATEAU in T.28.d.

These guns will barrage the North-western portion of the village from Zero till Zero plus 15 minutes. They will not fire outside the line of orchards surrounding the village.
(c) To link up both of above groups of guns by telephone to Headquarters,2nd Bn.Queen's Regt.
(d) Be prepared to send forward one/gun to (a) (b) (c) and (d) Strong Points (see para.6.) on receipt of orders from Brigade Headquarters.

He will establish his Headquarters at Advanced Brigade Headquarters, where he will keep the remainder of his guns in reserve.

8. ACTION OF TRENCH MORTAR BATTERY.

Officer Commanding,91st Trench Mortar Battery will arrange to place one gun in position in the Sunken Road at T.29.b.7.9. and one in position in the Sunken Road at T.30.a.1.9. on the night 31st March/1st April. These two guns will be placed under the Command of an Officer,and will be at the disposal of Officer Commanding,2nd Bn.Queen's Regt. for the operation mentioned in para.5.(b).

A carrying party of 50 men of 22nd Bn.Manchester Regt. will be placed at the disposal of Officer Commanding,91st Trench Mortar Battery, for carrying forward ammunition on night of Zero minus 1 day, details being arranged between Commanding Officers concerned.

Officer Commanding,91st Trench Mortar Battery will remain at Advanced Brigade Headquarters,where a reserve team of gunners will be held in readiness.

9. ACTION OF ROYAL ENGINEERS.

The Officer Commanding 528th (Durham) (Field) Coy. R.E. will arrange:-
(a) To lay out a tape line from B.4.d.3.5. to present Company Headquarters at B.5.d.35.60.
(b) To lay out a tape line along the line of assembly from C.1.c.0.2. - T.24.d.1.0. - T.24.c.4.2.

The flanks of Battalion Sectors will be conspicuously marked.

Both of these lines will be supported on 1 foot posts at intervals of not more than 20 paces.
(c) To be prepared to assist the Infantry on night following the attack in the formation of the Strong Points as laid down in para. 6. A carrying party of 100 men will be provided for this purpose.

(continued)

10. COMMUNICATIONS.

(a) In Advance of Battalion Headquarters.
Each of the assaulting Battalions will establish an Advanced Report Centre to which messages from the front line will be sent.

Relay posts of runners will be formed, at least two such posts being placed between Battalion Headquarters and the line of the first objective. The positions of these posts will be carefully reconnoitred beforehand and made known to all runners.

Separate telephone lines will not be laid to Companies; the principle to be adopted is that of laying a line to an Advanced Station previously made known to all concerned. This Advanced Telephone Station will serve the whole battalion front.

Every advantage will be taken of the exceptional facilities for visual signalling.

A power buzzer will be installed at the commencement of operations in the large crater at B.5.d.25.75. to work in conjunction with a listening set at crater B.10.b.4.5. whence messages so received will be transmitted to Brigade Headquarters by wireless. The power buzzer will subsequently be taken forward to the junction of road and railway in U.25.a.5.0.

This forms a most reliable means of transmitting information, and the positions of the set should be made known to all. Messages will be handed to the Officer in charge in clear.

Flares and pigeons will be distributed to attacking battalions as they become available. The former will not be used unless the aeroplane is at too great an altitude to see men waving to it.

(b) In rear of Battalion Headquarters.
Telephone and Visual back to Advanced Brigade Headquarters, thence telephone and wireless.

11. RELIEF OF POSTS.

Officers Commanding 2nd Bn. Queen's Regt., 1st Bn. South Staffordshire Regt., and 21st Bn. Manchester Regt. will be responsible for the defence of their respective Sectors after 9-30.p.m. on Zero minus 1 day. By this hour there will be established in front of each Battalion Sector 3 posts of 1 N.C.O. and 6 men apiece with one Lewis Gun, the whole being under the command of an Officer. Active patrolling will be carried out throughout the night until Zero minus 15 minutes. Password for the Brigade Sector "MAMETZ".

The posts lying in these sectors previously held by 2nd Bn. Royal Warwickshire Regt. 22nd Infantry Brigade will be withdrawn at 9-30.p.m.

Command of the Sector will be assumed by G.O.C. 91st Infantry Brigade at 9-30.p.m., on Zero minus one day.

The line of posts from T.30.a.1.8. - T.29.b.7.9. - T.29.a.6.9. - T.23.d.6.3. will continue to be held by 2nd Bn. Royal Warwickshire Regt. (Headquarters T.28.a.3.1.) under G.O.C. 91st Infantry Brigade.

12. ASSEMBLY.

(a) The line of assembly runs from C.1.a.0.2. where touch with 20th Infantry Brigade is made, to T.24.d.1.0. to T.24.c.4.2.
(b) All troops will be drawn up on the tape by Zero minus one hour.
(c) The route for the assembly march will be along the ERVILLERS - ST.LEGER road to B.4.a.9.9. to B.4.d.25.85. - along taped track to present Company Headquarters at B.5.d.55.60. where guides from the forward posts will be picked up. Battalion Commanders will arrange direct with Officer Commanding 2nd Bn. Royal Warwickshire Regt. during the day previous to the assembly march all details as to number of guides required.
(d) Battalions will pass the QUARRY at B.8.d.5.1. at the following hours:-

2nd Bn. Queen's Regt.	Zero minus 7 hours.
21st Bn. Manchester Regt.	Zero minus 6½ hours.
1st Bn. South Staffs. Regt.	Zero minus 6 hours.

An interval of 200 yards between Companies will be maintained throughout the assembly march, Battalion Commanders being responsible that adequate measures are taken to prevent touch being lost in the darkness.
(e) The assembly march will be carried out with the strictest secrecy. No smoking or noise will be permitted.
(f) Battalions will report completion of Assembly to Brigade Headquarters by the Code Word "HINDENBURG".

13. SYNCHRONISATION OF WATCHES.

    All units will send a watch to Brigade Headquarters at 5.p.m. on Zero minus one day. Attacking Battalions and 91st Machine Gun Company will be synchronised again by telephone at 11.p.m.

14. PERSONNEL TAKEN INTO ACTION.

    The same percentage of personnel as that detailed in Operation Order No.68 of 26th March,1917,will be left with the 1st Line Transport throughout the operations.

15. ADMINISTRATIVE INSTRUCTIONS will be issued later.

16. BRIGADE HEADQUARTERS, will remain at B.13.b.3.4. An Advanced Report Centre will be established in Old German Trench at B.3.d.9.7. where messages should be sent. Only Officers called to the telephone will make use of this trench, all other personnel remaining in the Sunken Road running just East of this Point.

17. ACKNOWLEDGE.

                                                    Captain,
                                A/Brigade Major, 91st Infantry Brigade.

Issued at 4.55.p.m.

Copy No 1 7th Division.   13 20th Inf.Bde.
        2 2nd Queen's R   14 22nd Inf.Bde.
        3 1st S.Staffs.R   15 62nd Inf.Bde.
        4 21st Manch.R   16 Bde. Transport Officer.
        5 22nd Manch.R   17 "D" Group, 7th D.A.
        6 91st T.M.Battery.   18 "C" Group, 7th D.A.
        7 91st Bde.Gren.Coy.   19 Supply Officer.
        8 91st Bd..Signals.   20 Brigade Major.
        9 91st M.G.Coy.   21 Staff Captain.
       10 C.R.A.   22 File.
       11 A.D.M.S.   23 War Diary.
       12 528 (Durham)Fd.Coy.   24 War Diary.
                                 25 2nd R. Warwick R.

SECRET.

Copy No. 13

Additions and Amendments to 91st Infantry Brigade
Operation Order No.69.

Sunday, 1st April, 1917.

-:-:-:-:-:-:-:-:-:-

1. ZERO day will be April 2nd; ZERO hour will be 5-15.a.m.
2. Reference para.5.(c) Line 11. For T.30.a.35.25. read
T.30.b.35.25.
    Reference para. 12(c) Line 3. For B.5.c.35.60 read B.5.d.35.60
3. ACKNOWLEDGE.

Brook.
Captain,
for Brigade Major, 91st Infantry Brigade.

Copies to all recipients of O.O.69.

Copy No. 23.

91st Infantry Brigade.

ADMINISTRATIVE INSTRUCTIONS (issued in connection with 91st Infantry Brigade Operation Order No.69.

1. **DRESS AND EQUIPMENT.**
   (a) The following Fighting Dress will be worn by all ranks except Specialists.
   - (1) Rifle and Equipment.
   - (2) 120 rounds S.A.A.
   - (3) Haversack on back containing rations as in para. 2(b).
   - (4) Leather Jerkin.
   - (5) Waterbottles filled.
   - (6) Waterproof Sheet with Jersey rolled inside fastened to waistbelt by supporting straps of pack.
   - (7) Two Mills Grenades one in each bottom pocket of the jacket.
   - (8) Box Respirator.
   - (9) 1 tin solidified paraffin (if available)

   (b) Fighting Dress for Specialists will be the same as in para. 1(a) except that Specialists will only carry 50 rounds S.A.A.
   Specialists include

   Bombers.   Runners.
   Signallers.   Lewis Gunners.
   Scouts.

   (c) Picks and shovels required will be drawn from Battalion Reserve.
   There will be a further supply of 100 shovels and 40 picks at the Brigade Dump at B.4.a.6.3.

2. **RATIONS.**
   (a) Every man will carry an iron ration but this is not to be consumed except by the order of an Officer.

   (b) Every man will also carry a full day's rations in his haversack.

   (c) An issue of rum will be made as shortly before Zero as is possible.

3. **SUPPLY OF S.A.A., BOMBS, &c.**
   There is a Brigade Dump of S.A.A. at T.27.d.8.1. and a more forward dump of S.A.A., Bombs, Wire and Stakes, in the SUNKEN ROAD at B.4.a.6.3.
   After objectives have been gained a dump will be established at U.25.a.5.5.

4. **TRANSPORT.**
   "A" Echelon, 1st Line Transport will move to a position in the neighbourhood of ERVILLERS to be arranged by the Brigade Transport Officer to be in position by 9 p.m. Zero minus 1 day.
   The Battalion Tool Limbers will accompany "A" Echelon.
   "B" Echelon will remain in its present position.
   The Brigade Transport Officer will arrange to have 6 pack animals loaded with S.A.A. and 6 with No.5.Mills Bombs in the QUARRY at T.27.d.8.1. ready to move forward at any moment.
   The Brigade Transport Officer will report to Headquarters, 22nd Manchester Regt. at T.27.d.9.9. one hour before Zero and will remain there during the operations.

5. **MEDICAL.**
   There are Advanced Dressing Stations at ST. LEGER and ERVILLERS with squads at Regimental Aid Posts. The Main Dressing Station is at the SUCRERIE, COURCELLES.

   (continued overleaf.)

6. PRISONERS OF WAR.
Prisoners will be sent under escort to the Cage at ERVILLERS where they will be handed over to the Vth Corps Officer in charge. All documents or papers taken from Prisoners or dead bodies will be collected in sandbags and sent to Brigade Headquarters.

Bde.Hd.Qtrs.

1st April, 1917.

Arkin Lawford   Lieut.
a/Staff Captain, 91st Infantry Brigade.

Copies to all recipients of O.O. 69.

SECRET.

Appendix 3.

Copy No. 11

91st Infantry Brigade Operation Order No. 70.

Monday, 2nd April, 1917.

Reference Maps – 51B S.W.
& 57C N.W.

-:-:-:-:-:-:-:-:-:-:-:-

1. The 91st Infantry Brigade will be relieved by 22nd Infantry Brigade to-night as under:-

    (a) 1st Bn. Royal Welsh Fusiliers will take over the front now held by 22nd Bn. Manchester Regt. 2nd Bn. Queen's Regt. and 21st Bn. Manchester Regt.
    (b) 2nd Bn. Royal Warwickshire Regt. will take over front now held by 1st Bn. South Staffordshire Regt. (also that of 9th Bn. Devon Regt., 20th Infantry Brigade).

2. All details with regard to (b) will be arranged between Commanding Officers concerned.

3. With regard to (a) –
   The 1st Bn. Royal Welsh Fusiliers will hold each Battalion Sector with 1 Company as under:-

    (a) 21st Bn. Manchester Regt. (to be relieved by "A" Company).
        2 platoons in outpost line.
        2 platoons and Company Headquarters in Strong Point T.24.d.7.5.
    (b) 2nd Bn. Queen's Regt. (to be relieved by "B" Company).
        2 platoons in outpost line.
        2 platoons and Company Headquarters in Factory.
    (c) 22nd Bn. Manchester Regt. (to be relieved by "C" and "D" Companies).
        "C" Company will put two platoons and Company Headquarters in Sunken Road T.17.d.5.7. – T.18.c.5.3. and two platoons to establish posts in advance of this line.
        "D" Company will be in reserve, and will take over from the Company of 22nd Bn. Manchester Regt. now in support in CROISILLES.

    Battalion Commanders will arrange guides, and will have the incoming Companies met at S. Corner of ST. LEGER WOOD at 7-30.p.m.
    3 Lewis Guns per Company will be taken in by the 1st Bn. Royal Welsh Fusiliers; these will be taken in in each case with Company Headquarters, the Company Commander placing them at his own discretion.

4. The 91st Machine Gun Coy. will be relieved by 22nd Machine Gun Coy. on night 3/4th April under arrangements to be made between Commanding Officers concerned.

5. The command of the Sector will pass to G.O.C. 22nd Infantry Brigade on completion of relief.

6. On relief, Units will march to billets as under:-

2nd Bn. Queen's Regt.	ERVILLERS to billets vacated by 1st Bn. Royal Welsh Fusiliers.
1st Bn. S. Staffs. Regt.	COURCELLES to former billets.
21st Bn. Manchester Regt.	COURCELLES to former camp.
22nd Bn. Manchester Regt.	ERVILLERS to billets vacated by 20th Bn. Manchester Regt.

    Quartermasters have been warned, and arrangements made for facilitating the billetting of 2nd Bn. Queen's Regt. and 22nd Bn. Manchester Regt.

-2-

7. Headquarters for to-night will be as under:-

  22nd Infantry Brigade. GOMIECOURT.
  91st Infantry Brigade. ERVILLERS. B.3.b.3.4.
  1st Bn.R.Welsh.Fuslrs. B.4.b.2.2.(Present Headquarters of 2nd Bn.Queen's Regt.)
  2nd Bn.R.Warwick.Regt. B.10.b.9.2.(Present Headquarters of 1st Bn.S.Staffordshire Regt.)

8. ACKNOWLEDGE.

               Captain,

           A/Brigade Major, 91st Infantry Brigade.

Issued at.. 7.p.m. (Previously Communicated)

  Copy No 1 7th Division.
     2 2nd Queen's R
     3 1st S.Staffs.R
     4 21st Manch.R
     5 22nd Manch.R
     6 91st M.G.Coy.
     7 1st R.Welsh Fus.
     8 2nd R.Warwick R
     9 22nd Inf.Bde.
     10 File.
     11 War Diary.
     12 War Diary.
     13 Brigade Major.
     14 Staff Captain.

Casualties
1st to 3rd April 1917.

Appendix 3A

	Killed		Wounded		Missing	
	Officers	O.R.	Officers	O.R.	Officers	O.R.
2nd Bn "Queens" Regt.	4	22	3	43	-	3
1st Bn S. Staffs Regt.	-	-	1	27	-	-
21st Bn Manchester Regt.	1	16	5	68	-	8
22nd Bn Manchester Regt.	2	3	2	26	-	10
Total.	7	41	11	164	-	21

Total. 18 Officers
226 O.R.

SECRET.

Appendix 3 B

Narrative of attack on CROISILLES carried out by 91st Infantry Brigade on 2nd April, 1917.

Reference Maps - FRANCE 51B. S.W. and 57C. N.W. Scale 1/20,000.

-:-:-:-:-:-:-:-:-

1. (a) **GENERAL PLAN.**

In conjunction with the 21st Division on the left and the 4th Australian Division on the right, the 7th Division was ordered to capture the villages of ECOUST LONGATTE and CROISILLES and to establish a line of posts on the slopes below the HINDENBURG LINE.

The task allotted to the 62nd Infantry Brigade, (21st Division) was to occupy the CROISILLES - LAGNICOURT-SUR-COJEUL Road from T.17.c.7.5. to T.3.a.3.4. and to establish posts on a line from T.17.b.6.1. to T.3.b.1.9.

The task allotted to the 20th Infantry Brigade was to capture the village of ECOUST-LONGATTE and the line of the railway from C.2.b.2.8. to U.25.b.4.3., and to establish posts on a line from C.3.b.0.3. to U.20.c.5.4.

Between these attacks the 91st Infantry Brigade was ordered:-

(i) to occupy the line of the railway and sunken road from U.25.b.4.3. to the factory at T.24.b.0.4. (inclusive) and to push patrols up to the road at T.18.c.5.3. in order to cut off the retreat of any enemy from CROISILLES and to obtain touch with 62nd Brigade, who were to send patrols to this point from T.17.d.0.9.

(ii) to establish a line of posts along the general line U.20.c.4.4. - U.19.d.8.7. - T.18.b.5.3.

(iii) to clear the village of CROISILLES after the operations in (i) above were complete.

(b) **ARTILLERY ARRANGEMENTS.**

A creeping barrage, arranged so as to be thickest on the flanks, was to open at ZERO hour on a line 200 yards in front of the assembly line, where it would remain for 3 minutes. It would then creep forward at the rate of 100 yards in 3 minutes to a line 200 yards beyond the first objective where it was to remain for 30 minutes. During this portion of the advance a stationary barrage was also to be kept on the first objective. At the expiration of 30 minutes the barrage was to creep forward at the same rate to its final protective position 200 yards in front of the outpost line to be taken up, where it was to remain until consolidation was complete.

CROISILLES was to be kept bombarded by Heavy Artillery from ZERO until the first objective was gained, special attention being directed to the outskirts of the village. The road leading from FONTAINE to CROISILLES and the trenches in U.19.b. and U.14.c. were to be barraged by Heavy Artillery from ZERO until consolidation was complete.

2. **BRIGADE ATTACK.**

The attack was to be carried out from a tape previously laid by the R.E. The line of assembly ran from C.1.a.0.2. - T.24.d.1.0. - T.24.c.4.2.

The attack was to be carried out by 3 Battalions, 2nd Bn. Queen's Regt. (left), 21st Bn. Manchester Regt. (centre) and 1st Bn. South Staffordshire Regt. (right) with right boundaries as under:-

2nd Bn. Queen's Regt.	U.13.c.4.3. - T.24.b.4.2. - T.24.c.9.1.	
21st Bn. Manchester Regt.	U.19.b.4.2. - U.25.a.3.9. - T.30.b.3.2.	
1st Bn. S. Staffs. Regt.	C.1.a.0.2. - U.20.c.4.3.	

(continued).

The 22nd Bn.Manchester Regt.(Headquarters J.27.d.9.9.) were to be in Brigade Reserve in ST.LEGER prepared either to clear the village or support the main attack. In the latter eventuality the 2nd Bn.Royal Warwickshire Regt.,22nd Infantry Brigade,were to be available for clearing the village. The original line of posts in front of ST.LEGER,from T.30.a.1.8. - T.29.b.7.9. - T.29.a.6.9. - T.22.d.6.3. was to be held by a company of 2nd Bn.Royal Warwickshire Regt.,22nd Infantry Brigade.

The 2nd Bn.Queen's Regt.(Headquarters B.4.b.2.1.) were to advance on a frontage of one company,with a second company following in support at a distance of 100 yards. A third company was detailed to deal with the enemy strong point at the "TOOTH"(T.23.d.8.3.),with the assistance of two Stokes guns (one in either fang) which had been placed in position on night 31st March/1st April. One platoon of the remaining company had been given to each of above companies,the remaining platoon being kept at Battalion Headquarters for carrying purposes. Three Vickers guns had been placed in the vicinity of the Cemetery in T.28.a. and two near the CHATEAU in T.28.d.,to cover the exposed left flank of 2nd Bn.Queen's Regt. by barraging the village during the advance on the first objective.

The 21st Bn.Manchester Regt. (Headquarters B.4.b.2.1.) was to attack on a frontage of two companies with a third company following in support,the remaining company being in reserve in the vicinity of J.29.Central.

The advance of the 1st Bn.South Staffordshire Regt. (Headquarters B.10.b.8.4.) was to be carried out in a similar manner to that of 21st Bn.Manchester Regt.

Each battalion was ordered to establish an advanced telephone station and relays of runners. This system was found to give excellent results.

Strong points were to be made at U.25.Central,U.25.a.5.6., T.24.d.6.5.,T.24.b.0.3. and T.18.b.5.5. These were to be constructed and garrisoned by battalions concerned,a specially equipped platoon being previously detailed for each strong point.

Liaison with the 62nd Infantry Brigade was maintained throughout by an exchange of officers between 2nd Bn.Queen's Regt. and 13th Bn.Northumberland Fusiliers (and subsequently also with 22nd Bn.Manchester Regt.)

3. ASSEMBLY.

The assembly march was carried out according to a table, the route being along the ERVILLERS - ST.LEGER road to the S.corner of ST.LEGER WOOD,thence along a taped track to the original Company Headquarters at B.5.c.5.6. where guides were assembled.

In the exceptionally clear moonlight one company of 2nd Bn. Queen's Regt.,while advancing down the exposed spur in T.30.a., was observed by the enemy who immediately put up a large number of "golden rain" rockets,and barraged the valley in B.5.a. somewhat severely. The limits of this barrage however were so well defined that succeeding battalions were able to keep clear of it. With this exception the forming up was carried out without incident.

4. THE ATTACK.

At ZERO hour (5-15.a.m.) the advance commenced. On the right the 1st Bn.South Staffordshire Regt. gained their first objective with little opposition,and brought heavy Lewis Gun fire to bear on parties of the enemy who were making good their escape across the open to the HINDENBURG LINE.

In the centre,the 21st Bn.Manchester Regt. were considerably handicapped by our barrage which opened on a line 50 yards in rear of the left company. As the barrage lifted, however,the line advanced,but the railway embankment in the vicinity of T.24.d.7.3. proved a formidable obstacle,being some 40 feet high,and covered with brambles. In the centre was a low culvert screened by brambles. The flanks of the embankment were wired,while above the culvert was a strong point with a machine gun emplacement,also wired. Numerous

(continued).

snipers posts were dug in along the top. As the front line
advanced it was met by heavy machine gun and rifle fire from the
top of the embankment and from a machine gun concealed in the
culvert. At the same time machine gun fire was opened from the
direction of CROISILLES, where the 2nd Bn.Queen's Regt. were
being held up. The top of the embankment was however gained
after a sharp struggle at 6-30.a.m., but the enfilade machine
gun fire from the left increased to such intensity that it was
impossible to maintain the position, and the line withdrew down
the embankment. The right company succeeded in getting a Lewis
Gun team over the embankment, and engaging a machine gun which
had apparently retired to a position covering the sunken road.
Finally, by a process of dribbling men over the embankment and
through the culvert, the line was established in the sunken road
by 10a.m.

On the left of the line the 2nd Bn.Queen's Regt. also
came under the barrage, all the officers of the leading company
becoming casualties. Considerable disorganisation ensued, a line
being dug some 80 yards in rear of the tape.

The advance was however re-organised and on going forward
came under Machine Gun fire from the "TOOTH" and the railway
at T.24.c.2.5. Under cover of a Lewis Gun section and covering
party placed to command the railway, the line of the railway was
carried at about 7.a.m.

By 7-30.a.m. the whole of the first objective had been
reached, and strong patrols sent out along the CROISILLES -
FONTAINE road in order to cut off the retreat of the enemy from
CROSILLES. Posts were established at T.18.c.6.3., T.18.d.0.8, and
T.18.b.5.3.(the latter being subsequently withdrawn to a better
position at T.18.d.5.4. owing to heavy enfilade machine gun fire).

Meanwhile the 1st Bn.South Staffordshire Regt. had pushed
forward posts to the second objective, which was also reached at
11a.m. by 21st Bn. Manchester Regt. and shortly afterwards by 2nd
Bn.Queen's Regt. Six Vickers guns were sent forward to the
railway which now formed an exceedingly strong support line.

The enemy strong point at the "TOOTH" had not succumbed to
the attack at ZERO hour. Under a stokes mortar bombardment, 2
sections 2nd Bn.Queen's Regt. had established themselves within
50 yards of the enemy when the point was found to be strongly
held, the approaches up the Sunken Roads and over the top being
covered by machine guns. Owing to the enfilade fire the situation
here was so unsatisfactory that it was decided to withdraw the
party, whose store of rifle grenades was exhausted, in order to
allow the strong point to be re-bombarded by the Artillery. This
took place at about 9-45.a.m. As the result of this bombardment
the "TOOTH" was evacuated 100 Germans (reported from two
different sources) being seen to leave the "TOOTH" and escape
through the village.

At about 10.a.m. and throughout the morning parties of the
enemy attempted to leave the village via the FONTAINE road
through T.18.c. These were turned back by the Lewis Gun post at
T.18.c.513. and casualties were inflicted on the enemy. The enemy
retired or left the village between the road running N. from the
Factory through T.24.b. and U.13.c. and d. The enemy appear
eventually to have escaped by using the road running through
T.17.c. and b. as small parties were continually seen during the
morning and fired on both by Lewis Guns from T.18.d.0.8. and
T.18.b.5.3. and by the Artillery. Owing to the distance it is
impossible to say what casualties were inflicted on the enemy,
but several of the latter were seen to fall at each burst of fire.

Had the 62nd Brigade succeeded in gaining touch with 2nd Bn.
Queen's Regt. at T.18.c.5.3. or even had a post at T.17.b.6.1.,
the right flank of their objective, there can be little doubt but
that a very large number of the enemy would have been effectually
cut off. A resume of the messages etc. on this point is attached
to this report.(Appendix "A").

5. CLEARING THE VILLAGE.

The situation of the 2nd Bn.Queen's Regt. now being
assured, I decided to put in the 22nd Bn. Manchester Regt. to clear
the village. Orders were accordingly issued for two companies
to form up on either side of the SENSEE River on a line 200 yards
N.E. of ST.LEGER WOOD and advance on the village at 11-30.a.m. under

(continued).

a stationery barrage on the defences of MOISLAINS. The objective was the Sunken Road from T.18.c.5.3. - T.17.d.4.8., and a strong bombing party was to be detailed to work round the defences of the village.

The line was seen to enter the village, after which the situation became most obscure. The left company pushed on towards its objective, engaging the enemy in a running fight. After a time however it became scattered and disorganised. The right company similarly became scattered and lost its direction, only one platoon reaching its objective in the Sunken Road. The bombing party were hung up by a strong point at T.23.a.5.5.

At 1-45.p.m. the support Company was ordered to take up a position in the southern end of the village, and shortly afterwards became involved in the fight.

Later in the afternoon a hostile machine gun was reported by 62nd Brigade at the cross roads at T.17.d.5.6. The Officer Commanding 22nd Bn. Manchester Regt. accordingly sent up the remainder of his reserves (2 platoons) under his Adjutant to deal with this post and also that at T.23.a.5.5. which was still holding out. This force, moving rapidly through the village found the cross roads occupied by a party of 2nd Bn. Queen's Regt. Turning N.E. they then returned via cross roads at T.17.c.7.6. in order to take the remaining point in the rear. Finding three dugouts occupied by the enemy, Lieut. Robinson placed his three Lewis Guns on the flanks and barraged the strong point and Sunken Road. He then rushed them, killing one officer and 3 men and taking 22 prisoners thus finally clearing the village.

The situation was not finally cleared however until the early morning of the 3rd, when touch was established at two points - with 62nd Infantry Brigade.

CONCLUSION.

During the night April 2nd/3rd the 2nd Bn. Queen's Regt. and 21st Bn. Manchester Regt. were relieved by 1st Bn. Royal Welsh Fusiliers and 1st Bn. South Staffordshire Regt. by 2nd Bn. Royal Warwickshire Regt. of 22nd Infantry Brigade. The 22nd Bn. Manchester Regt. remained in the line until relieved by 21st Division on night 4th/5th April.

In conclusion I would draw attention to two points, the first being the admirable manner in which the forming up was conducted by battalion commanders. To anyone who has visited the position by day it seems almost incredible that so large an assembly could have been carried out in bright moonlight at such a short distance from the enemy's position without arousing his suspicions. That the coughing and rattling and incidental noises almost inseparable from such an enterprise should have been suppressed to this extent is in my opinion most creditable.

This assembly was greatly facilitated by the excellent arrangements made by the Officer Commanding 528th (Durham) (Field) Coy. R.E. to whose skill in laying out the tape its success was largely due.

Secondly, I wish to state that, apart from the unfortunate accident at the commencement of operations, the work of the artillery was reported on most favourably by all. Both the barrage and the subsequent work (especially the 4.5" treatment of the "TOOTH") were most satisfactory.

The total casualties are shewn below:-

UNIT.	Killed.		Wounded.		Missing.	
	Off.	O.R.	Off.	O.R.	Off.	O.R.
2nd Bn. Queen's Regt.	4	25	3	43	-	-
1st Bn. S. Staffs. Regt.	-	-	1	26	-	-
21st Bn. Manch. Regt.	1	16	5	64	-	3
22nd Bn. Manch. Regt.	2	3	3x	26	-	10
TOTAL.	7	44	12x	159	-	13

x Includes 1 Still at Duty.

Bde. Hd. Qtrs.
13th April, 1917.

Brigadier General,
Commanding, 91st Infantry Brigade.

APPENDIX "A".

1. "BOLT (62nd Infantry Brigade).

    B.M.529.   2nd   AAA

    WAVE (2nd Bn.Queen's Regt) report 6.a.m. left held up by machine gun fire in outskirts of village

    WATER. (91st Infantry Brigade).
       7-10.a.m. "

2. Extract from telephone diary.

    " 7-35.a.m. G.O.C. to G.S.O.1.

    WAVE held up slightly - now pushing on to factory............
    .... Asks 62nd to push round and help...............Asks for heavies to continue on S.E. corner of village and 62nd to work round to back of factory."

3. " BOLT.

    B.M.530   2nd   AAA

    WAVE now on first objective and pushing out patrol to meet you as arranged

        WATER. 7-45.a.m. "   (priority).

4. "WATER

    B.M.30   2nd   AAA

    OX (13th Bn.Northumberland Fusiliers) has gained all his objectives and is on his look out for your patrols

    62nd Infantry Brigade. 8-35.a.m. "

5. Extract from report of Officer Commanding, 2nd Bn.Queen's Regt.

    "Touch with the unit on my left - i.e.62nd Brigade - was not obtained until about 2-30.p.m. in the afternoon when 2 officers of that Brigade visited my post at T.18.c.5.3.
        Had the post been established at T.17.a.9.2. at any time after 9-30.a.m. on the morning of 2nd April, it would have been impossible for any of the enemy to have retreated or got away from the village of CROISILLES. "

6. Extract from report of Officer Commanding, 22nd Bn.Manchester Regt.

    " A Company moved rapidly through the village to capture Machine Gun at T.17.d.5.7. and found a post of 2nd Bn.Queen's Regt. there. "

C O P Y.

Appendix 3 C

April 4th, 1917.

" Just a line to thank the 7th Division for the excellent way in which they co-operated with us in the attack on the 2nd and, by so doing, greatly assisted us in reaching our final object-ine - this is the third time since I have been in command of the 21st Division that we have been lucky enough to be associated with the 7th Division, and on at least two of these occasions, your Division has been very instrumental in enabling us to reach our objectives. I should especially like to convey my thanks to your left Brigade for the excellent manner in which they all played up to us. With all good wishes and many congratulations on your success ".

2.

7th Division No. G.292.

7th Divisional Artillery.
20th Infantry Brigade.
22nd Infantry Brigade.
91st Infantry Brigade.

I am directed by the Divisional Commander to forward the above copy of a private letter he has received from the General Officer Commanding, 21st Division.

He feels sure that all ranks will appreciate the spirit of comradeship in which the letter is written.

(signed) G.W. HOWARD. Lieut. Colonel.
7th April, 1917. General Staff, 7th Division.

S E C R E T.
****

Copy No. 10

7th DIVISION ORDER No. 144.

Reference -   3rd April, 1917.
Sheets 51B S.W.
      57C N.W.

1. (a)   The 7th Division will be relieved in the line, from its present right at C.4.c. 3.1. to the SENSEE River (exclusive) T.18.b. 4.3., by the 62nd Division during the 4th instant and night 4th/5th April.
          This relief will be completed by 8 a.m. 5th April.

   (b)   Orders for the relief of the 7th Division troops in the line from the SENSEE River (inclusive) to the present 7th Division left at T.17.d. 3.9. including the defence of CROISILLES by the 21st Division will be issued later.
          This relief will take place either tonight or tomorrow night.

2.   All details of relief as in 1 (a) will be made direct between the 22nd Infantry Brigade and the 185th Infantry Brigade.

3.   The 22nd Infantry Brigade will arrange to leave a proportion of machine gunners, Lewis gunners, and N.C.Os in the line for 24 hours after the completion of the relief.

4.   The command of the front as in 1 (a) will pass to the G.O.C. 62nd Division on completion of the relief.

5.   The C.R.E. will arrange direct with the C.R.E. 62nd Division for handing over any work in hand.
         R.E. Companies will be accommodated in their Brigade areas when relieved.

6.   The Artillery will remain in the line for the present.

7.   On relief, the 22nd Infantry Brigade will move to COURCELLES.

8./

8. On completion of the relief the 7th Division will be located as follows :-

    Divisional H.Q. - COURCELLES.

    20th Inf. Bde H.Q. - ABLAINZEVELLE.
    1 Battalion - ABLAINZEVELLE.
    1 Battalion - LOGEAST WOOD.
    2 Battalions - Tent Camps, ABLAINZEVELLE.

    22nd Inf. Bde H.Q. - COURCELLES.
    4 Battalions - COURCELLES.

    91st Inf. Bde H.Q. - BUCQUOY.
    1 Battalion. - BUCQUOY.
    1 Battalion - PUISIEUX.
    2 Battalions - Tent Camps, BUCQUOY.

    Pioneer Battalion - COURCELLES HALTE.
    (24th Manchester R)

9. The 220th Machine Gun Company will withdraw its guns at present in action protecting the Artillery, at 9 a.m. on April 5th.

10. ACKNOWLEDGE.

G. W. Howard.
Lieut-Colonel.
General Staff, 7th Division.

Issued at / p.m. to :-
A.D.C. (for G.O.C)	Copy No.1.
Office.	" 2 and 3.
"Q"	" 4.
7th Div. R.A.	" 5.
C. R. E.	" 6.
7th Signal Company.	" 7.
20th Inf. Bde.	" 8.
22nd Inf. Bde.	" 9.
91st Inf. Bde.	" 10.
Pioneer Battalion.	" 11.
A.D.M.S.	" 12.
Divisional Train.	" 13.
15th Squadron R.F.C.	" 14.
21st Division.	" 15.
4th Australian Division.	" 16.
62nd Division.	" 17.
War Diary.	" 18.

SECRET.   Copy No. 21

91st Infantry Brigade Operation Order No.71.

Saturday, 14th April, 1917.

Reference Maps - 51B. S.W.
                 57C. N.W.

-:-:-:-:-:-:-:-:-:-

1. (a) In conjunction with the VIIth Corps on the left and the 1st ANZAC Corps on the right the Vth Corps will be attacking the HINDENBURG LINE with objectives as shewn on attached map (issued with copies No.3,4,5,6, and 7 only).
    (b) The attack will probably take place at dawn on April 16th. ZERO day and hour will be notified later.

2. (a) The 7th Division will be in Corps Reserve for the operation, its role depending on the development of events.
        All units will be prepared to move at short notice and to take with them only the baggage supplies and stores laid down in War Establishments. No extra transport will be available.
        The 20th and 22nd Infantry Brigades will be concentrated at COURCELLES and the valley N.W. of MORY respectively by ZERO plus 3 hours.
    (b) The 91st Infantry Brigade will move to the ABLAINZEVILLE area in accordance with the attached March Table.

3. All units will send a watch to Brigade Headquarters at ZERO plus 3 hours to be synchronised.

4. Administrative Instructions will be issued later.

5. Brigade Headquarters will close at BUCQUOY at ZERO plus 2 hours at which hour it will open at ABLAINZEVILLE.

6. ACKNOWLEDGE.

                                                    Captain,
                                    A/Brigade Major, 91st Infantry Brigade.

Issued at 7/20 p.m.

Copy No 1 Bde. Major.   13 C.R.E.
       2 Staff Captain.   14 C.R.A.
       3 2nd Queen's R.   15 Supply Officer,
       4 1st S.Staffs.R   91st Inf.Bde.
       5 21st Manch.R   16 7th Divn. "G".
       6 22nd Manch.R   17 7th Divn. "Q".
       7 91st M.G.Coy.   18 20th Inf.Bde.
       8 No.3.Sectn.7th Div.Sig.Coy. 19 22nd Inf.Bde.
       9 91st T.M.Battery.   20 Town Major,
      10 91st Bde.Gren.Coy.   ABLAINZEVILLE.
      11 Bde.Transport Officer.   21 File.
      12 A.D.M.S.   22 & 23 War Diary.

MARCH TABLE.

(Issued with 91st Infantry Brigade Operation Order No.71.)

Unit.	Starting Point.	Time.	Destination.	Remarks.
2nd Bn.Queen's Regt.	Cross Roads BUCQUOY.	ZERO plus 1¼ hours.	ABLAINZEVILLE.	Take over Camp from 2nd Bn.Border Regt.
22nd Bn.Manch.Regt.	—do—	ZERO plus 1¼ hours.	LOGEAST WOOD.	" " " 9th Bn.Devon Regt.
Brigade Headquarters.) 91st T.M.Battery. 91st Bde.Gren.Coy.	—do—	ZERO plus 1¾ hours.	ABLAINZEVILLE.	Take over Billets from corresponding Units of 20th Infantry Brigade.
1st Bn.S.Staffs.Regt.	—do—	ZERO plus 2 hours.	—do—	Take over Billets from 8th Bn.Devon Regt.
91st Machine Gun Coy.	—do—	ZERO plus 2¼ hours.	—do—	" " " 20th Machine Gun Coy.

NOTE. - Units are responsible for making their own arrangements for taking over billets from outgoing Units.

Appendix 5

91st Infantry Brigade.

Summary of Intelligence - No.1.

From 12.noon.18th April,1917 to 12.noon.19th April,1917.

1. **ARTILLERY.**

    Enemy artillery was active on N.E.corner of ECOUST about 5.a.m. At 11.a.m. No.5.Post(Right Sector)was heavily shelled and forced to withdraw,to shelter of railway. - This post will be pushed out again to-night to a different position.
    Our Artillery did excellent shooting on enemy wire both with heavies and Field Guns,also on the centre of BULLECOURT.
    At 11-30.a.m. our 4.5's fired on the "tank" in the enemy wire from which the enemy were sniping all night up the BULLECOURT - ECOUST Road. At 11-45.a.m. the "tank" was hit and the ammunition inside apparently set on fire.

2. **MACHINE GUN AND RIFLE FIRE.** - Quiet.

3. **SNIPING.**

    During the night up the BULLECOURT - ECOUST Road from the "tank"

4. **PATROLS.**

    Two patrols went out from the left sector to reconnoitre the hostile wire from U.14.c.05525. to U.20.a.75.50. They report the presence of a hostile post with a machine gun at U.20.a.6.5. with a smaller post about 100 yards due N.of the latter.
    No.1.patrol went out at U.20.a.25.10. and struck the two enemy posts and then proceeded N.E.towards the wire.
    No.2.patrol went out at U.19.b.9.3. and struck the enemy's wire at about U.14.c.15.20.
    The patrols report that the wire is damaged but is still an obstacle to Infantry from U.14.c.15.20. to U.20.a.65.85.
    The ground in front of the wire from U.14.c.1.3. to U.20.a.45.95. is badly cut up by shell holes and it appears that our artillery firing on the wire has been firing short.
    From U.20.a.45.95. to U.20.a.6.5. there are comparatively few signs of our artillery fire.

5. **INTELLIGENCE.** - N I L , Visibility poor.

6. **GENERAL.** - N I L .

Bde.Hd.Qtrs.

19th April,1917.

Brigadier General,
Commanding,91st Infantry Brigade.

91st Infantry Brigade.

Appendix 6

Summary of Intelligence - No.2.

From 12.noon.,19th April,1917 to 12.noon.,20th April,1917.

1. OPERATIONS. - N I L.

2. ARTILLERY.
   (a) **Our Artillery.** - Both Field Guns and Howitzers appeared to be making excellent shooting on the wire in front of BULLECOURT.
   (b) **Enemy Artillery.** - During the morning and afternoon of the 19th Instant, the enemy shelled the Railway embankment about U.26.c.5.2. intermittently also the Cemetery at C.2.a.1.8. from the direction of HEND COURT.

   About 6.p.m. the enemy shelled the N.W.slopes of valley in U.26. heavily also from the Cemetery to C.2.b.2.5. with 5.9's, 4.2's and 77's.

   From 7.p.m. - 7-30.p.m. the enemy put down a heavy barrage round the Railway embankment from T.24.d. to U.25.a. This was repeated from 8-30.p.m. to 9.p.m. and about every hour he opened a short burst up to 5.a.m. this morning.

   L'HOMME MORT was shelled intermittently during this morning.

3. MOVEMENT.

   A party of 9 Germans was seen at dusk moving from North to South in the vicinity of U.14.c.2.9.

4. MACHINE GUNS.

   Machine Guns fired on our aeroplanes during the day otherwise quiet.
   Machine Guns are suspected at U.13.a.9.9. and U.20.b.4.2.

5. SNIPING.

   A sniper appeared to be using the Tank on S.E.of BULLECOURT during the evening.
   A sniper's post is suspected at about U.20.a.9.5.

6. PATROLS.

   A patrol from the Railway embankment at U.27.c. at 9-30.p.m. got to within a short distance of the enemy wire E. of Road in U.27.a.99.50. The enemy's Very Lights enabled them to get a good view of the wire and they report the wire as being well knocked about.

   A patrol left T.24.b.2.6. at 10.p.m. and worked up the road running thorugh T.24.b. and U.13.c. and d. until within about 30 yards of the German wire where two posts were located,one at U.13.d.8.9. and the other at U.14.c.0.8. There is a gap in the wire where the road runs through and in the gap is a machine gun, which fired on the patrol. The wire here is in good condition.

Bde.Hd.qtrs.

20th April,1917.

Brigadier General,
Commanding, 91st Infantry Brigade.

Appendix 7

91st Infantry Brigade.

Summary of Intelligence - No.3.

From 12.noon., 20th April,1917 to 12.noon., 21st April,1917.

1. **OPERATIONS.**

    Gas was discharged by Special Coy. R.E. at 3-40.a.m., against BULLECOURT. - The wind was S.W.

2. **ARTILLERY.**
   Our Artillery. - During the afternoon our heavies and 18 pdrs. fired on BULLECOURT and RIENCOURT and the wire in front of them.
   Between 2-30.p.m. and 4.p.m. our 4.5's were shooting short along the railway U.27.c.0.4. and U.27.d.3.5.
   At 3-30.p.m. our artillery did particularly good shooting and removed a good quantity of wire in front of BULLECOURT.
   Our heavies were firing short during the afternoon within 50 yards of post at U.20.d.85.12. and U.2 0.c.7.7.
   Enemy Artillery. - At 1.p.m. heavy shelling round right Battalion Headquarters (C.2.d.8.8.) and N.E. corner of ECOUST with 519's.
   At 3-30.p.m. enemy shelled railway embankment from BULLECOURT - ECOUST Road to 150 yards East of Road.
   At 5-45.p.m. enemy was again active with 5.9's and some shrapnel on N.E.corner of ECOUST.
   During the afternoon and evening the railway embankment in C.24.d. was heavily shelled.
   L'HOMME MORT was shelled intermittently during the afternoon.

3. **MOVEMENT.** - N I L .

4. **MACHINE GUNS.**
   A machine gun was firing from U.15.d.9.9. during the day.

5. **SNIPING.**

    There was a good deal of sniping last night probably from the centre of BULLECOURT.

6. **PATROLS.**

    Two patrols were sent out from the right Battalion and reached point U.25.a.9.4. and U.27.d.5.6. respectively. Both patrols report the wire in front of BULLECOURT to be badly damaged,but still to form a considerable obstacle.
    A third patrol from the right Battalion report the Sunken Road U.27.a.5.7. - U.20.d.9.5. was unoccupied by the enemy between 9.p.m. and midnight.
    A patrol from the left Battalion left U.19.b.8.2. at 9-10.p.m. and proceeding in a Northerly direction found a broad tape leading N.N.W. This was followed for about 80 yards where it ended.
    A newly dug but unoccupied post was discovered at about U.20.a.0.6. The patrol proceeded about 40 yards further and heard voices - with the aid of lights being fired some 200 yards away a high parapet about 15 yards long was seen at about U.20.a.35.90. Very lights were fired from this spot. It appears that this post was held by garrison of about 12 men.
    Another post with a garrison of about 8 men was discovered at U.19.b.85.90. There was no wire in front of this post.
    The patrol did not go through the wire of the HINDENBURG LINE as the post seemed to be a strongly held outpost line in front of it.

7. **MISCELLANEOUS.**

At 12-15.a.m. a fire was observed on a true bearing of 77° from C.2.d.8.8.

At 3-40.a.m. a golden rain rocket was fired from enemy trench N. of BULLECOURT. Our artillery were very active about this time.

Bde.Hd.Qtrs.

21st April,1917.

Brook, Capt.

Brigadier General,
Commanding, 91st Infantry Brigade.

Appendix 8.

S E C R E T.
****

Copy No. 14.

7th DIVISION ORDER No. 149.

20th April, 1917.

1. The 20th Infantry Brigade will relieve the 91st Infantry Brigade in the line on night of 21st/22nd April. On relief the 20th Infantry Brigade will come under the orders of 62nd Division.

2. All arrangements for this relief will be made between the Infantry Brigades concerned.

3. The command will pass to the 20th Infantry Brigade on completion of the relief.
Completion of relief will be reported to 62nd Division and repeated to 7th Division.

4. The 20th Machine Gun Company will relieve the 91st Machine Gun Company in the line on night of 22nd/23rd April.

5. To simplify the relief, the 20th Infantry Brigade will, on 20th instant, move 2 battalions into Camps at GOMIECOURT, whence they can proceed to the line on 21st instant.
"Q" will make the necessary arrangements for this move.

6. On relief the 91st Infantry Brigade will be quartered at ABLAINZEVELLE and LOGEAST WOOD, making use of the two Camps at GOMIECOURT as a staging place if required.

7. The 91st Infantry Brigade will leave a proportion of N.C.O's and Lewis gunners in the line for 24 hours after completion of the relief.

8. ACKNOWLEDGE.

Lieut-Colonel.
General Staff, 7th Division.

Issued at 11 a.m. to :-

A.D.C. (for G.O.C.)	Copy No 1.	20th Inf.Bde.	Copy No 12.
General Staff.	" 2 & 3.	22nd Inf.Bde.	" 13.
A.A. & Q.M.G.	" 4.	91st Inf.Bde.	" 14.
A.D.M.S.	" 5.	Pioneer Battalion.	" 15.
Divisional Train.	" 6.	7th Signal Coy.	" 16.
C. R. A.	" 7.	Div.M.G.Company.	" 17.
22nd Brigade R.F.A.	" 8	War Diary.	" 18.
35th Brigade R.F.A.	" 9.	D.A.D.O.S.	" 19.
Div. Ammunition Column.	" 10.	62nd Division.	" 20.
C. R. E.	" 11.		

SECRET.

Appendix 8A

Copy No. 22

91st Infantry Brigade Operation Order No. 72.

Friday, 20th April, 1917.

Reference Maps — Sheet 51B. S.W.
51C. N.W.

1. The 91st Infantry Brigade will be relieved in the line by the 20th Infantry Brigade on night 21/22nd April.

2. (a) Battalions will be relieved as follows:—

2nd Bn. Queen's Regt.	by	8th Bn. Devon Regt.
1st Bn. S. Staffs. Regt.	by	2nd Bn. Gordon Highlanders.
21st Bn. Manchester Regt.	by	9th Bn. Devon Regt.
22nd Bn. Manchester Regt.	by	2nd Bn. Border Regt.

   Guides to meet Commanding Officers and Company Commanders of relieving Units, to conduct them to Battalion Headquarters, will rendezvous as follows:—

2nd Bn. Queen's Regt.)	Cross Roads B.24.d.8.8.
22nd Bn. Manchester Regt.)	at 9-30.a.m., 21st instant.
1st Bn. S. Staffs. Regt.)	ST. LEGER Church,
21st Bn. Manchester Regt.)	at 9-30.a.m., 21st instant.

   All details of relief will be arranged between Battalion Commanders concerned.

   (b) On relief the 91st Infantry Brigade will proceed to ABLAINZEVILLE - LOGEAST WOOD Area.

3. The 91st Machine Gun Coy., will be relieved in the line by 20th Machine Gun Coy., on night 22/23rd April.

4. Each Battalion in the line will leave a proportion of N.C.O's and Lewis Gunners in the line for 24 hours after relief. The 91st Machine Gun Coy. will arrange to leave N.C.O's in the line in a similar way.

5. The greatest care will be taken in handing over all posts and positions and no post or position will be evacuated until properly relieved.

6. Billeting Instructions will be issued later.

7. Completion of relief will be reported to Brigade Headquarters by "B.A.B." Code.

8. ACKNOWLEDGE.

Major,
Brigade Major, 91st Infantry Brigade.

Issued at ..... p.m.

Copy No. 1. Bde. Major.	12. Q.M., 2nd Queen's R
2. Staff Captain.	13. Supply Off. 91st Inf. Bde.
3. 2nd Queen's R	14. 7th Division "G".
4. 1st S. Staffs. R	15. 7th Division "Q".
5. 21st Manch. R	16. 62nd Division "G".
6. 22nd Manch. R	17. 20th Inf. Bde.
7. 91st M.G. Coy.	18. 22nd Inf. Bde.
8. No. 3. Sec. 7th Div. Sigs.	19. 100th Inf. Bde.
9. 91st T.M. Battery.	20. Inf. Bde. (Anzacs).
10. 91st Bde. Gren. Coy.	21. File.
11. Bde. Transport Off.	22 & 23 War Diaries.

S.C/1823/11.

All Battalions.
Machine Gun Co.
7th Division "Q".
20th Inf.Bde.
Town Major, ABLAINZEVILLE.
Supply Officer.

Reference para.6 of Operation Order No.72 dated 20th instant.

1. (a) On relief on night 21st/22nd instant the Brigade will be disposed as under:-

Brigade Headqrs.	-	ABLAINZEVILLE.
2nd Queen's Regt.) 2 Coys. 22nd Manch. Regt.)	-	Camp at A.23.c.4.9.
1st S.Staffs Regt.	-	Camp at A.30.c.7.7.
21st Manchester Regt.	-	Billets at ABLAINZEVILLE.
22nd Manchester Regt. (less 2 Coys.)	-	Camp at ABLAINZEVILLE.

    (b) On night 22nd instant the 2nd Queen's Regt and 1st South Staffs Regt will move to camps at LOGEAST WOOD being clear of camps at GOMIECOURT by 2 p.m. and 2-30 p.m. respectively. 2 companies 22nd Manchester Regt will rejoin battalion at ABLAINZEVILLE, being clear of camp by 3 p.m.
    Troops can proceed across country, transport being sent via COURCELLES HALT.

2. Separate orders for the moves of 91st Machine Gun Co. will be issued later.

3. Quartermasters have been warned of the above moves.

Bde.Hd.Qtrs.   (sd)   O.F.MORSHEAD,   Captain,

20th April,1917.   Staff Captain,91st Infantry Brigade.

Appendix 9

S E C R E T.
****

Copy No. 14

7th DIVISION ORDER NO. 150.

27th April, 1917.

1. The 91st Infantry Brigade will relieve the 20th Infantry Brigade in the line on 29th instant and night 29th/30th.
   All arrangements for this relief will be made by the Infantry Brigade Commanders concerned.
   On relief the 91st Infantry Brigade will come under the orders of 62nd Division.

2. To facilitate the relief the 2 Camps North and South of GOMIECOURT will be available for the 91st Infantry Brigade to-morrow 28th inst.

3. On relief the 20th Infantry Brigade will move to LOGEAST WOOD and ABLAINZEVELLE, making use of the camps North and South of GOMIECOURT for staging purposes if required.
   Brigade Headquarters - ABLAINZEVELLE.

4. The command will pass to 91st Infantry Brigade at 9 a.m. on 30th inst.
   Completion of relief will be reported to 62nd Division and repeated to 7th Division.

5. The 20th Infantry Brigade will arrange to leave a proportion of Lewis gunners and N.C.O's in the line for 24 hours after completion of the relief.

6. The relief of the Machine Gun Companies will be carried out on the night of 30th April/1st May.

7. ACKNOWLEDGE.

G. W. Howard.

Lieut-Colonel.
General Staff, 7th Division.

Issued at   p.m. to :-

A.D.C.(for G.O.C.)	Copy No 1.	20th Inf.Bde.	Copy No 12.
General Staff.	" 2 & 3.	22nd Inf.Bde.	" 13.
A.A. & Q.M.G.	" 4.	91st Inf.Bde.	" 14.
A.D.M.S.	" 5.	Pioneer Battalion.	" 15.
Divisional Train.	" 6.	7th Signal Coy.	" 16.
C.R.A.	" 7.	Div. M.G.Company.	" 17.
22nd Brigade R.F.A.	" 8.	War Diary.	" 18.
35th Brigade R.F.A.	" 9.	R.A.D.O.S.	" 19.
Div. Ammunition Column.	" 10.	62nd Division.	" 20.
C.R.E.	" 11.		

SECRET.   Appendix 9A   Copy No. 22

91st Infantry Brigade Operation Order No. 73.

Friday, 27th April, 1917.

Reference Maps - 51B S.W. - 57C N.W. - 57D N.E. - Scale 1/20,000.

-:-:-:-:-:-:-:-:-:-:-:-

1. The 91st Infantry Brigade will relieve the 20th Infantry Brigade in the line on night 29/30th April, 1917.
   On relief the 91st Infantry Brigade will come under the orders of the 62nd Division.

2. The 22ND BN. THE MANCHESTER REGT. will take over the right of the line from 2ND BN. BORDER REGT.
   The 2ND BN. QUEEN'S REGT. will take over from 8TH BN. DEVON REGT. in support to right of the line.
   The 21ST BN. MANCHESTER REGT. will take over the left of the line from 9TH BN. DEVON REGT.
   The 1ST BN. SOUTH STAFFORDSHIRE REGT. will take over from 2ND BN. GORDON HIGHLANDERS in support to the left of the line.

3. The 21st Bn. Manchester Regt. will move on 28th April to Camp at A.23.c. This Camp will be cleared by outgoing unit by 4.p.m.
   The 22nd Bn. Manchester Regt. will move on 28th April to Camp at A.30.d. This camp will be cleared by outgoing unit by 4.p.m.
   Times of moves will be arranged by Battalion Commanders.
   Two Companies of 2nd Bn. Queen's Regt. will be attached to 22nd Bn. Manchester Regt., for the move, and further instructions will be issued later with regard to the accommodation of these two Companies.
   The 2nd Bn. Queen's Regt. (less two Companies) and 1st Bn. South Staffordshire Regt. will move forward direct to their positions in Support on the 29th instant, times of move being arranged by Battalion Commanders.
   All further arrangements for reconnaissances, reliefs and guides will be arranged between Battalion Commanders concerned.

4. The 91st Machine Gun Coy. will relieve the 20th Machine Gun Coy. in the line on night 30th April/1st May.
   All details of relief will be arranged between Commanding Officers concerned.
   Headquarters, 20th Machine Gun Coy. are at B.28.a.6.6.
   Further instructions regarding accommodation of 91st Machine Gun Coy. on night 29th April will be issued later.

5. The 20th Infantry Brigade are arranging to leave a proportion of N.C.O's, Lewis Gunners and Machine Gunners in the line for 24 hours after relief.

6. Completion of relief to be reported to 91st Infantry Brigade Headquarters at L'HOMME MORT by "B.A.B." Code.

7. ACKNOWLEDGE.

                                                    Major,
                              Brigade Major, 91st Infantry Brigade.

Issued at .... p.m.

                                          (Distribution over-leaf).

Copy No 1 Bde.Major.   12 Q.M.,2nd Queen's R
        2 Staff Captain.   13 Supply Officer,91st I.B.
        3 2nd Queen's R   14 7th Division "G"
        4 1st S.Staffs.R   15 7th Division "Q"
        5 21st Manch.R   16 62nd Division "G"
        6 22nd Manch.R   17 20th Inf.Bde.
        7 91st M.G.Coy.   18 22nd Inf.Bde.
        8 No.3.Sec.7th Div.Sigs.19 Bde. on Right (In line).
        9 91st T.M.Battery.   20 Bde. on Left (-do-).
       10 91st Bde.Gren.Coy.   21 File
       11 Bde.Transport Officer.22 War Diary.
                                23 War Diary.

Appendix 10

91st Infantry Brigade.

Summary of Intelligence - No.4.

From 12.noon.29th April,1917 to 12.noon.30th April,1917.

1. OPERATIONS. - N I L.

2. ARTILLERY.
    (a) Our Artillery has been active on BULLECOURT and the enemy trenches and wire.
    (b) Enemy Artillery shelled ECOUST and the Railway in T.26. fairly heavily about 4.a.m.
    A large number of apparent "duds" fell in and about CROISILLES during the night.

3. MACHINE GUNS AND SNIPERS. - Generally quiet.

4. PATROLS.
    A patrol left the post at U.13.c.5.1. at 10-15.p.m. and proceeded to within 30 yards of the enemy wire at about U.13.b.6.1. The wire appeared to be cut in several places.
    A further patrol proceeded to about the 95 Contour in U.20.a.9.6. and located enemy post short distance ahead. The strength of the post was about a machine gun team.
    A searchlight was sweeping the enemy wire and valley through U.20.a. and b. for a distance of about 350 yards.
    A working party was heard either picking or driving in stakes some distance to the left of the patrol.

5. INTELLIGENCE. - N I L.

6. GENERAL.
    The two Advanced Posts 3A at U.21.c.35.15. and 4A at U.21.c.10.35. were engaged with rifle fire from their front by party of enemy about 30 strong. The posts opened fire. Whilst their attention was engaged on enemy party in front, a party of about 20 Germans bombed first 4A Post from the rear and then worked down top of bank in S.E. direction to 3A Post. The men were taken by surprise and the only ones to return to Coy.H.Q. were 2 Sergeants,1 Lance Corporal and 1 man,all wounded. The remainder are missing. A man of No.3A Post states after firing on enemy and being wounded he came back to Coy.H.Q. via 4A Post which he found deserted. A patrol of 1 Officer and 1 Lance Corporal went up to U.26.b.6.9. at 5.a.m. but were unable to detect any movement or observe whether posts 3,4,3A and 4A were occupied. It is impossible to find out any further details until night fall.
    Our Machine Guns fired during the night on BULLECOURT and the HINDENBURG LINE and Support line.

Bde.Hd.Qtrs.
30th April,1917.

Brigadier General,
Commanding,91st Infantry Brigade.

7th DIVISION.

B. H. Q.

91st INFANTRY BRIGADE.

MAY 1917.

Army Form C. 2118.

WAR DIARY
INTELLIGENCE SUMMARY
(Erase heading not required.)

7th Dv
91st Infantry Brigade
May 1917

Vol 19

Place	Date	Hour	Summary of Events and Information	Remarks and references to Appendices
L'HOMME MORT	1-5-17		Fine. 22/Manchesters relieved by 8th 62nd Division also 2/Queens - 2/Manchesters. 1/S/Queens moved back to Camp at GOMIECOURT - Bde HQrs move back to GOMIECOURT. 2/Manchesters in line on left and 1/S Staff. in support in left coy under orders of 187th Inf Bde 62nd Division. Casualties 2/Manchesters 1 OR killed 2/Manchesters 1 OR wounded 2/Manchesters 3 OR wounded 1/S Staff. 1 O/rk. Reinforcements 1/S Staff in support.	Appendix 1 1A MB MB
GOMIECOURT	2-5-17		Fine. Casualties 2/Queens 1 O/rk wounded 2/Manchesters 3 O/rk. Reinforcements 2/Queens 6 O.R.	MB
	3-5-17		Fine. V Army carried out attack on BULLECOURT & HINDENBURG LINE to the East of it. III Army attacked with the first tank of the River SENSEE as objective - attack partly successful at first but enemy counter attack drove in troops used to starting line. 7th Division have not opposite BULLECOURT. Following more taken place. Bde HQrs. 2/Queens and 22/Manchesters 'D' MGC from BUCQUOY to COURCELLES from GOMIECOURT to COURCELLES. 2/Manchesters 11 OR. Casualties NIL. Reinforcements 2/Queens	MB
COURCELLES	4-5-17		Fine. 22/Manchesters and 1/S Staff relieve in line & support, and returned to BEHAGNIES and SAPIGNIES respectively. Casualties NIL. Reinforcements 1/S Staff 1 May 6 21 O.R.	MB

2449 Wt. W14957/M90 750,000 1/16 J.B.C. & A. Forms/C.2118/12.

Army Form C. 2118.

WAR DIARY
or
INTELLIGENCE SUMMARY

(Erase heading not required.)

Instructions regarding War Diaries and Intelligence Summaries are contained in F. S. Regs., Part II. and the Staff Manual respectively. Title Pages will be prepared in manuscript.

Place	Date	Hour	Summary of Events and Information	Remarks and references to Appendices
COURCELLES	5-5-17		Fine and very warm with thunderstorm in evening. Casualties & Reinforcements Nil.	MB
GOMIECOURT	6-5-17		Fine but cooler. Bde. Hqrs. moved to GOMIECOURT - 2/Queens to camp at B.26. 2/Manchester to camp at B.20. 9th MGC, 91st TMB and 91st Field Amb. Cn. to camp at G.6.B. Casualties Nil. Reinforcements 2/Queens 7.O.R. 1/S. Staff 2.O.R. 2/Manchester 10 O.R. 2/Manchester 7.O.R.	MB
"	7-5-17		Fine. 2/Queens moved up to MORY in reserve to 22nd Inf. Bde. for attack on BULLECOURT - 2/Manchesters moved to camp at B.28.a - Casualties 2/Manchester 1.O.R. wounded. Reinforcements. Nil. 9th MGC	MB
"	8-5-17		Hot - 2/Queens moved 2 Coys to ECOUST and 2 Coys to VRAUX. Reinforcements. 1/S. Staff 2 Officers 7.O.R. Casualties Nil	MB
"	9-5-17		Fine - 2/Manchester relieved 2/Queens 2/Queens moved back to B.28.a. Casualties Nil. Reinforcements Nil.	MB
L'HOMME MORT	10-5-17		Fine. Bde Hqrs moved to L'HOMME MORT - 2/Queens. 1/S. Staff, 9th MGC. 91st TMB. to Infantry Rge. in BULLECOURT sector. Casualties 2/Manchester 10 O.R. killed 13 O.R. 91st MGC Appendix 2	MB

2449 Wt. W14957/M90 750,000 1/16 J.B.C. & A. Forms/C2118/12

Army Form C. 2118.

WAR DIARY
or
INTELLIGENCE SUMMARY
(Erase heading not required.)

Instructions regarding War Diaries and Intelligence Summaries are contained in F. S. Regs., Part II. and the Staff Manual respectively. Title Pages will be prepared in manuscript.

Place	Date	Hour	Summary of Events and Information	Remarks and references to Appendices
L'HOMME MORT ECOUST	11-5-17		Fri. Bn HQrs moved to Cave at ECOUST. 2/Manchester moved to Railway embankment between ECOUST and BULLECOURT. 2/Manchester Casualties 2/Queen 1 Officer 2 OR Killed 1 Officer 150 R wounded. 2/Manchester 10 OR wounded. 2/Manchester 1/S Scoffs 10 R Killed 9 OR wounded. Reinforcements 1/S Scoffs 1 Officer 2/Manchester 6 OR wounded 2 OR missing.	Appendix 3. MR
ECOUST	12.5.17		Fine. very hot. 9th Inf Bde attacked BULLECOURT. 2/Queen on right 1/S Scoffs in left. 2 cos 2/Manchester attacked to each to mopping up purposes. 2/Manchester in Reserve. 3pm hours 3.45am. attack successful on right but failed on left. 3 cos 2/Manchester reinforced 1/S Scoffs - hrs [Lieut] H.R. CUMMING reinforced and patrols on left. Col. W. W. NORMAN DSO. assumed command after the Bde. assumed command. Reinforcements NIL	Appendix 4 " 5 " 6 " 7 " 8 MR
"	13.5.17		Fine. At 3.40am. the 2/R Warwick Regt. made a fresh attack on the old German front line trench in front of BULLECOURT supported by the 2/Manchester from the ridge. This attack was not successful. One Coy 2/Manchester attacked S.W. of village without success. Reinforcements NIL.	Appendix 9 MR
"	14.5.17		Fine. 1st Bn R. Welsh Fusiliers made four separate attacks on the S.W. corner of BULLECOURT but with little success. 2/Manchester 2/1 MGR and 2/Manchester during night 14/15 with any. Reinforcements NIL	MR
"	15.5.17		Fine. During night 16th/17th 17th "Inf Bde relieved 9th Inf Bde. All units 9th Inf Bde moved to BULLECOURT and 2/Manchester 2/1 MGR. Killed 2 Cap 2nd at AGNIET lès PETIT. Reinforcements 2/Manchester 2 OR.	Appendix 10 " 11 MR

2449 Wt. W14957/M90 750,000 1/16 J.B.C. & A. Forms/C.2118/12.

Army Form C. 2118.

WAR DIARY
or
INTELLIGENCE SUMMARY

(Erase heading not required.)

Instructions regarding War Diaries and Intelligence Summaries are contained in F. S. Regs., Part II and the Staff Manual respectively. Title Pages will be prepared in manuscript.

Place	Date	Hour	Summary of Events and Information	Remarks and references to Appendices
ACHIET LE PETIT.	16.5.17		Hot - Brigadier General R.T. PELLY D.S.O. assumed command of the Brigade. Reinforcements 2/Sh'wood 4 Officers.	Appendix to MS
"	17.5.17		Dull and cloudy. Battalion spent the day cleaning up. Casualties NIL. Reinforcements 2/Sh'wood 4 O.R. 1/S Staffs 3 O.R. 21/Manchester 30 O.R. 9 O.R. 9 M.G.C. 16 O.R.	MS
"	18.5.17		Fine. Casualties NIL Reinforcements NIL	MS
"	19.5.17		Fine. Casualties NIL Reinforcements NIL	MS
"	20.5.17		Fine. Brigade Church Parade service at 10.30 a.m. Casualties NIL. Reinforcements NIL	MS
"	21.5.17		Fine. Training carried out in accordance with Programme of Training. Casualties NIL. Reinforcements 2/Sh'wood 5 O.R. 1/S Staffs 5 O.R. 21/Manchester 66 O.R. 9 M.G.C. 5 O.R.	Appendix MS
"	22.5.17		Hot - ditto - CAPT. O.F. MORSHEAD M.C. appointed B'de Major vice MAJOR C.A.H. PALAIRET to Middx Regiment. LIEUT S.D'E. COLAM MC /John Highlanders appointed Staff Capt vice Captain O.F. MORSHEAD MC. Casualties reinforcements NIL	MS
"	23.5.17		Fine - ditto - Casualties - Reinforcements NIL	MS

Army Form C. 2118.

WAR DIARY
or
INTELLIGENCE SUMMARY

(Erase heading not required.)

Instructions regarding War Diaries and Intelligence Summaries are contained in F. S. Regs., Part II. and the Staff Manual respectively. Title Pages will be prepared in manuscript.

Place	Date	Hour	Summary of Events and Information	Remarks and references to Appendices
ACHIET LE PETIT	24.5.17		Fine – G.O.C. inspected 2/Queens and 1/S.Staffs on Ceremonial Parade. Casualties Nil. Reinforcements 1/S.Staffs 5 O.R. 2/Manchester 6 O.R.	MS
"	25.5.17		Fine - G.O.C. inspected 21st and 22/Manchester on ceremonial parade. Casualties Nil. Reinforcements Nil.	MS
"	26.5.17		Fine - Training carried out - Casualties Nil. Reinforcements 2/Queen 1 O.R.	MS
"	27.5.17		Fine - Brigade Church Parade service. Col. N. TALBOT C.F. Assistant Chaplain General 1/Manchester took the service. Casualties Nil. Reinforcements- 2/Queen 4 O.R. 2/Manchester 1 O.R. 1 O.R. 5 O.R.	MS
"	28.5.17		Fine - Relative training & bombing attack demonstration in afternoon. Casualties Nil. Reinforcements Nil.	MS
COURCELLES	29.5.17		Fine - Brigade march to COURCELLES. Casualties - Reinforcements 2/Queens Appendix 13 4 O.R. 1/S.Staffs 5 O.R. 2/Manchester 9 O.R.	MS
"	30.5.17		Fine - 2/Queens moved to IVORY and came under orders of 53rd Division & but in ECOUST-LONGATTE defences. Other battalions training. 91st TMB went to IVORY for trial purposes under 53 Division. Casualties Nil. Reinforcements Nil.	Appendix 14 MS
"	31.5.17		Fine - Training carried out - Casualties - 2/Queens 3 Men 10 R. wounded. Reinforcements- 1/S.Staffs 1 O.R. 2/Manchester 10 R. R. T. Pelley Brigadier General Comdg 91st Infantry Brigade	MS

2449 Wt. W14957/M90 750,000 1/16 J.B.C. & A. Forms/C.2118/12.

SECRET 　　　　　　　　　Appendix 1

　　　　　　　　　　　　　　　　　　　　B.M./494.

To all recipients of O.O.74.

　　　Reference 91st Infantry Brigade Operation Order No.74
of yesterday. X/Y night will be night 1st/2nd May, 1917.
　　　ACKNOWLEDGE.

　　　　　　　　　　　　　　　[signature] Major.
1.5.17.　　　　　　　Brigade Major, 91st Infantry Brigade.

SECRET.   Copy No. 21.

91st Infantry Brigade Operation Order No.74.

Monday, 30th April, 1917.

Reference Maps - 51B S.W. - 57C N.W. - Scale 1/20,000.

-:-:-:-:-:-:-:-:-:-:-

1. That portion of the line now held by the 91st Infantry Brigade which will form the Battle Front of the 62nd Division will be taken over by Units of the 62nd Division on the night X/Y Day, the frontages allotted to Brigades being as follows:-

   185th Inf. Bde. from U.28.c.2.3. to U.27.a.6.7.
   186th Inf. Bde. from U.27.a.6.7. to U.20.d.9.4.
   187th Inf. Bde. from U.20.d.9.4. to U.20.a.3.1.

   Boundaries will be as follows:-

   Between 185th and 186th Inf. Bdes. -
      From U.27.a.6.7. through C.2.a.6.7.
   Between 186th and 187th Inf. Bdes. -
      From U.20.d.9.4. through U.26.c.2.6.
   Between 187th Inf. Bde. and 21st Bn. Manchester Regt. -
      From U.20.a.3.1. through U.19.d.0.0.

2. Posts will be handed over as under:-

Description of Post.	Co-ordinate.	Garrison.	Handed over by.	Handed over to.
No.1A	U.28.c.1.4.	L.G. Section.	22nd Bn. Manch.R	2/7th West Yorks. 185th Inf.Bde.
No.1	U.27.d.2.5.	3 Sections.	-do-	-do-
No.2A	U.27.c.9.6.	(1 Platoon (1 Lewis Gun	-do-	-do-
No.2	U.27.c.3.7.	(1 Platoon (1 Lewis Gun	-do-	-do-
Coy.H.Q.	C.3.a.6.0.	(1 Platoon (1 Lewis Gun.	-do-	-do-
A Support.	U.26.d.7.5.	1 Section.	-do-	-do-
No.3.	U.27.a.3.5.	1 Section.	-do-	2/6th Duke of Wellingtons. 186th Inf.Bde.
No.4.	U.26.b.9.0.	(2 Sections (1 Lewis Gun	-do-	-do-
Coy.H.Q.	U.26.c.7.0.	(3 Platoons (3 Lewis Guns	-do-	-do-
No.5.	U.20.d.6.1.	1 Section	-do-	2/4th.K.O.Y.L.I. 187th Inf.Bde.
No.6.	U.20.d.2.5.	(1 Section (1 Lewis Gun	-do-	-do-
No.7.	U.20.c.6.4.	1 Section	-do-	-do-
C Support.	U.26.b.2.6.	(2 Sections (1 Lewis Gun	-do-	-do-
No.1.(Left Subsector).	U.20.c.5.9.	N.C.O. and 3 men.	21st Bn. Manch.R	-do-
Coy.H.Q.	U.25.a.7.5.	..	-do-	-do-

3. One guide per post will be detailed to meet incoming units at a time and place to be arranged between Commanding Officers concerned.

(continued).

4. Officers from relieving Units will report at the Headquarters of 22nd Bn.Manchester Regt. and 21st Bn.Manchester Regt. to-day, to arrange all further details of the relief.

5. The 2nd Bn.Queen's Regt. will be relieved by the 2/8th West Yorkshire Regt. under arrangements to be made between Commanding Officers concerned.

6. The 21st Bn.Manchester Regt. will remain in present position with the exception of the Posts detailed in para.2. The garrisons of these posts when relieved will be disposed elsewhere in the left Subsector at the discretion of the Officer Commanding, 21st Bn. Manchester Regt.
The 1st Bn.South Staffordshire Regt. and the guns of 91st Machine Gun Coy. at present in the left Subsector will remain in their present positions.

7. Completion of reliefs will be reported to Brigade Headquarters (by wire) by "B.A.B." Code.

8. Command of the Sector will pass from G.O.C.,91st Infantry Brigade on completion of reliefs by the Three Brigades of the 62nd Division on X/Y night when 1st Bn.South Staffordshire Regt., 21st Bn.Manchester Regt. and guns of 91st Machine Gun Coy.,in left Subsector will come under the orders of G.O.C.,187th Infantry Brigade whose Headquarters will be established in the vicinity of L'HOLLE MORT.

9. Officer Commanding,22nd Bn.Manchester Regt. will arrange to leave one man in each Post for 24 hours after completion of relief.

10. Administrative arrangements will be issued later.

11. ACKNOWLEDGE.

                                  Major,
                 Brigade Major,91st Infantry Brigade.

Issued at 7/0 p.m.

Copy No			
1	Bde.Major.	12	Supply Off,91st Inf.Bde.
2	Staff Captain.	13	7th Division "G".
3	2nd Queen's R	14	62nd Division "G".
4	1st S.Staffs.R	15	185th Inf.Bde.
5	21st Manch.R	16	186th Inf.Bde.
6	22nd Manch.R	17	187th Inf.Bde.
7	91st M.G.Coy.	18	62nd Inf.Bde.
8	No.3.Sec.7th Div.Sigs.	19	7th Aus.Inf.Bde.
9	91st T.M.Battery.	20	File.
10	91st Bde.Gren.Coy.	21	War Diary.
11	Bde.Transport Off.	22	War Diary.

Appendix 1 a

91st Infantry Brigade.

Summary of Intelligence - No.5.

From 12.noon., 30th April.1917 to 12.noon., 1st May, 1917.

1. **OPERATIONS.**

   Two posts were established in the Sunken Road in U.21.c. during the night.

2. **ARTILLERY.**

   (a) Our Artillery has been active on BULLECOURT and the HINDENBURG LINE throughout the day.
   (b) Enemy Artillery was active against the Railway Embankment in U.26. between 11-30.p.m., 30/4/17 and dawn this morning, mostly with 4.2's.
   The Left Battalion Headquarters were slightly shelled between 8.p.m. and 9.p.m.

3. **MACHINE GUNS.**

   Enemy machine guns were active against our Aeroplanes during the day.
   Bursts of traversing fire were fired during the night on the Right Battalion Sector; Machine Guns are reported to have been firing from U.20.b.3.4, U.20.b.4.2, and U.21.d.1.0.

4. **PATROLS.**

   A Patrol went out at 9-15.p.m. to clear up the situation in the Sunken Road in U.21.c. They found two of our men killed, one wounded and two suffering from shock in the Sunken Road, but no signs of the enemy except cap (sent herewith).
   This leaves 7 men and one Lewis Gun still missing from the raided posts.
   A patrol left the post at U.20.a.20.15. at 9-15.p.m. and proceeded towards the German wire. They reached the point about 80 yards from the wire (U.20.a.6.7.) and heard voices in the trench at about U.20.a.9.7. They were unable to proceed further owing to the brightness of the moon.

5. **GENERAL.**

   A Trench Mortar is reported by post at U.26.b.25.95. to have been active at 2.a.m. on 30/4/17 from about U.21.Central.
   At about 6.a.m. 30/4/17, smoke was seen rising from trenches about U.20.b.Central.
   At about 11-30.p.m., 30/4/17 the searchlight was again seen. It appears to be a double beam light. It was apparently being used for anti-aircraft purposes. Compass bearing from L'HOMME MORT 55° true.
   During bombardment of enemy line at dawn a great number of our shells dropped about 200 yards short on the left Battalion Sector. This appears to be a general fault.

   Brook Capt
   for Brigadier General,

Bde.Hd.Qtrs.
1st May, 1917.

SECRET

Appendix 2
Copy No. 23

91st Infantry Brigade Operation Order No. 75.

Wednesday, 9th May, 1917.

Reference Maps - ECOUST ST.MEIN - Scale 1/10,000.
51B S.W. & 57C N.W. - Scale 1/20,000.

-:-:-:-:-:-:-

1. The 91st Infantry Brigade will relieve the 20th Infantry Brigade in the line on night 10/11th May.

2. (a) The 2nd Bn. Queen's Regt. will take over the line on N.E. side of a line running from U.26 Central to U.26.a.2.5., held by elements of 2nd Bn. Border Regt. and 2nd Bn. Gordon Highlanders.
   The 2nd Bn. Queen's Regt. to be clear of the Cross Roads N.W. of VRAUCOURT (B.24.d.7.6.) by 9.p.m., 10th instant.
   (b) The 1st Bn. South Staffordshire Regt. will take over the line on S.W. side of the above line, held by elements of 2nd Bn. Border Regt. and 2nd Bn. Gordon Highlanders.
   The 1st Bn. South Staffordshire Regt. to be clear of the Cross Roads N.W. of VRAUCOURT (B.24.d.7.6.) by 10.p.m., 10th instant.
   (c) The 22nd Bn. Manchester Regt. will take over the line from 9th Bn. Devon Regt., and will have one Company on Railway Embankment N. of ECOUST on W. of ECOUST - BULLECOURT Road, and three Companies in ECOUST.
   (d) The 21st Bn. Manchester Regt. will move to Camp at MORY.

3. The 20th Infantry Brigade will have guides at the CRATER on VRAUCOURT - ECOUST Road, 500 yards S. of ECOUST to meet 2nd Bn. Queen's Regt. and 1st Bn. South Staffordshire Regt. to lead them to Battalion Headquarters of Battalions whom they relieve at the following times:-

   2nd Bn. Queen's Regt.   9-45.p.m., 10th inst.
   1st Bn. South Staffordshire Regt.   10-45.p.m., 10th inst.

   Times of moves, guides (except where stated above) and arrangements for reconnaissances and reliefs will be arranged between Battalion Commanders concerned.

4. The 91st Machine Gun Coy. and 91st Trench Mortar Battery will relieve the 20th Machine Gun Coy. and 20th Trench Mortar Battery respectively in the line on night 10/11th May, all details of relief to be arranged between Commanding Officers concerned.

5. Brigade Headquarters will close at COURCELLES at 5.p.m., and open at the same hour at L'HOMME MORT.

6. Completion of reliefs will be reported to 91st Infantry Brigade Headquarters by "B.A.B." Code.

7. ACKNOWLEDGE.

                                                     Major,
                                Brigade Major, 91st Infantry Brigade.

Issued at 10/50 p.m.

Copy No 1 Bde. Major.   13 C.R.E.
         2 Staff Captain.   14 C.R.A.
         3 2nd Queen's R   15 Supply Officer, 91st Bde.
         4 1st S. Staffs. R   16 7th Division "G".
         5 21st Manch. R   17 7th Division "Q".
         6 22nd Manch. R   18 20th Inf. Bde.
         7 91st M.G. Coy.   19 22nd Inf. Bde.
         8 No.3.Sec.7th Div.Sig.   20 Bde. on Right.
         9 91st T.M. Battery.   21 Bde. on Left.
        10 91st Bde. Gren. Coy.   22 File.
        11 Bde. Transport Off.   23 War Diary.
        12 A.D.M.S.   24 War Diary.

SECRET.

Appendix 3

Copy No. 25

91st Infantry Brigade Operation Order No. 76.

Thursday, 10th May, 1917.

Reference Maps - ECOUST-ST.MEIN - Scale 1/10,000.
51B S.W. and 57C N.W. - Scale 1/20,000.

-:-:-:-:-:-:-:-:-:-

1. On the 12th May, at an hour to be notified later, the 7th Division will continue its attack on BULLECOURT. This attack will be made in conjunction with an attack by the 5th Australian Division on the right, with the co-operation of troops of the 62nd Division on the left.
    The 91st Infantry Brigade will attack BULLECOURT from the S.E. on the morning of 12th May. ZERO hour will be notified later.
    (a) The attack will be carried out by the 2nd Bn. Queen's Regt. on the right (Headquarters in vicinity of U.28.a.3.1.) and 1st Bn. South Staffordshire Regt. on the left (Headquarters in vicinity of U.28.a.3.1.), the dividing line between the two Battalions being a line drawn through U.28.a.5.2. - U.28.a.1.5. - U.27.b.8.8. - U.21.d.9.6.
    The Officer Commanding, 21st Bn. Manchester Regt. will place two Companies at the disposal of The Officer Commanding, 2nd Bn. Queen's Regt. and two Companies at the disposal of The Officer Commanding, 1st Bn. South Staffordshire Regt. for this operation.
    (b) The Headquarters, 21st Bn. Manchester Regt. will move into Headquarters on the South of the Railway Embankment in U.27.d.4.3. 2 hours before ZERO.
    (c) The 22nd Bn. Manchester Regt. will be in reserve with one Company on Railway Embankment N. of ECOUST on W. of ECOUST - BULLECOURT Road, and three Companies in ECOUST.
    ~~As soon as the 21st Bn. Manchester Regt. have vacated the Railway Embankment, 2 Companies 22nd Bn. Manchester Regt. will move forward and hold the place vacated by 21st Bn. Manchester Regt. at U.28.c.~~
    (d) At ZERO hour the ANZAC Division on the Right will capture the HINDENBURG Support Line between U.22.d.5.3. to the Strong Point in the vicinity of U.22.c.6.4.

2. The two attacking Battalions will be formed up facing N.W. on a tape line through U.22.d.1.0. - U.27.b.6.0. an hour before ZERO.
    The attack will be made on a two Company front with a frontage of one platoon. Waves will follow each other closely and will be in close order or very slightly extended. The first two waves will be extended, the remainder may follow in platoon or section columns if thought desirable. Mopping-up parties, composed of 21st Bn. Manchester Regt., taken from the Companies attached to the two attacking Battalions will follow the waves with which they are acting and must be given definite areas for which they must be responsible directly the attacking waves have passed on. Sentries must be posted at once at each dug-out entrance and will not leave until properly relieved by their mopping-up party. Every man of the mopping-up parties must carry a bag of 8 bombs which will be used for clearing the dug-outs. The greatest care must be exercised by Officers in charge of these parties to see that no dug-out is left unguarded; they must familiarise themselves as soon as possible with their areas, and will not on any account leave them, or allow any of their men to leave, until they get definite orders to do so.

3. The Objective is shown by BROWN LINE on the attached map.
    On reaching the BROWN LINE strong points will be made at (approximately) U.22.c.9.3. U.22.c.6.3. U.22.c.3.1. and U.21.d.9.3. by the 2nd Bn. Queen's Regt. and at (approximately) U.21.d.4.3. U.21.d.4.1. U.21.d.2.4. and at the CRUCIFIX by the 1st Bn. South Staffordshire Regt.

As soon as/

-2-

As soon as these Strong Points are consolidated patrols are to be sent Northwards to the HINDENBURG LINE and if it is found empty it is to be consolidated and a strong block made on Sunken Road at U.21.d.5.6. by the 1st Bn.South Staffordshire Regt.

The protective barrage will lift from G.2. at Zero plus four hours to enable patrols to push forward to occupy this line from U.22.c.7.2. to U.21.d.5.6. if possible.

4. MACHINE GUNS.

The Machine Guns of the 91st Machine Gun Company in BULLECOURT must be prepared to move forward at the earliest opportunity under the orders of The Officer Commanding the Sector in which they are placed.

5. STOKES MORTARS.

The Officer Commanding, 91st Trench Mortar Battery will arrange for a Stokes Gun and personnel to be placed at the disposal of each of the Battalion Commanders of the attacking Battalions.

6. ARTILLERY ARRANGEMENTS.

(a) The attack will be covered by the Heavy Artillery of the V Corps assisted by the Heavy Artillery of the I ANZAC Corps, and by the Field Artillery affiliated to the 7th Division assisted by some batteries of the 1st Anzac Corps.

(b) The attack will be made under a barrage. Map showing barrages if forwarded herewith.

At Zero, a creeping barrage will be placed 100 yards in front of the forming up line and will remain on this line for two minutes and then will advance at the rate of 100 yards in 6 minutes through the village.

At Zero, the 4.5" Howitzers will open on G.1. the houses along the line of road 100 yards North of G.1. and on the road running east and west through BULLECOURT. These Howitzers will left and creep forward 50 yards in front of the 18 pdr. creeping barrage.

On lifting from the objective the creeping barrage will become protective and will search forward at irregular intervals, to cover the ground 1,000 yards in front of the objective.

(c) At Zero, the Heavy Artillery is going to barrage:-

    (i) The Sunken Road from U.22.d.0.3. to U.22.b.6.3., but not South of U.22.d.3.7. after Zero plus 4'.
    (ii) The road leading to the Factory from U.22.c.3.1., but not South of U.22.c.4.6. after Zero plus 4'.
    (iii) The Sunken Road from U.21.d.5.6. to U.22.a.5.3., but not South of U.21.d.8.9. after Zero plus 20'.
    (iv) Communication trench from U.27.b.6.8. to U.22.a.1.1., but not South of U.21.d.9.1. after Zero plus 6', nor South of U.22.c.0.5. after Zero plus 12'.
    (v) Communication trench from U.21.d.3.8. to U.16.c.7.0.
    (vi) Railway Station at U.22.b.6.3.
    (vii) Crucifix, but not after Zero plus 16'.
    (viii) G.1. from U.27.b.4.4. to 1.7. but not after Zero plus 2 minutes.
    (ix) Trench from U.21.d.1.7. to U.21.d.4.0.
    (x) Trench from U.27.b.1.9. to U.21.d.2.4. until Zero plus 20'.
    (xi) G.2. from U.22.c.8.4. to U.21.d.5.6., but not east of U.22.c.3.5. after Zero plus 6', and lift off the remainder at Zero plus 12'.
    (xii) Communication trench from U.21.a.9.4. to U.16.Central.
    (xiii) RIENCOURT and its vicinity.

(d) At Zero, an artillery feint barrage will be placed along the front of the 62nd Division and along the left front of the 7th Division. This feint barrage will lift at Zero plus 3'.

(e) Arrangements are being made for a crash of Liven's projectors to be made on the strong point at U.20.b.3.4. at Zero plus 1 minute.

7. MACHINE GUN BARRAGE/

-3-

7. **MACHINE GUN BARRAGE.**

The 62nd Division will be asked to make arrangements for machine gun fire in conjunction with the feint artillery barrage on their front.

Arrangements for machine gun fire on the front of the 7th Division not attacked will be made by The Officer Commanding, 220th Machine Gun Company, under verbal instructions which will be issued to him.

8. **ROYAL ENGINEERS.**

   (a) Strong Points will be established at:-

   (i)   U.27.b.2.8.
   (ii) U.27.b.1.6.
   (iii) U.27.b.5.6.
   (iv) U.27.b.6.3.

   (b) On Zero night, a communication trench will be dug from the railway embankment to the village, along the line of the road running N.E. from U.27.d.2.5.
   (c) The C.R.E. will arrange to construct this communication trench and for R.E. assistance to be given in the construction of the Strong Points mentioned above and of those mentioned in paragraph 3.

9. **LIAISON.**

   (a) Major W. Hayes, 2nd Bn. Queen's Regt. will report at Brigade Headquarters of 15th Australian Infantry Brigade at O.5.a.3.4. at ZERO hour to act as Liaison Officer.
   (b) The Officer Commanding, 1st Bn. South Staffordshire Regt. will detail an Officer to report at Brigade Headquarters of 185th Infantry Brigade at L'HALLE MORT at ZERO hour to act as Liaison Officer.
   (c) The Officer Commanding, 2nd Bn. Queen's Regt. will detail an Officer to report at Headquarters of Left Battalion of 15th Australian Infantry Brigade at U.22.d.7.9. at ZERO hour to act as Liaison Officer.
   (d) Major O.M. Komp, 21st Bn. Manchester Regt. and Major D.C. Twiss, 1st Bn. South Staffordshire Regt. will report at Advanced Brigade Headquarters at 10.p.m., 11th instant, to act as Observation Officers

10. **COMMUNICATION.**

    (a) <u>In Advance of Battalion Headquarters.</u>
    Each of the Assaulting Battalions will establish an Advanced Report Centre to which messages from the front line will be sent.

    Separate telephone lines will not be laid to Companies, the principle to be adopted is that of laying a line to an Advanced Station previously made known to all concerned. This Advanced Telephone Station will serve the whole Battalion Front.

    Every advantage will be taken of the facilities for visual signalling. A Power Buzzer will be installed at Battalion Headquarters on the Railway Embankment at U.28.c. where messages so received will be transmitted to Brigade Headquarters.

    This forms the most reliable means of transmitting information and the position of the Set should be made clear to all. Messages will be handed to the Officer in charge in clear.

    Flares and Pigeons will be distributed to attacking Battalions.

(b) In Rear/

(b) **In Rear of Battalion Headquarters.**
Telephone and Power Buzzer to Advanced Brigade Headquarters thence telephone and wireless.

(c) Each attacking Battalion will send half-hourly reports to Brigade Headquarters from ZERO hour onwards.

11. **SYNCHRONISATION.**

Watches will be synchronised by telephone at 7.p.m., on 11th May, and at midnight 11/12th May.

12. **ADMINISTRATIVE INSTRUCTIONS** will be issued separately.

13. The 22nd Infantry Brigade are arranging to place one Battalion at the disposal of the 91st Infantry Brigade from 12.noon. on "Y" Day. This Battalion will be situated in the vicinity of L'HOMME MORT.

14. **BRIGADE HEADQUARTERS** will move forward to Cellars in ECOUST at C.2.a.8.1. at 10.p.m.,11th instant.

15. **ACKNOWLEDGE.**

                                                        Major,

                Brigade Major,91st Infantry Brigade.

Issued at 2/30 a.m.,11th inst.

    Copy No 1 Brigade Major.
           2 Staff Captain.
  Ø   ¤ 3 2nd Queen's R
  Ø   ¤ 4 1st S.Staffs.R
  Ø   ¤ 5 21st Manch.R
  Ø   ¤ 6 22nd Manch.R
  Ø   ¤ 7 91st Machine Gun Coy.
           8 No.3.Secn.7th Div.Signals.
     ¤ 9 91st T.M.Battery.
        10 91st Bde.Grenade Coy.
        11 Brigade Transport Officer.
        12 Q.M.,2nd Queen's R
        13 A.D.M.S.
     ¤ 14 528th (Durham) Fd.Coy.R.E.
        15 C.R.E.
        16 Supply Officer,91st Inf.Bde.
        17 C.R.A.
     ¤ 18 7th Division "G".
        19 7th Division "Q".
        20 20th Inf.Bde.
        21 22nd Inf.Bde.
        22 15th Austn.Inf.Bde.
   Ø   23 185th Inf.Bde.
        24 File.
        25 War Diary.
        26 War Diary.

Ø Barrage Maps only issued to these Formations.
¤ Map of Objectives only issued to these Formations.

SECRET.   S.C/1933/3.
                                                       Copy No. 21

ADMINISTRATIVE INSTRUCTIONS WITH REFERENCE TO OPERATION ORDER No.76.

1. Brigade Standing Orders for Battle will come into force for this operation.

2. MEDICAL.
   (a) Aid Posts and relay posts have been established at C.7.a.2.5, C.7.d.8.4, C.13.a.8.4, B.24.b.8.4, B.5.w.8.4.
   (b) Advanced Dressing Stations ECOUST C.2.c.5.8. and C.3.c.1.2.
   (c) Main Dressing Station L'ABBAYE MORY.

3. (a) S.A.A., GRENADES, etc.
   Dumps containing Mills Nos.5 and 23, Hales No.24, 1" White Very Lights and S.A.A. have been formed as under :-
              U.28.a.3.1.   C.2.b.1.8.
              U.27.d.25.25.   U.28.c.8.2.
              C.2.c.2.1.
   (b) TRENCH MORTAR AMMUNITION.
   300 rounds are being stored at U.28.a.3.1.

4. R.E. STORES.
   Advanced R.E. dumps have been established at C.3.c.15.20 and at the point where the ECOUST to BULLECOURT communication trench crosses the railway in U.27.d.

5. WATER.
   (a) The following wells in ECOUST have been certified fit for drinking purposes:-
              C.2.b.07.05.   C.2.d.3.6.
              C.2.c.2.5.   C.2.c.5.9.
   (b) In addition to this a dump of 100 filled petrol tins will be established at U.28.a.3.1. and 100 at the Crater C.2.c.2.1.

6. PRISONERS.
   Prisoners will be sent back under escort to the Crater at C.2.c.2.1. where they will be handed over to a collecting post consisting of a sergeant and 12 men to be provided by 22nd Manchester Regt. by whom they will be evacuated to the A.P.M. at MORY. A receipt will in all cases be given to the escorts who will be returned forthwith to their unit.

7. TRANSPORT.
   (a) The Brigade Transport Officer will select a site in the vicinity of MORY for "A" Echelon 1st Line Transport and will arrange for its assembly there by 6 p.m. on 11th instant.
   (b) "B" Echelon will remain at SAPIGNIES.
   (c) Two mounted orderlies per battalion and Machine Gun Company will report to Brigade Transport Officer at L'HOMME MORT by 6 p.m. on 11th instant, and will remain there with him throughout the operations.

                                                       Captain,
Bde. Hd. Qtrs.
10th May, 1917.   Staff Captain, 91st Infantry Brigade.

Copies issued to :-
   1. Bde. Major.   8. No.3 Sec., 7th Div. Sigs.   15. Supply Officer.
   2. Staff Captain.   9. 91st T.M. Battery.   16. 7th Divn. "Q"
   3. 2nd Queen's R.   10. 91st Bde. Grenade Co.   17. 20th Inf. Bde.
   4. 1st S. Staffs R.   11. Bde. Transport Officer.   18. 22nd Inf. Bde.
   5. 21st Manch. R.   12. Q.M., 2nd Queen's R.   19. File.
   6. 22nd Manch. R.   13. A.D.M.S., 7th Div.   20. War Diary.
   7. 91st M.G. Coy.   14. 528 (Durham) Fld. Co.   21. War Diary.

SECRET.

Appendix 4

Copy No. 9

91st Infantry Brigade Operation Order No.77.

12th May, 1917.

Reference Maps - ECOUST ST.MEIN - Scale 1/10,000.
　　　　　　　　51B S.W. & 57C N.W. - Scale 1/20,000.

-:-:-:-:-:-:-:-

1. 　　The following reliefs will take place to-night, 12/13th May.
(a) 　Two Companies 21st Bn.Manchester Regt., will be withdrawn to ECOUST and will send representative to Staff Captain at 91st Infantry Brigade Headquarters to arrange accommodation.
　　　Two Companies to VRAUCOURT to select their own billets.
　　　Two Companies, 22nd Bn.Manchester Regt., will be re-organised on the line U.28.a.4.3. to U.28.a.3.0.
(b) 　The 2nd Bn.Queen's Regt., and 1st Bn.South Staffordshire Regt., with one Company 22nd Bn.Manchester Regt., attached will re-organise and hold the line in their respective Sectors.
　　　One Company 22nd Bn.Manchester Regt., will continue to hold its present position along Railway Embankment.
　　　These arrangements to take place as soon as possible under arrangements of Commanding Officers concerned.

2. 　　ACKNOWLEDGE.

　　　　　　　　　　　　　　　　　　C.A.H.PALAIRET. Major.

　　　　　　　　　　　　　　Brigade Major, 91st Infantry Brigade.

Copy No. 1 Brigade Major.
　　　　 2 2nd Queen's R
　　　　 3 1st S.Staffs.R
　　　　 4 21st Manch.R
　　　　 5 22nd Manch.R
　　　　 6 91st M.G.Coy.
　　　　 7 7th Div.
　　　　 8 File.
　　　　 9 War Diary.
　　　　10 War Diary.

SECRET.

Appendix 5

Copy No...17...

91st Infantry Brigade Operation Order No.78.

12th May, 1917.

Reference Maps - ECOUST ST.MEIN - Scale 1/10,000.
FRANCE 51B S.W. & 57C N.W. - Scale 1/20,000.

-:-:-:-:-:-:-:-:-:-

1. The 91st Infantry Brigade, with 2nd Bn.Royal Warwickshire Regt., attached will complete the capture of BULLECOURT to-morrow, 13th instant.

2. ZERO hour will be 3-40.a.m.

3. The attack will be carried out by the 2nd Bn.Royal Warwickshire Regt., attacking from the S.W. and by the 22nd Bn.Manchester Regt.(less two Companies) from the N.E. with the objective G.1. from U.27.b.65.25.(Road inclusive) - U.27.b.05.65.(Road inclusive).

4. At Zero hour a barrage will be put down on a line 150 yards South of the trench known as G.1. and will remain on that line for two minutes. The barrage will then creep forward at the rate of 100 yards in 3 minutes to objective and will remain on objective for two minutes and then lift on to G.2.

5. (a) The 2nd Bn.Royal Warwickshire Regt., will be formed up by 3.a.m., on a tape to be laid 150 yards N.of the Railway Line from U.27.d.40.65 - U.27.a.65.15. Headquarters 2nd Bn. Royal Warwickshire Regt., will be at U.27.c.35.55.
(b) The 22nd Bn.Manchester Regt.(less Two Companies) will be formed up by 2-50.a.m. facing S.W. 50 yards N.of the Road running from U.27.b.15.85. - U.27.b.75.50. and will advance on to G.1. immediately the barrage lifts on to G.2. (Headquarters 22nd Bn.Manchester Regt., will be at U.28.a.3.1.)

6. The attack will be made with a barrage.

7. The 2nd Bn.Royal Warwickshire Regt., are responsible for clearing the communication trench joining G.1. at U.27.b.4.4. and also for placing sentries over the dug-outs in G.1. They will also gain touch with the troops of the 185th Infantry Brigade who captured the CRUCIFIX to-day. The 185th Infantry Brigade are re-inforcing the garrison at the CRUCIFIX during the night.

8. The Officer Commanding, 1st Bn.South Staffordshire Regt., will withdraw all troops within 150 yards of the Road at U.27.b.65.15.before Zero.

9. The Officer i/c 91st Stokes Mortars and 2" Trench Mortars will arrange to barrage G.1. from Zero to Zero plus 3 fire being concentrated on enemy strong points U.27.b.55.20. and U.27.b.4.4.

10. As soon as G.1.has been taken and consolidated the 2nd Bn.Royal Warwickshire Regt., will be withdrawn and the trench garrisoned by two Companies, 22nd Bn.Manchester Regt.

11. Watches will be synchronised at 12.midnight.

12. ACKNOWLEDGE.

C.A.H.PALAIRET. Major.
Brigade Major, 91st Infantry Brigade.

Issued at 11.p.m.

Copy No 1 Brigade Major.
2 Staff Captain.
3 2nd Queen's R
4 1st S.Staffs.R
5 21st Manch.R
6 22nd Manch.R
7 91st M.G.Coy.
8 91st T.M.Bty.
9 91st Bde.Sigs.
10 7th Division.
11 C.R.A.
12 C.R.E.
13 185th Inf.Bde.
14 173 Inf.Bde.
15 2nd R.Warwick.R
16 File.
17 War Diary.
18 War Diary.

SECRET.

Appendix 6

Copy No. 17

91st Infantry Brigade Operation Order No.79.

13th May, 1917.

Reference Maps - ECOUST ST.MEIN - Scale 1/10,000.
FRANCE 51B. S.W. - 57C N.W. - Scale 1/20,000.

-:-:-:-:-:-:-:-:-

1. One Company 21st Bn.Manchester Regt., will this evening capture the first line of German Trench between U.27.b.62.25. (Road inclusive) and U.27.b.05.65.(Road inclusive) and that portion of the RED PATCH lying between it and the Road from U.27.b.75.45.(Road inclusive) to U.27.b.05.85.(Road inclusive).

2. ZERO hour will be 6.p.m.

3. The Company will assault in two waves 50 yards apart, each wave consisting of two Lewis Gun Teams, one on either flank, a Section of Rifle Grenadiers and Bombers on the inner left flank, and a section of Riflemen on the inner Right flank.
   The Rifle Grenadier Section will direct and proceed up the first German Line starting from U.27.b.65.25. and a Lewis Gun on its left flank working between German Line and wire, a section of Riflemen on its Right Flank with a Lewis Gun on its extreme Right Flank.

4. FIRST WAVE.
   The task of the Rifle Grenadiers and Bombers will be to clear the trench. The task of the Lewis Gunners to bring fire to bear on any enemy attempting to obstruct the advance of the Rifle Grenadiers. The Riflemen will support the latter and clean up the RED PATCH between German Line and Road.

5. The 2nd Wave will support the first wave clear dug-outs with "P" Bombs and assist in the capture of any Strong Points which may be encountered.

6. The above attack will be supported by 2" Trench Mortars and Stokes Mortars which will this afternoon take up positions as follows:- Stokes Mortars in Syrong Point No.3. at U.27.b.8.2. 2" Trench Mortars on the Road at U.27.b.85.45. From these positions these Mortars will during the evening direct their fire on German First Line and Strong Points in immediate front. They will at Zero hour open a rapid barrage on the same points and as the assaulting Company passes through their line, they will follow up and support the advance.

7. The Officer Commanding, Company 21st Bn.Manchester Regt., will select a suitable line in resr of above Trench Mortar positions as a forming up line and will be formed up by 5-45.p.m., 13th instant.
   The Officer Commanding, 1st Bn.South Staffordshire Regt., will arrange for a party under an officer to closely follow up the attack and to report its movements to him. He himself will be responsible for conveying all information gained to Brigade Headquarters and will submit reports every half hour whether containing positive or negative information.

8. As early as possible this evening the elements of 22nd Bn.Manchester Regt.,which are in BULLECOURT will be withdrawn to a position in Reserve in the vicinity of U.28.a.3.1.

9. The 2nd Bn.Queen's Regt.,and 1st Bn.Douth Staffordshire Regt.,will maintain their present positions.

10. An artillery protective barrage will be placed on the portions on the HINDENBURG LINE N.W. of the Sunken Road and

above U.21.d.3.3. and will also block Communication Trenches and approaches N.of German 2nd Line from U.22.d.3.8. - U.22.a.05.10.

11. The assaulting troops will establish Strong Points at the CRUCIFIX and at U.27.b.05.65. under cover of a barrage of Stokes and 2" Mortars.

12. The above operation will be under the direction of Lieut. Colonel A.B.BEAUMAN,D.S.O.,1st Bn.South Staffordshire Regt.,who will supply the Officer Commanding Company,@1st Bn.Manchester Regt.,with any firther information as may be necessary to make obvious alterations in the above scheme.

13. Watches will be synchronised at 5.p.m.

14. ACKNOWLEDGE.

            C.A.H.PALAIRET. Major.

        Brigade Major,91st Infantry Brigade.

Copy No		
1	Bde.Major.	10 C.R.A.
2	Staff Captain.	11 C.R.A.
3	2nd Queen's R	12 7th Divn.
4	1st S.Staffs.R	13 185th Inf.Bde.
5	21st Manch.R	14 No.3.Sec.Div.Sigs.
6	22nd Manch.R	15 173rd Inf.Bde.
7	91st M.G.Coy.	16 File.
8	91st T.M.Bty.	17 War Diary.
9	2" Mortars.	18 War Diaru.

SECRET.

Appendix 7

Copy No. 15

INSTRUCTIONS FOR CAPTURE OF RED PATCH.

13th May, 1917.

Reference Map - ECOUST ST.MEIN - Scale 1/10,000.

-:-:-:-:-:-:-:-:-

1. In the event of the operation ordered in 91st Infantry Brigade Operation Order No.79 for the capture of the RED PATCH not proving successful, the 1st Bn. Royal Welsh Fusiliers attached to 91st Infantry Brigade will carry out the following operations on the 14th instant.

   (a) Attack with two Companies from the line of the Road U.27.b.25.85. - U.27.b.75.50. facing S.W. and capture the trench known as G.1. at the same time clearing the enemy out of the RED PATCH and establishing strong points at U.27.b.05.70. and U.27.b.4.4. and a defensive flank facing W. from U.27.b.1.8. - U.27.b.05.70.
   (b) There will be no artillery preparation or barrage.
   (a) Zero hour will be 2.a.m.

2. (a) In the event of (a) being unsuccessful the 1st Bn. Royal Welsh Fusiliers will as soon as possible attack the RED PATCH from the East with the remaining two companies and will work up the RED PATCH towards the N.W. establishing Strong Points and a defensive flank as ordered in 1(a) above.
   (b) This attack will be made under a rifle grenade, stokes mortar and 2" mortar bombardment under arrangements to be made by Officer Commanding, 1st Bn. Royal Welsh Fusiliers and the Stokes Mortars and Medium Trench Mortars who are at U.28.a.3.1., the Headquarters, 2nd Bn. Queen's Regt.
   (c) Zero hour will be settled by Officer Commanding, 1st Bn. Royal Welsh Fusiliers, who will inform Brigade Headquarters if possible.

3. Should 1(a) be only partially successful The Officer Commanding, 1st Bn. Royal Welsh Fusiliers will clear up the situation with the remaining two Companies and will ensure the capture of the RED PATCH.

4. In the event of the above operations being undertaken the Officer Commanding, 1st Bn. Royal Welsh Fusiliers will arrange so that the situation can be reported in every ½ hour to Brigade Headquarters.

5. ACKNOWLEDGE.

C.A.H.PALAIRET. Major.

Brigade Major, 91st Infantry Brigade.

Copy No. 1 Bde.Major.
2 2nd Queen's R
3 1st S.Staffs.R
4 21st Manch.R
5 1st R.Welsh Fus.
6 22nd Manch.R
7 7th Div.
8 C.R.A.
9 91st T.M.Bty.
10 O.C.2" Mortars.
11 185th Inf.Bde.
12 173rd Inf.Bde.
13 2/1st H.A.C.
14 File.
15 War Diary.
16 War Diary.

SECRET.

Copy No. 12

Appendix 8

91st Infantry Brigade Operation Order No.80.

13th May, 1917.

Reference Maps - 57B.N.W. & 51C S.W. - Scale 1/20,000.

-:-:-:-:-:-:-:-:-:-

1. The following reliefs and moves will take place to-night 13/14th May,1917:-
   (a) 2/1st H.A.C. will take over the front now held by 1st Bn.South Staffordshire Regt.,and one Company 22nd Bn.Manchester Regt.attached.
   BULLECOURT AVENUE id at the disposal of 2/1st H.A.C. between 9.p.m. and 11.p.m. for the purposes of this relief.
   All further details to be arranged between Commanding Officers concerned.
   (b) 22nd Bn.Manchester Regt.,less one Company holding the Railway Embankment,and one Company attached to 1st Bn.South Staffordshire Regt.,will be withdrawn at dusk via valley from C.4.Central to C.9. Central the Company holding Railway Embankment will be relieved by one Company,21st Bn.Manchester Regt.,under arrangements to be made between Commanding Officers concerned.
   (c) The 1st Bn.Royal Welsh Fusiliers will take up a position of assembly in the vicinity of U.28.a.3.1. where Battalion Headquarters will be established. Officer Commanding,2nd Bn.Queen's Regt.,will arrange to have four guides at the Windmill,C.8.d.2.7. at 9.p.m. to conduct the Battalion to position of assembly.
   (d) 21st Bn.Manchester Regt.,less one Company will move to ECOUST under orders issued separately.
   (e) 2nd Bn.Queen's Regt.,and 91st Machine Gun Coy.,will remain in the line.

2. A proportion of Officers,N.C.O's and Lewis Gunners of 1st Bn. South Staffordshire Regt.,will remain in the line after relief and will rejoin their Battalion on night 14/15th May.

3. On relief 1st Bn.South Staffordshire Regt.,and 22nd Bn.Manchester Regt.,will proceed to Camps at MORY. Quartermasters have been warned to provide guides at L'ABBAYE MORY at 10-30.p.m.

4. Completion of reliefs will be reported by B.A.B.Code.

5. Brigade Headquarters will remain in present position.

6. ACKNOWLEDGE.

O.F.MORSHEAD. Captain,

for Brigade Major,91st Infantry Brigade.

Issued at 4.45.p.m.

Copy No.1 Bde.Major.
2 2nd Queen's R
3 1st S.Staffs.R
4 21st Manch.R
5 22nd Manch.R
6 91st M.G.Coy.
7 7th Div."G".
8 1st R.Welsh Fus.
9 2/1st H.A.C.
10 22nd Inf.Bde.
11 File.
12 War Diary.
13 War Diary.

SECRET.

Appendix 9

Copy No. 17

91st Infantry Brigade Operation Order No.81.

14th May, 1917.

Reference Maps – ECOUST ST.MEIN – Scale 1/10,000.
FRANCE 57C N.W. & 57B N.W. – Scale 1/20,000.

-:-:-:-:-:-:-:-:-:-

1. (a) The front now held by 2nd Bn.Queen's Regt., 1st Bn.South Staffordshire Regt., and 1st Bn.Royal Welsh Fusiliers and elements of 21st and 22nd Bns.Manchester Regt., will be taken over to-night by 20th Bn.Manchester Regt., and 2/1st H.A.C. in accordance with attached relief table.
   (b) Officer Commanding, 1st Bn.South Staffordshire Regt., will arrange to notify elements of 21st and 22nd Bns.Manchester Regt., now in BULLECOURT. The former will rejoin their Battalion in ECOUST, the latter will remain attached to 1st Bn.South Staffordshire Regt., for night 14/15th May, and will rejoin their Battalion on 15th instant.
   (c) The 91st Machine Gun Coy., will be relieved by 22nd Machine Gun Coy., under arrangements to be made between Commanding Officer concerned. Actual guns will not be moved.

2. (a) Dividing Line between Battalions now runs approximately as follows:- U.28.a.3.1. – U.28.a.1.5. – U.27.b.98.90. – U.22.c.0.5.
   (b) Battalion Headquarters of both sectors will be at U.28.a.3.1.
   (c) The following are the present locations of Vickers Guns:-

Left Sector.	Right Sector.
U.27.b. 9. 9.	U.28.a.15.55.
U.27.b.95.90.	U.28.a.65.60.
U.27.b.5 . 99	U.28.a.70.65.
U.28.a.3.1.	U.28.a.75.70.
U.28.c. 7. 4.	U.28.a.80.75.
	U.28.a.45.95.

3. The 21st Bn.Manchester Regt.(less elements now in BULLECOURT) and 91st Trench Mortar Battery will remain in their present positions.

4. A proportion of Officers, N.C.O's, Vickers and Lewis Gunners and runners will remain in the line for 24 hours after relief. They will rejoin their Battalions on night 15/16th May.

5. All aeroplane photographs, situation maps, S.A.A., grenades, Very Lights etc., will be carefully handed over to relieving Units.

6. A picquet will be placed by Officer Commanding, 1st Bn.South Staffordshire Regt., on the Northern end, and by Officer Commanding, 21st Bn.Manchester Regt., on the Southern end of BULLECOURT AVENUE with written orders to allow no persons (including wounded) to enter the trench without a permit from Brigade Headquarters between the hours of 8-30.p.m. and 11.30.p.m.

7. On relief units will be disposed as under:-
   (a) 2nd Bn.Queen's Regt. VAULX – ECOUST Road in C.24.b. (Headquarters C.24.b.8.8.).
   (b) 1st Bn.South Staffordshire Regt. defensive line running East of L'HOMME MORT. Thence to former billets in SAPIGNIES and BEHAGNIES in their own time on 15th instant.
   (c) 1st Bn.Royal Welsh Fusiliers to defensive line running East of L'HOMME MORT. Thence in their own time on 15th instant to Camp at B.20.d.
   Only that portion of trench lying to the S.E. of the MORY – ECOUST Road will be occupied by 1st Bn.Royal Welsh Fusiliers and that portion lying N.W. of above Road by 1st Bn.South Staffordshire Regt. Quartermasters have been warned to have Cookers at L'HOMME

2.

MORT by 11.p.m.
(d) 91st Machine Gun Coy. to former Camp at A.30.d.

8. Completion of Relief will be reported by B.A.B.Code.

9. Brigade Headquarters will remain in its present position.

10. ACKNOWLEDGE.

           C.A.H.PALIARET. Major.

      Brigade Major, 91st Infantry Brigade.

Issued at 4-15.p.m.

Copy No			
1	Brigade Major.	10	Lieut. Lawford.
2	2nd Queen's R	11	22nd Inf.Bde.
3	1st S.Staffs.R	12	7th Div."G".
4	21st Manch.R	13	7th Div."Q".
5	22nd Manch.R	14	186th Inf.Bde.
6	1st R.Welsh Fus.	15	173rd Inf.Bde.
7	2/1st H.A.C.	16	File.
8	20th Manch.R	17	War Diary.
9	91st M.G.Coy.	18	War Diary.

RELIEF TABLE.

(Reference Operation Order No.81.)

UNIT.	Relieves.	Guides at. Place.	Time.	ROUTE.
20th Bn.Manch.Regt.	2nd Queen's Regt.	Company Guides. WINDMILL C.8.d.1.8. Platoon Guides at Reg.Aid Post. C.4.c.5.1.	9-30.p.m. 10. 0.p.m.	Valley through C.9.Central and C.4.Central.
2/1st H.A.C.	1st S.Staffs.Regt. 1st R.Welsh Fus. and elements of 21st and 22nd Bns.Manch.Regt.	Junction BULLECOURT AVENUE - ECOUST to NORIEUL Road C.3.c.1.3. M	8-30.p.m.	BULLECOURT AVENUE.
22nd Machine Gun Coy.	91st Machine Gun Coy.	-	-	Not to make use of BULLECOURT AVENUE.

M to be provided by Brigade Headquarters.
Battalion to be taken over by 1st Bn.South Staffordshire Regt.
Guides at TANK CRATER.

SECRET.

Appendix 10

Copy No. 20

91st Infantry Brigade Operation Order No.82.

15th May, 1917.

Reference Maps - ECOUST ST.MEIN - Scale 1/10,000.
51B S.W. & 57C N.W. - Scale 1/20,000.

-:-:-:-:-:-:-

1. (a) The 7th Division will be relieved by the 58th Division on night 15/16th May and on relief will be withdrawn to back area.
   (b) The 91st Infantry Brigade will be relieved by 174th Infantry Brigade in accordance with the attached relief table.
   (c) The relief of the Machine Guns in the line will take place on night 16/17th May under arrangements to be made by 174th Infantry Brigade.

2. All Units will arrange to leave one Officer per Company, one N.C.O. per platoon and one Lewis Gunner per team in the line for 24 hours after relief.

3. All aeroplane photographs, diagrams and papers relating to the defence of the line, and all Bombs, S.A.A., Very Lights and R.E.Stores will be carefully handed over to relieving Units.

4. (a) On relief the 1st Bn.Royal Welsh Fusiliers, 20th Bn. Manchester Regt., and 2/1st H.A.C. will proceed to Camp at B.20.d. Guides and Cookers will be at Cross Roads VAULX Sugar Factory after 10.p.m.
   (b) 21st Bn.Manchester Regt., will proceed to VAULX Sugar Factory where it will bivouac for the night. Cookers and guides will be at VAULX Sugar Factory after 10.p.m.
   21st Bn.Manchester Regt., will move to ACHIET-LE-PETIT on 16th instant under separate orders.

5. The Command of the Sector will pass to G.O.C., 174th Infantry Brigade on completion of relief when Brigade Headqtrs. will close at ECOUST and open at ACHIET-LE-PETIT.

6. Completion of relief to be reported by B.A.B.Code.

7. ACKNOWLEDGE.

O.F.MORSHEAD. Captain,

for Brigade Major, 91st Infantry Brigade.

Issued 6.45.p.m.

Copy No			
1	2nd Queen's R	11	Lt.Lawford.
2	1st S.Staffs.R	12	7th Div."G".
3	21st Manch.R	13	7th Div."Q".
4	22nd Manch.R	14	22nd Inf.Bde.
5	1st R.Welsh Fus.	15	186th Inf.Bde.
	~~173rd Inf.Bde.~~	16	173rd Inf.Bde.
6	20th Manch.R	17	174th Inf.Bde.
7	2/1st H.A.C.	18	File.
8	22nd M.G.Coy.	19	220th M.G.Coy.
9	No.3.Sec.Div.Sigs.	20	War Diary.
10	91st T.M.Bty.	21	War Diary.

RELIEF TABLE.

(Issued with Operation Order No.82.).

UNIT.	Relieves.	Guides. Place.	Time.	Route.	Remarks.
2/8th London Regt.	1st R.Welsh Fus. 2/1st H.A.C. 20th Manch.R 21st Manch.R (less 2 Coys).	(a) Coy.Guides. Windmill. C.8.d.a.8. (b) Platoon Guides.	Leading Company. 9-15.p.m. Leading Platoon 10.p.m.	BULLECOURT AVENUE.	Companies to follow at ½ hour intervals.
2/5th London Regt.	1 Company, 21st Manch.R on Railway Embankment. U.27.c. & d. (H.Q.U.27.c.3.6.).	Road Junction C.2.c.3.4.	8-45.p.m.	-	Battln.H.Q.C.2.d.3.6. 1 Coy. ECOUST. 2 Coys.L'HOMME MORT Defences.
174th T.M.Battery.	91st T.M.Bty.	-	-	-	Arrangements to be made between C.O's concerned.

NOTE. - All outgoing Units will proceed via Valley through C.3.Central and C.4.Central.

BULLECOURT AVENUE is closed for repairs after 11-30.p.m.,15/15th May.

No troops will be allowed to enter the Northern End after 8-30.p.m.

Appendix 11

CASUALTIES for period 11th May to 15th May 1917.

Unit.	Killed		Wounded		Missing	
	Off.	O.R.	Off.	O.R.	Off.	O.R.
2nd Bn. The Queen's R.	1	32	3	121	-	10
1st Bn. South Staffs. R.	2	32	7	89	-	32
21st Bn. Manchester R.	3	18	7	108	-	28
22nd Bn. Manchester R.	2	14	1	78	1	13
91st Machine Gun Coy.	-	1	-	17	-	1

Appendix 12

91st Infantry Brigade.

Narrative of Operations against BULLECOURT – 11th to 15th May, 1917.

Reference Maps – ECOUST ST. MEIN – Scale 1/10,000.
51B, S.W. & 57C N.W. – Scale 1/20,000.

1. (a) **GENERAL PLAN.**

    In conjunction with the 5th Australian Division on the Right and with the co-operation of troops of the 62nd Division on the left, the 7th Division was ordered to continue its attack on BULLECOURT on the 12th May, 1917.

    The task allotted to the 5th Australian Division was to capture the HINDENBURG Support Line between U.22.d.5.3. to the Strong Point in the vicinity of U.22.c.8.4. and there to effect touch with the attacking troops of the 7th Division.

    The 62nd Division was ordered to capture the German Strong point at the CRUCIFIX (U.27.b.1.9.) and to obtain touch with the left assaulting battalion of the 7th Division.

    The task allotted to the 7th Division was:-
    1. To occupy and consolidate the line of the Road through the village running U.27.b.1.7. – U.27.b.2.9. – U.27.b.35.75. – U.21.d.50.05. – U.21.d.75.05. – U.27.b.95.90. – U.22.c.75.15.

    2. To establish a line of posts along the Northern outskirts of the village.

    3. To send forward patrols Northwards to ascertain whether the HINDENBURG Support Line was held by the enemy.

    The 91st Infantry Brigade was ordered to carry out this task.

    (b) **ARTILLERY ARRANGEMENTS.** – These were –

    1. At ZERO a creeping barrage to be placed 100 yards in front of the forming up line and to remain on this line for two minutes and then to advance at the rate of 100 yards in 6 minutes through the village.

        The 4.5" Howitzers to open on the Old German Front Line, the houses along the line of the road 100 yards North of this trench and on the road running East and West through BULLECOURT.

        These Howitzers to lift and creep forward 50 yards in front of the 18 pdr. creeping barrage.
        On lifting from the objective the creeping barrage to become protective and to search forward at irregular intervals to cover the ground 1,000 yards in front of the objective.

    2. In addition the Heavy Artillery to barrage the various approaches to the village, the HINDENBURG Support Line and the Communication Trench and the Village of RIENCOURT and its vicinity.

    3. The 62nd Divisional Artillery to place a feint barrage along the 62nd Division Front and the Left front of the 7th Division. This feint barrage to lift at ZERO plus 3.

2. BRIGADE ATTACK/

2. BRIGADE ATTACK.

The attack was to start in a North Westerly direction from a tape line previously laid through U.22.d.1.0. - U.27.b.6.0. and to be carried out by two Battalions, 2nd Bn. Queen's Regt. (Right) and 1st Bn. South Staffordshire Regt. (Left), with dividing line through U.28.a.5.2. - U.28.a.1.5. - U.27.b.8.8. - U.21.d.9.6.

The Headquarters of both Battalions to be at U.28.a.3.1.

Battalions were to attack on a two Company front with a frontage of one platoon; waves to follow each other closely and to be in close order or very slightly extended.

Two Companies of 21st Bn. Manchester Regt. were to be attached to each of the assaulting Battalions for mopping-up purposes and were to follow the waves with which they were acting.

The 22nd Bn. Manchester Regt., was to be in reserve with one Company of the Railway Embankment N. of ECOUST or WEST of ECOUST-BULLECOURT Road and three Companies and Battalion Headquarters in ECOUST.

Strong points were to be established as under:-

By 2nd Bn. Queen's Regt. at U.22.c.9.3. - U.22.c.6.3. - U.28.a.3.1. and U.21.d.9.3.

By 1st Bn. South Staffordshire Regt. at U.21.d.4.3. - U.21.d.4.1. - U.22.d.2.4. - and at the CRUCIFIX U.27.b.1.9.

By the Royal Engineers. - at U.27.b.2.8. - U.27.b.1.6. - U.27.b.5.0. - U.27.b.6.3.

Four Vickers Guns and 1 Stokes Mortar were to be placed at the disposal of each Battalion Commander.

Liaison was to be maintained with the Brigades on the flanks by interchange of Officers.

3. ASSEMBLY.

On the night 10/11th May, the 91st Infantry Brigade relieved the 20th Infantry Brigade, the two attacking Battalions taking over the posts in BULLECOURT in their respective Sectors.

Brigade Headquarters was opened at L'HOMME MORT on the 10th May, moving to Caves at ECOUST on the 11th May.

On the night 11/12th May, a forming up tape was laid out by 528th (Durham) Field Coy. R.E.

In the early morning of the 12th instant the two attacking Battalions proceeded to form up with the first waves on this tape. The forming up was successfully carried out although some casualties were suffered from the steady enemy bombardment on the S.E. Corner of BULLECOURT.

4. THE ATTACK.

At ZERO hour (3-40.a.m.) the advance commenced. The 2nd Bn. Queen's Regt. reached its objective at 4-15.a.m. meeting with little opposition, the enemy concentrating his artillery fire on the Old German Front Line. As soon as the objective was gained Lewis Gun posts were pushed out to the front, and the line just North of the Road consolidated. Close touch was maintained with the Australians on the Right at U.22.c.9.2. and with the 1st Bn. South Staffordshire Regt. on the left.

On the left the advance of the 1st Bn. South Staffordshire Regt. did not progress so favourably. At ZERO hour the enemy put down a very heavy barrage on the S.E. of BULLECOURT and numerous machine guns and snipers opened fire from the S.W. of the village. As a result the attacking troops on the South side of the main Road suffered heavy casualties, made very little progress and became very disorganised. The troops attacking on the Right of the Road obtained a certain amount of cover and in spite of considerable casualties pushed on steadily, and by 7.a.m. positions were firmly established on the N. and N.W. of the village and touch gained with the 2nd Bn. Queen's Regt. on the Right.

By 9.a.m./

By 9.a.m.,The Officer Commanding,1st Bn.South Staffordshire Regt. became convinced,from reports received from his Company Commanders,that the part of the village South of the main Road was strongly held. Considering that a fresh attack was necessary he sent forward his reserve Company. This Company meeting with very heavy machine gun fire was unable to proceed and consequently dug in under heavy fire in the centre of the village.

At 12.noon, on the 12th May,in view of the situation the Brigadier General Commanding sent forward 3 Companies of the 22nd Bn.Manchester Regt.,and ordered them to place themselves under the Command of The Officer Commanding,1st Bn.South Staffordshire Regt. By this time the enemy's barrage and machine gun fire had become so intense that it was impossible to deploy troops in daylight for an attack,and The Officer Commanding,1st Bn.South Staffordshire Regt.,therefore decided to hold these three Companies in reserve.

During the remainder of the day,no further advance could be made,but the positions already gained were firmly consolidated.

During the afternoon of the 12th May,The Brigadier General Commanding went forward to BULLECOURT to confer with his Battalion Commanders as to the renewal of the attack and to ascertain the general situation.

At 8.p.m.,Brigadier General H.R.Cumming relinquished Command of the Brigade and handed over to Colonel W.W.Norman, D.S.O.

At nightfall the four Companies of the 21st Bn.Manchester Regt.,were withdrawn,3 Companies to bivouacs near VAULX Sugar Factory,and one to the Railway Embankment N.of ECOUST.

At 8-30.p.m.,it was decided to renew the attack at 3-40.a.m. on the 13th May. For this purpose the 2nd Bn.Royal Warwickshire Regt.,was to be lent to the 91st Infantry Brigade to attack the S.W.portion of the village,with two Companies of the 22nd Bn. Manchester Regt.,co-operating from the North Side of the main Road through the village.

Accordingly the 2nd Bn.Royal Warwickshire Regt.,moved up and established its Headquarters on the Railway Embankment at U.27.c.4.7. and the Headquarters of the 22nd Bn.Manchester Regt., were moved forward to U.28.a.3.1.

ZERO hour was fixed for 3-40.a.m. and a tape laid out by the R.E. from U.27.d.4.7. to U.27.a.75.20. on which the 2nd Bn. Royal Warwickshire Regt. formed up. This attack was ordered upon the assumption that the 62nd Division had captured the strong point at the CRUCIFIX as had been reported at 6-50.a.m., on the 12th May.

Previous to the forming up a patrol of the 21st Bn. Manchester Regt.,was sent forward to ascertain whether the front line trench was held. The Officer in Command of this patrol reported at 3-10.a.m. that the patrol had entered the trench and proceeded some distance along it without finding any trace of the enemy.

The 2nd Bn.Royal Warwickshire Regt. advanced at 3-40.a.m. under heavy hostile shelling but were unable to make any appreciable progress except on the extreme right where a small party worked round the wire and went forward into the middle of the village.

The two Companies of the 22nd Bn.Manchester Regt. attacking from the North were unable to advance at ZERO hour being held up by our own barrage which opened heavily on the road through the village instead of on the German front line trench. So soon as this barrage lifted the attacking companies pushed forward but were again held up by heavy machine gun fire from what appeared to be three strong points in the old front line trench. Several attempts were made against the centre strong point but all failed.

At 10.a.m.,on the 13th May,the 2nd Bn.Royal Warwickshire Regt. was withdrawn.

During the day/

During the day of the 13th May, several attempts were made by the 1st.Bn.South Staffordshire Regt. to bomb up the trench towards the CRUCIFIX from U.27.b.7.2. None of these attacks were successfull owing to the very heavy machine gun fire brought to bear upon the attacking troops from the trench on the S.W. side of the village which was still strongly held by the enemy.

At 7.p.m., a composite Company of the 21st Bn.Manchester Regt., was sent forward and placed under the orders of The Officer Commanding,1st Bn.South Staffordshire Regt. This Company again attacked and attempted to clear the South West portion of the village. The attack was, as before, held up by machine gun fire from commanding positions in the front line trench and by a heavy fire of rifle grenades and bombs. Several attempts were then made to bomb up the trench but were completely unsuccessful.

On the 13th May, orders were issued that the 2/1st H.A.C. would be lent to the 91st Infantry Brigade to relieve the 1st Bn. South Staffordshire Regt., who had suffered heavy casualties.

At 8-10.p.m., an S.O.S. signal was reported and orders were accordingly sent for the 2/1st H.A.C. to stand fast in ECOUST.

On the S.O.S. turning out to be a false alarm, the 2/1st. H.A.C. were sent forward, but owing to the lateness of the hour, The Officer Commanding,1st Bn.South Staffordshire Regt. considered that there was not sufficient time to complete the relief before daylight and the 2/1st H.A.C. were accordingly withdrawn again to cellars in ECOUST.

At 11.p.m., on the 13th May, the 1st Bn.Royal Welsh Fusiliers were sent forward to BULLECOURT (with Headquarters at U.28.a.3.1.) with orders to attack and clear the South-western part of the village on the morning of the 14th May.

This attack was launched at 2-10.a.m., by two companies, but was not successful. The Companies were promptly re-organised and at 4.a.m., a second attack was made which again met with little success, owing to heavy machine gun fire from the front line trench. Posts were established however at U.27.b.30.60. facing the CRUCIFIX and at U.27.b.42.45.

At 6-15.a.m., on the 14th May, the remaining two Companies of 1st Bn.Royal Welsh Fusiliers were sent forward to renew the attack. This attack was held up by the garrison of the front line trench and the companies concerned sustained very heavy casualties and were obliged to dig in at points nearly surrounding the enemy strong point at U.27.b.65.20. A further attack was made by one of these Companies at 2-30.p.m. This attack was partially successfull but owing to the lack of bombs and S.A.A. (due to the main dump at U.28.a.3.1. being destroyed by enemy shell fire) the troops had ultimately to fall back on their original positions in the face of a heavy hostile counter-attack.

During the whole of the 14th May, the enemy kept up a steady artillery bombardment on our forward posts and on the whole village.

At 4-15.p.m., on 14th May, orders were issued for the 20th Bn. Manchester Regt. to relieve the 2nd Bn.Queen's Regt. during the night 14/15th May and for the 2/1st.H.A.C. with one Company of the 21st Bn.Manchester Regt. to relieve the 1st Bn.South Staffordshire Regt and 1st.Bn.Royal Welsh Fusiliers, the areas allotted to each being:-

20th Bn.Manchester Regt. - from U.22.a.8.2. to U.27.b.9.9.

2/1st H.A.C. - from U.27.b.9.9. to U.27.b.35.75.

21st Bn.Manchester Regt. - posts in the vicinity of U.27.b.2.7. and those facing the old German front line and along the trench running from U.27.b.8.2. to U.27.b.8.4.

The relief was carried out successfully in spite of continuous heavy shelling.

During the relief orders were received that the 1st.Bn. Royal Welsh Fusiliers were to renew the attack and accordingly two Companies of this Battalion remained behind and prepared to attack.

From midnight onwards/

From midnight onwards the enemy put down a heavy barrage of H.E. and Gas Shells on ECOUST and on the Communication Trench to BULLECOURT.

At 3-55 a.m., before our further attack had been launched, the enemy delivered a counter-attack on the posts held by the 2/1st H.A.C., 1st Bn. Royal Welsh Fusiliers and 21st Bn. Manchester Regt., and drove their posts back, one platoon at U.27.b.2.7. with 2 Lewis Guns being completely scuppered. However by a speedily organised counter-attack the enemy was held and a line established along the road running South from the Church to U.27.b.7.2.

During the day of the 15th May this line was generally improved and consolidated.

During the night 15/16th May, the Brigade was relieved by the 174th Infantry Brigade, 58th Division. The relief passed off without incident in spite of a continuous bombardment.

The line of posts handed over was approximately as follows:-

The line of the Road U.22.c.8.2. – U.27.b.9.9. – U.27.b.75.45. – U.27.b.6.2.

5. CONCLUSION.

The success of the operations was largely impaired for two reasons:-

(1) The constant heavy enemy shelling rendering all telephonic communication impossible and the passage of orderlies with written messages almost impracticable.

(2) Misleading reports as exemplified by –
(a) the report that the Strong point at the CRUCIFIX was in our hands on the morning of the 12th May.
(b) the report that the most easterly strong point in the front line trench was surrounded.

The following are the casualties suffered by the Brigade from 11/15th May –

UNIT.	Killed.		Wounded.		Missing.	
	Off.	O.R.	Off.	O.R.	Off.	O.R.
2nd Bn. Queen's R	1	32	3	121	–	10
1st Bn. S. Staffs. R	2	32	7	89	–	32
21st Bn. Manch. R	3	18	7	108	–	28
22nd Bn. Manch. R	2	14	1	78	1	13
91st Machine Gun Coy.	–	1	–	17		1

Bde. Hd. Qtrs.

27th May, 1917.

R.T. Pelly, Brigadier General,
Commanding, 91st Infantry Brigade.

Appendix 12

SECRET.

Copy No. 19

91st Infantry Brigade Operation Order No. 83.

Sunday, 27th May, 1917.

Reference Maps - 57C & 57D. - Scale 1/40,000.

1. The 91st Infantry Brigade will move to COURCELLES on the 29th May, in accordance with the attached March Table.

2. The defence of the VRAUCOURT - ST.LEGER Line from L'HOMME MORT (exclusive) to the Vth Corps left boundary is allotted to the 22nd Infantry Brigade from 30th May, to 6th June on which day the 91st Infantry Brigade will be responsible for its defence. Orders for relief will be issued later.

3. Administrative Instructions for the move are issued separately.

4. Brigade Headquarters will close at ACHIET-LE-PETIT at 2-30.p.m. and open at COURCELLES at the same hour.

5. ACKNOWLEDGE.

Captain,
A/Brigade Major, 91st Infantry Brigade.

Issued at 10.15.p.m.

Copy No 1 Bde.Major.	11 Bde.Transport.Off.
2 Staff Captain.	12 Supply Officer, 91st Inf.Bde.
3 2nd Queen's R'	13 7th Division "G".
4 1st.S.Staffs.R.	14 7th Division "Q".
5 21st.Manch.R'	15 20th Inf.Bde.
6 22nd Manch.R'	16 22nd Inf.Bde.
7 91st M.G.Coy.	17 186th Inf.Bde.
8 No.3.Sec.Div.Sigs.	18 File.
9 91st T.M.Bty.	19 War Diary.
10 91st Bde.Gren.Coy.	20 War Diary.

MARCH TABLE.

(Issued with Operation Order No.83).

UNIT.	Starting Point.	Time of passing Starting Point.	Route.	To take over billets from.
21st Bn. Manchester Regt.	Cross Roads G.8.c.5.4.	10.0 a.m.	FOREST LODGE. (Logeast Wood).	2/6th Duke of Wellington's Regt. A.15.d.2.7.
2nd Bn. Queen's Regt.	-do-	10.20 a.m.	-do-	2/4th Duke of Wellington's Regt. A.15.d.6.9.
1st Bn. S. Staffs. Regt.	-do-	10.40 a.m.	-do-	2/5th Duke of Wellington's Regt. A.16.c.6.
22nd Bn. Manchester Regt.	-do-	11-10 a.m.	-do-	2/7th Duke of Wellington's Regt. A.21.b.6.5.
91st T.M. Battery. } 91st Bde. Gren. Coy. }	-do-	11-30 a.m.	-do-	186th T.M. Battery. A.16.c.4.
91st Machine Gun Coy.	Leave-Present Camp.	2-0 p.m.	-do-	213th Machine Gun Coy. A.16.c.6.8.
91st Infantry Brigade Headquarters.	-do-	2-15 p.m.	-do-	186th Infantry Brigade Headquarters.

SECRET.

Appendix 14

Copy No. 18

91st Infantry Brigade Operation Order No.84.

Tuesday, 29th May, 1917.

Reference Map - FRANCE 57C N.W.

-:-:-:-:-:-:-:-

1. The 2nd Bn. Queen's Regt., will be placed at the disposal of the 58th Division for work on the ECOUST - LONGATTE defences.

2. The 2nd Bn. Queen's Regt., will move on the morning of the 30th instant to Camp in the neighbourhood of B.20.d.

3. On arrival The Officer Commanding, 2nd Bn. Queen's Regt., will report at Headquarters, 58th Division (B.28.a.)

4. A party will be detailed by Officer Commanding, 2nd Bn. Queen's Regt., to draw 25 tents and 100 shelters from Ordnance, 5th Corps Troops (ACHIET-LE-GRAND) at 9-30.a.m., 30th instant.

5. Four wagons of 7th Divisional Train will report at Ordnance, 5th Corps Troops, ACHIET-LE-GRAND at 9-30.a.m., 30th instant, for the purpose of moving tents and shelters to B.20.d. Loading Party will accompany these wagons.

6. An Officer will meet the Staff Captain at Road Junction, B.20.b.9.5. at 10.a.m., 30th instant, to select site of Camp.

7. ACKNOWLEDGE.

Captain,

A/Brigade Major, 91st Infantry Brigade.

Issued at 8/45. p.m.

Copy No 1 Bde.Major.　　　11 Bde.Transport Off.
　　　　　2 Staff Captain.　　12 Supply Officer, 91st Inf.Bde.
　　　　　3 2nd Queen's R　　 13 7th Division "G".
　　　　　4 1st S.Staffs.R　　14 7th Division "Q".
　　　　　5 21st Manch.R　　　15 58th Division.
　　　　　6 22nd Manch.R　　　16 No.3.Coy.Div.Train.
　　　　　7 91st M.G.Coy.　　 17 File.
　　　　　8 No.3.Sec.Div.Sigs.
　　　　　9 91st T.M.Bty.　　 x18 War Diary.
　　　　　10 91st Gren.Coy.　 19 War Diary.

"C" Form
MESSAGES AND SIGNALS.   Army Form C. 2123.
                              (In books of 100.)
                              No. of Message..........

Prefix....Code....Words....	Received From......	Sent, or sent out At......m.	Office Stamp.
Charges to collect	By........	To........	29/5/17
Service Instructions.	Priority	By........	

Handed in at...... Office......m. Received......m.

TO   91st Inf Bde

| Sender's Number | Day of Month | In reply to Number | AAA |
| G104 | 29 | | |

You will place one Bn and 1 field Company RE at the disposal of 58th Divn for work on the ECOUST-LONGATTE defences aaa these troops will be billeted in the neighbourhood of MORY under arrangements to be notified by "Q" and will move during the morning of 30th aaa the aforesaid troops will report to Headquarters 58th Divn (229D) on 22nd Infantry Bde will relieve his battalion on June 6th aaa ACKNOWLEDGE aaa added 91st Infy Bde and CRE 7th Divn and 58th Divn

FROM

PLACE & TIME   7th Divn 4 pm

* This line should be erased if not required.

"C" Form
MESSAGES AND SIGNALS.

Army Form C. 2123.

Prefix AM Code Words 191
Charges to collect
Service Instructions.
Handed in at MBD Office ... m. Received 5.00 m.
Office Stamp A-29.V.17.

TO: Water

*Sender's Number	Day of Month	In reply to Number	AAA
AB 429	29		

Refce G104 aaa The battalion and the field coy will both be camped in B20D aaa The field coy will take their bivouac shelters etc from COURCELLES aaa The battalion will draw 25 tents and 100 shelters from Ordnance 7th corps troops and will take no tents or shelters from COURCELLES aaa The train will detail 4 wagons to report at Ordnance corps troops at 9.30 am tomorrow and Water will arrange for a loading party to be there at the same time this party proceeding

FROM
PLACE & TIME

"C" Form
MESSAGES AND SIGNALS.

Army Form C. 2123.

Prefix	Code	Words	Received.	Sent, or sent out	Office Stamp.
	£ s. d.		From	At ...... m.	
Charges to collect			By	To	
Service Instructions.				By	

Handed in at .... Office .... m. Received .... m.

TO

*Sender's Number	Day of Month	In reply to Number	AAA

with the wagons when loaded aaa the battalion and beta coy will be rationed by Sup aaaa water RE tram rptd bde corps troops and G

FROM
PLACE & TIME Sup 5pm

"C" Form
MESSAGES AND SIGNALS.
Army Form C. 2123.

Prefix	Code	Words	Received From	Sent, or sent out At	Office Stamp
Charges to collect			By	To	29.V.17
Service Instructions				By	

Handed in at **EO** Office ___ m. Received ___ m.

TO Sigs 2DS

Sender's Number	Day of Month	In reply to Number	AAA
EO 920	29th	W 2	

ACHIET-LE-GRAND

Cooks Tools (Ordnance)

FROM Sigs EO.
PLACE & TIME

7th DIVISION

B. H. Q.

91st INFANTRY BRIGADE.

JUNE 1917.

WAR DIARY or INTELLIGENCE SUMMARY

Army Form C. 2118.

HQ 91 July B/6

91st Infantry Brigade
June 1917.

Place	Date	Hour	Summary of Events and Information	Remarks and references to Appendices
COURCELLES	1-6-17		Fine. 1/S.Staff and 22/Manchester carried out attack practice between ACHIET LE PETIT and LOGEAST WOOD in conjunction with contact aeroplane. Sheets of paper were used as an experiment instead of flares and proved very satisfactory. The Brigadier went up in an aeroplane after the practice and saw to finish the shoot proper. In the afternoon the Brigadier delivered a lecture to Officers and Serjeants on "The Attack in open warfare". Casualties - Officers NIL. 1/S.Staff 1 O.R. 21/Manchester 8 O.R. 22/Manchester 6 O.R. 2/S.Manchester 7 O.R. Reinforcements NIL.	MB
"	2-6-17		Fine. Brigadier and Brigade Major attended decoration 17th Canadian Brigade attack South of LENS returning at 8 p.m. LT-COL A.B.BEAUMAN D.S.O. 1/S.Staffs returned from leave. COL W.W. NORMAN D.S.O. 2/Manchesters went on leave. Casualties 2/Manchester 2 O.R. missing. Reinforcements 2/Manchester 1 O.R.	MB
"	3-6-17		Fine. Brigadier and Brigade Major visited the Officers in camp at R road in the afternoon. Casualties NIL. Reinforcements 21/Manchester 3 O.R. 22/Manchester 10 O.R.	MB
"	4-6-17		Fine. G.O.C. 7th Division went round with Brigadier and Brigade Major in morning and saw Battalion training schemes in afternoon went into R.F.C. Wing to discuss practice attack for tomorrow. Casualties NIL. Reinforcements 1/S.Staffs 10 Off 4 O.R. 21/Manchester 6 O.R. 91st M.G.C. 1 Officer.	Appendix 1. MB
"	5-6-17		Fine. 22/Manchester carried out an exercise in LOGEAST WOOD exemplifying wood fighting, contact aeroplane worked in conjunction, very lights were fired in plan of attack but did not shew very satisfactory. Staff Captain reported on leave. Appendix 2. Casualties 2/Queens 1 O.R. wounded. Reinforcements 2/Queens 1 Officer 1 O.R.	

Army Form C. 2118.

WAR DIARY
or
INTELLIGENCE SUMMARY

(Erase heading not required.)

Place	Date	Hour	Summary of Events and Information	Remarks and references to Appendices
Courcelles	6.6.17		Reg.t of the Brigade on & Brigade Major lectures to officers & NCO's of 2/1st Manchester on the elements of open warfare. The Brigadier & Brigade Major inspected 2nd L.G.R. as we have in afternoon. 2/2nd Manchesters took over S.P. L.G.R. & Carpolnic front Royal Welsh Fus. at 2.00 p.m. 2/2 Queens returned from Road (work station Ecoyst Line) 1st Stafford sent 3 coys to Ruins to form a reserve to B.R. Casualties: Nil. Reinforcements Queens 1 or, 1st S. Staffs 1 or. 3 M. Manchesters 1 or.	Appendix 3 M.
	7.6.17		The Brigadier General Henderson C.B. inspected officers & NCO's early morning. Visited Bn. Bayonet class & Bullseye Rif.le & was I/c officers received. Peer at Whitchenae Ring Succeepp. Casualties 2/Queens 1 OR, 1st S. Staffs – 21st Manc. 1 OR wounded. Reinforcements – 9th M.F.C. 6 OR	M.
	8.6.17		Not engaged. Brigadier General went round with training in morning. Brigade Major reconnoitred trees during day at Busseux – Casualties 9th M.G.C. 2 OR wounded. Reinforcements 1st S. Staff 1 or.	M.
	9.6.17		Not engaged. Brigadier General & Brigade Major round Bn ts training in afternoon. Casualties Nil. Reinforcements 2/Queens 1 or, 1st S. Staffs 1 or –	M.

WAR DIARY or INTELLIGENCE SUMMARY

Army Form C. 2118.

Place	Date	Hour	Summary of Events and Information	Remarks and references to Appendices
Courcelles	10-6-17		Int. Div Const. lectured in the morning on attack formations. Rain in afternoon. Casualties Nil. Reinforcements Officers 6 or. 2nd Manrs 1 or. 22nd Manrs 6 or. 91/92 M.G. Co. 1 or.	Nil.
	11-6-17		Very bad thunderstorm in morning. Brigadier General + Brigade Major Shot — Casualties 22nd Manrs 1 or. wounded. Men out all day to — Casualties Nil. Reinforcements Nil.	Nil.
	12-6-17		Brigadier General + Brigade Major went round battalions training in afternoon. Very hot — Casualties Nil. Reinforcements Nil.	Appendix 17 Nil.
	13-6-17		all Bns out on field firing range at PUISIEUX. Brigadier continued watching till 11-30. Aventeuil. General + Brigade Major went to AUXI-LE-CHATEAU in afternoon. Brig. General + Bde Major. Casualties Nil.	Nil.
	14-6-17		"Free Platoon" Demonstration by G.H.Q. Casualties Nil. Reinforcements 1st S. Staffs 1 or. 2nd Manrs 3 or. Lot. Bde Major went to see Divl. Plyr. Tr. + Bayonet fighting class. Capt. Henson (T.M.S) demonstrated with Ballon he designed + Stokesmortans. Col. Norman D.S.O. approved Brigadier General 87th Bde. Casualties Nil. Reinforcements 2 Queens 6 or. 1st S. Staffs 6 or. 2nd Manrs 6 or. 2nd Manrs 22nd Manrs 7 or. 91/92 M.G. Co. 10 3/6 2 or.	Nil.

WAR DIARY or INTELLIGENCE SUMMARY

Army Form C. 2118.

Place	Date	Hour	Summary of Events and Information	Remarks and references to Appendices
COURCELLES	5-6-17		Brigade Major reconnoitres COURCELLES Valley with Lt. Killip on R.E. for Bullet & Bayonet Range. Brigadier General went round Transport lines. Bde Major decides site of operation by Scoy Queens at MOYENNEVILLE. Casualties Nil. Reinforcements Nil.	M.
	6-6-17		Brigadier General & Bde Major conducted rehearsal for next day's reconnaissance in COURCELLES to Ellis Col Norman O.C.'s left joins 8th Brigade. Lt Col Lomax assumed to take command of 21st Manchesters. Brig General & Bde Major attend 1st Staffords Boxing Competition. Casualties Nil. Reinforcements Nil	M.
	7-6-17		Bde Major out early to lay course of QUEENS Demonstration. Brigadier General took command of Demonstration & PU/S/15/VX fired 9 in rt ranges. Bde Major attended Tank Demonstration at ARRAS. Staff Capt to Brigadier Cdre. Casualties Nil - Reinforcements Nil	M.
	8-6-17		Bde Major. Thunderstorm in evening. Casualties Nil. Reinforcements Nil.	M.

Army Form C. 2118.

WAR DIARY
or
INTELLIGENCE SUMMARY

(Erase heading not required.)

Instructions regarding War Diaries and Intelligence Summaries are contained in F. S. Regs., Part II and the Staff Manual respectively. Title Pages will be prepared in manuscript.

Place	Date	Hour	Summary of Events and Information	Remarks and references to Appendices
COURCELLES	24-6-17		Heavy Thunderstorm. Brigadier General to Bde Hqrs. Lt Col Jefferson at Dinner. Rifle meeting by the Queens. Left the Army Commander's on PURSUIT at Regimental Range Conference of Commanding Officers in evening. Capt. Booth attached to Divl. Casualties Nil. Reinforcements 3 Queens 3 or. 1/9 Staffs 1 or.	
	25-6-17		Brigadier General, Bde Major, Lt Col Beauman DSO, & also Jenkins DSO went up to L. MORT HOMME to see 174th Bde. Brigadier General, Staff went up to Queens to see Jefferson. Operation orders for relief issued. Casualties Nil. Reinforcements 2 Queens 40 or. 1st S. Staffs 2 offs.	Offensive Rt. 5
	26-6-17		Brigade Major to let round line — from MORT HOMME AEC out up Pelican Av. to Sunken Rd. Back along railway to Factory. Av. up to Front line & back to St Leger. 1st S. Staffs were up to S. Leger in evening. Casualties 3 Queens 1 or. wounded. Reinforcements Nil	Offensive Rt. 6

Army Form C. 2118.

WAR DIARY
or
INTELLIGENCE SUMMARY
(Erase heading not required.)

Place	Date	Hour	Summary of Events and Information	Remarks and references to Appendices
COURCELETTE	22.6.17		Brigadier General + Bde Major relieves to Bde in morning. Jumping competition between Bde. Sir + Trench in afternoon. Bde won. 21st + 22nd Manchesters moved up to MORY CORPS E. 1st S/Staffs relieved 2 Lbns on Regt. on left sector with Casualties. 21st Manch 2 or killed 1 or wounded Reinforcements 3 Queens 2 Offs. 1st S Staffs 7 or. 21st Manch 13 or. 22nd Manch 10 or. 9th M.G Co. i or. Brig. General + Bde Major entered up CROISILLES west sector.	Nil
	23.6.17		left sector — up FACTORY AVENUE, along front line, back up HUN PLANE to LONG TRENCH. Back down FACTORY AV. + along Fahre Reserve line to KNUCKLE AV. then across open to 13.2 HQ. in Railway Embankment. QUEENS (2 two coys in St LEGER LINE) move up to St LEGER, T.M. B. 9 M.G Coy have formed up. 9/24 Para Coys attacked Bgd. Casualties 1st S Staffs 1 or killed Reinforcements Nil	Nil

WAR DIARY or INTELLIGENCE SUMMARY

Army Form C. 2118.

Place	Date	Hour	Summary of Events and Information	Remarks and references to Appendices
MORT HOMME	24.6.17		B.H.Q. moved up to Mort Homme. Stake over from 74th B.Gr. B.Gr Major & Intell officer went up to Reg. Batt. H.Q. in afternoon. Also up Fusilier Av, to front line. Fusiliers Arrgs. but worn thin. Shallow. Weather 2 reinforcements 1st Staffords on way back. Casualties 21st Manc. 10 killed 2 or. wounded, 22nd Manc. 4 or. wounded. Reinforcements 1st S. Staff 2 or.	nil
	25.6.17		Cloudy with bright intervals. Warm. Brigadier General & Brigade Major up Pelican Avenue to right sector & subsequently visited 2nd Gordons, the Battalion on our right, at the Crucifix - Bullecourt. Visited H.Q. of 21st & 22nd Manchester Regiments and the 1st S.A Staffords on the way back. Casualties 1st S.Staff 10 killed, 8 wounded, 21st Manc. 10 killed, 10 wounded, 22nd Manc 6 or. wounded. Reinforcements Nil. Sunny & cool. Brigade Major and G.S.O.3 visited right sector Brigadier General inspected detail camps - in afternoon Brigade Major visited H.Q. of 100th Brigade on left. Casualties 21/9 Manc 1 or. wounded at duty. Reinforcements 1st S. Manc 1 M.G.	nil
	26.6.17			nil
	27.6.17		Sunny morning overcast in afternoon - Brigadier General and Staff Captain round left sector support line and back by Knuckle Avenue. In afternoon Brigade Major up Pelican Avenue & round by Crucifix to Bullecourt Avenue and back along Railway to Ecoust. 21st Manchesters relieved 1st South Staffords in left sector. Casualties 2nd Manc 1 or. wounded 22nd Manc 3 or. wounded Reinforcements 2 Officers 1st S. Staff 2 or. 1 or.	nil Appendix

Army Form C. 2118.

WAR DIARY
or
INTELLIGENCE SUMMARY

(Erase heading not required.)

Instructions regarding War Diaries and Intelligence Summaries are contained in F. S. Regs., Part II. and the Staff Manual respectively. Title Pages will be prepared in manuscript.

Place	Date	Hour	Summary of Events and Information	Remarks and references to Appendices
MORT HOMME	28.6.17		Heavy rain in night 27-28. Hot overcast day. Heavy thunderstorm in morning. Brigadier General visited Brigade Major round machine gun positions with O.C. 9th Machine Gun Co (Major Hamilton-Gotley) in morning. Conference at 6 p.m. with Divisional Commander and O.C. 1st S. Staffords with reference to a proposed raid – 2nd Queens relieved 22nd Manchesters in right sector. Casualties Nil. Reinforcements Nil.	M.
	29.6.17		Sunny warm. The V Corps Commander visited the Brigadier at Brigade H.Q. and V Corps Intelligence Officer called. Saw Brigade Major in morning. Brigadier General went round line in afternoon. Casualties 2nd Yorks 1 or killed 1 or wounded. Reinforcements 1/5 S. Staffs 6 or. Brigadier General and Brigade Major to Conference at Divisional H.Q. in afternoon.	M.
	30.6.17		Dull cold with rain at intervals. Brigadier General round the line in the morning. Brigadier General to Divisional H.Q. in afternoon. R.E. Pioneers worked part of the front line at night. Casualties 1st S. Staffs 3 or wounded 21st Hussars 1 or wounded. Reinforcements Nil.	M.

A. T. Beckley O.C.
Actg 9th Inf Bde

Appendix 1.

Programme of Training - 91st Infantry Brigade.

Date.	Unit.	Time.	Locality.	Nature of Training.
4/6/17.	1st Bn.S.Staffs.Regt.	8-30.a.m. - 12-30.p.m.	COURCELLES.	Physical Training and Bayonet Fighting - Close Order Drill - Section Training - Training of Specialists - Platoon Training - Hasty consolidation and wiring. - Musketry.
	21st Bn.Manchester Regt.	8-30.a.m. - 12-30.p.m. 2.p.m. - 4-30.p.m.	-do-	Physical Training and Bayonet Fighting - Battalion Drill - Open Warfare. One Company Musketry - Training of Specialists.
	22nd Bn.Manchester Regt.	8-30.a.m. - 1.p.m.	-do-	Companies Extended Order and Attack Practices - Company Drill - Attack - Training of Specialists - One Company using Range.
5/6/17.	1st Bn.S.Staffs.Regt.	8-30.a.m. - 12-30.p.m.	COURCELLES.	Physical Training and Bayonet Fighting - Close Order Drill - Section Training - Training of Specialists - Musketry - Battalion Drill.
	21st Bn.Manchester Regt.	8-30.a.m. - 12-30.p.m. 2.p.m. - 4-30.p.m.	-do- -do-	Advanced Guard to ERVILLERS - Flank Guard from ERVILLERS. One Company Musketry - Training of Specialists.
	22nd Bn.Manchester Regt.	8-30.a.m. - 1.p.m.	-do-	Bayonet Fighting - Box Respirator Drill - Digging and Constructing Strong Points - Ceremonial - Training of Specialists - Headquarters on Range.
6/6/17.	1st Bn.S.Staffs.Regt.	8-30.a.m. - 12-30.p.m.	COURCELLES.	Physical Training and Bayonet Fighting - Close Order Drill - Section Training - Musketry - Company Training - Extended Order and Artillery Formation - Open Order attack practice.

Date.	Unit.	Time.	Locality.	Nature of Training.
6/6/17. (contd.).	21st Bn.Manch.Regt.	8-30.a.m. - 12-30.p.m. 2.p.m. - 4-30.p.m.	COURCELLES.	Physical Training and Bayonet Fighting - Battalion Drill - Outposts - One Company Musketry - Training of Specialists
	22nd Bn.Manch.Regt.	8-30.a.m. - 1.p.m.	-do-	Arm Drill - Artillery Formations and Extensions for attack - Battalion Drill Training of Specialists - One Company on Range.
7/6/17.	2nd Bn.Queen's Regt.	9.a.m. - 12-30.p.m. 2.p.m. - 3-30.p.m.	COURCELLES.	Physical Training and Bayonet Fighting - Arm Drill - Company Drill - Attack and consolidating a Syrong Point - One Company firing on Range - Training of Specialists. One Company on Range - Training of Specialists
	1st Bn.S.Staffs.Regt.	8-30.a.m. - 12-30.p.m.	-do-	Physical Training and Bayonet Fighting - Close Order Drill - Section Training - Musketry - Training of Specialists - Company Training - Attack on a Syrong Point.
	21st Bn.Manch.Regt.	8-30.a.m. - 12-30.p.m.		Village attack on AYETTE. Lewis Gunners on Range - Training of Specialists.
	22nd Bn.Manch.Regt.	8-30.a.m. - 1.p.m.	COURCELLES.	Extended Order - Attack on Strong Points Attack - One Company firing on Range - Training of Specialists.
8/6/17.	2nd Bn.Queen's Regt.	9.a.m. - 12-30.p.m. 2.p.m. - 3-30.p.m.	COURCELLES. -do-	Physical Training and Arm Drill - Training of Specialists - Company attack in Open - Casuals on Range. Battalion Drill.

Date.	Unit.	Time.	Locality.	Nature of Training.
8/6/17. (contd).	1st Bn. S. Staffs. Regt.	8-30.a.m. - 12-30.p.m.	COURCELLES.	BATTALION EXERCISE.
	21st Bn. Manchester Regt.	8-30.a.m. - 12-30.p.m.	-do-	~~BATTALION EXERCISE~~
	22nd Bn. Manchester Regt.	8-30.a.m. - 1.p.m.	-do-	Repitition.
9/6/17.	2nd Bn. Queen's Regt.	9.a.m. - 12.30.p.m.	COURCELLES.	BATTALION EXERCISE.
	1st Bn. S. Staffs. Regt.	8-30.a.m. - 12-30.p.m.	-do-	Companies at disposal of Company Commanders. - Repitition of previous training
	21st Bn. Manchester Regt.	8-30.a.m. - 12-30.p.m. 2.p.m. - 4-30.p.m.	-do-	Physical Training and Bayonet Fighting Battalion Drill - Attack on Strong Points. One Company on Range - Training of Specialists.
	22nd Bn. Manchester Regt.	8-30.a.m. - 1.p.m.	-do-	~~Bayonet Fighting - Box Respirator Drill - Arm Drill - Ceremonial.~~ BATTALION EXERCISE

NOTES.
2nd Bn. Queen's Regt. — Short Lectures under Company Arrangements every day on the day's work. Box Respirator Drill to be carried out once a week.
1st Bn. S. Staffs. Regt. — Classes for young Officers in Bombing and Lewis Gun daily from 2.p.m. - 3.p.m. Barr and Stroud Range Finder Instruction for N.C.O's daily from 2.p.m. - 3.p.m. One Company firing on Range each day.
Company Conferences daily from 6.p.m. - 6-30.p.m.
22nd Bn. Manch. Regt. — Specialists parade with Companies on Battalion Parades. Lewis Gunners fire on Range with their Companies and parade with Companies for tactical exercises. Barr and Stroud Range Finders taken on Range for instructional purposes.
Afternoons spent in Recreational Training.
Conferences daily from 2.p.m. to 3.p.m. on explanation of work for next day.

SECRET.

Appendix 2

Copy No. 18

91st Infantry Brigade Order No. 2.

5th June, 1917.

Reference Maps – 51B S.W. – Scale 1/20,000.
57C N.W. – Scale 1/20,000.

1. In the event of the first line system of defence being penetrated the defence of the ST.LEGER – VRAUCOURT line from L'HOMME MORT – the SENSEE RIVER (both exclusive) will devolve upon the 91st Infantry Brigade.

    This line will be continued to the N. by the 21st Division and to the S.E. by the 62nd Division.

2. (a) The Officer Commanding, 22nd Bn. Manchester Regt., will detail two Companies to relieve two Companies 1st Bn. Royal Welsh Fusiliers now forming the permanent garrison of this Sector.
   (b) The Officer Commanding, 91st Machine Gun Coy., will similarly relieve eight guns in the line now found by 22nd Machine Gun Coy.

    Above reliefs to be completed by 5.p.m., June 6th, 1917.

3. Should the 91st Infantry Brigade be ordered to hold this line, the order "DEFENCE MOVE" will be given, on receipt of which the following moves will take place:-

    (a) 21st Bn. Manchester Regt. (and one Company, 22nd Bn. Manchester Regt.), Right front Battalion, from L'HOMME MORT (exclusive) to B.4.d.8.5. (inclusive). Three Companies in front line, and two Companies in Sunken Road in B.10.b. and d.
    (b) 22nd Bn. Manchester Regt. (less one Company) Left front Battalion, from B.4.d.8.5. to the SENSEE RIVER (both exclusive). Two Companies in the Front Line and one Company in Reserve in ST.LEGER QUARRY.

      The Company forming permanent garrison of the Right Sector will stand fast and come under the orders of the Officer Commanding, 21st Bn. Manchester Regt.
    (c) 1st Bn. South Staffordshire Regt. (less one Company working under 58th Division) Right Reserve Battalion at MORY.
    (d) 2nd Bn. Queen's Regt., Left Reserve Battalion in position of assembly in B.14.b.
    (e) 91st Machine Gun Coy. (less 8 guns already holding line) Headquarters and 4 guns in Reserve at MORY and 4 guns in ST.LEGER.
    (f) "A" Echelon 1st Line Transport will concentrate at BEUGNIERS under the Brigade Transport Officer. "B" Echelon remaining in its present position.

4. On completion of above moves each Unit will send a representative to Brigade Headquarters to report their exact location. Position of Brigade Headquarters will be notified later.

5. Sketch Map of the position is attached.

6. Officers Commanding Battalions will arrange to reconnoitre the position and its approaches and suitable places for Battalion Headquarters.

   ACKNOWLEDGE.

   Captain,
   Brigade Major, 91st Infantry Brigade.

Issued at 4.45.p.m.

(Distribution over-leaf.)

SECRET.

91st Infantry Brigade Order No.R.

Copy No.....

Copy No 1	Bde.Major.	10	Gren.& L.G.School.
2	Staff Captain.	11	Eden Transport Officer.
3	2nd Queen's R.	12	Supply Officer.
4	1st S.Staffs.R.	13	7th Division.
5	21st Manch.R.	14	22nd Inf.Bde.
6	22nd Manch.R	15	21st Division.
7	91st M.G.Coy.	16	62nd Division.
8	No.3.Sec.Div.Sigs.	17	File.
9	91st T.M.Battery.	18 & 19	War Diary.

M.G. Post 15
Post 14
Post 13
Post 12
M.G. Post 11

Support Post E
Support Post D
Post 10

Support Post C
Post 9
Support Post B

Support Post A
M.G. Post 8

Post 7

M.G. Post 6
M.G. Post 5

Post 4
M.G. Post 3

M.G. Post 2
M.G. Post 1

Scale 1:10000

SECRET.   Appendix 3   Copy No. 13

91st Infantry Brigade Order No. 1.

4th June, 1917.

1. 2nd Bn. Queen's Regt., will be relieved by 2nd Bn. Royal Warwickshire Regt., 22nd Infantry Brigade on June 6th, 1917. Relief to be complete by 12. noon.

2. On relief the 2nd Bn. Queen's Regt. will return to their former billets in COURCELLES and will again come under the orders of 91st Infantry Brigade.

Captain,

Brigade Major, 91st Infantry Brigade.

Copy No 1 Bde. Major.   8 91st T.M. Battery.
       2 Staff Captain.   9 Supply Officer.
       3 2nd Queen's R   10 7th Division.
       4 1st S. Staffs. R   11 58th Division.
       5 21st Manch. R   12 22nd Inf. Bde.
       6 22nd Manch. R   13 File.
       7 91st M.G. Coy.   14 & 15 War Diary.

SECRET. *Appendix 4*

Copy No. 14.

91st Infantry Brigade Order No. 3.

12th June, 1917.

Reference Maps – FRANCE 57C. N.W.) – Scale 1/20,000.
"   57B. S.W.)

1. (a) Responsibility for the defence of the L'HOMME MORT – ST.LEGER Line will be assumed by the 22nd Infantry Brigade on the 13th instant.
   (b) Two companies 22nd Bn. Manchester Regt., and 8 guns of 91st Machine Gun Coy., now forming garrison of this line will be relieved by two Companies 2/1st H.A.C. and 8 guns 22nd Machine Gun Coy., on 13th instant, relief being complete by 8.p.m.

2. On completion of the above relief the 91st Infantry Brigade will be prepared, in the event of an enemy attack, to:–

   (a) Counter-attack the enemy on the High Ground West of CROISILLES, should he break through the right of the VIth Corps. (Scheme "A").

   (b) To reinforce the troops holding the Vth Corps front, for the defence of the front line and the village of ECOUST – LONGATTE (Scheme "B").

3. In the event of Scheme "A" being put into operation
   (a) Units will move via COURCELLES HALT and HAMELINCOURT Cross Roads in the following order:–

   1. Brigade Headquarter Report Centre to MAISON ROUGE.
   2. 2nd Bn. Queen's Regt., to Area between T.25.d.5.5. and B.1.b.7.7.
   3. 22nd Bn. Manchester Regt., to vicinity of Sunken Road in N.W. Corner of Square B.1.b.
   4. 91st Machine Gun Coy., and 91st Trench Mortar Bty., to S.E. Corner of Square B.1.a.
   5. 21st Bn. Manchester Regt., to N.E. Corner of Square B.1.c.
   6. 1st Bn. South Staffordshire Regt., to S.E. Corner of Square B.1.c.

   (b) "A" Echelon 1st Line Transport will accompany Units to above assembly positions. "B" Echelon will remain in its present position.
   (c) All Commanding Officers will report to Brigade Headquarters Report Centre in advance of their Units.

4. The attack will be carried out by 2nd Bn. Queen's Regt. (Left) and 22nd Bn. Manchester Regt. (Right), the dividing line being a line from Road Junction T.26.b.8.2. to Cross Roads T.21.d.8.5.
   The line JUDAS FARM – ST. LEGER MILL will mark the Right Boundary of the attack.
   The objective will probably be the present 2nd Line, which joins the L'HOMME MORT – ST. LEGER Line at T.29.a.1.3. and runs N.W. through T.22.d.2.4. – T.22.d.1.9. – T.22.b.3.6. – T.16.c.5.2.

5. Officers Commanding Units will carry out the necessary reconnaissances forthwith.

6. ACKNOWLEDGE.

O. F. Morshead
Captain,

Brigade Major, 91st Infantry Brigade.

(Distribution over-leaf).

Issued at 8.30 p.m. to

Copy No 1 Staff Captain.
2 2nd Queen's R
3 1st S.Staffs.R
4 21st Manch.R
5 22nd Manch.R
6 91st M.G.Coy.
7 No.3.Sec.Div.Sigs.
8 91st T.M.Battery.
9 Gren.& L.G.School.
10 Bde. Transport Officer.
11 7th Division.
12 22nd Inf.Bde.
13 File.
14 War Diary.
15 War Diary.

SECRET.   Copy No. 17

Appendix 5

91st Infantry Brigade Order No.4.

18th June, 1917.

Reference Maps — 51B S.W. — Scale 1/80,000.
              57C N.W. — Scale 1/20,000.

1. (a) The 91st Infantry Brigade will re-assume responsibility for the defence of the L'HOMME MORT — ST.LEGER Line from 10pm, on the 20th June, 1917.
   (b) Two Companies 2nd Bn.Queen's Regt., and 8 guns 91st Machine Gun Coy., will relieve 2 Companies 2/1st H.A.C. and 8 guns 22nd Machine Gun Coy., respectively, relief being complete by 8.p.m., June 20th.

2. On completion of relief the defence scheme in force will revert to that laid down in paras.3 and 4 of 91st Infantry Brigade Order No.2., dated 5th June,1917,"2nd Bn.Queen's Regt." being substituted throughout for "22nd Bn.Manchester Regt." and vice versa.

3. ACKNOWLEDGE.

                                                        Olhionshead
                                                        Captain,
                                        Brigade Major, 91st Infantry Brigade.

Issued at.../..p.m. to

           Copy No 1 Staff Captain.   10 Bde.Transport Officer.
                  2 2nd Queen's R   11 Supply Officer.
                  3 1st S.Staffs.R   12 7th Division.
                  4 21st Manch.R   13 22nd Inf.Bde.
                  5 22nd Manch.R   ~~14 21st Division~~
                  6 91st M.G.Coy.   ~~15 62nd Division~~
                  7 No.3.Sec.Div.Sigs.   16 File.
                  8 91st T.M.Battery.   17 War Diary.
                  9 Gren.& L.G.School.   18 War Diary.

SECRET.   Appendix 6   Copy No. 22

91st Infantry Brigade Order No. 5.

Wednesday, 20th June, 1917.

Reference Map - HENDECOURT, Edition 1.
Scale 1/20,000.

1. (a) The 7th Division is to relieve the 58th Division on the Vth Corps Front.
   (b) The 91st Infantry Brigade will relieve the 174th Infantry Brigade on the Left Sector in accordance with the attached table, all further details being arranged between Commanding Officers concerned.
   (c) The 20th Infantry Brigade will be on the Right (Headquarters of Left Battalion - U.27.d.6.3.), and the 19th Infantry Brigade on the Left (Headquarters of Right Battalion in Quarries at U.13.c.0.8.).
   The 22nd Infantry Brigade will be in Reserve at MORY.

2. Dividing Lines run as follows:-

   (a) Between 20th Infantry Brigade and 91st Infantry Brigade - ECOUST - CRUCIFIX - FACTORY Road.
   (b) Between 91st Infantry Brigade and 19th Infantry Brigade - From U.14.a.C.1.,S.W. along N.W. side of track to FACTORY.
   (c) Between Battalion Sub-sectors - A line from U.25.a.5.6. to U.20.a.5.0. to U.20.b.0.3. (inclusive to Left Sub-sector).

3. All maps, aeroplane photos, work and defence schemes will be taken over on relief.

4. The outgoing Units are arranging to leave a proportion of Officers, N.C.Os and Lewis Gunners in the line for 24 hours after completion of relief.

5. The two companies of 2nd Bn. Queen's Regt., and 8 guns of 91st Machine Gun Company now holding the MORT HOMME - ST. LEGER Line will be relieved by a similar party of 175th Infantry Brigade by 9.a.m., June 24th. Further details as to relieving Unit will be issued later.

6. (a) Transport and Details will be temporarily accommodated in Camp at B.27.a.5.7., under arrangements to be made by the Staff Captain.
   (b) No furniture or tentage will be removed from the present Area.
   (c) Each Unit will leave one man per Company to hand over present billets to incoming Units.
   (d) A Brigade Store will be formed at ERVILLERS to accommodate surplus stores while the Brigade is in the Line. The exact position will be notified later.

7. The Command of the Sector will pass to G.O.C., 91st Infantry Brigade at 9.a.m., on 24th June, at which hour Brigade Headquarters will close at COURCELLES and open at L'HOLME MORT.

8. ACKNOWLEDGE.

Captain,
Brigade Major, 91st Infantry Brigade.

Issued at 10. p.m. to

Copy No 1 2nd Queen's R   12 O.C., Left Group R.A.
        2 1st S.Staffs.R   13 528 (Durham) Fd.Coy.R.E.
        3 21st Manch.R   14 Supply Officer.
        4 22nd Manch.R   15 7th Division.
        5 91st M.G.Coy.   16 20th Inf.Bde.
        6 Staff Captain.   17 22nd Inf.Bde.
        7 No.3.Sec.7th Div.Sigs. 18 19th Inf.Bde.
        8 91st T.M.Battery.   19 175th Inf.Bde.
        9 91st Bde.Gren.School. 20 174th Inf.Bde.
       10 Bde.Transport Officer. 21 File.
       11 A.D.M.S.   22 & 23 War Diary.

Table issued with 91st Infantry Brigade Order No.5.

Date.	Unit.	From	To	To relieve.		Operation to be completed by :-	Remarks.
				Unit.	Hd.Qtrs.		
June 21st.	1st Bn.S.Staffs.Regt.	COURCELLES.	ST.LEGER.	5th London Rifle Bde.	T.28.d.2.0.	7.p.m.	On relief 1st Bn.S.Staffs.Regt. come under orders of 175th Inf.Bde. for tactical purposes.
June 22nd.	21st Bn.Manch.R and 22nd Bn.Manch.R	COURCELLES.	Camp at MARY COPSE.			8.p.m.	Billetting representatives to meet Staff Capt. at MARY COPSE at 3.p.m. 21st June.
	1st Bn.S.Staffs.Regt.	ST.LEGER.	Left Sub-Sector.	7th London Regt.	U.19.a.4.3.	Daylight June 23rd.	
June 23rd.	2nd Bn.Queen's R (less 2 Coys.)	COURCELLES.	ST.LEGER.	7th London Regt.	T.28.d.2.0.	7.p.m.	On completion of relief 2nd Bn. Queen's R come under orders of 175th Inf.Bde. for tactical purposes.
	91st T.M.Bty. 91st M.G.Coy. (less 8 guns.) 91st Bde.Gren.School.	COURCELLES.	Camp at B.27.a.5.7.			8.p.m.	
	21st Bn.Manch.R	MARY COPSE.	Support Battalion.	6th London Regt.	T.24.d.7.2.	Daylight June 24th.	
	22nd Bn.Manch.R	MARY COPSE.	Right Sub-Sector.	8th Post Office Rifles.	U.25.b.5.3.	Daylight June 24th.	
June 24th.	91st M.G.Coy.	B.27.a.5.7.	Line.	174th M.G.Coy.	B.4.d.5.3.	Daylight June 25th.	
	91st L.T.M.Bty.	B.27.a.5.7.	Line.	174th L.T.M.B.	U.26.c.1.7.	Daylight June 25th.	

SECRET.   Appendix 7

Copy No. 20.

91st Infantry Brigade Order No.6.

Tuesday, 26th June, 1917.

Reference Map - HENDECOURT, Edition 1.
- Scale 1/20,000.

1.   On night June 27/28th -
  (a) The 21st. Bn. Manchester Regt., will relieve 1st. Bn. South Staffordshire Regt., in the Left Sector.
  (b) 1st Bn. South Staffordshire Regt., will relieve 21st. Bn. Manchester Regt., in Brigade Support.

2.   On night June 28/29th -
  (a) The 2nd Bn. Queen's Regt., will relieve 22nd Bn. Manchester Regt., in the Right Sector, and detachment of 21st. Bn. Manchester Regt., in MEBUS at U.20.b.90.25, which will thence-forward be garrisoned by the Battalion holding Right Sector.
  (b) 22nd Bn. Manchester Regt., will be withdrawn into Brigade Reserve at ST.LEGER.

3.   All details of above reliefs will be arranged between Commanding Officers concerned, a copy of Battalion Relief Orders being forwarded to this office.

4.   Consequent on above reliefs, the table of R.E. Carrying parties given in para. 3. of B.M./1408 of 25th June, is cancelled, and the following substituted :-

Date.	Time.	Strength.	Unit.	Rendezvous.
Night, June 27/28th.	9-30.p.m.	100 O.R.	2nd Bn. Queens.R'	S.Side of Rly.Emb. U.26.a.75.05.
	10-0 p.m.	100 O.R.	-do-	-do-
Night June 28/29th.	9-30.p.m.	100 O.R.	1st. Bn. S. Staffs.R'	Junction of Road & Rly. U.25.a.5.6.
	10-0 p.m.	100 O.R.	-do-	-do-
Night June 29/30th.	9-30.p.m.	100 O.R.	1st Bn. S. Staffs.R'	Junction of Road & Rly. U.25.a.5.6.
	10-0 p.m.	100 O.R.	22nd Bn. Manch.R'	-do-
	9-30.p.m.	100 O.R.	-do-	S.Side of Rly.Emb. U.26.a.75.05.

5.   ACKNOWLEDGE.

Ohmorehead
Captain,

Brigade Major, 91st. Infantry Brigade.

Issued at 8.45.p.m. to

    Copy No 1 2nd Queen's R'   11 A.D.M.S.
            2 1st S. Staffs.R'   12 O.C. Left Group, R.A.
            3 21st. Manch.R'   13 528 (Durham) Fd. Coy.
            4 22nd Manch.R'   14 Supply Officer.
            5 91st. M.G.Coy.   15 7th Division.
            6 No.3.Sec.7th Div.Sigs. 16 22nd Inf.Bde.
            7 91st T.M.Battery.   17 100th Inf.Bde.
            8 91st Bde.Gren.School.   18 File.
            9 Staff Captain.   19 War Diary.
           10 Bde.Transport Officer. 20 War Diary.

SECRET/

21st Battalion The Manchester Regiment.

OPERATION ORDER NO. 65   Copy No. 6

26th JUNE, 1917.

Ref: ECOUST ST MEIN 1:10.000 Ed. 4
51 B. S.W. and special maps issued.

1. On night 27/28th June LAKE will relieve SEA in the front line of Left Sub-Sector.
   Companies will relieve as follows:-
   A. Company LAKE will relieve B. Company SEA in support in trench from L. 4. - L. 3.
   B. Company LAKE will relieve A. Company SEA on left of line.
   D. Company LAKE will relieve D. Company SEA in centre of line.
   C. Company LAKE will relieve C. Company SEA on right of line.
   Route.- FUSILIER AVENUE and track alongside this trench.

2. Company Commanders having reconnoitred their new positions on 26th June will arrange for a Sergeant per platoon to proceed to platoons of SEA on afternoon of 27th to act as Liason officers during relief.

3. Guides from C. Company SEA will be at Battalion Headquarters T. 24. d. 7. 9. at 9.15 p.m. to guide C. Company LAKE.
   O. C. A. Company LAKE will provide one guide per post to report to O.C. B. Company SEA at 9.15 p.m.
   Officers Commanding B, C, & D. Companies LAKE will each detail one man per Company to remain behind and show relieving Companies of SEA their available accomodation etc.
   These men to report to Battalion Headquarters as soon as their duty is complete.

4. All trench stores etc will be taken over by Company Commanders of LAKE who will render a list of stores taken over to Battalion Headquarters as soon as possible .
   They will hand over to relieving Company Commanders of SEA all trench stores in their present positions, receipts to be forwarded to this office.

5. One Lewis Gun Section complete from A. Company will report for duty with B. Company on afternoon of 27th June.

6. Rations for 28th will be distributed after relief by a party from "DETAILS". All water-bottles are to be filled before proceeding to line. A fresh supply of water will be sent up on night of 28th.

7. Relief complete will be reported to Battalion Headquarters by wire. The word "ARGENTINE" will be used.

8. Battalion Headquarters and Regimental Aid Post will both remain in their present positions.

9. On night 28/29th June party of C. Company LAKE in MEBUS at U. 29. b. 90. 25 will be relieved by WAVE. Guides will be arranged by Battalion Headquarters.

10. These orders are on no account to be taken into the front line.

Lieut: & Adjt,
21st Bn. Manchester Regiment.

11. Acknowledge

ADDENDUM TO OPERATION ORDER NO. 5   No. 6

27th JUNE, 1917.

1. ROUTE.

B. Company LAKE will leave their present position at
9.30 p.m. and proceed to front line via FACTORY LANE
and track alongside.

C. Company LAKE will leave the embankment at 9.30 p.m.
and proceed to front line via FUSILIER AVENUE and
track alongside.

D. Company LAKE will leave the sunken road at 10 p.m.
and proceed to front line via FUSILIER AVENUE and track
alongside.

                                          Lieut: & Adjt,
                                 21st Bn. Manchester Regiment.

DISTRIBUTION.
Copy No. 1. Commanding Officer.
        2. O.C. A. Company.
        3.   B.   "
        4.   C.   "
        5.   D.   "
        6. 91st Infantry Brigade.
        7. 1st S. Staffordshire Regt.

Issued at 11.45 a.m. by Runner.

SECRET.   COPY NO. 6

OPERATION ORDERS
by
Lieut.-Colonel. A.B.BEAUMAN. D.S.O.
Commanding, - Bn. South Staffordshire Regiment.
In the Trenches.   Wednesday, 27th June, 1917.
==

Map ref. ECOUST - ST. MEIN. 1/10.000. Ed.4. Combined CHERISY Sheet
51.B. S.W. 2. and 4.

1. On the night 27/28th SEA will be relieved by LAKE in front line of
   Left Sub-Sector.

2. Companies will be relieved as follows :-

   A. Coy. SEA, relieved by B.Coy. LAKE in front line.
   B. Coy. SEA, will relieve A.Coy. LAKE in Supporting Posts.
   C. Coy. SEA, relieved by C.Coy. LAKE in front line.
   D. Coy. SEA, relieved by D.Coy. LAKE in front line.

   O.C. "C" Coy. SEA, will detail 1 guide per platoon and one for Coy. H.Q.
   to be at Bn. H.Q., T.24.d.8.2. by 9-15 p.m. to guide up C. Coy. LAKE.

   Relief of B. Coy. except for forward posts will be complete by 9-0 p.m.
   1 guide per post will report to O.C., B. Coy. by 9-15 p.m.

3. On completion of relief C. and D. Companies will move out over the top
   by the side of FUSILIER AVENUE, and will occupy the following positions,

       C. Coy. to SUNKEN ROAD from U.19.c.0.3. - U.25.a.5.7.
              (Coy. H.Q., U.19.c.3.1.)
       D. Coy. to SUNKEN ROAD in T.30.c.
              (Coy. H.Q., T.30.c.3.8.)

   A. Coy. will move out over the top by the side of FACTORY AVENUE, and
   will occupy a position in RAILWAY EMBANKMENT T.24.d.
              (Coy. H.Q., about T.24.d.7.4.)

4. O.C., Companies will hand over a list of Bombs, Rifle Grenades, S.A.A.,
   Very Lights, with their Companies, and will forward a duplicate copy
   to Bn. H.Q.
   They will arrange to have all these put in definite places where
   Companies of LAKE can find them.

5. A. C. and D. Companies will find their CQMS's. in the positions which
   they are going to take up. As soon as all the Company is in, each
   CQMS will be sent down to the Cookers at the FACTORY T.24.b.0.4. to
   bring up hot dinners for the men.

6. Relief complete will be reported by the word ARGENTINESEA.

7. ACKNOWLEDGE.

                                    (Signed) A.W. LEE. Lieut. & Adjutant.
Issued at 12-30 p.m.   - Bn. South Staffordshire Regiment.

   COPIES.
       O.C., A. Coy.   WATER. ✓
       O.C., B. Coy.   LAKE.
       O.C., C. Coy.   FILE.
       O.C., D. Coy.

SECRET.   WAVE OPERATION ORDERS.   No 48

1. The Battn will relieve RIVER and detachment of LAKE in the right sector tomorrow 28th inst
2. An advance party of Signallers under Sgt Aldridge and the Provost Sgt will parade at 4.30 p.m. and proceed to Battn Hd Qrs of RIVER at U.25.b.7.2. The O.C. RIVER will detail one Signalling N.C.O. & two signallers to take over Signal Station at Chateau ST LEGER by 5 p.m.
3. The Battn will parade in fighting order in road outside Hd Qrs at 9.15pm. and will march off by Coys 200 yds interval in the order D,C,A,B, Hd Qrs. Route - track down valley via B.5.d.3.8. to T.30.b.2.7. and Aid Post, to Railway Cutting in U.25.a.& b.
4. Lewis Guns will proceed 15 mins in advance of "D" Coy under L.G.O and will be unloaded at T.30.b.2.7. whence they will be carried by teams who will collect guns in passing. Three buckets for guns will be taken to gun position, two buckets per gun will be dumped at Coy Hd Qrs and one per gun at Battn Hd Qrs.
5. Guides from posts or detachments shewn on the attached table will meet incoming Coys and conduct them to their positions. Relief will be carried out accordingly.
6. Completion of relief will be reported by using code word CAR followed by the letter of the incoming Coy.
7. Daily reports will be rendered at undermentioned times.
    Situation.   3.30 a.m. & 3.30 p.m.
    Intelligence.   9.0 a.m.
    Casualty.   9.0 a.m.
The BAB code (edn 2) will be used for all telephone messages.
8. In the event of an alarm O.C. B Coy will be prepared to send two patrols to front line to ascertain situation and report,
    (1) Patrol under officer to proceed to left front Coy via FUSILIER ALLEY (or KNUCKLE AVENUE)
    (2) Patrol under N.C.O. to proceed to PELICAN AVENUE to right front Coy. O.C. "B" Coy will make necessary arrangements for launching a counter attack or to reinforce front line according to situation. "C" Coy will make necessary arrangements for holding line of the Railway.
9.   ADMINISTRATIVE.
Great coats in packs will be stacked by Coys in courtyard
    a. near Cookers by 2 p.m. Surplus stores and Pioneers' materials will be ready there by the same time. Each Coy will detail a loading party of 4 men. "C" Coy will stack packs etc. in their billets.

    b. All surplus foodboxes, officers' valises and stores will be stacked in courtyard by 7 p.m. "C" Coy will have these at their billet by 6.50 p.m. Personnel for Details Camp will march with this transport.

    c. Transport for food boxes etc. for trenches will be ready for loading in Hd Qrs courtyard by 8 p.m. A representative of each Mess will march with this vehicle and be responsible for his own load.
10. The Aid post adjoins Battn Hd Qrs
    8 S.Bs will be accommodated in front line, 4 in each Coy's sector.
    There are bomb dumps at each Coy Hd Qrs at the head of PELICAN AVENUE and at Battn Hd Qrs.
    Support Coys are responsible for rations and water of Coy and

- 2 -

and posts occupying their respective front line.

M Strode Lt & A/Adjt

Copies to :-

WATER	Qr Mr.
RIVER	T.O.
LAKE	R.S.M.
Bn Hd Qrs	S/Sgt
All Coys & H.Q.Sec.	
L.G.O.	War Diary. (2)

-- RELIEF TABLE. --

Guide from	for post	incoming Coy WAVEn	meet at	time.	Route of relief.
RIVER	R. 14	A.	Hd Qrs "A" Coy RIVER.	10p.m. /15	Tape near Fusilier Alley.
"	R. 7.	A.	"	"	"
"	R. 6.	A.	"	"	"
"	R. 16	A.	"	"	"
"	R. 17	A.	"	"	"
"	R. 18	A.	"	"	"
"	R. 19	A.	"	"	"
LAKE	Road Block Post.	A.	"	"	"
LAKE	MEBUS Detachment.	A.	"	"	"
RIVER	B Coy	B.	Batt H.Q.	10.25	Rly Cutting.
	C "	C	do	10.20	"
"	R. 1.	D	Batt H.Q.	10.15	Pelican Avenue
"	R. 2.	"	"	"	"
"	R. 3.	"	"	"	"
"	R. 4.	"	"	"	"
"	R. 5.	"	"	"	"
"	R. 10	"	"	"	"
"	R. 12.	"	"	"	"

TOTAL No. of GUIDES - RIVER....16
LAKE.....2.

SECRET.

OPERATION ORDERS

Wednesday 27/6/17.

Ref Map ECOUST 1:10,000.

① The Battn will be relieved to-morrow night the 28th inst by the 2nd QUEENS Rgt and on completion of relief will proceed to ST LEGER.

② A.B.C.D. Coys of 22nd MANCHESTER Rgt will be relieved by A.B.C.D. Coys of 2nd QUEENS Rgt respectively.

③ Front line Companies will be relieved by posts. Guides for D Coy to be at Bn HQ by 9.45 pm. One guide per post. Relief of D Coy will proceed via PELLICAN AVENUE in the following order:— Posts R1, R2, R3, R4, R5, R10, R12, Coy HQ. B Coy will furnish guides for A Coy posts. These guides will be at A Coy HQ at 9.45 pm. Relief of A Coy will be conducted over the top in following order:— Posts R19, R18, R17, R16, R7, R6, R14. One guide for C Coy and one guide for B Coy will be at Battn HQ at 9.45 pm. O.C. Coys will ensure that each guide clearly understands for which post he is the guide.

④ Each Company will detail 1 N.C.O to remain behind for 24 hrs after relief is complete. One officer for D Coy and one officer at Bn HQ will also stay for 24 hrs.

⑤ N.C.O's in charge of posts will hand over a list of trench stores in their posts and see that all stores are clean and correct. Any information regarding enemy movement, habits, dangerous places etc, that will be of value to relieving troops to be handed over. O.C. Coys will hand over all stores, dispositions maps etc, in their possession.

⑥ All Lewis guns, Lewis gun panniers, mess boxes, trench kits petrol tins and camp kettles will be dumped at the ration dump.

⑦ O.C Companies will report personally to Battn HQ the relief complete of their Companies.

J.L. Ludlow Lt Col
O.C. 22nd Manchester Regt

Brigade HQ

SECRET.

SAHIBI ORDER.

The Officer Commanding,

    All Battalions.
    Machine Gun Coy.
    T.M.Battery.
    Supply Officer.

The following will probably be the programme of events later in the present week:-

Thursday,(21st inst).		1st Bn.S.Staffs.Regt. to ST.LEGER in afternoon.
Friday,(22nd inst).	(a)	21st Bn.Manch.Regt.and 22nd Bn. Manch.Regt. to MORY COPSE in afternoon.
	(b)	1st Bn.S.Staffs.Regt. relieve Left Battalion of 174th Inf.Bde. in evening.
Saturday,(23rd inst).	(a)	H.Q. and 2 Coys.,2nd Bn.Queen's Regt. to ST.LEGER in afternoon.
	(b)	91st T.M.Bty.,Gren.School and H.Q. & 8 guns of 91st M.G.Coy., to MIVILLERS in afternoon.
	(c)	22nd Bn.Manch.Regt. relieve Right Battalion,174th Inf.Bde.,and part of 175th Inf.Bde.(left of MOUNT-CRUCIFIX - FACTORY ROAD) in evening.
	(d)	21st Bn.Manch.Regt.,relieve Battalion in Support in evening.
	(e)	Bde.H.Q. to MORY HOUSE in evening. M.G.Coy., take over in evening.
Sunday,(24th inst).		
Monday,(25th inst).		2 Coys.,2nd Bn.Queen's Regt.,and 8 guns 91st M.G.Coy.,relieved in ST. LEGER Line and rejoin their Units.

NOTES.-
(1) Parties of 21st Bn.Manch.Regt.,now finding aerial working parties "A" & "B" will probably be relieved after work on Wednesday,(20th instant).
(2) Daily parties will not be found by this Brigade after Thursday,(21st instant).
(3) If more than 8 guns of 91st Machine Gun Coy.,are required in the line,guns will be taken forward from ST.LEGER Line on night 24/25th instant.

Ollivershead

Bde.Hd.Qtrs.
                                                            Captain,

18th June,1917.   Brigade Major,91st Infantry Brigade.

SECRET.
****
Copy No. 14

7th DIVISION ORDER No. 161.

Reference -
  Sheets 57.c.
       51.b.
  Scale 1/40,000.   18th June, 1917.

1. The 7th Division is to relieve the 58th Division on the V Corps front. The command will pass to G.O.C. 7th Division at 10 a.m. 24th June.

2. Arrangements for the relief will be as follows:-

(a) The 20th Infantry Brigade will remain holding the right Sector.
Headquarters at MORT HOMME.

(b) The 91st Infantry Brigade will take over the left Sector as under :-

On night 22nd/23rd June, one battalion will relieve the left battalion of 174th Infantry Brigade.
On 23rd June and night 23rd/24th June :-
  (i) One battalion will relieve the right battalion of 174th Infantry Brigade and that portion of 175th Infantry Brigade west of the ECOUST-CRUCIFIX-FACTORY Road.
  (ii) One battalion will relieve the battalion in support in the left sub-sector. One battalion will relieve the battalion in reserve in ST.LEGER.

The command will pass to the 91st Infantry Brigade on completion of the relief.

The two companies Infantry and Machine Gun Company at present holding the MORT HOMME - ST. LEGER Line will be relieved by the 58th Division on 25th instant.

Headquarters at MORT HOMME.

(c) The 22nd Infantry Brigade will be in reserve and will relieve the 175th Infantry Brigade in MORY vicinity on the 25th instant.
Headquarters - Old Divisional Advanced Headquarters at MORY.

(d) All arrangements for the above reliefs will be made direct between the Brigade Commanders concerned.

(e) /

2.

(e) The C.R.E. will arrange direct with C.R.E. 58th Division for the relief of the Field Companies. He will arrange to take over all schemes of work on hand.

3. The relief of the Machine guns in the left Sector and the Machine guns of the 58th Divisional Machine Gun Company (214th Machine Gun Company) will take place on the night of 24th/25th June.
   The 220th Machine Gun Company will arrange to relieve the Machine guns of 214th Machine Gun Company.

4. The C.R.A. 7th Division will assume command of the artillery covering the front at 10 a.m. on 24th instant.
   Arrangements for the relief of Trench Mortar Batteries will be made by the C.R.A.

5. To faciliate the above reliefs moves as under will be made :-

   On 21st June :-
   One battalion 91st Infantry Brigade to ST.LEGER.

   On 22nd June :-
   Two battalions 91st Infantry Brigade to MORY COPSE.

6. The 174th and 175th Infantry Brigades are going to leave one officer per company, one N.C.O. per platoon, and one representative of each Lewis gun team, in the line for 24 hours after completion of the relief.

7. The relief of all units not mentioned in the above order will be arranged by "Q".

8. Divisional Headquarters will open at BEHAGNIES (H.2.a. 4.8) at 10 a.m. on 24th instant.

9. ACKNOWLEDGE.

G. W. Howard.
Lieut-Colonel.

General Staff, 7th Division.

Distribution overleaf :-

Issued at 8.30 p.m. to:-

   A.D.C. (for G.O.C) Copy No.1.
   General Staff.   " 2 and 3.
   A.A.&Q.M.G.   " 4.
   A.D.M.S.   " 5.
   Divisional Train.   " 6.
   C.R.A.   " 7 to 10 and
               23 to 29.
   C.R.E.   " 11.
   20th Infantry Brigade. " 12.
   22nd Infantry Brigade. " 13.
   91st Infantry Brigade. " 14.
   Pioneer Battalion.   " 15.
   7th Signal Company. " 16.
   Div.Machine Gun Company. " 17.
   War Diary.   " 18.
   D.A.D.O.S.   " 19.
   58th Division.   " 20.
   62nd Division.   " 21.

S E C R E T.
****
7th Division No.
G. 562.

Copy No. 14

AMENDMENTS TO 7TH DIVISION ORDER No. 161.

20th June, 1917.

The following amendments will be made to 7th Division Order No. 161:-

1. Paragraph 2 (b) -

    The two Companies and Machine gun Company holding the MORT HOMME- ST. LEGER LINE will be relieved on 24th instant, and not on 25th as stated in the order.

2. Paragraph 2 (c) -

    The 22nd Infantry Brigade will carry out its relief on 24th instant, and not on 25th instant as mentioned in the order.

3. ACKNOWLEDGE.

G. W. Howard.
Lieut-Colonel.
General Staff, 7th Division.

Issued at 9 a.m.
to all recipients of 7th Division Order No.161,

7th DIVISION.

B. H. Q.

91st INFANTRY BRIGADE.

JULY 1917.

WAR DIARY or INTELLIGENCE SUMMARY

Army Form C. 2118.

HQ 91 Indy Bde
JULY 1917

Place	Date	Hour	Summary of Events and Information	Remarks and references to Appendices
L'HOMME MORT	1-7-17		Overcast, mainly some rain. Brigadier General & Brigade Major went with O.C. 1st South Staffs to select site for Battalion for forthcoming raid. In afternoon Brigade Major round line to see result of morning and found same not very satisfactory. Casualties - 21st Manchesters killed 2 or wounded 10 or. Reinforcements - 21st Manchesters 7 off 8 or. 2nd Manchesters 3 off and 9 or.	N.
	2-7-17		Full morning. Sunny afternoon. Brigadier General went round left sector with Divisional Commander in morning. Staff Capt round right sector in morning. In afternoon Brigade Major to H.Q. 20th Brigade to listen by Somerville from B.H.Q. in musketry. Casualties - 2 Queens 3 or wounded (1 at duty). 1st S. Staffs 1 or killed 1 or wounded at duty. 21st Manchesters 2 or wounded. Reinforcements Nil	N.2.
	3-7-17		Sunny, hot sheggy. Brigade Major went round line to further reconnoitre mine. Brigadier General visited 2nd Manchesters in St. Leger. 1st S. Staffs relieved 21st Manchesters in left sector in the evening. Casualties. 21st Manchesters 2 or wounded. Reinforcements Nil	App "A" N.2
	4-7-17		Rain early. Fine in afternoon. Brigadier General and Brigade Major round left sector in morning and visited all Battalion H.Q. on way back. Divisional Commander General Stanley Clarke came in afternoon to discuss raid. Casualties 21st Manchesters 10 off 5 or - 2 Queens wounded 1 or at duty. Reinforcements 82nd S Staffs also present. Casualties 21st Manchester wounded 1 or at duty. 2nd Manchesters 10 off 5 or - 2 Queens relieved by 2 Manchesters in right sector. 2 Queens to St LEGER.	N.

Army Form C. 2118.

WAR DIARY
or
INTELLIGENCE SUMMARY
(Erase heading not required.)

Place	Date	Hour	Summary of Events and Information	Remarks and references to Appendices
L'HOMME MORT	5.7.17		Cool & Overcast. Brigadier General & Brigade Major visit O.C. 1st S. Staffs in morning to rehearsal of raid. The Army Commander, Corps & Divisional Commander with members of their respective Staffs present at the rehearsal. Afterwards Brigadier & Brigade Major to a rehearsal by 2nd Gordons 20th Brigade of their proposed raid. Casualties Nil. Reinforcements 2 Queens 3 o.r.	N.
	6.7.17		Hot & Sunny. Brigadier & Brigade Major visit O.C. 16th Siege Battery, O.C. 1st S. Staffords & Attwood round left sector in morning reconnaissance for raid. C.R.E. called. Operation orders for raid issued. Casualties 2nd Queens 1 o.r. wounded. 1st S. Staffs 1 o.r. wounded at duty. 2 & 2nd Manchesters 1 o.r. Killed 1 o.r. wounded 8 o.r. b. at camp. Reinforcements Nil.	App "B" M.
	7.7.17		Sunny very hot. Brigadier Brigade Major & final rehearsal of raid in morning. Col. Howard and Major Boyd (new B.S.O.2) called 2nd Queens moved from St Leger Chateau to camp on ERVILLERS - St LEGER Road on account of shelling in St LEGER. Staff Captain round line in afternoon. 20th Inf. Bde. took over line on night from 22nd Inf. Brigade. Casualties 1st S. Staffs. wounded 3 o.r. 2 at duty. 21st Manchesters wounded 2 o.r. 22nd Manchesters wounded 3 o.r. 91st Machine Gun Co wounded 1 o.r. Reinforcements 1st S. Staffs 1 W. 21st Manchesters 1 Officer.	M.

WAR DIARY or INTELLIGENCE SUMMARY

Army Form C. 2118.

Place	Date	Hour	Summary of Events and Information	Remarks and references to Appendices
L'HOMMÉ MORT	8/9/17		Very heavy thunderstorms and rain during night 7/8th. Rain morning. Sunny afternoon. Divisional Commander called and it was decided to postpone raid of 1st S. Staffs. Orders issued accordingly. Orders also issued for relief of 1/1 S.S. Staffs on night of 9th-10th. Divisional Commander anxious about defence of the Hump and posts in that vicinity ordered the advanced shortroad. Further wiring carried out by 528th Field Co at night - Casualties 22nd Manchesters 1 or. wounded. 91st Machine Gun Co wounded 1 or. - Reinforcements 21st Manchesters 46 ors - 22nd Manchesters 62 ors	App 'C' M.
	9/9/17		Full day raining - Brigade Major round line up Knuckle Avenue and along Queens Avenue. Inspect new work and New Cut. Implement on the 21st Manchesters. L.O.C. with O.C. 528 Field Co and O.C. 1/5 S. Staffs to see Hindenburg Support line near HENIN - 21st Manchesters relieved 1st S. Staffs in line left of Queens Avenue. 22nd Manchesters took over up to Queens Avenue - Casualties 1/5 S. Staffs wounded 1 or. (self inflicted) 22nd Manchesters killed 1 or. wounded 1 or. Reinforcements 1/5 S. Staffs 10 ors. 21st Manchesters 2 ors.	App 'D' M.
	10/9/17		Sunny & cool. 4 O.C. & Staff Capt round trenches early. 2nd Queens working on new communication trench (Queens Avenue) at night. Brigade Major went up to see the Knuckle. Gas Bombardment on Boesleux work. Pioneers wiring in front of the Knuckle. Casualties Machine Gun Corps 2 ors (gas wounds), 1 or. Support lines at night. 1 or. S. Staffs 12 or. 21st Manchesters 3 Officers Reinforcements 1 or. S. Staffs 12 or. 21st Manchesters 3 Officers	A. M.

Army Form C. 2118.

WAR DIARY
or
INTELLIGENCE SUMMARY
(Erase heading not required.)

Instructions regarding War Diaries and Intelligence Summaries are contained in F. S. Regs., Part II. and the Staff Manual respectively. Title Pages will be prepared in manuscript.

Place	Date	Hour	Summary of Events and Information	Remarks and references to Appendices
1. HOHAE MORT	11-7-17		Sunny Cool. Brigade Major & Staff Captain to Trenches at Knuckle Avenue and back by Queens Avenue now dug through. Orders for relief on nights 12/13 & 15/16 issued. Casualties 2nd Queens killed 1 o.r. wounded 1 o.r. 21st Manchesters wounded 1 o.r. (accidental) - M.G. Co wounded 1 o.r. Reinforcements 21st Manchesters 4 o.r.	A.2.
	12-7-17		Sunny very hot - Brigadier round line in morning to see Queens Avenue - went Pelican Avenue and along front line to Queens Avenue back by Knuckle Avenue also visited 22nd Manchesters H.Q. - 2nd Queens relieved 22nd Manchesters in evening the latter moving back to Tangier Camp - 1st South Staffords out digging Stafford Avenue at night - Brigade Major in evening to see rehearsal of 1st South Stafford raid - Casualties 21st Manchesters wounded 10 o.r. - Reinforcements Nil	App "E" A.2.
	13-7-17		Fine very hot. Brigade Major to H.Q. 2nd Queens in line to meet Divisional Commander but could not proceed round line on account of shoot by heavy artillery on the Mebus opposite place of proposed raid - from Brigadier Brigade Major in afternoon tree demonstration of blowing up a dug out by 528 Field Co. R.E. Report received from 2nd Queens at 11.30 p.m. that Enemy had moved stakes Mebus No 1 - and hot had accordingly been withdrawn - Casualties Nil - Reinforcements Nil	A.2.
	14-7-17		Very hot - rain in afternoon - In the evening 1st South Staffords made a raid which was not successful. Casualties wounded 2nd Queens wounded 1 o.r. 91st Machine Gun Co 2 o.r. 1 Officer 9 o.r. Reinforcements 21st Manchesters 1 o.r.	App "F" A.2.

Army Form C. 2118.

WAR DIARY
or
INTELLIGENCE SUMMARY
(Erase heading not required.)

Instructions regarding War Diaries and Intelligence Summaries are contained in F.S. Regs., Part II. and the Staff Manual respectively. Title Pages will be prepared in manuscript.

Place	Date	Hour	Summary of Events and Information	Remarks and references to Appendices
L'HOMME MORT	15/7/17		Hot Muggy. Brigade Major round Trenches in morning. Saw new Aid Post dug out in left sector; also along STRANGEWAYS. Saw new Trench dug by 1st South Staffords. Divisional Commander called with G.S.O.1. Heard about raid Brigadier planned to detail cant. to interview O/C Woof & raiding party of 1/C South Staffords. Casualties 2nd Queens Killed 1 or. wounded 8 or. 1st South Staffs Killed 5 or. wounded 1 offr. 15 or. Reinforcements Nil	App "G" K2.
	16.7.17		Sunny warm. Brigadier & Staff Captain round the line in the morning. In the afternoon the Brigadier & Brigade Major saw demonstration by "J" Special Company R.E. of firing burning oil out of projectors. Brigade Major with O.C. 2nd Queens in the evening to reconnoitre a suitable site for Reserve line but were unable to complete this owing to darkness. Casualties Nil. Reinforcements Nil.	N.L.
	17.7.17		Fine & hot. Brigadier and Staff Captain to visit Brigade on our left. Brigade Major & O.C. 528 Field Co. R.E. up the line in evening and completed the siting of the Manchester Reserve line, then on to inspect the new wire along Queens Avenue. Sites for winter camps for Brigade HQ. and two battalions decided on the new DRILLERS to work on same directed to begin. Casualties 22nd Manchesters wounded 1.O.R. accidental. Reinforcements 1st S. Staffords 1 Offr. 27 or. 91st Machine Gun Co 5 or.	N.L.

WAR DIARY
or
INTELLIGENCE SUMMARY

(Erase heading not required.)

Army Form C. 2118.

Place	Date	Hour	Summary of Events and Information	Remarks and references to Appendices
MONT L'HOMME MORT	18.7.17		Fine, very hot + heavy. Very quiet all day. The 22nd Infantry Brigade relieved the 20th Brigade on our right. Officer came in evening to superintend discharge of gas tonight but the wind proved unfavourable. Casualties 1st South Staffords wounded 1 o.r. Reinforcements Nil.	A.2.
	19.7.17		Cold but sunny. Brigadier and Brigade Major round the line in the morning by Knuckle Avenue + along to Dog Trench. Back by Queens Avenue etc. Queens H.Q. Staff Captain rode inspect progress of new huts for Camps and to Logeast Wood to inspect huts & the move up from there. Casualties 2nd Queens wounded 3 o.r. (two at duty). Reinforcements 22nd Manchesters 1 Off-Reinforcements Nil.	A.2.
	20.7.17		Breezy and Sunny. Brigadier round the line in the morning with General Haldane, the new Corps Commander. Brigade Major to inspect Brigade Bombing School. Also to see Bangalore Torpedo experiment in Left Sector in the afternoon. 2nd Queens relieved by 22nd Manchesters in the evening. Casualties 22nd Manchesters wounded 2 o.r. (accidental). Reinforcements Nil	App "H" A.2.
	21.7.17		Brigade Major round line with Divisional Commander who appeared himself so pleased with the state of the line. Brigadier Armiford Brigade Bombing Range from School. Capt. Watson 9th K.O.Y.L.I. from Cambridge Staff Course attached to Brigade Staff Captain to inspect arrangement of huts from Logeast Wood for winter Camps. Hot + Sunny day. Casualties 1st S. Staffs wounded 1 o.r. (accidental) Reinforcements Nil.	A.2.

WAR DIARY
or
INTELLIGENCE SUMMARY

(Erase heading not required.)

Army Form C. 2118.

Place	Date	Hour	Summary of Events and Information	Remarks and references to Appendices
L'HOMME MORT	22.7.17		Fine & sunny. Relief and Bde Major to visit Queens in morning. Staff Captain to railway entrainment to support battalions. Brigadier and Brigade Major to Puisieux Ridge to watch demonstration in afternoon by Queens. Bde Major stayed at Queens. Reinforcements 22nd Manchester 1 officer.	App "I"
	23.7.17		Very fine. Staff Captain round line in morning. Brigadier and Bde Major to Puisieux Range in afternoon to witness demonstration of attack by Queens. 21st Manchester's relieve 1st S. Staffs in left subsector. Casualties 1st S. Staffs wounded 2 O.R. Reinforcements 21st Manchester 7 O.R. 22nd Manchester 1 off. 36 O.R.	App "I"
	24.7.17		Fine but close. Brigadier & Bde Major round lines in morning. Staff Captain to Support Battalions' camps. Casualties 1st S. Staffs killed 1 O.R. wounded 2 (1st at duty). Reinforcements 1st S. Staffs 1 off. 22 O.R.	App "I"
	25.7.17		Hot & close - sharp thunderstorm in afternoon. Brigadier & Staff Captain to Support Battalions Camps. Brigade Major round the line with G.S.O.I. Casualties 21st Manchester killed 1 O.R. wounded 2 O.R. (1st at duty) Reinforcements 9 Int. G. Coy 1 O.R.	App "I"
	26.7.17		Close two day. Brigadier round line in morning; Brigade Major in afternoon. So this two battalions to HERSECOURT by rail arriving at noon. Casualties 21st Queens wounded 2 O.R. 21st Manchester wounded 5 O.R. Reinforcements nil.	App "I"

WAR DIARY or INTELLIGENCE SUMMARY

Army Form C. 2118.

Place	Date	Hour	Summary of Events and Information	Remarks and references to Appendices
L'HOMME MORT	27.7.17		Very fine, hot. Brigade Major went lines in morning with 4.O.C. 22nd Bn. Div. Comm., C.R.A. & R.E. called at Bde H.Q. Brigadier to Camps in afternoon. Wide demonstration entrained by working party 2nd Queens & 1st S. Staff. Casualties 21st Manchesters wounded 1 Officer (at duty), 22nd Manchesters wounded 6 Officers (3 at duty) 3 O.R. (2 at duty); Reinforcements 2nd Queens 11 O.R. 91 nom. 9 Coy. 1 O.R.	App
	28.7.17		Exceptionally hot. Brigadier & Bde Major went line in morning. Brigadier to Bde School to lecture on termination of course in afternoon. Casualties 22nd Manchesters wounded 1 O.R. 1st S. Staff wounded 1 O.R. (self inflicted) 22nd Manchester wounded 1 O.R.	App "K"
	29.7.17		Reinforcements nil. Sharp storm in morning, still air dry. Brigade major to Queens HQ in afternoon. 2O/C Captain to Support Battalion Camps. Casualties 2nd Queens wounded 1 Officer (at duty) 21st Manchesters killed 1 O.R. Reinforcements 1 D. Staff 11 O.R. 22nd Manchesters 1 Off. 6 O.R. 22nd Manchesters 8 O.R. Bde at night.	App
	30.7.17		Brigadier & Brigade Major went lines in morning. Staff Captain up to Camps in afternoon to recommend light duty minimum. Casualties 2nd Queens killed 1 O.R. 10 O.R. wounded 1 O.R. (at duty). Reinforcements 2nd Queens 6 O.R.	App

Army Form C. 2118.

WAR DIARY
or
INTELLIGENCE SUMMARY

(Erase heading not required.)

Instructions regarding War Diaries and Intelligence Summaries are contained in F. S. Regs., Part II. and the Staff Manual respectively. Title Pages will be prepared in manuscript.

Place	Date	Hour	Summary of Events and Information	Remarks and references to Appendices
L'HOMME MORT	3/7/17		Still Warm - Army Commander and Divisional Commander visited the line with the Brigadier - Army Commander expressed his satisfaction at the state of the sector held by the Brigade. Major Bree Battalion in support in the afternoon - Staff Captain amongst winter camps. 1st South Staffords relieved 21st Manchesters in left sub sector the latter moving back to PATRICIA CAMP. Casualties Queens 1 or wounded at 9 a/s. Reinforcements Nil	K.

M.T. Pilly
Brigadier General
Commanding 91st Infantry Brigade

SECRET.

91st Infantry Brigade Order No. 7.

Copy No. 19.

Reference Map – HENDECOURT, Edition 1.
— Scale 1/20,000.

Monday, 2nd July, 1917.

"A"

1. The following reliefs will take place as under:—
   (a) On night July 3rd/4th, 1st Bn. South Staffordshire Regt., will relieve 21st Bn. Manchester Regt., in the Left Sub-sector, 21st Bn. Manchester Regt., being withdrawn into Brigade Support.
   (2) On night July 4/5th, 22nd Bn. Manchester Regt., will relieve 2nd Bn. Queen's Regt., in the Right Sub-sector, 2nd Bn. Queen's Regt., being withdrawn into Brigade Reserve in ST.LEGER.

2. All details of reliefs will be arranged between Commanding Officers concerned, a copy of Battalion Relief Orders being forwarded to this office.

3. Completion of relief will be reported to Brigade Headquarters.

4. ACKNOWLEDGE.

Captain,
Brigade Major, 91st Infantry Brigade.

Issued at ... p.m. to
Copy No. 1 2nd Queen's R.
        2 1st S. Staffs. R.
        3 21st Manch. R.
        4 22nd Manch. R.
        5 91st M.G. Coy.
        6 No. 3 Sec. 7th Div. Sigs.
        7 91st T.M. Battery.
        8 91st Bde. Gren. Coy.
        9 Staff Captain.
       10 Bde. Transport Officer.
       11 A.D.M.S.
       12 O.C. Left Group, R.A.
       13 528 (Durham) Fd. Coy.
       14 Supply Officer.
       15 7th Division.
       16 22nd Inf. Bde.
       17 64th Inf. Bde.
       18 File.
       19 War Diary.
       20 War Diary.

SECRET.

Copy No 16

"B"

91st Infantry Brigade Order No. 8.

Friday, 6th July, 1917.

Reference Map - HENDECOURT, Edition 1.
- Scale 1/20,000.

1. (a) A Raid will be carried out by 1st Bn. South Staffordshire Regt. on enemy trenches between U.20.b.4.7. and U.20.b.35.95. on night 8/9th July, 1917, with the object of obtaining an identification, killing or capturing the hostile garrison and destroying the suspected tunnel dug-out by means of "P" Bombs.
    (b) Simultaneously with this Raid the 2nd Bn. Gordon Highlanders will be carrying out a raid in the vicinity of U.22.a.4.4.

2. ZERO hour will be notified later.

3. (a) The Artillery programme is shewn on barrage map attached.
    (b) Continuance of the barrage after ZERO plus 30 minutes can be secured by sending the word "RABBIT....minutes" to Brigade Headquarters.
    (c) A Liaison Officer will be at Advanced Battalion Headquarters U.20.b.3.3. throughout the operations.

4. The Officer Commanding, 91st Machine Gun Company will arrange:-
    (a) To barrage the following areas from ZERO till ZERO plus 30 minutes or until cessation of our Artillery barrage:-
        (i) The enemy front line from U.14.d.1.4. to U.14.a.7.1.
        (ii) FAG ALLEY from U.15.a.0.9. to U.14.a.85.95.
        (iii) TRIDENT ALLEY from U.16.c.0.4. to U.21.a.85.40.
        (iv) The area bounded by U.21.a.5.7. - b.5.2. - d.1.5. - a.2.9.
    (b) To have a Liaison Officer at Advanced Battalion Headquarters U.20.b.3.3. throughout the operations.

5. (a) The Officer Commanding, 91st Trench Mortar Battery will arrange to place a slow barrage on the area bounded by U.14.a.9.2. - U.14.a.5.0. - U.14.d.3.4. - U.14.a.9.2.
    (b) The Officer Commanding, X7 (Medium) Trench Mortar Battery will bombard:-
        (a) The enemy front line in U.14.a. and c.
        (b) The enemy front line in U.21.a. and c. East of MEBUS at U.21.a.3.1.
    Both of above batteries will open fire at ZERO and cease fire at ZERO plus 30 minutes or on the cessation of our Artillery barrage.

6. Watches of 1st Bn. South Staffordshire Regt., 22nd Bn. Manchester Regt., and 91st Machine Gun Coy., will be synchronised by telephone at 5-15 p.m. on July 8th. Officers Commanding 91st Trench Mortar Battery and X7 Trench Mortar Battery will arrange to have a representative at one of above Battalion Headquarters at that hour.

7. Prisoners will be sent to Brigade Headquarters.

8. Return of Raiding Party will be reported by Fullerphone.

9. The Officer Commanding, 1st Bn. South Staffordshire Regt., will submit his scheme, based on above programme, to Brigade Headquarters for approval.

10. ACKNOWLEDGE.

Captain,

Brigade Major, 91st Infantry Brigade.

(Distribution over-leaf).

Issued at.....p.m. to :-

    Copy No 1 2nd Queen's R¹
            2 1st. S.Staffs.R¹
            3 21st. Manch.R¹
            4 22nd Manch.R¹
     x   5 91st M.G.Coy.
     xx   6 91st T.M.Bty.
     x   7 Div.T.M.Officer.
            8 O.C.,Left Group,R.A.
            9 7th Division.
          10 C.R.A.
     x   11 528th.(Durham) Fd.Coy.
          12 20th Inf.Bde.
     x   13 64th Inf.Bde.
          14 File.
          15)
          16) War Diary.

     x *Barrage Map not attached*

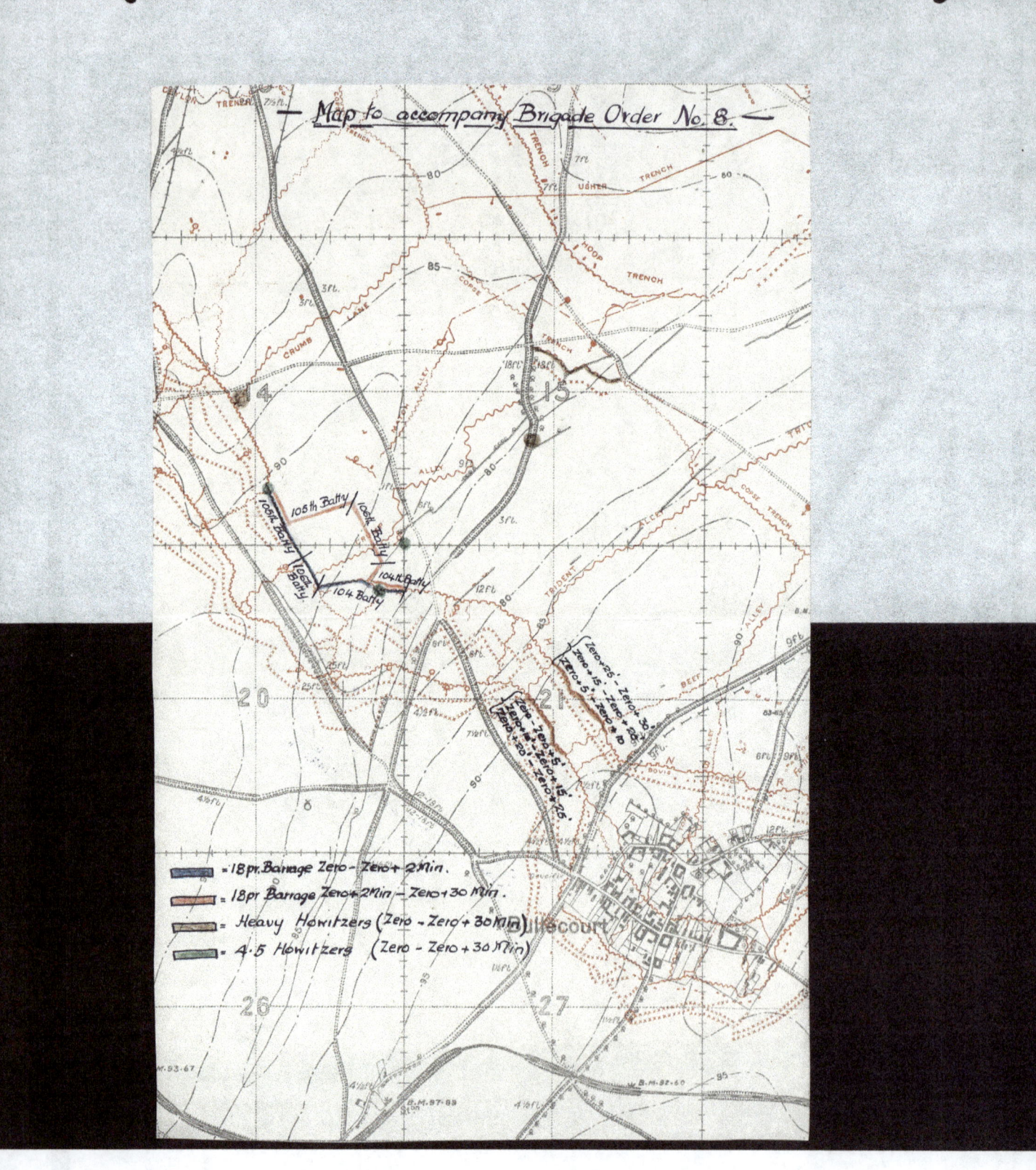

SECRET.

Copy No. 16

Amendment to 91st Infantry Brigade Order No.8.

"C"

8th July, 1917.

-:-:-:-:-:-:-:-:-

The Operation referred to in Brigade Order No.8., dated 6th July, 1917, is indefinately postponed.

[signature]
Captain,
Brigade Major, 91st Infantry Brigade.

Issued at 1-45.p.m. to All recipients of B.O.8. and 2nd Lieut. WOOD.

SECRET.

91st. Infantry Brigade Order No. 9.

Copy No. 19 "D"

Sunday, 8th July, 1917.

Reference Map — HENDECOURT — EU.1.
Scale 1/20,000.

1. On night 9/10th July, 1917:-
   (a) The 21st. Bn. Manchester Regt., will relieve 1st. Bn. South Staffordshire Regt., on that portion of the Brigade Front lying to the N.W. of the junction of QUEEN'S AVENUE, with the front line at U.20.a.9.6. (15 yards S.W. of MEBUS 5.)
   (b) The 22nd Bn. Manchester Regt., will take over that portion of the Front now held by 1st Bn. South Staffordshire Regt., lying to the S.E. of above point.

2. On night 10/11th July, 1917, the 22nd Bn. Manchester Regt., will be relieved on that portion of the Brigade Front on the Right of PELICAN AVENUE by 8th Bn. Devonshire Regt. (Headquarters U.27.d.6.5.).

3. All arrangements for above reliefs will be made between Commanding Officers concerned, a copy of Battalion Orders being sent to Brigade Headquarters.

4. Completion of reliefs will be reported to Brigade Headquarters by Fullergram.

5. On completion of relief the 1st. Bn. South Staffordshire Regt., will be withdrawn to PATRICIA CAMP (B.9.a.3.3.) and will be in Brigade Reserve.

6. After above reliefs the boundaries of the Right Sub-sector will run as follows:-
   (a) <u>Right Boundary.</u>

   PELICAN AVENUE from the front line to the Road at U.26.b.6.3. Thence the Road to the Railway Embankment at U.26.d.7.0., all inclusive.

   (b) <u>Left Boundary.</u>

   QUEEN'S AVENUE (inclusive) from the front line to KNUCKLE AVENUE at U.19.b.80.25. Thence KNUCKLE AVENUE (exclusive) to the Railway at U.25.a.7.6.

7. ACKNOWLEDGE.

O. Moorshead
Captain,
Brigade Major, 91st Infantry Brigade.

Issued at 9/15 p.m. to.
Copy No. 1. 2nd Queen's R.
2. 1st S. Staffs. R.
3. 21st. Manch. R.
4. 22nd. Manch. R.
5. 91st. M.G. Coy.
6. 91st. T.M. Bty.
7. 91st. Bde. Gren. School.
8. No. 3. Sec. Div. Sigs.
9. Staff Captain.
10. A.D.M.S.
11. Left Group, R.A.
12. 528th (Durham) Fd. Coy.
13. Supply Officer.
14. 7th Division.
15. 20th Inf. Bde.
16. 110th Inf. Bde.
17. Div. T.M. Officer.
18. File.
19. War Diary.
20. War Diary.

SECRET.   Copy No..20   "E"

91st Infantry Brigade Order No.10.

Wednesday, 11th July, 1917.

Reference Map - HENDECOURT - Edn.1.
             - Scale 1/20,000.

1. (a) On night July 12/13th, 2nd Bn. Queen's Regt., will relieve 22nd Bn. Manchester Regt., in the Right Sub-sector.
    (b) On night July 15/16th, 1st Bn. South Staffordshire Regt., will relieve 21st Bn. Manchester Regt., in the Left Sub-sector.

2. (a) On completion of relief on night July 12/13th, 22nd Bn. Manchester Regt., will be withdrawn to TANGIER CAMP (B.9.a.3.3.) and will be in Brigade Support.
        1st Bn. South Staffordshire Regt, will pass into Brigade Reserve.
    (b) On completion of relief on night July 15/16th, 21st Bn. Manchester Regt., will be withdrawn to PATRICIA CAMP, and will be in Brigade Reserve.

3. All details of above reliefs will be arranged between Commanding Officers concerned, a copy of Battalion Orders being sent to Brigade Headquarters.

4. Completion of reliefs will be reported to Brigade Headquarters by Fullergram.

5. ACKNOWLEDGE.

                                                                Captain,
                                            Brigade Major, 91st Infantry Brigade.

Issued at 4/15 p.m. to -

    Copy No 1 2nd Queen's R'
            2 1st. S. Staffs. R'
            3 21st Manch. R'
            4 22nd Manch. R'
            5 91st. M.G. Coy.
            6 91st. T.M. Bty.
            7 91st. Bde. Gren. School.
            8 No. 3. Sec. Div. Sigs.
            9 Staff Captain.
           10 A.D.M.S.
           11 Left Group, R.A.
           12 528th (Durham) Field Coy. R.E.
           13 Supply Officer.
           14 7th Division.
           15 20th Inf. Bde.
           16 110th Inf. Bde.
           17 Div. T.M. Officer.
           18 File.
           19 War Diary.
           20 War Diary.

S E C R E T.

Copy No. 16.

Amendments and Additions to 91st Infantry Brigade Order No.8.

Friday, 13th July, 1917. "F"

Reference Map :- HENDECOURT Edn.1.
 - Scale 1/20,000.

1. (a) Para.1(a) and para.6. for "night 8/9th July" read "night 14/15th July".
    (b) Para.3(a). Certain minor alterations in the Barrage Scheme have been made, details of which have been issued to Officer Commanding, 1st Bn. South Staffordshire Regt.
    (c) Para.3(b) is cancelled and the following substituted:-
    "The Artillery will continue to fire at a reduced rate until zero plus 60 minutes if required. Officer Commanding, 1st Bn. South Staffordshire Regt. will report to Brigade Headquarters by Fullerphone when the barrage is no longer required."
    (d) Para.4. For "zero plus 30 minutes" read "zero plus 60 minutes."
    (e) Para.5. is cancelled and the following substituted:-
    "(a) The Officer Commanding, 91st Trench Mortar Battery will arrange to place a slow barrage on the area bounded by U.14.c.9.2. - U.14.a.5.0. - U.14.d.3.4. - U.14.a.9.2. He will also arrange to bring a hurricane bombardment from 4 guns to bear on the objective of the raid from Zero to Zero plus 1 minute.
    (b) Two 2" Trench Mortars are firing on TUNNELL TRENCH from U.14.d.0.7. - U.14.d.2.2. and one 2" Trench Mortar at U.21.c.25.23. is engaging the 2 MEBUS at U.21.a.32.10. and U.21.a.42.13.
    The fire of all Trench Mortars will continue until Zero plus 60 minutes or until cessation of our Artillery barrage."

2. Zero hour will be 11-30.p.m.

3. The Officer Commanding, 2nd Bn. Queen's Regt., and 21st Bn. Manchester Regt., will arrange for MEBUS Nos. 4 and 6 to be cleared for use throughout the operations as Raid Headquarters and Advanced Dressing Station respectively.

4. The Officer Commanding, 528th (Durham) Field Coy. R.E. will detail two parties of 3 men each for destroying dug-out entrances on either flank, and 2 pairs of men for dealing with the MEBUS on either flank.

5. Smoke is being released at zero hour if weather conditions are favourable on the area between U.21.c.3.1. and U.20.d.9.5., under arrangements to be made by the Divisional Gas Officer.

6. ACKNOWLEDGE.

Captain,
Brigade Major, 91st Infantry Brigade.

Issued at 9. p.m. to :-

All recipients of B.O.8., and 110th Infantry Brigade.

REPORT ON RAID CARRIED OUT BY 1ST BN. SOUTH STAFFORDSHIRE REGT.,
NIGHT 14/15th JULY, 1917.

The Objective, composition of Raiding Party, Artillery, Trench Mortar and Machine Gun programme are set out in the Operation Orders, a copy of which is attached.

"G"

NARRATIVE.

11-15.p.m.   By this hour our wire had been cleared and the Raiding Party were formed up in the Sunken Road at U.20.b.2.6., ready to advance.

11-30.p.m.   Artillery and Trench Mortar Bombardment commenced
(ZERO).   and party started to move forward. Enemy's Machine Guns and Trench Mortars immediately opened fire, the latter paying special attention to the Sunken Road where our party formed up.
             The three parties in the assaulting line (Right, Centre and Left parties) moved up close behind the barrage to within 60 yards of the enemy trench.
             The carrying party in rear became somewhat broken up and cut off from the front line by a heavy barrage of Trench Mortar and pineapple Bombs. Throughout the 2 minutes bombardment the enemy continued to man his parapet and kept up a steady rifle and Machine Gun fire on our advancing line, causing several casualties.

11-32.p.m.   The barrage lifted.
             THE RIGHT PARTY attempted to rush the MEBUS at U.20.b.4.6., but were held up by a Machine Gun located in the trench a few yards to the North of the MEBUS. The leader of this party (Sergeant ALLCHURCH) and one man managed to work their way up to within bombing distance of the gun which they succeeded in putting out of action with Mills Grenades.
             Meanwhile a party of about 12 Germans were discovered working round the right flank of the remainder of the Right party. A lively encounter took place the enemy being driven off with Rifle Grenades and Rifle fire.
             THE CENTRE PARTY was also held up by heavy Machine Gun fire but the leader, 2nd Lieut. T.N.WOOF, M.C., and one man succeeded in getting into the enemy trench. A strong party of Germans came down the trench from the North into whom our men threw bombs. The enemy retaliated with Stick Bombs and 2nd Lieut. WOOF finding that the remainder of the party were not in the trench withdrew with his only man to a shell hole outside the parapet, from which they continued to bomb the trench, in the hopes of being able to cover the advance of the remainder.
             THE LEFT PARTY came under heavy fire from the MEBUS at U.20.b.2.8., near which a Machine Gun was mounted. A trench all round the MEBUS was also manned.
             They found another post between the MEBUS and the trench due East of the MEBUS (presumably at the saphead shewn on aeroplane photographs).
             During their advance they had encountered a post of 6 men about 30 yards West of the MEBUS who fled at their approach.
             The party told off for the attack of the MEBUS kept its garrison occupied, Sergeant HORAN getting on the roof and bombing from there until wounded, while the remainder pushed on.
             Before reaching the trench they encountered strong sunken wire which delayed their progress.
             The N.C.O. in charge of this party reports that they got through the wire, but were unable to get into the enemy trench owing to the fire of a Stokes Gun which was continuing its fire on their objective. The Stokes Gun was making very good shooting, most of its bombs dropping in the trench, where the enemy were heard shouting and running about in considerable confusion.

                                                      (continued).

-2-

This party assert that had it not been for the Stokes Gun, they could have effected an entry into the trench.

12-15.a.m. As the enemy's Machine Gun and Rifle fire were holding things up and there seemed little chance of carrying out the plan through as arranged, The Officer Commanding, 1st Bn.South Staffordshire Regt., ordered the recall signal to be made and the party returned to our lines.

GENERAL.
1. The Raiding party consider that the bombardment should have been heavier or that there should have been none at all. As it was it is thought that it caused the enemy to be on the alert without driving him to ground.

2. The enemy's trench was about 5 feet deep.

3. Several snipers were out in NO MAN'S LAND.

4. Useful information as to the enemy's dispositions was obtained.

5. Considerable casualties are known to have been inflicted on the enemy, and a Machine Gun was put out of action.

6. Our casualties were :-

RAIDING PARTY.

Unit.	Killed.	Wounded.	Missing.
1st Bn.S.Staffs.Regt.	5	1 Officer. 15 O.R.	1

TROOPS HOLDING THE LINE.

Unit.	Killed.	Wounded.	Missing.
2nd Bn.Queen's Regt.	1	8	-
21st Bn.Manch.Regt.	-	3 (includes 1 still at duty).	-

Bde.Hd.Qtrs.
15th July,1917.

R.T.Pelly
Brigadier General,
Commanding,91st Infantry Brigade.

SECRET.   Copy No. 20

91st Infantry Brigade Order No. 11.

Thursday, 19th July, 1917.

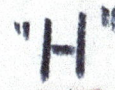

Reference Map - HENDECOURT, Edn.1.
– Scale 1/20,000.

1. (a) On night July 20th/21st, the 22nd Bn. Manchester Regt., will relieve 2nd Bn. Queen's Regt., in the Right Sub-sector.
   (b) The 2nd Bn. Queen's Regt. (less one Company) will be withdrawn to TANGIER CAMP and will be in Support to the Right Sub-sector.

2. (a) On night July 23rd/24th, the 21st Bn. Manchester Regt., will relieve 1st Bn. South Staffordshire Regt., in the Left Sub-sector.
   (b) The 1st Bn. South Staffordshire Regt. (less one Company) will be withdrawn to PATRICIA CAMP and will be in Support to the Left Sub-sector.

3. All details of above reliefs will be arranged between Commanding Officers concerned, a copy of Battalion Orders being sent to Brigade Headquarters.

4. Completion of reliefs will be reported to Brigade Headquarters by Fullergram.

5. ACKNOWLEDGE.

                                                    Ohhorshind
                                                    Captain,
                                        Brigade Major, 91st Infantry Brigade.

Issued at 6 p.m. to

        Copy No 1 2nd Queen's R'
                 2 1st S.Staffs.R'
                 3 21st Manch.R'
                 4 22nd Manch.R'
                 5 91st M.G.Coy.
                 6 91st T.M.Bty.
                 7 91st Bde.School.
                 8 No.3.Sec.Div.Sigs.
                 9 Staff Captain.
                10 A.D.M.S.
                11 Loft Group, R.A.
                12 528th (Durham) Fd.Coy.R.E.
                13 Supply Officer.
                14 7th Division.
                15 22nd Inf.Bde.
                16 110th Inf.Bde.
                17 Div.T.M.Officer.
                18 File.
                19 War Diary.
                20 War Diary.

SECRET.

Copy No. 17

91st Infantry Brigade.

DEFENCE SCHEME.

Reference Maps –
- FRANCE 51B. S.W. – Scale 1/20,000.
  " 57C. N.W. – Scale 1/20,000
  Sketch Map attached.

"1"

1. **DISPOSITIONS.**

    (a) The Brigade Sector extends from U.21.c.45.15. to U.14.a.0.0. and is held by two battalions, the remaining battalions (less one company each) being in Support to their respective sectors at PATRICIA and TANGIER Camps, B.9.a.3.3. Reliefs take place every 6 days.
    The extent of the Sector, Dispositions and Machine Gun and Trench Mortar Emplacements are shown on attached map.

    (b) One Company of each Supporting Battalion is allotted to its corresponding front line Battalion for work in the forward area. These Companies are quartered in the RAILWAY LINE and are relieved every two days.

    (c) 4 Machine Guns of Divisional Machine Gun Company (shown in green on attached map) are allotted to this Sector. The remaining 8 guns of 91st Machine Gun Company are in reserve at Details Camp B.9.c.

    (d) There are at present 7 Stokes Mortar Emplacements in the front line. Two guns are kept in the front line, two in STRANGWAYS RESERVE and the remainder at Headquarters, 91st Trench Mortar Battery, (U.26.c.0.8.)

    (e) MANCHESTER RESERVE will shortly be dug, and will accommodate the counter-attack company of the Right Sector.

    (f) Dugouts capable of holding Company Headquarters, a Support Platoon and a Machine Gun Team will shortly be constructed in QUEEN'S AVENUE, KNUCKLE AVENUE and STAFFORD AVENUE. As these become available, one platoon will be withdrawn to them from each front line company, its function being to man the fire bays in the Communication Trench while the counter-attack company acts.

    All of the above trenches are in process of being fire-stepped and wired on both sides for flank defence.

2. **ARTILLERY.**

    The front is covered by the 22nd Brigade, R.F.A. A Liaison Officer is attached to each front line Battalion and Battalions are in direct communication with the batteries covering their front.
    The S.O.S. Lines are shown on attached map.

3. **ACTION IN CASE OF ATTACK.**

    (a) The front line is the main line of resistance. Should the enemy succeed in effecting an entrance, he will be driven out by a local counter-attack delivered IMMEDIATELY by the Commander on the spot.

    (b) The Officer Commanding Counter-attack Company of the Sector concerned will send forward patrols to ascertain the situation, and will at once organise a counter-attack without waiting for further orders.
    Pending completion of the dugout referred to in para. 1(f) above, one platoon of the counter-attack company of the Right Sector will be sent up to man the fire bays in QUEEN'S AVENUE.

    (c) The Reserve Company will be moved up, under the orders of the Battalion Commander concerned, to take the place of the counter-attack company; its role will depend on the development of events.

    (d) The Company/

(d) The Company on loan from the Support Battalion (vide para.1.(b) above) will hold the RAILWAY LINE until the arrival of the remainder of its Battalion, when it will again come under the orders of its own Battalion Commander.

In case of necessity this Company may be employed by the forward Battalion Commander, after reference to Brigade Headquarters (unless the telephone wire is cut, in which case this is not necessary). In any event notification of its employment will be sent by runner to Brigade Headquarters and to The Officer Commanding Support Battalion concerned.

(e) The garrisons of all supporting posts will hold on.

(f) On the order "DEFENCE MOVE", both Supporting Battalions will assemble in the Valley in B.10.a. and d., The Commanding Officers reporting in advance to Brigade Headquarters. Each Supporting Battalion will send forward a Liaison Officer to its corresponding front line battalion.

If required to move up in support, the route for either battalion will be via the HOG'S BACK to the area in the vicinity of T.30.d.8.5. The route and locality are labelled, and Battalion Commanders will have this reconnoitred at the earliest opportunity.

(g) On the order "DEFENCE MOVE", The Officer Commanding, 91st Machine Gun Company will bring up his reserve guns, placing two at the disposal of each sub-sector commander and retaining four in reserve at his Headquarters.

On seeing the S.O.S.Signal on the Brigade Front, all machine guns will open bursts of fire on their S.O.S.Lines.

(h) All WORKING PARTIES in the front line system will man the fire bays of the Communication Trench or STRANGEWAYS RESERVE, according to their locality, the Officer in charge reporting to the nearest Company Commander.

4. Preparedness for attack is the best defence. Battalion Commanders will ensure that all subordinate commanders realise the probable situations they may have to meet, and have definite plans formulated to deal with them.

5. ACKNOWLEDGE.

Bde.Hd.Qtrs.

Captain,

22nd July, 1917.   Brigade Major, 91st Infantry Brigade.

Copies to -

Copy No			
1	2nd Queen's R	10	22nd Bde.R.F.A.
2	1st S.Staffs.R	11	528th (Durham) Fd.Coy.
3	21st Manch.R	12	7th Division.
4	22nd Manch.R	13	20th Inf.Bde.
5	91st M.G.Coy.	14	22nd Inf.Bde.
6	91st T.M.Bty.	15	110th Inf.Bde.
7	No.3.Sec.Div.Sigs.	16	File.
8	Staff Captain.	17	War Diary.
9	C.R.A.	18	War Diary.

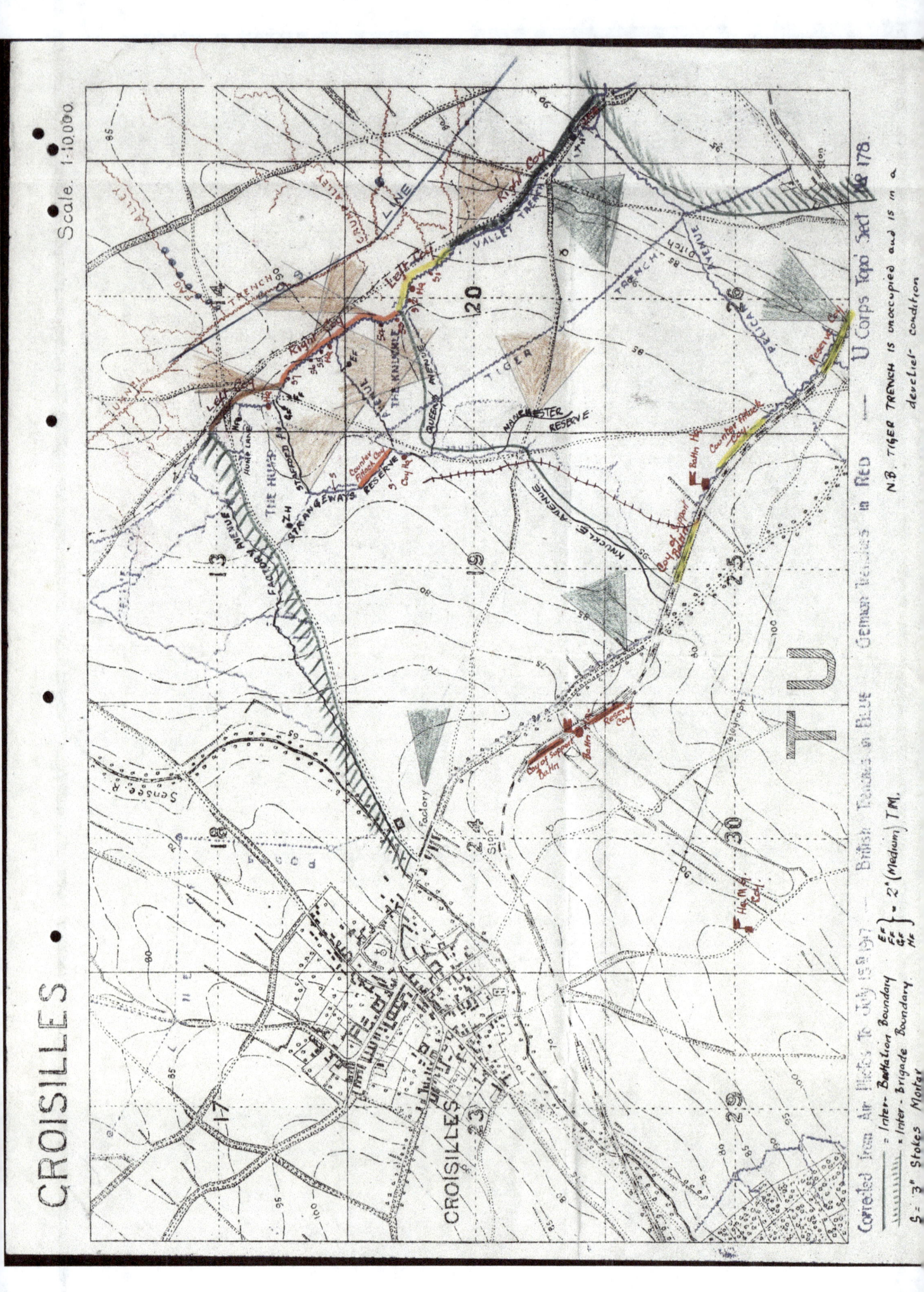

S E C R E T.

Copy No. 20

91st Infantry Brigade Order No.12.

Friday, 27th July, 1917.

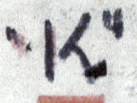

Reference Map - CHERISY -
Scale 1/10,000.

1. (a) On night July 28/29th, 2nd Bn. Queen's Regt., will relieve 22nd Bn. Manchester Regt., in the Right Sub-sector.
   (b) The 22nd Bn. Manchester Regt. (less one Company) will be withdrawn to TANGIER CAMP and will be in support to the Right Sub-sector.

2. (a) On night July 31st/Aug. 1st., 1st Bn. South Staffordshire Regt., will relieve 21st Bn. Manchester Regt., in the Left Sub-sector.
   (b) The 21st Bn. Manchester Regt., (less one Company) will be withdrawn to PATRICIA CAMP and will be in support to the Left Sub-sector.

3. The outgoing battalions will in each case be responsible for all work in the front line system on the night of relief.

4. All details of above reliefs will be arranged between Commanding Officers concerned, a copy of Battalion Orders being sent to Brigade Headquarters.

5. Completion of reliefs will be reported to Brigade Headquarters by Fullerphone.

6. ACKNOWLEDGE.

Captain,
Brigade Major, 91st Infantry Brigade.

Issued at 1/30 p.m. to -
Copy No 1 2nd Queen's R¹
        2 1st S. Staffs. R¹
        3 21st Manch. R¹
        4 22nd Manch. R¹
        5 91st M.G. Coy.
        6 91st T.M. Bty.
        7 91st Bde. School.
        8 No.3.Sec. 7th Div. Sigs.
        9 Staff Captain.
       10 A.D.M.S.
       11 Left Group, R.A.
       12 528th (Durham) Fd. Coy. R.E.
       13 Supply Officer.
       14 7th Division.
       15 22nd Inf. Bde.
       16 110th Inf. Bde.
       17 Div. T.M. Officer.
       18 File.
       19 War Diary.
       20 War Diary.

S E C R E T.

7th Division No.
G.938

7th Div.R.A.
C. R. E.
20th Infantry Brigade.
22nd Infantry Brigade.
91st Infantry Brigade.
"Q"

With reference to this office No. G.631 dated 23rd June, on the night 9th/10th July the boundary between the right and left Sectors will be altered as follows :-

PELICAN AVENUE as far as the road at U.26.b. 6.3., thence the road to the railway embankment at U.26.d. 7.0. (all inclusive to the left Sector).

All arrangements for this alteration will be made by the Brigade Commanders concerned. The completion of the re-adjustment will be reported to Divisional Headquarters.

Lieut-Colonel.
7th July, 1917. General Staff, 7th Division.

SECRET

Copy No. 13.

20th INFANTRY BRIGADE ORDER No 146.

Ref: Map
ECOUST ST MEIN 1/10,000.

9th July, 1917.

1. On the night of 10th/11th July, 1917, the 8th DEVON REGIMENT will relieve the 22nd Manchester Regiment 91st Infantry Brigade on that portion of the front between the present left post of the 20th INFANTRY BRIGADE about U.21.d.0.2. and PELICAN AVENUE.

2. All arrangements for this relief will be made between Commanding Officers concerned.

3. Completion of this relief will be reported to Brigade Headquarters by wire by the code word "MACKEREL".

4. The left boundary of the Brigade Sector will, on completion of the above relief, run as follows:-

   PELICAN AVENUE as far as the road at U.28.b.6.3., thence the road to the railway embankment at U.28.d.7.0. (all inclusive to the Left Sector).

5. ACKNOWLEDGE.

Issued at 2.50 p.m.

A.N.Neland
Major.
Brigade Major.
20th Infantry Brigade.

Copy No 1. Brigade Major.
2. Staff Captain.
3. 8th Devon Regt.
4. 9th Devon Regt.
5. 2nd Border Regt.
6. 2nd Gordon Highlanders.
7. 20th Coy. M.G. Corps.
8. 20th T.M. Battery.
9. Brigade Signals.
10. Brigade Bomb Coy.
11. War Diary.
12. War Diary.
13. 91st Infantry Brigade.
14. 7th Division.
15. 95th Field Coy, R.E.
16. 35th Brigade R.F.A.
17. 7th Division Artillery.

SECRET.

LAKE
OPERATION ORDERS NO. 71.

Copy No. 6.

Ref: HENDECOURT 1:20:000 Ed.1.
51 B. S.W.

15th JULY, 1917.

1. On the night 15/16th July LAKE (less B. Company) will be relieved in the Left Sub-Sector by SEA.

2. The following is the detail of relief by Companies:-

    A. Coy LAKE will be relieved by A. Coy SEA who will move forward from the RAILWAY EMBANKMENT at 8.30 p.m.
    D. Coy LAKE will be relieved by B. Coy SEA who will move forward from the RAILWAY EMBANKMENT at 8.45 p.m.
    C. Coy LAKE will be relieved by D. Coy SEA who will move forward from the RAILWAY EMBANKMENT at 10.30 p.m.

3. B. Company LAKE will remain in its present position and come under the orders of Officer Commanding SEA on completion of relief.

4. On completion of relief Companies will move out via KNUCKLE AVENUE to BATTALION HEADQUARTERS where O.C. DETAILS will arrange to guide Companies to PATRICIA CAMP.

5. All trench stores including picks and shovels will be handed over to relieving Companies of SEA. Receipts to be obtained and handed in to BATTALION HEADQUARTERS when Companies march out.

6. The Transport Officer will arrange for 1 Limber per Company for Lewis Guns and Officer's Mess Kit to be at BATTALION HEADQUARTERS at the following times:-
    D. Company 9.30 p.m.
    A.   "   10.0 p.m.
    C.   "   12 midnight.
he will also arrange for the conveyance of CANTEEN & HEADQUARTER Stores.

7. Relief complete will be sent to BATTALION HEADQUARTERS by Fullergram code word DERWENTWATER. Company Commanders will also report personally to BATTALION HEADQUARTERS.

8. ACKNOWLEDGE.

Issued at 2.30 p.m. by RUNNER.

Lieut: & Adjt,
LAKE.

Copies to:-
1. Commanding Officer.
2. O.C. A. Company.
3.   B.   "
4.   C.   "
5.   D.   "
6. WATER.
7. WAVE.
8. SEA.
9. Q.M. & T.O.
10. R.S.M.
11. War Diary.
12.   do.
13. File.
14.   do.

7th DIVISION.

B. H. Q.

91st INFANTRY BRIGADE.

AUGUST 1917.

WAR DIARY
or
INTELLIGENCE SUMMARY   HQ 91 Infy Bde

Army Form C. 2118.

(Erase heading not required.)

Place	Date	Hour	Summary of Events and Information	Remarks and references to Appendices
L'HOMME MORT	1/8/17		Hot and cold. Staff Captain round the line up KNUCKLE AVENUE and by QUEENS AVENUE and visited both Battalion Headquarters – Divisional Commander visited Brigade Headquarters in morning – Brigadier visited reserve Battalion – Casualties – (Manchesters wounded 1 or (accidental)) Reinforcements Nil	Nil
	2/8/17		Hot – cold. Brigadier – Brigade Major went round the line in the morning The Staff Capt. went to Divisional HQ for conference connected with leave. – In the afternoon the Brigadier inspected all transport & animals of all units preparatory to the Corps commanders inspection. Casualties Nil. Reinforcements Nil.	Nil
	3/8/17		Hot & cold. Brigadier round line with G.O.C. 21st Division in the morning. Brigadier General commanding 64th Infantry Brigade called at Brigade Headquarters in afternoon. Brigadier and Brigade Major went to detail camp where Brigadier delivered lecture to Officers N.C.Os of 21st & 22nd Manchesters – 1st South Staffords repulsed an enemy patrol in the vicinity of the Lost wounding & taking prisoner the Patrol Leader. Casualties 1st South Staffords wounded 2 or. Reinforcements 2nd Queens 1 off	Nil
	4/8/17		Fall & cloudy. Brigade Major round the line with Brigade Major 64th Infantry Brigade. Staff Captain to inspect billets in MINFER area to which the Brigade is moving – The Brigadier visited reserve Battalion. Casualties Nil. Reinforcements Nil	Nil
	5/8/17		Dull & close. The Divisional commander called at Brigade HQ and had long conference with the Brigadier. Staff Captain of 64th Brigade called to see the Staff Captain for which Brigade and men to visit area issued. Casualties 1st S. Staffords wounded 1 or. Reinforcements Nil	Appx I Nil.

Army Form C. 2118.

WAR DIARY or INTELLIGENCE SUMMARY

(Erase heading not required.)

Place	Date	Hour	Summary of Events and Information	Remarks and references to Appendices
L'HOMME MORT	6/8/17		Hot + fine. Staff Captain to arrange billets in new area Pommier - Berles-au-Bois - Bienvillers and Berles-au-Bois. Brigadier round the line with Brigade Signalling Officer. Brigade Major visited Battalions in reserve. Casualties 2nd Queens killed 1 or wounded 3 or. Reinforcements 2nd Queens 54 or. 1st S. Staffords 92 or.	A.1.
	7/8/17		Hot and cloudy. Brigade Major went round line. 21st Manchesters moved to billets at Pommier. 12th Manchesters to billets at Bienvillers. Assistant Staff Capt and Brigade Transport Officer to new Bde. H.Q. at Pommier. 2nd Queens and 1st South Staffords relieved in the line by 9th + 10th Bns K.O.Y.L.I. respectively and moved out to TANGIER + PATRICIA Camps. Machine Gun + Trench Mortar Battery wounded 1 or. 9th + 10th [?] Staffords wounded 1 or. 9 or 2 [?]. Machine Gun Co wounded 1 or. Reinforcements Nil.	A.1.
POMMIER	8/8/17		Fine. Thunderstorm. Brigade H.Q. moved to POMMIER. Brigade Major proceeded on short leave to Paris. Brigade Signal Officer proceeded on leave to England. Casualties Nil. Reinforcements 21st Manchesters 8 or.	A.1.
	9/8/17		Heavy Showers with fine intervals - 2nd Queens and 1st S. Staffords moved to billets at Berles-au-Bois. Brigadier and Staff Captain rode round the training area and to select training grounds. 91st Machine Gun Co. moved to Camp at Bretencourt. 91st Trench Mortar Battery and 91st Brigade Lewis Gun + Bombing School moved to billets at Bienvillers. Brigadier had conference of Battalion Commanders re new programme of training. Casualties Nil. Reinforcements 2nd Queens 5 6 or.	A.1.
	10/8/17		Showery. Brigadier + Staff Captain to see Battalions training in the morning. The Divisional Commander called at Brigade H.Q. Casualties Nil. Reinforcements 21st Manchester Regt 3 or. 22nd Manchester Regt 3 or.	A.1.

15/9/17 should read? 15/8/17

E TICK THE APPROPRIATE BOX ON THE OPPOSITE SIDE OF THIS MARKER. THIS
WITH THE COPIES YOU REQUIRE INFORMATION SHEETS ARE AVAILABLE FROM THE
TANCE. *****************************

Army Form C. 2118.

WAR DIARY
or
INTELLIGENCE SUMMARY
(Erase heading not required.)

Instructions regarding War Diaries and Intelligence Summaries are contained in F. S. Regs., Part II. and the Staff Manual respectively. Title Pages will be prepared in manuscript.

Place	Date	Hour	Summary of Events and Information	Remarks and references to Appendices
POMMIER	11/8/17		Showery. Brigadier and Staff Captain round all Battalions to inspect drafts received during July and August. A.S.O.1 called at Brigade HQ in the afternoon. Arrangements made with VIIth Corps School for the use of their range for units of this Brigade. Casualties Nil. Reinforcements Nil.	A2.
	12/8/17		Fine morning. Heavy showers in afternoon. The Brigadier to visit P.P.C.L.I. formerly commanded by him on the anniversary of its formation. Casualties Nil. Reinforcements 2/. Queens 1 MO. 36 or. 1/. Manchesters 56 or. 2/. Manchesters 35 or. 9/. Machine Gun Co 2 or.	A2.
	13/8/17		Showery all day. Brigadier round training area in morning. One Battalion training. Staff Captain round ranges with Divisional Musketry Officer. The Divisional Commander called at Brigade HQ. Brigade Major returned from leave Paris in the evening. Casualties Nil. Reinforcements 2/. Queens 149 or.	A2.
	14/8/17		Showery. Brigadier & Brigade Major round the training area in morning. Casualties Nil. Reinforcements 22/. Manchesters 1 or.	A2.
	15/8/17		Showery. Brigadier & Brigade Major round battalions in morning training. In afternoon M. Bazillon of the 3 Army School lectured to the officers of the 1/. R.W. of the Brigade. Casualties 21/. Manchester two 2 or. accidentally wounded. Reinforcements 2/. Queens 36 or. 1/. S. Staffords 13 or. 21/. Manchesters 2 or. (from Hospital)	A2.
			9/. Machine Gun Co 3 or.	

WAR DIARY
or
INTELLIGENCE SUMMARY

Army Form C. 2118.

(Erase heading not required.)

Place	Date	Hour	Summary of Events and Information	Remarks and references to Appendices
Pommier	16/8/17		Slight showers & bright. GOC & Bn. round training area in morning. Casualties nil. Reinforcements nil.	off...
do.	17/8/17		Hot. Division Commander round training area with B.F.C. & Bn. in morning. 1 officer, 2nd half 1 off. Casualties nil. Reinf. 2nd Queens.	off...
do	18/8/17		Hot. GOC & Bn. round training. Col: Brownlow, Cmdt 2nd Army School, lectured to officers & NCOs of the Bn. at Berles at 5:30 pm. Reinf:- 21st huhrs. 1 off.	off...
do	19/8/17		Hot. Bn. reconnoitred area for Bde scheme in morning. Cas: nil. Reinf. 2nd Queen Rgt 2 off, 1st S. Staffs. 6 OR, 21st huhrs 42 OR	off o/h.
do	20/8/17		Hot. GOC round training in morning. Cas: nil & all off down to Coy cmdrs lecture. Grosville, 4:30. Rein: 21st huhrs. 1 OR from Hosp.	off...
do.	21/8/17		Hot. GOC & Bn. to gas lecture by Divnl Gas off. (all Cos, 2nds in Cmd & Coy Cmdrs attending) in morning. Representative of huhrs, Guardian to lunch - writing up record of huhrs Battles. (2nd Queens) returned from 1 month's leave. Cas. nil. Reinfs. 83 OR. 22nd huhrs.	off...
do	22/8/17		V. Hot. GOC & Bn. visited 628th 7th Coy RE, 9th M.F.C. & 91st LTMB in morning Casnl. Reinfs. 215th huhrs.	off...
do.	23/8/17		Hot. had rain in evening. Bde scheme in morning - half-frogging Battn. Back at 1. Cas. nil. [14 OR, 90th S.C. 10 R	off...
do.	24/8/17		Fine - showery. Bde route-marched to FICHEUX to watch demonstration by 22nd I.B. Back at 8 pm. Cas. nil. Reinf. 4 OR. 1st SS.	off...
do	25/8/17		Fine & cool. 7th Divisional Fair at HENDECOURT - general holiday. S. Staffs off. Bde easily leading throughout. Challenge Cup won by 1st Bn Cas & Reinforcements ret.	off o/h (Qr M Z) o/h.
do.	26/8/17		Fine day - much rain in evening. Cas: 1 & Reinf: 6 nil.	off...
do.	27/8/17		Torrential rain throughout day. Orders for move & entrainment noted. Bulletin. & Intelligence officers (Lt. N. in advance. Bde Signal officer detailed by car to northern area to reconnoitre staff. Lt Ryott, 1st SS. staffs joined HQ staff for attachment & proceeded N with Bde Intelligence officer. Cas nil. Reinf. 6 OR. 2nd Queens. 64 OR. 1st SS. staffs. 21st huhrs 69 (1 if huh) 2nd huh. 15 OR 91st h.S.C. 1 off.	off I off...

2449 Wt. W4957/M90 750,000 1/16 J.B.C. & A. Forms/C.2118/12.

Army Form C. 2118.

WAR DIARY
or
INTELLIGENCE SUMMARY
(Erase heading not required.)

Instructions regarding War Diaries and Intelligence Summaries are contained in F. S. Regs., Part II. and the Staff Manual respectively. Title Pages will be prepared in manuscript.

Place	Date	Hour	Summary of Events and Information	Remarks and references to Appendices
GREVAS	28/8/17		V. High Wind. Bde Sport marched to MONDICOURT area ≈ (vide B.O.) Major G. O. Raughton D.S.O. 22nd Br Ache R.) joined 2nd Border Rgt (20th I.B.) as 2nd in Comd. Major W. Hayes D.S.O. 2nd Queens Rgt joined H.Q. Staff for attachment B.M. G.O.C. employed as President G.C.M. at BLAIREVILLE. Conference of G.O. 5.30 P.M. at Bde H.Q. re new profiles. Casualties and Reinforcements — Nil.	≈ Bde O. No. 14 AAA (Appx III) ETB
OUDERDOM	29/8/17		Fine morning. Hard rain afternoon. Entrained for FLANDERS ≈ commencing at MONDICOURT. Entrainment supervised by Staff left first train containing Bde H.Q. arrived MONDICOURT (vide B.O.) (near POPERINGHE) at 6.30 P.M. Detraining carried out by B.M. Maj. Hayes 2/Lt Lamdell (A/ASTO) Bde H.Q. and all units in vicinity of OUDERDOM. Casualties. Nil. Reinfts 2nd Queens 20R	≈ Bde O. No. 15 and (Appx IV) ETB
do	30/8/17		1st South Stafford 2 Off. 22nd Bn Fusrs Rgt 1 Off. (Yeo Hosp) 11 OR. cold. Detrainment continued throughout day. Last train completed 10.30 P.M.	ETB.
do	31/8/17		Lt Lawford (A.M. S.C.) rejoined from leave. Casualties + Reinforcements Nil. Overcast and cold. Some showers. G.O.C. and B.M. went round Bns in morning Casualties. 2nd Queens wounded 1 Off. Rnfts Nil.	ETB

M. Sugborough Mit
for Brig Gend Comdg: 91st Inf Bgt 1517.

SECRET.

Appendix I

Copy No. 22

91st Infantry Brigade Order No. 13.

Sunday, 5th August, 1917.

Reference Map – LENS, Sheet 11. 1/100,000.
VI) Corps Trench Map – CROISILLES – 1/10,000.

1. The 7th Division (less Artillery) will be withdrawn from the line into Divisional Reserve about ADINFER.

2. The 91st Infantry Brigade will be relieved by 64th Infantry Brigade, 21st Division, as under :—
(a) 2nd Bn. Queen's Regt. in the Right Sub-sector will be relieved by 9th Bn. K.O.Y.L.I., on night August 7/8th. On completion of relief, 2nd Bn. Queen's Regt. will be withdrawn to TANKERS CAMP.
(b) 1st Bn. South Staffordshire Regt. in the Left Sub-sector will be relieved by 10th Bn. K.O.Y.L.I. on night August 7/8th.
KNUCKLE AVENUE South of its junction with QUEEN'S AVENUE will not be used for the purposes of this relief.
On completion of relief, 1st Bn. South Staffordshire Regt. will be withdrawn to PATRICIA CAMP.
(c) The Machine Guns in the line will be relieved by guns of 64th Machine Gun Company on August 7th, relief being complete by 3.p.m.
On relief, 91st Machine Gun Company will be withdrawn to billets in ERVILLERS, and the 4 guns of 220th Machine Gun Company at present in the Sector will rejoin their Company.
(d) The 91st Light Trench Mortar Battery will be relieved by the 64th Light Trench Mortar Battery on August 7th, relief being complete by 12. noon.
On relief, 91st Light Trench Mortar Battery will be withdrawn to billets in ERVILLERS.

3. One Officer per Company, one N.C.O. per platoon, and one representative of each Lewis Gun team will be left in the line for 24 hours after relief.

4. All maps, diagrams, aeroplane photographs and trench stores will be handed over on relief and a receipt forwarded to this office by 8.a.m., 8th August.

5. (a) Details of reliefs will be arranged between Commanding Officers concerned.
(b) Completions of reliefs will be reported to Brigade Headquarters by Fullergram.

6. The Tunnelling Company fatigues on KNUCKLE and QUEEN'S AVENUE dug-outs will continue to be found by this Brigade up till 2.p.m., August 7th. The N.C.Os and men of 64th Infantry Brigade who will furnish the 2.p.m. shift will report to Battalion Headquarters concerned for guides at 1.p.m., August 7th.

7. (a) On relief the Brigade will be withdrawn to the BERLES-AU-BOIS AREA in accordance with the attached March Table.
(b) Each Unit will send a billetting party under an Officer to report to the Town Major's Office of the village it is to occupy one day in advance.
(c) Lorries will report as follows :—

7th August.

1 Lorry to H.Q., 22nd Bn. Manchester Regt. (nearest point on Road) ... ... 7-30.a.m.
1 Lorry to H.Q., 21st Bn. Manchester Regt. (nearest point on Road) ... ... 7-30.a.m.

9th August.

1 Lorry to H.Q., 2nd Bn. Queen's Regt. (nearest point on Road). 7-30.a.m.
1 Lorry to H.Q., 1st Bn. South Staffordshire Regt. (nearest point on Road). ... 7-30.a.m.
X 1 Lorry to H.Q., 91st Trench Mortar Battery, E.8.a.6.3.
7-30.a.m.

This Lorry/

-2-

X This Lorry to be available half for 91st Trench Mortar Battery and half for 91st Machine Gun Company.

All Lorries will be available for double journey.

(d) The position of Supply Refilling Point in the new area will be notified later.

(e) Ordnance Refilling Point will be at BRETENCOURT from August 10th inclusive.

8. The Command of the Sector will pass to G.O.C., 64th Infantry Brigade at 10.a.m., August 8th, at which hour Brigade Headquarters will close at L'HOMME MORT and open at POMMIER.

9. ACKNOWLEDGE.

J. Moorshead
Captain,
Brigade Major, 91st Infantry Brigade.

Issued at 8/30 p.m.

Copy No. 1. 2nd Queen's R.
2. 1st S. Staffs. R.
3. 21st Manch. R.
4. 22nd Manch. R.
5. 91st M.G. Coy.
6. 91st T.M. Bty.
7. O.C. Bde. School.
8. No. 3 Sec. Div. Sigs.
9. Staff Captain.
10. Bde. Transport Officer.
11. 21st Field Ambulance.
12. 22nd Bde. R.F.A.
13. 528th (Durham) Fd. Coy. R.E.
14. Supply Officer.
15. 7th Division.
16. 20th Infantry Brigade.
17. 22nd Infantry Brigade.
18. 64th Infantry Brigade.
19. 252nd Tunnelling Coy. R.E.
20. 220th M.G. Coy.
21. File.
22. War Diary.
23. War Diary.
24. No. 3 Coy. Div. Train.

SECRET.   Copy No. 22

AMENDMENTS TO 91ST INFANTRY BRIGADE ORDER NO.13.

Tuesday, 7th August, 1917.

1. 1. The destination of 528th (Durham) Field Coy. R.E., and 91st Light Trench Mortar Battery will be BRETENCOURT instead of BIENVILLERS. These Units will march independently via HAMELINCOURT.

2. The destination of the 91st Machine Gun Company will be Camp at RANSART instead of BIENVILLERS. Route:- DOUCHY - ADINFER - RANSART. Time of starting remains unchanged.

3. The necessary alterations will be made to the MARCH TABLE.

4. ACKNOWLEDGE.

Captain,
Brigade Major, 91st Infantry Brigade.

Issued at 11-30.p.m. to
All recipients of Brigade Order No.13.

MARCH TABLE.
(to accompany Brigade Order No.13.)

Date.	Unit.	From.	To.	Starting point.	Time.	Route.
6/8/17.	1 Sec.528th Fd.Coy.R.E. 21st Bn.Manch.Regt.	ST.LEGER. PATRICIA CAMP.	POMMIER. POMMIER.	Crater,ERVILLERS. -do-	9-0.a.m. To be W. of ERVILLERS by 9-30.a.m.	COURCELLES - AYETTE - DOUCHY - thence - Troops - by track S. of ADINFER' WOOD' - MONCHY' - BIENVILLERS Transport. - ADINFER' - MONCHY' - BIENVILLERS.
7/8/17.	22nd Bn.Manch.Regt.	TANGIERS CAMP.	BIENVILLERS.	-do-	To be W. of ERVILLERS by 10.a.m.	-do-
8/8/17.	Brigade Headqtrs.	L'HOMME MORT.	POMMIER.			-do-
9/8/17.	2nd Bn.Queen's Regt.	TANGIERS CAMP.	BERLES-AU-BOIS.	Crater,ERVILLERS.	8-25.a.m.	Troops as above to MONCHY,thence via fair weather track leaving MONCHY' - BIENVILLERS Road at a point 1 mile due N. of H of HANNESCAMPS. Transport.- via ADINFER' - RANSART - Cross Roads 1200 yards due S. of X of BASSEUX.
	1st Bn.S.Staffs.Regt.	PATRICIA CAMP.	BERLES-AU-BOIS.	-do-	8-50.a.m.	-do-
	91st M.G.Coy.) 91st T.M.Bty.) Bde.School.	ERVILLERS.	BIENVILLERS.	-do-	9-15.a.m.	As for 21st Bn.Manch.Regt.
	No.2.Coy.Div.Train.	E.15.a.3.4.	POMMIER.	-do-	9-30.a.m.	-do-
	528th Field Coy.R.E. (less one Section)	ST.LEGER.	BIENVILLERS.	-do-	9-40.a.m.	-do-
	1 Sec.528th Fd.Coy.R.E.	POMMIER.	BIENVILLERS.		10.a.m.	
	21st Field Ambulance.	FERMAGNIES.	BIENVILLERS.	Road Junction immediately East. of D' in ACHIET-LE-GRAND.	9-30.a.m.	BIHUCOURT - BUCQUOY - HANNESCAMPS.

All movement E. of COURCELLES to be by Companies at 200 yards interval: 500 yards will be maintained between Units.

1st Line Transport.will accompany Units.

SECRET.

85

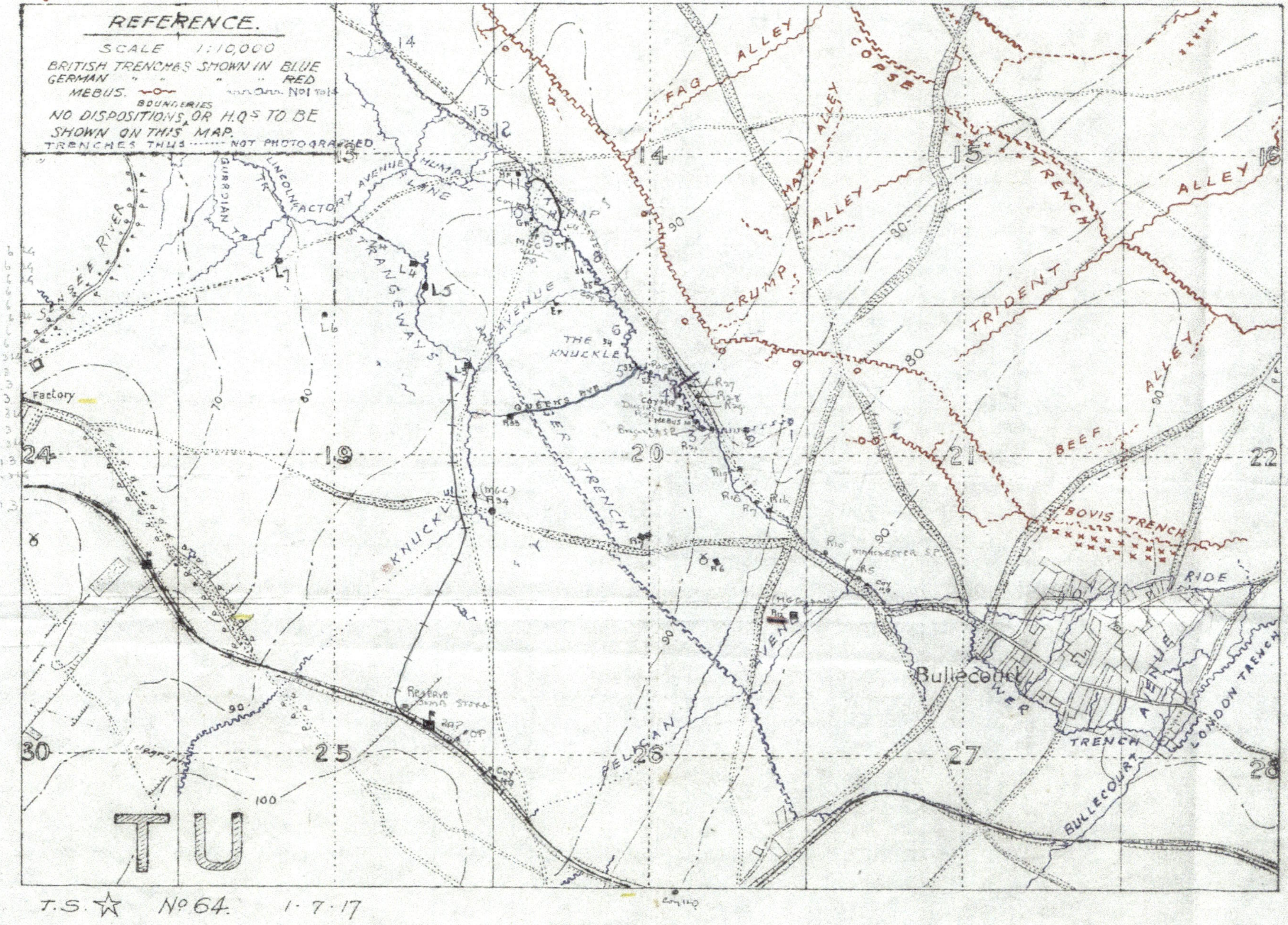
REFERENCE.
SCALE 1:10,000
BRITISH TRENCHES SHOWN IN BLUE
GERMAN " " " RED
MEBUS.
BOUNDARIES
No 1 to 14
NO DISPOSITIONS, OR H.Q.S TO BE SHOWN ON THIS MAP.
TRENCHES THUS ...... NOT PHOTOGRAPHED.
FAG ALLEY
COPSE
MATCH ALLEY
ALLEY
CRUMP
TRENCH
TRIDENT
ALLEY
BEEF
BOVIS TRENCH
RIDE
LONDON TRENCH
BULLECOURT TRENCH
AVENUE
TOWER
Bullecourt
PELICAN
AVENUE
TIGER TRENCH
KNUCKLE
THE KNUCKLE
QUEENS AVE
AVENUE
STRANGEWAYS
FACTORY AVENUE
LINCOLN TR
GUARDIAN TR
HUMP LANE
RIVER
Factory
WINCHESTER S.P.
Reserve Bomb Store
RAP
OP
Coy
TU
13 14 15 16 19 20 21 22 24 25 26 27 28 30
T.S. ☆ No 64. 1·7·17

Reference Sketch Map attached.

GENERAL IDEA.

During the first phase of offensive operations the line of VICTORY TRENCH has been captured and consolidated.
The 91st Infantry Brigade, holding 600 yards of this trench with its left resting on the OLD MILL (B.9.c.10.55.), has been ordered to continue the advance and to capture the LUDENDORF LINE from B.4.c.9.0. – B.3.d.9.6., in conjunction with other troops operating on either flank.

---oOo---

SPECIAL IDEA.

The attack will be carried out in two phases. In the first phase the 2nd Bn. Queen's Regt. (Right) and 21st Bn. Manchester Regt. (Left) will establish the line of KAISAR GRABEN. In the second phase the 22nd Bn. Manchester Regt. (Right) and 1st Bn. South Staffordshire Regt. (Left) will pass through the 2nd Bn. Queen's Regt., and 21st Bn. Manchester Regt. respectively and advance to the capture of HANS CRESCENT and the LUDENDORF LINE.
There will be an interval of 75 minutes between the two phases.

A copy of Brigade Orders for the attack and one copies of sketch map are appended.

---oOo---

SECRET.

Copy No. 8

91st Infantry Brigade Order No.500 (a).

Reference Sketch Map attached.

Monday, 20th August, 1917.

-:-:-:-:-:-:-:-:-:-:-:-

1. On August 23rd, 1917, the 91st Infantry Brigade, in conjunction with troops on either flank, will attack and capture the LUDENDORF LINE from E.4.c.9.0. to E.3.d.9.6.

2. The attack will be carried out in two phases at 75 minutes interval as under.

3. PHASE "A".
(a) The 2nd Bn. Queen's Regt. (Right) and 21st Bn. Manchester Regt. (Left) will make good the line of KAISAR GRABEN.
(b) The attack will be carried out from a tape laid out from E.15.b.00.85. - E.9.c.15.60., on night 22/23rd August, under separate orders.
(c) Boundaries will be as shewn in BLUE on attached map.
(d) Battalion Headquarters will remain in VICTORY TRENCH throughout the operations.
(e) (i) The attack of 2nd Bn. Queen's Regt., will be carried out with two companies in the front line (objective KAISAR GRABEN), one company in Support (objective WOTAN ALLEY) and one company in reserve (objective HAMBURG TRENCH).
    (ii) The attack of 21st Bn. Manchester Regt., will be carried out in Normal Attack Formation; the two leading companies going through to KAISAR GRABEN, the support companies remaining in HAMBURG TRENCH.
(f) All positions will be consolidated on capture, and patrols pushed out in advance of the HANNESCAMPS - BIENVILLERS Road.
(g) The 22nd Bn. Manchester Regt., and 1st Bn. South Staffordshire Regt., will be formed up in artillery formation opposite their respective sectors, 500 yards S.W. of the BIENVILLERS - FONQUEVILLERS Road by Zero (a) hour, when they will move forward to occupy the assembly positions vacated by 2nd Bn. Queen's Regt., and 21st Bn. Manchester Regt., respectively.

4. PHASE "B".
(a) The 22nd Bn. Manchester Regt. (Right) and 1st Bn. South Staffordshire Regt. (Left) will advance in artillery formation of platoons from the TAPE LINE at Zero (b) minus 15 minutes, the leading companies crossing KAISAR GRABEN and deploying on a line 50 yards N.E. of the HANNESCAMPS - BIENVILLERS Road under cover of the patrols referred to in para.3 (f) above.
(b) The attack will be carried out in each case with two companies in the front line (objective LUDENDORF LINE), one company in support (objective shell hole positions between LUDENDORF LINE and HANS CRESCENT) and one company in reserve (objective HANS REDOUBT and HANS CRESCENT).
(c) Boundaries will be as shewn in BLUE on attached map.
(d) All captured positions will be consolidated and patrols pushed out in advance of the LUDENDORF LINE.
(e) Battalion Headquarters of 22nd Bn. Manchester Regt., will be established at WILLOW PATCH "C" and of 1st Bn. South Staffordshire Regt., at WILLOW PATCH "B" until Zero (a) when they will both move forward to VICTORY TRENCH. At Zero (b) both Battalion Headquarters will be established in KAISAR GRABEN.

5. Zero hours will be as follows :-

    Phase "A" (Zero (a))   10-0 a.m.
    Phase "B" (Zero (b))   11-15.a.m.

6 ARTILLERY ARRANGEMENTS/

6. ARTILLERY ARRANGEMENTS.
   (a) PHASE "A". - A Field Gun barrage will open at Zero (a) hour on a line 200 yards N.E. of the TAPE LINE, where it will remain for 3 minutes, allowing the leading wave to crawl forward as close as possible. It will then advance at the rate of 200 yards in 3 minutes to a line 200 yards N.E. of KAISAR GRABEN, where it will remain (at a reduced rate) until Zero (b) hour.
   (b) PHASE "B". - At Zero (b) hour above barrage will resume its advance at the same rate to a line 200 yards N.E. of the LUDENDORF LINE, where it will pause for 15 minutes to allow of patrols being organised. It will then continue its advance to a line 500 yards in advance of the LUDENDORF LINE where it will remain at a reduced rate as a protective barrage.
   (c) Remainder of Artillery Programme Imaginary.

7. Machine Gun and Trench Mortar Programme (Imaginary).

8. CONTACT PATROLS.
   (a) Flares will be lit as follows :-
      (i) by 2nd Bn. Queen's Regt., and 21st Bn. Manchester Regt. on reaching HAMBURG TRENCH, WOTAN ALLEY and KAISAR GRABEN successively.
      (ii) by 22nd Bn. Manchester Regt., and 1st Bn. South Staffordshire Regt. on reaching HANS CRESCENT and LUDENDORF LINE successively.
      (iii) by all troops at 11-30.a.m.
      (iv) on demand from the aeroplane (succession of dashes on Klaxon Horn or firing white very lights)
   Organised troops in trenches should light flares in pairs at 20 yards interval. Shell hole groups should each light one flare.
   (b) Ground sheets, signalling shutters and aeroplane lamps will be taken forward.

9. In the event of a hostile counter-attack, the support company of 22nd Bn. Manchester Regt., and 1st Bn. South Staffordshire Regt. will hold on to their shell hole positions, the reserve company carrying out a counter-attack without waiting for orders. One support company of 2nd Bn. Queen's Regt., and 21st Bn. Manchester Regt., will be previously earmarked to replace these companies in HANS CRESCENT, and will be under the command of the front line Battalion concerned from Zero (b) hour onwards.

10. All units will send a watch to Brigade Headquarters at 8.a.m. August 23rd, for synchronisation.

11. Brigade Headquarters will be established at WILLOW PATCH "B" throughout the operations.

12. ACKNOWLEDGE.

(signed) O.F.MORSHEAD. Captain,
Brigade Major, 91st Infantry Brigade.

Copies to -

    No 1. 2nd Queen's R
       2 1st S.Staffs.R
       3 21st Manch.R
       4 22nd Manch.R
       5 12th Squadron, R.F.C.
       6 File.
       7 War Diary.
       8 War Diary.
       9)
      10) Spare
      11)
      12)

NOTES.

(1) It is hoped to ~~issue~~ 400 flares per battalion, with different colours for ~~the~~ two phases.

(2) STANDING CROPS will represent shelled areas and will in all cases be avoided.

    The Officer Commanding, 21st Bn. Manchester Regt. will arrange to picquet these in the vicinity of E.9. Central throughout the operations. The Officer Commanding, 1st Bn. South Staffordshire Regt., and 22nd Bn. Manchester Regt. will similarly picquet those lying between their first assembly positions and the BIENVILLERS - FONQUEVILLERS Road.

(3) (a) The Officer Commanding, 1st Bn. South Staffordshire Regt. will arrange to lay the tape referred to in para. 3 (b) of Brigade Order No. 500 (a).
(b) The Officer Commanding, 21st Bn. Manchester Regt., will arrange for a drum and flag barrage in accordance with 6 (a) of above order.
(c) The Officer Commanding, 22nd Bn. Manchester Regt., will similarly arrange for the barrage for Phase (b).
(d) The Officer Commanding, 21st Bn. Manchester Regt., will arrange for a bugler to report to the Brigade Major at the OLD MILL at 9.a.m.

(4) Battalion Commanders concerned are responsible for making sufficient gaps in the wire to admit of their operations taking place.

(5) Dress - Fighting Order. No bombs will be carried.

(6) Battalion Commanders and Staff need not remain at Battalion Headquarters. A nominal Headquarters must however be maintained for the reception of messages.

(7) A copy of Battalion Orders will be forwarded to this office by 6.p.m., 22nd instant.

(8) On the conclusion of operations the DISMISS will be sounded, and troops will be marched back to billets. Officers will assemble at No.4. concrete standard (E.9.b.5.0.0) for a conference.

-:-:-:-:-:-:-:-:-:-:-

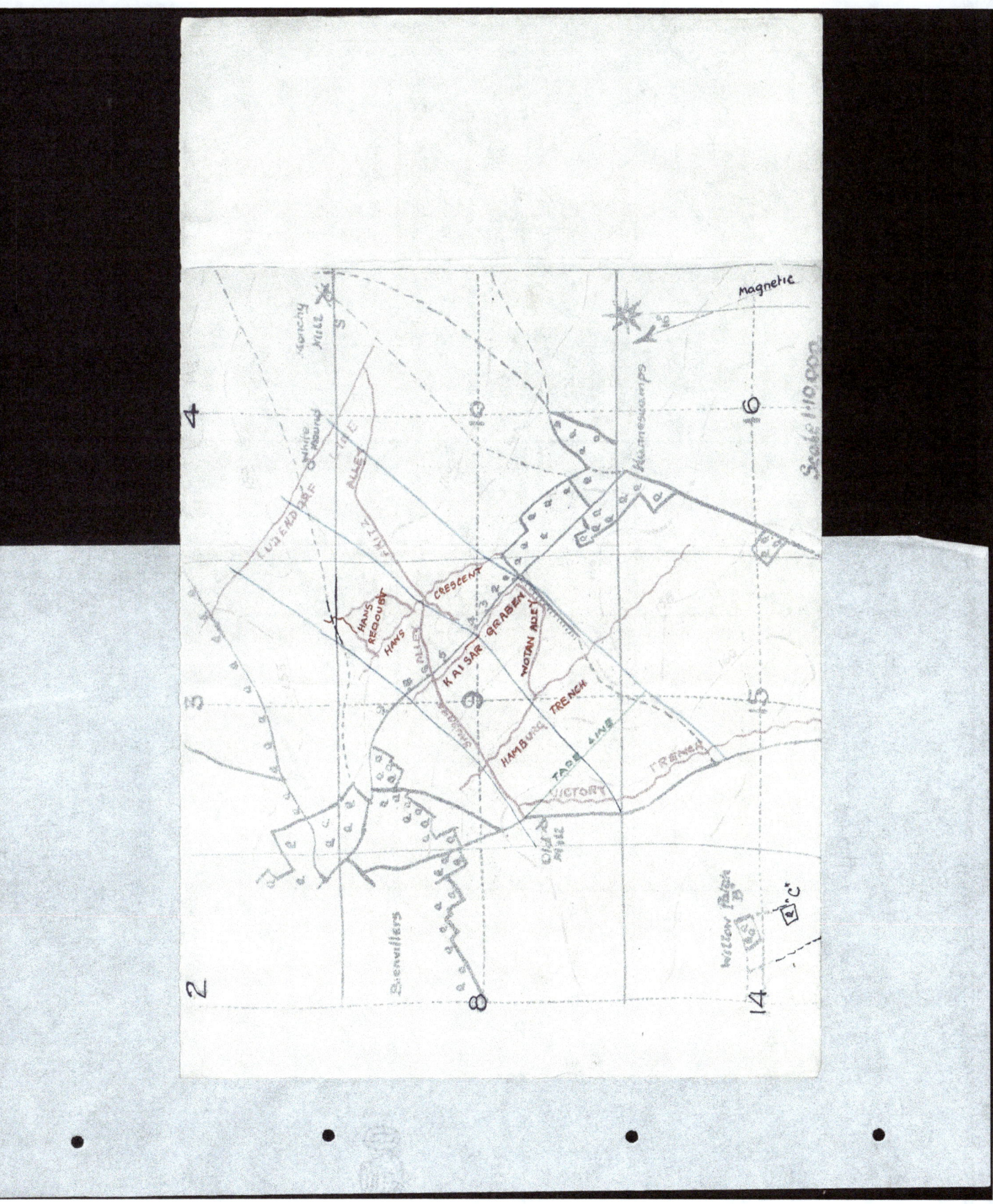

SECRET.

Appendix III
Copy No. 18

91st Infantry Brigade Order No.14.

Monday, 27th August, 1917.
Reference Map - LENS Sheet 11, Edition 2.1/100,000.
-:-:-:-:-:-:-:-:-:-

91st Inf.Bde. H.Q. 2nd Queen's (R.W.S.Regt.) 1st S.Staffs R. 21st Manch.Regt. 22nd Manch.Regt. 91st M.G.Coy. 91st L.T.M.Bty. No.3 Sec., 7th Div.Sig.Co. No.3 Coy., 7th Div.Train. 21st Fld.Amblce. 22nd Fld.Amblce. 220th M.G.Coy. 54th Fld.Coy., R.E.	1. The 7th Division will be transferred by rail from VI Corps area to II Corps area. 2. (a) On August 28th, 1917, the 91st Infantry Brigade Group (consisting of the marginally-named units) will move to the MONDICOURT area in accordance with attached March Table. (b) Separate orders will be issued for the entrainment which will take place at MONDICOURT on August 29th and 30th. 3. Units will march closed up and will halt for the last ten minutes of each hour. 4. Brigade Headquarters will close at POMMIER at 11 a.m. and open at GRENAS at 12 noon. 5. ACKNOWLEDGE.

Ofkershead
Captain,
Brigade Major, 91st Infantry Brigade.

Issued at 12:30 p.m. to -
Copy No. 1 2nd Queen's R.
2 1st S.Staffs R.
3 21st Manch.R.
4 22nd Manch.R.
5 91st M.G.Coy.
6 No.3 Sec., 7th Div.Sig.Co.
7 91st L.T.M.Batty.
8 Staff Captain.
9 Bde. Transport Officer.
10 21st Fld.Amblce.
11 22nd Fld.Amblce.
12 54th Fld.Coy., R.E.
13 Supply Officer.
14 No.3 Coy., 7th Div.Train.
15 7th Division.
16 220th M.G.Coy.
17 File.
18 War Diary.
19 War Diary.

M A R C H   T A B L E (to accompany 91st Inf.Bde.Order No.14)

Unit.	From	To	Starting Point.	Time.	Route.	Remarks.
21st Bn.Manchester Regt.	POMMIER	MONDICOURT	POMMIER Church.	9-30 a.m.	Route A	
2nd Bn.Queen's (R.W.S.Regt.)	BERLES	POMMIER	Rd. junction ½ mile N. of POMMIER.	9-40 a.m.	Route A	
1st Bn.S.Staffs Regt.	BERLES	MONDICOURT	-do.-	10-0 a.m.	Route A	
91st Machine Gun Coy.	RANSART	MONDICOURT	X roads ¼ mile N. of first A of RANSART.	9-15 a.m.	Route A	
220th Machine Gun Coy.	RANSART	PAS	-do.-	9-30 a.m.	BERLES - POMMIER - ST.AMAND - HENU.	
54th Fld.Coy., R.E.	RANSART	PAS	-do.-	9-45 a.m.	-do.-	
22nd Bn.Manchester Regt.	BIENVILLERS.	GRENAS	BIENVILLERS Church.	9-30 a.m.	Route B.	
21st Field Ambulance.	BIENVILLERS.	Pommier	-do.-	9-50 a.m.	Route B.	
22nd Field Ambulance.	HENDECOURT.	PAS			Route B.	Not to enter BIENVILLERS before 10 a.m
No.3 Coy., 7th Div.Train.	POMMIER	PAS			ST.AMAND - HENU.	to be clear of POMMIER by 11 a.m.
91st T.M.Battery.	BRETONCOURT.	GRENAS			via ARRAS - DOULLENS road.	March independently

Route A : RANSART - BERLES AU BOIS - POMMIER - HUMBERCAMP - GAUDIEMPRE - HAUTE - MONDICOURT.
Note - Road from HUMBERCAMP Church - H of HUMBERCAMP is impassable for transport.

Route B : HENDECOURT - ADINFER - MONCHY - BIENVILLERS - SOUASTRE - HENU - PAS - GRENAS (via track from A of PAS).

SECRET

Appendix IV

Copy No. 18

91st Infantry Brigade Order No. 15.

Monday, 27th August, 1917.

Reference Maps - LENS Sheet 11, Edition 2, 1/100,000.
HAZEBROUCK Sheet 5A, Edition 2, 1/100,000.

—:—:—:—:—:—:—:—:—:—:—:—:—:—

1. The 91st Infantry Brigade Group will entrain at MONDICOURT for HOPOUTRE in accordance with the attached table.

2. (a) Entraining States shewing men, horses and vehicles (G.S. wagons, limbered wagons, two-wheeled vehicles and bicycles to be shewn separately) will be submitted to Brigade Headquarters GRENAS, by all units by 6 p.m. August 29th.
(b) Transport of all units will arrive at the station 3 hours before the time of departure and personnel 1½ hours before.

3. O.C., 21st Manchester Regt. will detail 1 Company, with cooker and team, to report to R.T.O., MONDICOURT, at 7 a.m. on August 29th for billets. This Company will be employed on loading, working in reliefs of 50, until the last train on August 30th.

4. (a) Baggage and Supply Wagons will be loaded full and will accompany units. Supply Wagons will rejoin Divisional Train on August 31st.
(b) Units will entrain with rations for 31st instant.

5. (a) Covered vans will hold 8 horses or 40 men.
(b) Flat trucks will carry either 1 G.S. Wagon and 1 two-wheeled vehicle or 4 axles in the case of limbered vehicles. No men will travel on flat trucks.
(c) Brake vans will not be used for men or baggage.

6. (a) Breast and head ropes for horse trucks should be provided by units. Lashings for vehicles are provided.
(b) Not more than 4 men will travel in each horse truck.

7. Lamps are usually provided in the covered vans, but not in the Officers compartments.

8. The yard at the detraining station must be cleared as soon as possible after detrainment.

Ollivershead
Captain,
Brigade Major, 91st Infantry Brigade.

Issued at 7.15 p.m. to -
Copy No. 1 2nd Queen's R.
2 1st S. Staffs R.
3 21st Manch. R.
4 22nd Manch. R.
5 91st M.G. Coy.
6 No. 3 Sec., 7th Div. Sig. Coy.
7 91st L.T.M. Battery.
8 Staff Captain.
9 Bde. Transport Officer.
10 21st Fld. Amblce.
11 22nd Fld. Amblce.
12 54th Fld. Coy., R.E.
13 Supply Officer.
14 No. 3 Coy., 7th Div. Train.
15 7th Division.
16 220th M.G. Coy.
17 File.
18 War Diary.
19 War Diary.

ENTRAINMENT TABLE (to accompany 91st Inf.Bde. Order No.15).

Serial No. of Train.	Date.	Time of departure.	CONTENTS of TRAIN. UNIT.	Serial No. of Unit
1.	Aug.29th.	10-30 a.m.	Brigade Headquarters. 1 Coy., 1 cooker & team, 2nd Queen's Regt. No.3 Sec., 7th Div. Signal Coy. 91st Machine Gun Coy. 91st Light Trench Mortar Battery.	730 731(a) 735 736 737
4.	Aug.29th.	2-30 p.m.	2nd Queen's Regt. less 1 Coy.	731
7.	Aug.29th.	6-30 p.m.	1st South Staffs Regt. less 1 Coy.	732
10.	Aug.29th.	10-30 p.m.	21st Manchester Regt. less 1 Coy.	733
13.	Aug.30th.	2-30 a.m.	22nd Manchester Regt. less 1 Coy.	734
16.	Aug.30th.	6-30 a.m.	220th Machine Gun Coy. 54th Field Coy., R.E.	708 781
19.	Aug.30th.	10-30 a.m.	1 Coy., 1 cooker & team, 22nd Manch. Regt. 1 Coy., 1 cooker & team, 1st S.Staffs R. 22nd Field Ambulance.	734(a) 732(a) 787
22.	Aug.30th.	2-30 p.m.	21st Field Ambulance. No.3 Coy., 7th Divl. Train. 1 Coy., 1 cooker & team, 21st Manch. Regt.	706 777 733(a)

All trains will consist of 1 coach, 30 covers, 17 flats.

7th DIVISION.

B. H. C.

91st INFANTRY BRIGADE.

SEPTEMBER 1917.

Army Form C. 2118.

September 1917

Headquarters
9th Infantry Brigade

WAR DIARY
or
INTELLIGENCE SUMMARY
(Erase heading not required.)

Vol 23

Place	Date	Hour	Summary of Events and Information	Remarks and references to Appendices
OUDEZEELE	1/9/17		Overcast and cold. Some showers in afternoon. Orders arrived in morning for withdrawal of Bde to STEENVOORDE area in afternoon. (9th M.G. Coy) Head of column arrived 9.30 p.m. Billets scattered but comfortable. Bde H.Q. STEENVOORDE. Coln N.F. Rfts, 1/1 Staffords, Y.O.R., 9th M.G. Coy, 3 O.R.	Bds o/o and 76 ① EHB
STEENVOORDE	2/9/17		Fine & cool. Brigadier went on leave in early morning. 2/1st and 22nd N.F. Rfls Regt moved to CAËSTRE in afternoon. 2nd Queens arrived no 2nd Border Regt billets (also in STEENVOORDE area) Cas. & Rfts. Nil.	EHB
LE NIEPPE	3/9/17		Fine and warm. Bde group moved to WALLON-CAPPEL area in afternoon. (9 V.D.R.O.) 2nd Army Commander inspected units on march. Billets very scattered. Bde H.Q. LE NIEPPE. Casualties and Reinforcement Nil.	Bde o/o attd 17 ② EHB
do.	4/9/17		Fine and Sunny. B.M. and Maj. Hayles visited units in morning. Casualties & Rfts. Nil.	EHB
do.	5/9/17		Fine and Sunny. Lt. Col. Woodward D.S.O. Coy. 22nd N. Fus 2 Clrs. Regt. went on leave. Casualties Nil. Reinforcement 2nd Queens 2 O.R. 1st South Staffords 134 O.R. 21st N. Clrs. Regt. 10 Y. 7. O.R. 22nd N. Clrs. 3 O.R. (Fun hospital)	EHB
do.	6/9/17		Overcast. Warm. Some rain. Wet and Stormy evening. Major G.R. Meineike-Smith, Coy 9th M.G.Coy. went on leave. 2/1st Bedrs. 22nd N Clrs, 9th M.G. Coy. 9th T.M. Batty moved their billets according to scheme for closer groupg of troops. 1st South Staffords Casualties and Reinforcement Nil.	EHB
do.	7/9/17		Diffused Sunshine. Hot. Lt. W. A.B. Beaumont D.S.O. Coy 1st South Staffords went on leave. Major Hayles presented to G.O.C. at H.Q.; 2nd South Staffords Staff Capt 9 o/s.C. round with 2 Majs. Coln N.F. 2/1st H.A.C. dined at Bde. H.Q. Casualties & Reinforcement Nil.	EHB
do.	8/9/17		Misty Morning. Hot and Sunny afternoon. Maj. Hayles left Bde for attachment to 9th Div. H.Q. Lt. Col. Solomon D.S.O. M.C. Coy. 2/1st H.A.C. attached. 1st South Staffords 1 off (to hosp.) 2 O.R. 9th M.G. Coy. 1 O.R.	EHB

WAR DIARY
or
INTELLIGENCE SUMMARY

Army Form C. 2118.

Place	Date	Hour	Summary of Events and Information	Remarks and references to Appendices
LE NIEPPE	7/9/17		Fine and sunny. B.M. motored to BOISDINGHEM to reconnoitre training facilities in new area. Lt. Col. Unwin, G.S.O.1, 7th Div called at Bde in morning.	C.F.B.
do.	10/9/17		B.M. & B.T.O. attended Bde eliminating trials for III Army Cross Horse Show in afternoon. Cas: Nil. Rfts 20 2nd Indian Regt. 1 Offr. (Pro. Lingh) 91 O.R. M.G. Coy 1 O.R.	C.F.B.
do.	11/9/17		Dull early; hot and sunny later. Lt. Col Veasley Coy 7th Div. Train inspected Train (1st line) of units in morning. Casualties and Rafts – Nil.	C.F.B.
do.	12/9/17		Hot and sunny. Brig Gen Stoehr (22nd Indian Bde) returned from leave in afternoon. Cas Nil. Rafts 1st S. Stafford 1 Offr & O.R.	C.F.B.
			Fine and sunny. B.M. and Bde Commdr motored to YPRES to reconnoitre conditions in line Brigade returned from leave in afternoon. Cas Nil. Rafts 1st S. Stafford 1 Offr & O.R.	
ARQUES	13/9/17		2/1st Indian Regt 1 Offr. 22nd Indian Regt. 1 Offr. Dull. Rain in afternoon. Bde group moved to RENESCURE en route for TILQUES area. W. & L. B.D. at 10.50 A.M. Orders were received for 22nd & 2nd Indian Regt to proceed to CASSEL to entrain for ETAPLES in conjunction with 1st Bn R.W.F. to quell disturbances at the Base Depot. They turned about and marched to CASSEL accordingly.	Bde O No 18 attd (3) C.F.B.
do.	14/9/17		Bde H.Q. ARQUES. Billets scattered but good. Cas & Rfts. Nil. Dull heavy wind. A.G.1 a.m. attended demonstration by Bn Hrs of Canadian Mule animal in morning. G.O.C. 7th Div called at Bde H.Q. in afternoon. Bde T.O. went on leave. Cas and Reinforcements. Nil.	C.F.B.
BOISDINGHEM	15/9/17		Fine and sunny. Bde group resumed its march to TILQUES area. Billets very scattered and not good. Casualties & Rfts. Nil.	V.O. R.D. Bde O No 18 attd (3) C.F.B.
do.	16/9/17		Dull early: sunny later. B.G.C. and B.M. reconnoitred ground by Bde Scheme. tricd. Bleuron Bde very S. Stafford Dr. Lt. Woodham and 22nd Indian Regt returned to Bde. Enemy Casualties nil. Reinforcements Nil.	C.F.B.

WAR DIARY or INTELLIGENCE SUMMARY

Army Form C. 2118.

Place	Date	Hour	Summary of Events and Information	Remarks and references to Appendices
BUSSINGHEM	17/9/17		Dull. Sunshine at intervals. B.G.C. and B.M. watched an attack by 2nd Queens in morning. G.O.C. 9. Div. called at Bde. H.Q. in afternoon. Conference of Cmdg. offrs. at H.Q. Bde. at 5.30 P.M. Casualties nil. Reinforcements 1st South Staffords 3 O.R. 21st Middx. 9. 40.R. 22nd Middx. Regt 2 O.R.	C/S
do.	18/9/17		Rain all day. High Wind. 22nd Middx. Regt. returning from ETAPLES, detrained at WIZERNES at 6 A.M. and proceeded to billets in brigade area. Detrainment supervised by S.C. 2 O/S.C. Brigade scheme No. 1 carried out by 3rd South Staffords and 2nd Middx. Regt. 3 O.R. 10.30 A.M. Army Manoeuvres quietly. enemy 9. 1st 2nd 3rd Coys. returned from leave. Casualties Nil. Rnfts 2nd Queen 2 O.R.	* Brig. Sch. No. 1 not held. C/S
do.	19/9/17		Sunny. High Wind. Brig. scheme No. 1. See above carried out by 2nd Queen. 22nd Middx. Regt.	C/S
do.	20/9/17		Zero 10.10 A.M. B.M. attended funeral in afternoon for Brig. Sch. No. 2. S.C. 2 Sig. offr. went on Int. Course to PARIS. Cas. Nil. Rnfts. 1st South Staffords 6 O.R. Sunny. High Wind. Brig. Scheme No. 2 * Carried out by 2nd Queen. 1st South Staffords 2nd Middx. Regt. Zero 10.30 A.M. B.M. reconnoitred ground for Div. scheme in afternoon. G.O.C. 9. Div. called at Bde H.Q. Casualties Nil. Reinforcements 2nd Queen 2 O.R.	* Brig. Sch. No. 2 and C/S
do.	21/9/17		Fine and Sunny. Brigade scheme No. 2. (See above) carried out by 2nd Queen. 2nd Bn. Indian 3.72 Rnfts. 1st S. Staffords 1 off. 2nd Rnfts 10 R (from Italy)	CHB
do.	22/9/17		Zero 6.30 A.M. Casualties Nil. Reinforcements 2nd Queen 38 O.R. 1st S. Staffords 1 off. 2nd Rnfts 10 R (from Italy) Fine - Sunny at intervals. B.G.C. M. and Bns training in camps in morning. Lt. Col. Howard G.S.O. 5 called at H.Q. Casualties Nil. Reinforcements 21st Middx. 10 R (from Italy)	LEHB
do.	23/9/17		Fine and Sunny. Lt. Col. Longbourne D.S.O. Cdg. 2nd Queen left to resume command of 17th S. Staff. Bde. (5th Div.) Casualties Nil. Reinforcements 1st S. Staffords 2 O.R.	C/S
do.	24/9/17		Fine and Sunny. Hot. Brigade took part in Div. scheme * at which the C. in C. was present. S.C. 9. Sig. offr. Returned from PARIS in evening. Casualties Nil. Reinforcements 21st Middx. 10 R 22nd Middx. 50 R	* 9.10.16. 9.30 P.M. C/S
do.	25/9/17		Fine & Sunny. Hot. B.G.C. watched Div. scheme carried out G.2.O. & 2.2nd 1.S.S. B.M. watched scheme in afternoon from contact aeroplane. Casualties nil Rnfts. 2nd Queen 8. O.R. 1st S. Staffords 1 off. 18 O.R. 22nd Middx.	C/S

2449 Wt. W14957/Mgo 750,000 1/16 J.B.C. & A. Forms/C.2118/12.

Army Form C. 2118.

WAR DIARY
or
INTELLIGENCE SUMMARY

(Erase heading not required.)

Instructions regarding War Diaries and Intelligence Summaries are contained in F. S. Regs., Part II. and the Staff Manual respectively. Title Pages will be prepared in manuscript.

Place	Date	Hour	Summary of Events and Information	Remarks and references to Appendices
BERTDINGHEM	26/9/17		Dull. Sunshine at intervals. Bde took part in Div Sch. Major Brent 1.3 R 2nd in cmd 22nd inches annual command of 2nd Bn Royal War Rgt (22.1.B) Casualties Nil. Reinforcements 1 NCO, 14 OR 21st Inches Rgt 1 Off. 20 OR (1 Bn. Inf) 22nd Inches Rgt 1 Off	¾ Div Sd R.O. 19. II. 7 inst. ETB
do	27/9/17		Fine and Sunny. Hot. B.G.C and B.M. attended conference at Div H.Q. at 6 PM. Casualties Nil. Reinforcements 21st Inches Rgt 1 Off. 1 Off. hospital	ETB
ELNES	28/9/17		Dull. Sunny afternoon. Bde front Coy 9.11 m.g Coy moved by motor route to ELNES - HAVRIETES area ¾ Fd Bd. Billets good but scattered. B.G.c and B.M. left at 8 AM by car to reconnoitre forward area. Bde H.Q at ELNES, Coy M.G. Regts 2nd Queen 4 Offr. 213 Inches 3 or 22nd Inches 3 PM	¾ Div. 130. No 19. AM ETB
ST HUBERTUS - HOEK	29/9/17		Fine and Sunny. Bde front marched to ARQUES to entrain for ABEELE. TRANSPORT entrained at VIZERNES. On arrival at ABEELE Bde front marched to camp in vicinity of ST HUBERTUR VAN ISK. A.S.C.B.M left by car at 3 PM to forward area, accompanied by Lt.Col Beaum = Sig M. Casualties Nil. Reinforcements Nil.	¾ B.O. No 20 off ETB
do	30/9/16		Misty Early. Hot and Sunny Later. B.M. took party forward to reconnoitre fort line. Wheps Lorries visited Bde H.Q in morning. Conference with 2nd Off B 20. 26 B.Le at 3 PM to discuss forthcoming operations. Cas: Nil. Refs 2nd Queen. 1 off.	Off B

Ghostlady Cotton
for Brigadier General
Commanding 89th Infantry Bde.

SECRET.   Copy No. 18

91st Infantry Brigade Order No.16

Saturday, 1st September, 1917.
Reference Maps - BELGIUM & FRANCE Sheets 27 & 28 1/40,000

91st Inf.Bde.
  H.Q.
2nd Queen's Regt.
1st S.Staffs R.
21st Manch.R.
22nd Manch.R.
91st M.G.Coy.
91st L.T.M.B.
No.3 Coy.,7th
  Div.Train.
528 (Durham) Fld.
  Co.,R.E.
21st Fld.Amblce.

1. (a) The 91st Infantry Brigade Group, consisting of the marginally named units, will move to the STEENVOORDE area this afternoon.
   (b) The march will probably be continued to-morrow, September 2nd to the LEDERZEELE area.

2. Units will pass the starting point (Cross Roads G.22.b.6.3.) as follows:-

Brigade Hd.Qtrs.)	
91st L.T.M.Batt.)	4-25 p.m.
2nd Queen's Regt.	4-30 p.m.
22nd Manchester Regt.	4-44 p.m.
21st Manchester Regt.	4-58 p.m.
1st S.Staffs Regt.	5-12 p.m.
91st M.G.Coy.	5-26 p.m.
No.3 Co.,7th Div.Train	5-32 p.m.
21st Field Ambulance.	5-38 p.m.
528 (Durham) Fld.Co., R.E.	5-46 p.m.

3. (a) Route for all units via BUSSEBOOM cross-roads - Cross Roads G.15.b.1.7. - Rd.junc.G.15.c.0.8. - Cross Roads G.20.a.4.4. - Rd.junc. G.19.b.4.9. - HOPOUTRE (L.17.central) - ABEELE - STEENVOORDE.
   (b) The head of the column will not reach ABEELE before 6-20 p.m.

4. (a) Intervals of 200 yards between companies, and between the rear company and the 1st Line transport, will be maintained East of the REMINGHELST - POPERINGHE road.
   (b) West of this road companies will march closed up.

5. All units will halt for the last ten minutes of each hour.

6. O.C., 21st Field Ambulance will arrange for the road in rear of the column to be patrolled by a motor ambulance throughout the march.

7. Watches will be synchronised by bearer.

8. On arrival in the new area units will be met by their advanced parties and conducted to their billeting areas.

9. Position of Refilling Point will be notified later.

10. Brigade Headquarters will close at OUDERDOM at 4 p.m. and open at STEENVOORDE at the same hour.

11. Acknowledge.

Captain,
Brigade Major, 91st Infantry Brigade.

Issued at 2 p.m. to -

Copy No.1 2nd Queen's Re	10 21st Fld.Amblce.
2. 1st S.Staffs R.	11 528 (Durham) Fld.Co.R.E.
3 21st Manch.R.	12 Supply Officer.
4 22nd Manch.R.	13 No.3 Coy.,7th Div.Train.
5 91st M.G.Co.	14 7th Division.
6 91st L.T.M.Batt.	15 20th Inf.Bde.
7 No.3 Sec.7th Div Sigs.	16 File
	17 War Diary.
8 Staff Captain.	18 War Diary.
9 Bde.Transport Off.	

SECRET.   App. 2   Copy No. 19

91st Infantry Brigade Order No.17.

Sunday, 2nd September, 1917.
Reference Map - HAZEBROUCK Sheet 5A Edition 2 1/100,000.

1. The 91st Infantry Brigade Group will move to the WALLON CAPPEL Area to-morrow, September 3rd, 1917, in accordance with the attached March Table.

2. Each unit will send a billeting party to meet the Staff Captain at the Area Commandant's Office, STAPLE, at 11 a.m.

3. O.C., 21st Field Ambulance will arrange for the road in rear of the main column and also for that in rear of 21st Bn. Manchester Regt to be patrolled by an ambulance throughout the march.

4. A synchronised watch will be circulated in the course of the morning to all units moving via CASSEL.

5. Brigade Headquarters will close at STEENVOORDE at 1-15 p.m. and open at LE NIEPPE at the same hour.

6. Acknowledge.

Captain,
Brigade Major, 91st Infantry Brigade.

Issued at 9 p.m. to -

Copy No. 1 2nd Queen's Regt.
2 1st S. Staffs Regt.
3 21st Manch. Regt.
4 22nd Manch. Regt.
5 91st M.G. Coy.
6 91st L.T.M. Batty.
7 No.3 Sec., 7th Div. Sig. Co.
8 Staff Captain.
9 Bde. Transport Officer.
10 21st Field Ambloe.
11 528 (Durham) Fld. Co., R.E.
12 Supply Officer.
13 No.3 Coy., 7th Div. Train.
14 12th M.V.S.
15 7th Division.
16 20th. Inf. Bde.
17 File.
18 War Diary.
19 War Diary.

MARCH TABLE (to accompany 91st Inf.Bde.Order No.17).

Unit.	Starting Point.	Time.	Destination.	Route.	Remarks.
Brigade Headquarters.) 91st L.T.M.Battery)	Cross Roads ½ mile S. of the N. of STEENVOORDE.	2-0 p.m.	LE NIEPPE.	Via CASSEL, OXELAERE, BAVINCHOVE.	
2nd Bn.Queen's Regt.	-do.-	2-5 p.m.	Area S.W. of ZUYTPEENE.	Via CASSEL and ZUYTPEENE.	
1st S.Staffs Regt.	-do.-	2-20 p.m.	Les TROIS ROIS (½ mile East of N. of EY HOUCK)	Via CASSEL, OXELAERE, BAVINCHOVE.	
No.3 Coy.,7th Div.Train.	-do.-	2-35 p.m.	Area 1 mile N.W. of LE NIEPPE.	-do.-	
21st Field Ambulance.	-do.-	2-41 p.m.	Area immediately S.W. of EY of EY HOUCK.	-do.-	
528(Durham)Fld.Co.,R.E.	-do.-	2-47 p.m.	Area immediately E. of 1st S.Staffs Regt.	-do.-	
12th M.V.S.	-do.-	2-52 p.m.	LE NIEPPE.	-do.-	
91st M.G.Company.			Area 1 mile S. of X of LONGUE CROIX		Not to enter ABEELE - CASSEL road before 2-30 p.m.
22nd Manchester Regt.	Cross Roads 200 yards N. of L of LE BELARDE.	2-50 p.m.	LE NIEPPE.	LONGUE CROIX - STAPLE	
21st Manchester Regt.	-do.-	2-45 p.m.	Area S. of LES SIX of LES SIX RUES.	-do.-	

Units will march closed up. Intervals of 500 yards between battalions and 20 yards between smaller units will be maintained. All units will halt for the last ten minutes of each unit hour.

Copy No. 16

SECRET.

91st Infantry Brigade Order No. 18.

Wednesday, 12th September, 1917.

Reference Maps –
FRANCE, Sheet 27 – Scale 1/40,000.
" " 27A.S.E. – Scale 1/20,000.
HAZEBROUCK 5A, Edition 2. – Scale 1/100,000.

1. The 91st Infantry Brigade Group will move to the TILQUES AREA on September 13th and 15th in accordance with the attached march tables.

2. (a) Spaces of 500 yards in rear of Battalions and 200 yards behind smaller Units will be maintained throughout the march.
   (b) All Units will halt for the last 10 minutes of each hour.
   (c) A synchronised watch will be circulated to units on morning of September 13th and 15th.

3. Billetting Parties for all Units except 91st Machine Gun Coy., and 528th (Durham) Field Coy, R.E., will report to Area Commandant BOISDINGHEM by 11.a.m. on September 14th.

4. (a) Baggage wagons will report to Battalions by 7-30.a.m. on September 13th and 15th.
   (b) Lorries (1 apiece per Battalion, 91st Machine Gun Coy., and 91st Trench Mortar Bty.) will report to Units by 7-30.a.m. on September 13th and 15th. Half of the Lorry for 91st Machine Gun Coy., will be available for 21st Field Ambulance to whom it will be re-directed by 91st Machine Gun Coy. The Lorry for 91st Trench Mortar Bty., will be similarly shared by Brigade Headquarters.

5. A certificate that area stores, billets and tents are left intact and clean on vacation will be rendered by all units by 9.a.m. on the day following each move.

6. (a) Refilling Point will be at HAUT-ARQUES (about S.10.c.) on September 13th and 14th, thereafter in vicinity of NORDAL (exact location to be notified later).
   (b) Railhead for leave purposes will be ARQUES on September 14th and 15th, thereafter LUMBRES.
   (c) Railhead for Courses will be EBLINGHEM on September 14th and 15th, thereafter ST.OMER. Men proceeding on Courses may be sent to ST.OMER by train from WIZERNES at 19-44.

7. Brigade Headquarters will close at LE NIEPPE and ARQUES at 10.a.m. on September 13th and 15th, and open at the same hour at ARQUES and BOISDINGHEM respectively.

8. ACKNOWLEDGE.

Captain,

Brigade Major, 91st Infantry Brigade.

Issued at 8/30.p.m. to –

Copy No 1 2nd Queen's R
2 1st S.Staffs.R
3 21st Manch.R
4 22nd Manch.R
5 91st M.G.Coy.
6 91st L.T.M.Bty.
7 No.3.Secn.7th Div.Sigs.
8 Staff Captain.
9 Bde. Transport Officer.
10 21st Field Ambulance.
11 528th (Durham) Field Coy. R.E.
12 Supply Officer.
13 No.3.Coy. 7th Div.Train.
14 7th Division.
15 File.
16 War Diary.
17 War Diary.

March Table for September 13th, 1917.

Issued with 91st Infantry Brigade Order No.18.

Unit.	Destination.	Starting Point.	Time.	Route.	Remarks.
91st Inf.Bde.Hdqrs. } 91st L.T.M.Bty. }	ARQUES. S.15.c.45.45. ARQUES. S.15.c.	Entrance to Bde. H.Q. R.11.a.2.7.	10.a.m.	Via main CASSEL ST.OMER Road.	
91st Machine Gun Coy.	ARQUES. S.15.c.	-do-	10.4.a.m.	-do-	
22nd Bn.Manch.Regt.	ARQUES. S.15.d.	-do-	10.11a.m.	-do-	
2nd Bn.Queen's Regt.	HAUT ARQUES. S.16.c.	-do-	10.23.am.	-do-	
21st Field Ambulance.	HAUT ARQUES. S.10.c.5.1.	-do-	10.35.am.	-do-	Not to enter rain road before 2nd of Queens Regt. is clear of MAISON BLANCHE.
528th (Durham) Fd.Coy. R.E.	HAUT ARQUES. S.16.b.3.8.	-do-	10-45.am.	-do-	Not to pass MAISON BLANCHE before 21st Field Amb. are clear.
No.3.Coy.Div.Train.	HAUT ARQUES. S.10.c.9.5.	-do-	11.a.m.	-do-	
21st Bn.Manch.Regt.	H.19.c.5.8.	LE HIEPPE Church.	9-15.a.m.	-	
1st Bn.S.Staff.Regt.	COIN PERDU. H.20.d.8.8.	MAISON BLANCHE.	10-30.am.	-	

Reference Map:
HAZEBROUCK, 5A, Edition 2.
Scale 1,100,000.

March Table for September 15th, 1917.

Issued with 91st Infantry Brigade Order No. 18.

Unit.	Destination.	Starting Point.	Time.	Route.	Remarks.
91st Inf.Bde. H.Q. } 91st L.T.M.Bty. }	BOISDINGHEM. BARBINGHEM.	Junction of Road & track ¼ mile S. of O. of ST.OMER.	10-0 a.m.	Via LONGUENESSE - TATINGHEM - QUELMES - VERNOVE.	
2nd Queen's Regt.	BOISDINGHEM, & ZUTOVE.	-do-	10-4 a.m.	-do-	
21st Field Amb.	LA HATTINE.	-do-	10-16.a.m.	-do-	
No.3.Coy.Div. Train.	NORDAI.	-do-	10-26.a.m.	-do-	
21st Manch.Regt.	MORINGHEM, GRAND MERQUES & PETIT DIEQUES.	ST.MARTIN AU LAERT Church.	12.noon.	Via ZUDAUSQUES.	
1st S.Staffs.Regt.	ZUDAUSQUES, LIHEUSE, NOIR CARME & ADSOIL.	-do-	12-12.p.m.		
2nd Manch.Regt.	ACQUIN, LE NOUVRE & LE POUVRE.	As for Bde. H.Q.	10-31.a.m.	Via LONGUENESSE and SETQUES.	
91st M.G.Coy.	LUIBRES.	-do-	10-43.a.m.	-do-	Proceed to Area allotted by DIV.M.G.Officer.
528th (Durham) Fd.Coy.R.E.	HALLINES.	Cross Roads ½ mile S. of A of ARQUES.	8-30.a.m.	WIZERNES.	Proceed to Area allotted by C.R.E.

BRIGADE SCHEME NO. 1.

Reference Map - FRANCE 27A S.E. Scale 1/20,000.

Appx. 4.

GENERAL IDEA.

Phase (a). Simple advance of Two Battalions, in normal formation, on a 600 yards front, from PETIT DIFQUES - MORINGHEM Road, over ridge 26 (i.e. ridge running N.E. from Windmill Q.26.c.0.0.) and ridge 33 (i.e. ridge immediately S. of ridge 26) to ZUDAUSQUES - CORMETTE road.

Phase (b). The two Battalions return behind a flag barrage over same course, assuming that the line of the track and bank from Q.32.d.0.4. - Q.33.b.0.9. is held by two other battalions, with the object of capturing ridge 26 and establishing and consolidating the line of the banks from Q.25.d.6.3. - Q.26.a.8.1.

—:—:—:—:—

SPECIAL IDEA.

Phase (a). 1. By Zero hour "A" Battalion (on the right) and "B" Battalion (on the left) will be in position with the leading wave on a tape line (imaginary) running from the corner of field at Q.25.d.5.7. - corner of field at Q.26.a.25.55.

2. Boundaries (for both phases) will be as follows :-

 (a) Right flank of "A" Battalion:- A line from corner of field at Q.25.d.5.7. - Windmill Q.26.c.0.0. - corner of field W.3.a.5.8.
 (b) Between "A" and "B" Battalions:- A line from Q.26.a.0.0. - end of bank Q.32.b.5.6. - end of bank Q.33.d.2.2.
 (c) Left of "B" Battalion:- A line from corner of field Q.26.a.25.55. - Q.27.c.0.0. - end of bank Q.33.d.85.40.

3. At Zero hour the line will commence to move forward, the inner flanks of Battalions directing, and the advance will continue at normal walking pace until the ZUDAUSQUES - CORMETTE Road is reached, when Battalions will halt and reform.

Phase (b). 1(a) At Zero hour (which will be notified on the field) a flag barrage will open on the line of the bank from Q.32.b.0.1. - Q.27.c.0.0., where it will remain for two minutes, allowing the infantry to creep up to within 50 yards of it.
 (b) At Zero plus 2 minutes it will advance by 50 yard bounds at the rate of 100 yards in 4 minutes, making a pause of 5 minutes after every 300 yards advance to allow the mopping up (imaginary) to take place.
 (c) On reaching the PETIT DIFQUES - MORINGHEM Road it will halt and become a stationary protective barrage.

2. At Zero minus 15 minutes the advance of the infantry will commence by platoons in artillery formation from the line of the ZUDAUSQUES - CORMETTE Road. Before reaching the crest of ridge 33, normal attack formations will be assumed, and the advance will be continued to a line 50 yards beyond the line of the track and bank held by our most forward troops, where the line will halt and await the barrage (see para. 1.)

NOTES.
1. During the course of the advance drummers representing gas shell will appear, on hearing which all ranks will instantly assume gas protection. The cessation of drumming will signify that safe conditions again prevail.
2. Special attention will be paid to the use of compasses throughout the advance.
3. In phase (b), in order to clear NO MAN'S LAND quickly, intervals of 15 yards only between waves will be maintained until the rear wave is clear of the bottom of the valley, when normal intervals will be gradually resumed.
4. Dress:- Fighting Order, no bombs.

—————oOo—————

BRIGADE SCHEME NO. 2.

Reference Map:- FRANCE Sheet 27A S.E. - Scale 1/20,000.

GENERAL IDEA.

1. The line of the MORINGHEM - BOISDINGHEM Road is held by our forward posts, the spur running from Q.31.a.0.4. - P.36.d.0.2. being held by the enemy.

2. The Brigade is ordered to make good the ridge along the line of the track from CHATEAU W.1.d.7.4. - W.7.a.25.90.

3. (a) PHASE "A".
"A" Battalion is accordingly ordered to capture and consolidate the line of the track from V.6.Central to W.1.a.1.3., thence the main road to its junction with track at W.1.a.5.3.
  (b) PHASE "B".
"B" Battalion (Right) and "C" Battalion (Left) are then ordered to pass through "A" Battalion to the final objective, which is to be consolidated.
  (c) "D" Battalion (imaginary) remains in Brigade reserve.

SPECIAL IDEA.

PHASE "A".

1. "A" Battalion will be formed up by Zero hour with its leading wave on the MORINGHEM - BOISDINGHEM Road from P.36.c.0.6. - P.36.b.25.35.
"B" and "C" Battalions will be in positions of assembly in the valley in P.35.b. and 36.a.

2. (a) At Zero hour a flag barrage will open on a line 200 yards S.E. of the MORINGHEM - BOISDINGHEM Road, where it will remain for two minutes to allow the infantry to advance as close as possible.
  (b) At Zero plus 2 minutes it will commence to advance by 50 yard bounds every two minutes until a total advance of 300 yards from the original barrage line has been effected. Thenceforward the rate will be decreased to 50 yards in 3 minutes until it reaches a line 200 yards in advance of the first objective where it will remain until Zero plus 60 minutes.

PHASE "B".

1. As "A" Battalion moves forward at Zero hour, "B" and "C" Battalions will take up their respective positions on the MORINGHEM - BOISDINGHEM Road from P.36.c.0.6. - P.36.b.25.35.

2. Boundaries will be as follows:-

  (a) Right of "B" Battalion:- A line from P.36.c.0.6. to Road junction V.6.a.7.4., thence S.E. along track through V.6.Central.
  (b) Between "B" and "C" Battalions:- A line joining P.36.c.65.95. to tree at V.6.b.75.40. Thence to W.7.a.50.95.
  (c) Left of "C" Battalion:- P.36.b.25.35. - Road junction P.36.d.9.3. - Road junction W.1.a.5.3. - W.1.d.15.20.

3. (a) At Zero plus 45 minutes, "B" and "C" Battalions will advance by platoons in artillery formation, the right flank of "B" Battalion directing.
  (b) Normal attack formations will be assumed immediately before crossing the ridge running through Q.31.c.0.3. and P.36.d.0.0.
  (c) The advance will be continued through "A" Battalion to a position as close to the barrage as possible, where the line will halt and await the lifting of the barrage.

4. At Zero plus 60 minutes the barrage will resume its advance by 50 yard bounds every 4 minutes until the final objective is reached, when it will become a stationary protective barrage on a line 200 yards in advance of the final objective.

NOTES.

1. <u>Formation of "A" Battalion.</u>

    2 Companies in front, 2 Companies in rear, finding "moppers up"

  <u>Formation of "B" and "C" Battalions.</u>

    2 Companies in front.
    1 Company "mopping up".
    1 Company Reserve.

2. A sketch map follows shewing positions of known pepper boxes, Strong Points and Machine Gun Emplacements.

3. Coloured flags will represent Known' as well as Unknown Strong Points.

4. Enemy will wear caps with the peak to the rear.

5. "Moppers up" will be previously detailed to definite areas by each Battalion. They will wear Field Service caps.

6. Each Battalion will be accompanied to the position of assembly by a pack convoy of 15 animals under the Officer detailed in B.M./1599/2 dated 18th September, 1917 for pack work. This convoy will carry any form of ammunition or R.E. Stores except S.A.A. in boxes (Lewis Gun magazines may be carried) and will, for the purposes of this scheme, move forward under battalion arrangements to the battalion objective, when gained.

    The Officer i/c pack train will previously reconnoitre the best route for this.

7. Gas shell will be represented by Drums as in Scheme 1.

8. Casualties will be instructed to lie down with their caps off and head towards the enemy.

9. Special attention will be paid to the use of compasses during the advance.

10. At the conclusion of operations (Bugle calls "STAND FAST" and "DISMISS") all Officers will assemble for a pow-wow at Road Junction W.1.a.5.3., troops being marched back to billets under the N.C.Os.

11. Dress:- Fighting Order, without bombs.

-:-:-:-:-:-:-:-:-:-:-:-:-

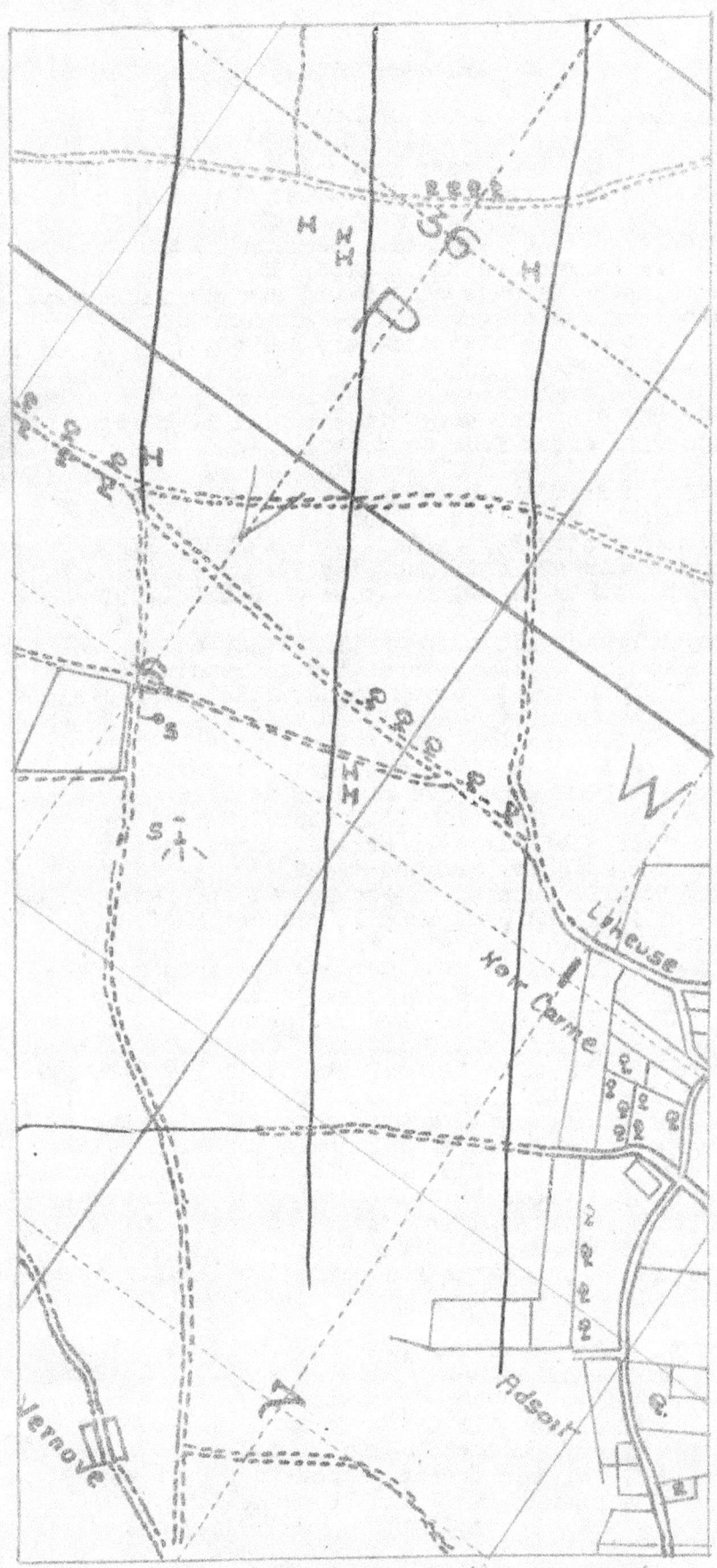

Notes:- H = Haystacks representing pepperbox
S = Strong point
Haystacks will NOT be marked by red flags

Scale 1:10,000

SECRET.

Copy No. 17

App. 6

91st Infantry Brigade Order No.P1.

Friday, 21st September, 1917.

Reference attached Map.

1. (a) The 7th Division will take part in an attack on the high ground West of WISQUES at 11.a.m., on September 25th, 1917, with objectives and boundaries as shewn on attached Map "A".
   (b) The 91st Infantry Brigade will be attacking on the Right and the 20th Infantry Brigade on the Left of the Divisional front. The 22nd Infantry Brigade will be in Divisional Reserve.
   (c) The Nth Brigade, of Y Division will be simultaneously attacking on the Right of the 91st Infantry Brigade with objectives as shewn on attached Map "A".

2. The attack of the 91st Infantry Brigade will be carried out by four Battalions with objectives as under:-

   (a) 1st Bn. South Staffordshire Regt. — RED LINE.
   (b) 2nd Bn. Queen's Regt. (Right) and
       21st Bn. Manchester Regt. (Left). — YELLOW LINE.
   (c) 22nd Bn. Manchester Regt. (assisted
       by 2nd Bn. Queen's Regt.) — GREEN LINE.

3. (a) The Artillery barrage will open at 11.a.m., on a line 150 yards in advance of the forming up line, where it will remain for two minutes, allowing the infantry to creep up as close as possible. At 11-2.a.m. it will commence to advance at the rate of 100 yards in 4 minutes until it reaches the RED LINE (11-23.a.m.), where it will remain for 6 minutes. At 11-29.a.m., it will resume its advance at the rate of 100 yards in 6 minutes until reaching a line 200 yards in advance of the RED LINE where it will remain until 12-17.p.m. on the 91st Infantry Brigade front, and until 12-35.p.m., on the 20th Infantry Brigade front.
   (b) At 12-17.p.m., it will resume its advance at the rate of 100 yards in 6 minutes till 12-32.p.m., when it reaches the YELLOW LINE as far East as W.21.a.7.1., thence rejoining its original line at W.15.d.2.1. Thenceforward it will advance at the same rate, with its right pivoting on point W.21.a.7.1., until reaching the remainder of the YELLOW LINE (at 12-56.p.m.), where it will remain for 6 minutes. At 1-2.p.m., it will lift off the YELLOW LINE and advance at the rate of 100 yards in 8 minutes to a line 200 yards in advance of the YELLOW LINE where it will remain until 2-15.p.m.
   (c) At 2-15.p.m., the barrage will commence to roll forward at the rate of 100 yards in 8 minutes on an alignment parallel to the YELLOW LINE from W.16.c.7.4. - W.15.d.9.0., until the GREEN LINE is reached (at 2-51.p.m.) where it will remain for 8 minutes. It will then resume its advance to a protective barrage line 200 yards in advance of the final objective.
   (d) Throughout the above programme the barrage will advance by 50 yard bounds.

4. (a) (i) The 1st Bn. South Staffordshire Regt., will be formed up by 10-30.a.m., in normal attack formation with the leading wave on the tape line. (See Map "A" attached).
      (ii) At 11.a.m., the line will crawl forward as close as possible to the barrage, and the advance will be carried out in accordance with the barrage programme in para.3(a) above.
      (iii) The objective when gained will be consolidated in depth.

   (b) (i) At 10-30.a.m., the 2nd Bn. Queen's Regt., and 21st Bn. Manchester Regt., will be in a position of assembly in the vicinity of W.8.c.0.0. and W.8.d.8.4. respectively.
      (ii) Thence the advance will be carried out, on a two Company front in each case, in artillery formation of platoons in file, the leading platoons crossing the tape line at 11-45.a.m.
      (iii) The deployment into normal attack formation will be carried out after the leading wave has passed through 1st Bn. South Staffordshire Regt., unless an earlier deployment has been rendered necessary by heavy Machine Gun Fire.

(iv) The advance will be continued as close to the barrage as possible, when the line will halt and await the lifting of the barrage.

(v) At 12-17.p.m., the advance will be continued in accordance with the barrage programme in para.3(b) above, to the objectives as shewn on attached Map "A".

(vi) The objectives when gained will be consolidated in depth.

(c) (i) The 22nd Bn.Manchester Regt., will be in a position of assembly in the valley about W.8.b.0.2. by 10-30.a.m.

(ii) Thence the advance will be carried out in Artillery formation of platoons in file, the leading platoon crossing the LEULINGHEM - QUELMES Road at 1-15.p.m. The flanks of the advance will be as for 21st Bn.Manchester Regt.

(iii) The deployment into Normal Attack Formation will take place after the leading line has crossed the valley in W.21.b.

(iv) The advance will be continued as close as possible to the protective barrage (200 yards in advance of the YELLOW LINE) where the leading line will halt and wait for the barrage to roll back across the battalion front. As the barrage clears, the line will advance to the capture of the GREEN LINE, where touch will be established with the 20th Infantry Brigade on the left and the 2nd Bn.Queen's Regt. on the right.

(v) The objective when gained will be consolidated in depth.

(d) Simultaneously with the operation indicated in para.c(iv) above, The Officer Commanding, 2nd Bn.Queen's Regt., will conform by advancing his left flank, pivoting on the junction of the YELLOW and GREEN LINES.

5. After the capture of the final objective the 21st Bn. Manchester Regt., will be withdrawn into Brigade Reserve in W.8.d. under separate orders.

6. (a) Battalion Headquarters will be established as under:-

2nd Bn.Queen's Regt.	W.8.c.6.0.
1st Bn.South Staffordshire Regt.	track junction W.14.b.8.9.
21st Bn.Manchester Regt.	In immediate vicinity of Bde.Hd.Qtrs.
22nd Bn.Manchester Regt.	Road junction W.8.b.2.4.

(b) Previous notice will be given to Brigade Headquarters before Battalion Headquarters moves forward, stating the proposed position; A guide will also be sent from the new position. A representative will remain at the former Headquarters until the forward Headquarters is opened.

7. (a) (i) Two sections of 91st Machine Gun Company are allotted to the Brigade.

(ii) The Officer Commanding, 91st Machine Gun Coy., will detail an Officer to accompany the rear wave of 1st Bn. South Staffordshire Regt., and proceed to reconnoitre a position for two guns in the vicinity of W.15.c., whence fire can be brought to bear on the valley in W.21.c. The guns will be brought forward when the most satisfactory position has been located and notified to Brigade Hd.Qtrs.

(iii) Officers will be similarly detailed to proceed with the rear wave of 2nd Bn.Queen's Regt., and 22nd Bn. Manchester Regt., to select positions on the forward slopes of Hill 120 so as to command the spur through W.21.d.0.0., the valley through W.27.b.0.5. and 5.0., and the spur through W.28.a.0.3.

(iv) A further two guns will be placed in selected positions in rear of the RED LINE.

(b) The remaining 8 guns will co-operate in the Divisional Machine Gun barrage scheme under the Divisional Machine Gun Officer.

-3-

7. (c) (i) The guns detailed in sub-para.(a)(ii) and (iv) will cover the consolidation of the RED and YELLOW LINES.
(ii) The guns detailed in sub-para.(a)(iii) will cover the consolidation of the GREEN and YELLOW LINES.
(iii) ALL guns will be prepared to open fire, in response to an S.O.S.Call or Rocket, on their final S.O.S.Lines a scheme for which will be drawn up by The Officer Commanding, 91st Machine Gun Coy., immediately the forward gun positions are selected.

(d) The Officer Commanding, 91st Machine Gun Coy., will establish his Headquarters in the immediate vicinity of Brigade Headquarters.

8. (a) The Officer Commanding, 91st Light Trench Mortar Battery will detail one gun and team to proceed with the rear wave of 2nd Bn. Queen's Regt., and one gun and team with the rear wave of 21st Bn. Manchester Regt., to deal with any obstructions that may arise. On reaching the YELLOW LINE emplacements will be constructed for defensive purposes.
These guns will be carried slung (without tripods) and will each be provided with a carrying party of 10 men by the Battalion concerned.
(b) He will also detail 6 men each to 1st Bn.South Staffordshire Regt., and 22nd Bn.Manchester Regt., for attachment to mopping up parties to assist in blowing in the doors of pepperboxes. Each man will carry 4 rounds of Stokes ammunition.
(c) The remainder of 91st Light Trench Mortar Battery will remain in Brigade Reserve in the vicinity of Brigade Headquarters.

9. (a) The Officer Commanding, 528th (Durham) Field Coy.R.E., will detail two sections to assist in the consolidation of the YELLOW LINE when captured. These sections will move forward under the orders of Brigade Headquarters accompanied by their own pack detachment. They will be in a position of assembly in the vicinity of W.8.c.0.0. by 10-30.a.m., a Liaison Officer being sent to Brigade Headquarters by that hour.
(b) The platoon of pioneers detailed by The Officer Commanding, 24th Bn.Manchester Regt., will assist the 1st Bn.South Staffordshire Regt., to consolidate the RED LINE. They will make their own arrangements for tools and stores and should be in a position of assembly in QUELMES by 11.a.m. The Platoon Commander will report in advance to Headquarters, 1st Bn.South Staffordshire Regt., at 10-30.a.m.

10. (a) (i) All Battalions will be connected to Brigade Headquarters by telephone.
(ii) In no case will more than one telephone line per Battalion be run out forward.
(iii) Each Battalion will establish runner posts forward, the positions of which will be laid down as far as possible beforehand, and marked with a signal flag when occupied.
(iv) Full advantage will be taken of the exceptional facilities for visual signalling. A Brigade Receiving Station will be opened at W.15.a.0.5. at 11-30.a.m.; any messages so received will be distributed thence by telephone to the addressee.
(v) Three sets of pigeons per Battalion will be issued, if available, for distribution to the attacking Companies.

(b) (i) The leading troops will light flares at 11-45.a.m., 1-15.p.m., 3.p.m., and when called for by a contact aeroplane.
(ii) Groundsheets and panels will be laid out at Battalion Headquarters and communication with aeroplanes practised.

(c) Liaison Officers will be exchanged as under. Each Officer will be accompanied by two orderlies, and should report to the Battalion Headquarters concerned by 10-30.a.m.:-

1st Bn.South Staffordshire Regt.   - 2nd Bn.Border Regt.
 (H.Q. W.8.d.80.05.)
 Nth Bn.The Blankshire Regt.(Imaginary).

21st Bn.Manchester Regt.   - 8th Bn.Devonshire Regt.
 (H.Q. W.15.d.4.0.)

22nd Bn.Manchester Regt.   - 9th Bn.Devonshire Regt.
(H.Q. W.21.b.8.7.)

2nd Bn.Queen's Regt.   - 9th The Blankshire Regt.
(Imaginary).

(d) Two S.O.S. rifle grenades each will be issued to 22nd Bn. Manchester Regt., and 2nd Bn.Queen's Regt., and two to 1st Bn.South Staffordshire Regt. The Officer Commanding, 1st Bn.South Staffordshire Regt., will arrange for a look-out station to be posted with orders to repeat at once any S.O.S. signal observed on the Brigade front.

11. A watch will be circulated to Battalions, 91st Machine Gun Coy., and 91st Light Trench Mortar Bty., before 10-30.a.m.

12. Administrative instructions will be issued later.

13. Brigade Headquarters will open at Road junction W.8.a.9.0. at 10-30.a.m.

14. ACKNOWLEDGE.

Moorhead

Captain,

Brigade Major, 91st Infantry Brigade.

Copies to -

    Copy No 1 2nd Queen's R
            2 1st S.Staffs.R
            3 21st Manch.R
            4 22nd Manch.R
            5 91st M.G.Coy.
            6 91st L.T.M.Bty.
            7 No.3.Secn.7th Div.Sigs.
            8 Staff Captain.
            9 Brigade Transport Officer.
           10 A.D.M.S.
           11 528th (Durham) Fd.Coy.R.E.
           12 24th Bn.Manch.R
           13 7th Division.
           14 20th Inf.Bde.
           15 File.
           16 War Diary.
           17 War Diary.

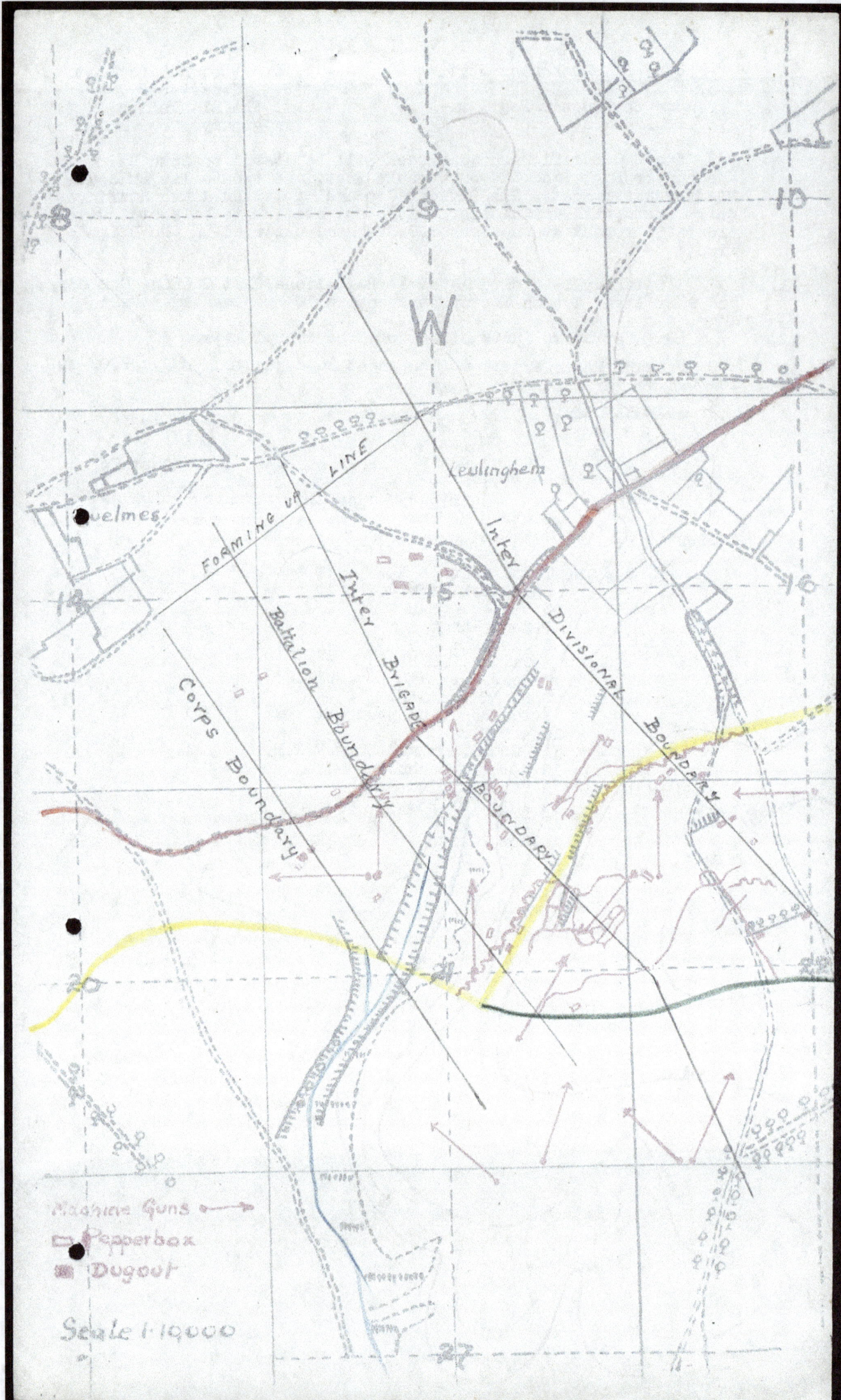

APPENDIX 1
to 91st Infantry Brigade Order No.21.

Notes for Regulation of Divisional Practice Attack, September 25th, 1917.

Reference Map Sheet 27 SE. 1/20,000.

1. (a) Units will move to their assembly positions in their own time with the following modifications.
   (1) O.C., 22nd Bn. Manchester Regt will make arrangements direct with Div.M.G.Officer (WESTBECOURT) as to the use of the AQUIN - GUILLES road.
   (2) The 21st Bn. Manchester Regt will not enter EUMAUSQUES before 9-45 a.m.
   (b) Lewis Gun limbers may be taken to the assembly positions, but will be clear of the theatre of operations by 11 a.m. They may, if desired, park on the N.W. outskirts of GUILLES. Units will make their own arrangements for picking them up on the conclusion of operations; no limber will be taken S.E. of GUILLES before 3-30 p.m.
   (c) Officers Mess Carts may rendezvous in vicinity of Road junction W.22.d.3.3., where the Pow-wow will take place.

2. (a) 2nds-in-Command of battalions and companies and the 2nd-in-Command of 91st Machine Gun Co. will be detailed to act as Umpires. Actual Commanders may be sent in lieu of above if desired.
   (b) Umpires will be mounted for each attack and will wear two white armbands, to be provided under Divisional arrangements.
   (c) Copies of Instructions for Umpires and a sun print of the theatre will be issued later to each Umpire.
   (d) All Umpires will rendezvous on 23rd September at 10-30 a.m. at road junction W.15.a.2.8. for a rehearsal.

3. Troops taking part in the attack will carry haversack rations.

4. (a) The Barrage will be represented by flags.
   (b) The flags will remain up on the line of the final protective barrage until 3-42 p.m., when they will be lowered. They will not be raised again unless called for by the S.O.S. signal.

5. (a) The skeleton enemy will wear F.S. caps reversed.
   (b) The Nth Bn. The Blankshire Regt will be represented by men in single file carrying red flags.
   (c) Hostile M.G's, dugouts, Trench Mortars, etc., will be marked by name-boards. Enemy Machine Guns will be represented by a rattle.
   (d) Trenches to be captured have been double-spitlocked. All existing trenches dug on the theatre will be ignored.

6. "A" Echelon only of the Brigade Pack train will be in attendance, less the 5 pack subsections of 91st M.G.Coy. which will be controlled under orders of Divl.M.G.Officer.

7. (a) The taking and evacuation of prisoners will be practised.
   (b) Casualties and Medical arrangements will be practised. Casualties will lie down with the helmet off, and head towards the enemy.
   (c) No Rifle Grenades, bombs, etc. will be actually used.
   (d) Carrying parties will be detailed, and will carry ration boxes etc. to represent loads.
   (e) Contact aeroplanes will be in attendance, and possibly a further number of aeroplanes to repel hostile counter-attacks.
   (f) No pigeons will be available for use in the attack.
   (g) Smoke candles will be available for local use against pepperboxes.

8. O.C., 91st T.M.Battery will liaise with Battalion Commanders regarding the carrying out of his duties.

(continued)

- 2 -

9.   Battalions will forward their orders for the attack by 12 noon on September 24th.

10. (a) At the conclusion of operations the "stand fast" will be sounded, when troops will eat their haversack rations. After an interval the Officers call, followed by the "No Parade" will be sounded, when mounted officers will rendezvous at W.22.central and troops will return to billets.
    (b) Battalions will hand in to the Brigade Major at the Pow-wow all written messages received from front line commanders throughout the operations. These will be returned the same evening.

11.   On Wednesday 26th inst. the 2nd Bn.Queen's Regt. will furnish a skeleton enemy for the attack of the 20th and 22nd Inf.Bdes., under separate orders. 2nds-in-Command of battalions will also probably be required as Umpires.

Bde.Hd.Qtrs.
22nd September, 1917.

Captain,
Brigade Major, 91st Infantry Brigade.

APPENDIX 3
to 91st Infantry Brigade Order No.F1.

ADMINISTRATIVE INSTRUCTIONS.

Reference Map Sheet 27 S.E. 1/20,000.

1. Dress and Equipment.

   (a) (i)   Rifle and equipment less pack.
        (ii)   220 rounds S.A.A.
        (iii) Haversack on back containing Iron Ration and haversack ration.
        (iv)   Groundsheet rolled, with cardigan jacket inside, and fixed to the back of the waist belt by the supporting straps of the pack.
        (v)   Box respirator and P.H. helmet.
        (vi)   Two sandbags, if available, under flap of haversack.

   (b) Lewis Gunners (except Nos.1 and 2), signallers and runners will carry 100 rounds S.A.A.

   (c) Rifle grenadiers will carry 50 rounds S.A.A. and 8 Rifle Grenades (Mills 23 as they and the cups are available).

   (d) Aeroplane flares (as available) will be distributed among the front line troops.

   (e) Smoke candles (as available) will be distributed among the second wave.

   (f) The rear wave of battalions will carry 4 tools per section, at the rate of 1 pick to 1 shovel in the case of the 1st Bn.S.Staffs Regt. and 21st Bn.Manchester Regt. and two shovels to a pick for the remaining battalions.

   (g) Moppers up will carry 100 rounds S.A.A. 1 "P" bomb, 2 Mills No.5, and 4 Rifle Grenades.

2. Rations & Water.

   (a) Every man will carry an iron ration which is not to be consumed except on the order of an officer.
   (b) Every man will also carry a haversack ration.

   Supply Refilling Point will be established at P.9.c.4.7. Supplies will be delivered to Brigade Transport Camps at P.30.a.2.2.(imaginary).

   Tanks (assumed) will be established filled at W.1.b.5.2.

3. S.A.A.,Bombs, R.E. Material.

   A Brigade Dump will be established at W.14.a.4.8.
   After the objectives have been gained a forward dump will be established W.21.b.1.5.

4. Transport.

   The Brigade Pack Transport will assemble by 10-30 a.m. under the command of 2/Lieut.S.Perry,2nd Queen's Regt.,a/Bde.Transport Officer,S.W. of the road at W.8.a.5.5. The a/Bde.Transport Officer will arrange to have an orderly at Brigade Headquarters.
   The pack train will be made up of the normal 3 subsections of 6 animals each from each Battalion and 8 animals from Bde.Hd.Qtrs. and will be ready loaded in accordance with Schedule "A" attached.
   So soon as the situation permits the train will move up to the forward Brigade Dump proceeding via W.8.a.9.0. - to track junction at W.14.b.8.9. - W.15.d.4.9. - W.21.b.1.5. From this point forward Battalions and T.M.Battery will carry all ammunition and stores by carrying parties using the Yukon Pack where available for this purpose.
   The Brigade Transport Officer will arrange for the watering of Pack Animals by Battalion sections at ZOUDAUSQUES and will keep Brigade Headquarters notified of the number of animals available for work.

(continued)

- 2 -

5. **Stragglers Posts.**

   Posts will be established at the Road Junction W.14.a.6.4. and W.15.a.1.8. O.C., 2nd Queen's Regt. will detail a party of 1 N.C.O. and 5 o.r. for the former post and to patrol the road between that post and W.13.b.3.4. O.C., 1st S. Staffs Regt. will detail a similar party for the second post and to patrol the road between that and No.1 Post.

6. **Prisoners of War.**

   (a) Units will report by the quickest means available the first identification established. Only fresh identifications will subsequently be reported.

   (b) Prisoners will be sent to the Divl. P.of W. cage at Cross Roads W.1.b.8.3. under an escort not exceeding 10% of their strength. On arrival there they will be handed over to the Officer in charge and a receipt obtained. Escorts will then rejoin their units.

7. **Medical.**

   There will be an advanced Dressing Station at W.7.d.1.3. with bearers at Regimental Aid Posts. The main Dressing Station will be at MORINGHEM.

   No unwounded men are to escort wounded men.

   Walking cases will make their own way back to the Regimental Aid Posts, Stretcher cases will await the arrival of the Stretcher bearers.

8. **Veterinary.**

   The 12 M.V.S. will establish an Aid Post at P.26.a.9.0. and an advanced collecting station at P.22.d.5.5.

9. **Casualties.**

   All units will render an estimated Casualty return to Brigade Headquarters by 3 p.m. giving officers and other ranks separately.

10. **Water.**

    Water in captured territory will not be consumed until it has been examined by a Medical Officer and passed fit for drinking.

11. **Personnel.**

    Not more than 20 Officers, excluding the Medical Officer and Pack Train Officer, will accompany each Battalion into action.

12. **Documents.**

    (a) All ranks are forbidden to take into action any documents other than a map of the theatre of operations which must contain no information calculated to be of use to the enemy.
    (b) Each Battalion will detail 4 men to search dugouts for enemy documents, maps or letters, which will be collected in sandbags and despatched direct to Brigade Headquarters. These men will wear a brassard of pull through flannellette on their right arm.

13. **ACKNOWLEDGE.**

Bde. Hd. Qtrs.
23rd September, 1917.

R. Crawford
Lieut.,
for Staff Captain, 91st Infantry Brigade.

SCHEDULE "A".

Unit.	No.1 Subsection.	No.2 Subsection.	No.3 Subsection.
2nd Queen's Regt.	2 animals S.A.A. 2 " Wire. 2 " Picks and Shovels. x	2 animals Mills No.23. 2 " Stokes. 2 " L.G.Magazines.	2 animals Picks and Shovels. x 2 " Sandbags (if available). 2 " Halos No.24.
1st S.Staffs Regt.	4 animals Stokes ammunition. 2 " S.A.A.	2 animals Stokes ammunition. 2 " L.G.Magazines. 2 " Mills No.23.	2 animals Stokes ammunition. 2 " Mills No.5. 2 " Stokes.
21st Manchester Regt.	2 animals S.A.A. 2 " Wire. 2 " Picks and Shovels. x	2 animals Mills No.23. 2 " Stokes. 2 " L.G.Magazines.	2 animals Stokes. 1 " Very Lights and Pistols. 2 " Wire. 1 " Sandbags (if available).
22nd Manchester Regt.	--ditto--	--ditto--	2 animals L.G.Magazines. 2 " Wire. 2 " Halos No.24.
Brigade Headquarters.	8 animals S.A.A.		

x proportion 2 shovels to 1 pick.

S E C R E T.

Copy No. 17

Additions and Amendments to 91st Infantry Brigade Order No. P.1.

23rd September, 1917.

-:-:-:-:-:-:-:-:-:-:-

1. Para.1(a) - for Sept.25th,1917 read Sept.24th,1917.

2. Para.9(a), Line 2. - for "two sections" read "one section".
   " " Line 3. - for "those sections" read "this section".

3. Para.9(b) is cancelled.

4. (a) Para.10(a)(iv), Line 3. - after W.15.a.0.5. insert -
   "Call Q.3."
   (b) Para.10(a)(iii) - add "A Brigade Runner Post will be
   established at W.15.a.1.7., to which
   messages for Brigade Headquarters
   will be sent."
   (c) Para.10(a) insert sub-para -
   "(vi) A Power Buzzer will be established at
   W.15.a.1.7. (Call C.X.) which will be in
   communication with Brigade Headquarters."

5. Para.10(d), lines 1 and 2. - For "two" read "four".

6. (a) Appendix 1., para.(b) After "Lewis Gun Limbers" insert
   "and limbers for carrying tools for
   distribution among the men."
   (b) " " para. 11 is cancelled.

7. Appendix 3. 1(a)(ii) for "220 rounds S.A.A." read "150
   rounds S.A.A."

Captain,

Brigade Major, 91st Infantry Brigade.

Copies to all recipients of B.O. P.1.

SECRET.

Appx 7

Copy No. 15

91st Infantry Brigade Order No.P.2.

Tuesday, 25th September, 1917.

Reference Map "A".

-:-:-:-:-:-:-:-:-

1. (a) The 7th Division will take part in an attack on the high ground West of WISQUES at 11.a.m., on September 26th, 1917, with objectives and boundaries as shewn on attached Map "A".
(b) The 22nd Infantry Brigade will be attacking on the Right and the 91st Infantry Brigade on the Left of the Divisional Front. The 20th Infantry Brigade will be in Divisional Reserve.
(c) The Qth Brigade of Z Division is attacking on the left of the 91st Infantry Brigade with objectives as shewn on Attached Map "A".

2. The attack of the 91st Infantry Brigade will be carried out by 3 Battalions with objectives as under :-

    (a) 22nd Bn.Manchester Regt.   -   RED LINE.
    (b) 2nd Bn.Queen's Regt.   -   YELLOW LINE.
    (c) 1st Bn.South Staffordshire Regt. - GREEN LINE.
The 21st Bn.Manchester Regt., will be in Brigade Reserve.

3. (a) The Artillery barrage will open at 11.a.m., on a line 150 yards in advance of the forming up line, where it will remain for two minutes, allowing the infantry to creep up as close as possible. At 11-3.a.m., it will commence to advance at the rate of 100 yards in 4 minutes until it reaches the RED LINE (11-23.a.m.), where it will remain for 6 minutes. At 11-29.a.m., it will resume its advance at the rate of 100 yards in 6 minutes until reaching a line 200 yards in advance of the RED LINE where it will remain until 11-53.a.m., on the 22nd Infantry Brigade front, and until 12-10.p.m., on the 91st Infantry Brigade front.
(b) At 12-10.p.m., it will resume its advance in conjunction with the left flank of the 22nd Infantry Brigade, at the rate of 100 yards in 6 minutes till reaching the YELLOW LINE (At 12-32.p.m.), where it will pause for 6 minutes before moving on to its protective barrage 200 yards beyond the YELLOW LINE.
(c) At 1-20.p.m., the barrage will commence to roll forward at the rate of 100 yards in 8 minutes on an alignment parallel to the YELLOW LINE from W.16.c.7.4. - W.15.d.9.0. Until the GREEN LINE is reached (at 1-58.p.m.) where it will remain for 8 minutes. It will then resume its advance to a protective barrage line 200 yards in advance of the final objective, where it will remain until 2-34.p.m. It will thenceforward only be put down in response to an S.O.S.Signal.
(d) Throughout the above programme the barrage will advance by 50 yard bounds.

4. (a) (i) The 22nd Bn.Manchester Regt.(Hd.Qtrs. W.8.d.80.05) will be formed up by 10-30.a.m., with the leading wave on the tape line (see Map "A" attached).
    (ii) At 11.a.m., the line will crawl forward as close as possible to the barrage, and the advance will be carried out in accordance with the barrage programme in para.3(a) above.
    (iii) On reaching its objective the 22nd Bn.Manchester Regt., will maintain itself until the 2nd Bn.Queen's Regt., have passed through, when the RED LINE will be consolidated in depth.

    (b) (i) At 10-30.a.m., the 2nd Bn.Queen's Regt.(Hd.Qtrs.W.2.d.3.0.) will be in a position of assembly in the Valley in the vicinity of W.2.d.5.1.
    (ii) Thence the advance will be carried out in Artillery Formation of Platoons in file, the leading platoon crossing the LEULINGHEM - QUESQUES Road at 11-45.a.m.

(iii) The deployment/

(iii) The deployment into Normal Attack Formation will take place as the leading platoon reaches the RED LINE, unless an earlier deployment is rendered necessary by heavy Machine Gun fire.

(iv) The advance will be continued as close as possible to the protective barrage, when the line will halt and await the lifting of the barrage.

(v) At 12-10.p.m., the advance will be continued in accordance with the barrage programme in paras.3(b) above.

(vi) On reaching the YELLOW LINE the 2nd Bn. Queen's Regt., will maintain itself until the 1st Bn. South Staffordshire Regt., has passed through, when the YELLOW LINE will be consolidated in depth.

(c) (i) The 1st Bn. South Staffordshire Regt. (Hd.Qtrs. Road junction W.8.b.1.4.) will be in a position of assembly in the Valley at W.2.d.2.1. at 10-30.a.m.

(ii) Thence the advance will be carried out in Artillery Formation of Platoons in file, the leading platoon crossing the LEULINGHEM - QUELMES Road at 12-50.p.m.

(iii) The deployment into Normal Attack Formation will be carried out after the leading line has crossed the valley in W.15.d.

(iv) The advance will be continued as close as possible to the protective barrage, when the line will halt and await the lifting of the barrage.

(v) At 1-20.p.m., the advance will be continued in accordance with the barrage programme in 3(c) above.

(vi) The objective when gained will be consolidated in depth.

(d) The 21st Bn. Manchester Regt. (Hd.Qtrs W.8.a.8.8.) will be in a position of assembly at W.8.a.8.8. at 10-30.a.m. Their role will depent on subsequent developments.

5. Previous notice will be given to Brigade Headquarters before Battalion Headquarters moves forward, stating the proposed position; a guide will also be sent from the new position. A representative will remain at the former Headquarters until the forward Headquarters is opened.

6. (a) Two sections of 91st Machine Gun Coy., are allotted to the Brigade. The remaining 8 guns will co-operate in the Divisional Machine Gun barrage scheme under the orders of the Divisional Machine Gun Officer.

(b) (i) The Officer Commanding, 91st Machine Gun Coy., will detail an Officer to accompany the rear wave of the 22nd Bn. Manchester Regt., to reconnoitre a position for 2 guns in the vicinity of W.15. Central whence the valley in W.15.d. can best be covered.

The guns will be brought forward when the most satisfactory position has been selected.

(ii) An Officer will similarly accompany the rear wave of 2nd Bn. Queen's Regt., with 2 guns to reconnoitre a position in the vicinity of the YELLOW LINE whence a good field of fire can be obtained for defence of the YELLOW LINE. While the reconnaissance is proceeding the guns will remain in the valley in W.15.d.

(iii) An Officer, with 4 guns, will similarly accompany the rear wave of 1st Bn. South Staffordshire Regt., and will reconnoitre positions on the top of the hill for two guns for all round defence, and for a further two on the right of the Brigade front to cover the front in Squares W.22.c. and 21.d.

The above four guns will remain in the valley in W.15.d. while the reconnaissance is in progress.

(c) The above guns/

-3-

(c) The above guns will remain under Brigade control. The Battalion Commander concerned will however be notified (in addition to Brigade Headquarters) of the exact positions selected.

(d) The above guns will cover the consolidation of their respective objectives, and will be prepared to open barrage fire in response to an S.O.S. call or rocket on their final S.O.S. lines, a scheme for which will be drawn up by Officer Commanding, 91st Machine Gun Coy.; immediately the forward gun positions have been selected.

(e) The Officer Commanding, 91st Machine Gun Coy., will establish his Headquarters in the immediate vicinity of Brigade Headquarters.

7. (a) The Officer Commanding, 91st Light Trench Mortar Battery will detail two guns and teams to proceed with the rear wave of 22nd Bn. Manchester Regt. These guns will take up positions in vicinity of the RED LINE whence fire can be brought to bear on the groups of pepperboxes at W.21.b.3.9. and W.15.d.2.3. At 12-6.p.m., he will open a hurricane bombardment on these targets for 4 minutes.

The Officer Commanding, 22nd Bn. Manchester Regt., will detail 20 men (with Yukon Packs if available) for carrying Stokes ammunition.

(b) The above guns will advance with the rear wave of 2nd Bn. Queen's Regt., and will take up defensive positions in the YELLOW LINE.

(c) The Officer Commanding, 91st Light Trench Mortar Battery will also detail 6 men to each assaulting Battalion to assist mopping up parties in blowing in the doors of pepperboxes. Each man will carry 4 rounds of Stokes ammunition.

(d) The remainder of 91st Light Trench Mortar Battery will remain in Brigade Reserve in the vicinity of Brigade Headquarters.

8. The Officer Commanding, 528th (Durham) Field Coy. R.E., will detail one section to assist 2nd Bn. Queen's Regt., in the consolidation of the YELLOW LINE. This section accompanied by its own pack detachment should report to Brigade Headquarters by 12.noon.

9. (a) (i) All Battalions will be connected to Brigade Headquarters by telephone.
(ii) In no case will more than one telephone line per Battalion be run forward.
(iii) 8 extra runners per Battalion will be detailed to report to Brigade Headquarters by 10-30.a.m. They will rejoin their units on the conclusion of operations.
(iv) Each Battalion will establish runner posts forward, the positions of which will be laid down as far as possible beforehand, and marked with a flag when occupied. A Brigade runner post will be established at W.15.a.1.7. Brigade Runner Routes will be marked with a small red flag charged with a white cross.
(v) A Brigade visual receiving station (Call C.R.) will be established after 11.a.m., in the vicinity of W.15.a.1.7. Messages received here will be distributed thence by telephone to the addressee.
(vi) A Power Buzzer will be established at W.15.a.1.7. (Call C.X.) which will be in communication with Brigade Headquarters.

(b)(i) The leading troops will light flares at 11-35.a.m., 12-45.p.m., 2-15.p.m. and when called for by contact aeroplane.
(ii) Groundsheets and panels will be laid out at Battalion Headquarters and communication with aeroplanes practised.

(c) Liaison Officers/

(c) Liaison Officers will be exchanged as under. Each Officer will be accompanied by two orderlies and should report to the Battalion Headquarters concerned by 10-30.a.m. :-

    22nd Bn.Manchester Regt.   -   2nd Bn.Royal Warwickshire Regt.

    2nd Bn.Queen's Regt.   -   22nd Bn.Manchester Regt., to watch and report on progress of advance.
                              2/1st H.A.C.

    1st Bn.South Staffs.Regt.   -   2nd Bn.Queen's Regt. to watch and report on progress of advance.
                              20th Bn.Manchester Regt.

Headquarters of above units of 22nd Infantry Brigade will be notified later.

10.   A watch will be circulated to Battalions,91st Machine Gun Coy., and 91st Light Trench Mortar Battery., before 10-30.a.m.

11.   Administrative Instructions follow ~~are issued herewith.~~

12.   Brigade Headquarters will open at Road Junction W.C.a.9.0. at 10-30.a.m.

13.   ACKNOWLEDGE.

Khorshead
Captain,
Brigade Major, 91st Infantry Brigade.

Copies to -

    Copy No 1   2nd Queen's R
              2   1st S.Staffs.R
              3   21st Manch.R
              4   22nd Manch.R
              5   91st M.G.Coy.
              6   91st L.T.M.Bty.
              7   No.3.Secn.7th Div.Sigs.
              8   Staff Captain.
              9   Brigade Transport Officer.
            10   A.D.M.S.
            11   528th (Durham) Fd.Coy.R.E.
            12   7th Division.
            13   22nd Inf.Bde.
            14   File.
            15   War Diary.
            16   War Diary.

APPENDIX 1.
to 91st Infantry Brigade Order No.P.2.

Notes for Regulation of Divisional Practice Attack, September 26th, 1917.

1. Paras.1,3,4(a),5,6,7, and 10 of Appendix 1 to Brigade Order No.P.1., hold good for this operations

2. Umpires (as before) will be detailed to report at the same place and time as on September 24th.

3. No S.O.S.Rocket Grenades will be available.
    The Officer Commanding, 91st Light Trench Mortar Battery will arrange to have a Stokes Gun with the new S.O.S. shell in the GREEN LINE for the counter-attack which may be expected to develop there towards the conclusion of operations.

4. The role of the 21st Bn.Manchester Regt., throughout will be imaginary. A proportion of Officers will be detailed to attend as spectators.

5. Map "A" was issued with 91st Infantry Brigade Order No.P.1.

6. No Stokes shell (other than the S.O.S.Signal) will actually be fired.

Captain,

Brigade Major, 91st Infantry Brigade.

Copies to all recipients of B.O. P.2.

SECRET

ADMINISTRATIVE INSTRUCTIONS
in connection with
91st Infantry Brigade Order No.P.2.

Paras. 1, 2, 6, 7, 8, 9, 10, 11, 12 of Administrative Instructions in connection with 91st Infantry Brigade Order No.P1. hold good for this operation.

3. **S.A.A., Bombs, R.E. material**

   A Brigade Dump will be established at W.15.a.0.7.
   After the objectives have been gained a forward dump will be established at W.21.b.1.9.

4. **Transport.**

   Pack Train will be practised as before and will assemble at N.E. side of Road at W.8.a.5.5.

   All animals of the Pack Train will carry Gas Helmets in the Alert position and Drivers must be prepared to adjust them in the event of the train passing through a Gas area.

   Para.4(a)

   Carrying parties of 20 other ranks each to accompany Battalion Hd.Qrs. will be detailed as under :-

   22nd Bn.Manchester Regt. to carry 5,000 rounds S.A.A., Bombs, Very Lights, etc., (as available).
   2nd Bn.Queen's Regt. to carry 2,000 rounds S.A.A., Bombs, Very Lights, Wire and Stakes, (as available).
   1st Bn.S.Staffs Regt. to carry 2,000 rounds S.A.A., Bombs, Very Lights, Wire and Stakes, (as available).

   (Note - The material for these carrying parties will be provided regimentally.)

   21st Bn.Manchester Regt will detail a carrying party of 50 o.r. to report to O.C. pack train by 10-30 a.m. to carry stores forward should the tactical situation not admit of the pack train being sent forward.

5. **Stragglers Posts.** will be established at :-

   (1) Cross Roads W.8.a.9.1.
   22nd Manchester Regt. and 2nd Queen's Regt. will each send one N.C.O. and one Regimental Policeman to this Post.

   (2) Road Junction W.9.b.1.2.
   21st Manchester Regt. and 1st S.Staffs Regt. will each send one N.C.O. and one Regimental Policeman to this Post.

   Orders will be issued to the senior N.C.O. at each Post on the ground.

Bde.Hd.Qtrs.
25th September, 1917.

Captain,
Staff Captain, 91st Infantry Brigade.

SECRET.   Appx. 8.
                                              Copy No. 16

        91st Infantry Brigade Order No.19.

                                27th September, 1917.
Reference Map -
    HAZEBROUCK 5A, Edition 2, Scale 1/100,000.

1.   The 91st Infantry Brigade Group less 91st Machine Gun
        Company will move to the ELNES - WAVRANS Area on September
        28th, in accordance with attached March Table.

2.   (a) Spaces as laid down in Brigade Routine Order No.274,
        para.3., dated 17th September, 1917, will be maintained
        throughout the march.
        (b) All Units will halt for the last 10 minutes of each
        hour.
        (c) A synchronized watch will be circulated to Units in
        the morning of the 28th instant.

3.   Billeting parties will report to Staff Captain at the
        Church ELNES at 10-30.a.m.

4.   (a) Baggage wagons will report to Battalions at 6.a.m.,
        on 28th September.
        (b) Particulars of Lorries available for the move will be
        issued later.

5.   A certificate that Area Stores, billets and tents are
        left intact and clean on vacation will be rendered by all
        Units by 6.p.m., 28th September.

6.   (a) Refilling Point will be on Road between ELNES and
        WAVRAN. Railhead will be notified later.
        (b) Units will refil in the evening of 28th September.

7.   Brigade Headquarters will close at BOISDINGHEM at 9.a.m.,
        September 28th.

8.   ACKNOWLEDGE.

                                              Captain,
                              Brigade Major, 91st Infantry Brigade.

Issued at......p.m.
    to - Copy No 1 2nd Queen's R
              2 1st S.Staffs.R
              3 21st Manch.R
              4 22nd Manch.R
              5 91st M.G.Coy.
              6 91st L.T.M.Bty.
              7 No.3.Sec.Div.Sig.Coy.
              8 Staff Captain.
              9 Bde. Transport Officer.
             10 21st Field Ambulance.
             11 528th (Durham) Fd.Coy.
             12 Supply Officer.
             13 No.3.Coy.Div.Train.
             14 7th Division.
             15 File.
             16 War Diary.
             17 War Diary.

MARCH TABLE
(Issued with 91st Infantry Brigade Order No.19).

Unit.	Destination.	Starting Point.	Time.	Route.	Remarks.
22nd Manch.R	ELNES - WAVRAN Area.	400 yards S.E. of Church, ACQUIN.	9-15.a.m.	ACQUIN - LUMBRES - ELNES.	
2nd Queen's R	-do-	-do-	9-35.a.m.	-do-	
21st Manch.R	-do-	-do-	9-48.a.m.	-do-	
1st S.Staffs.R	-do-	-do-	10-14.a.m.	-do-	
91st Inf.Bde.H.Q. 91st L.T.M.Bty.	-do-	-do-	10-30.a.m.	-do-	
No.3.Coy.Div.Train	-do-	-do-	10-35.a.m.	-do-	
21st Field Amb.	-do-	-do-	10-45.a.m.	-do-	
526th.(Durham) Fd.Coy.	-do-	-	-	SEREQUES - LUMBRES - ELNES.	To be clear of LUMBRES by 10.a.m.

SECRET

3.C./915.

Reference 91st Infantry Brigade Order No.19. of to-day, the following lorries will be available for the move to-morrow 28th September. :-

1 Lorry. - 2nd Bn. Queen's Regt.
1   "   - 1st Bn. S. Staffs. Regt.
1   "   - 21st Bn. Manchester Regt., and 91st Light Trench Mortar Battery. (Half of the lorry to be available for the latter).
1   "   - 22nd Bn. Manchester Regt.

Lorries will report at 5-30.a.m., and be available for a double journey.

Officer Commanding, 21st Bn. Manchester Regt., will be responsible for directing the lorry on to 91st L.T.M.Bty.

Supply Railhead on 28th September, will be EBLINGHEM, and from 29th September inclusive OUDERTOM.

Bde. Hd. Qtrs.

27th Sept. 1917.

Captain,
Staff Captain, 91st Infantry Brigade.

Copies to all recipients of B.O.19. (except 7th Division).

SECRET.   Copy No. 16

91st Infantry Brigade Order No.20.

28th September, 1917.

Reference Map:-
HAZEBROUCK, 5A, Edition 2, Scale 1/100,000.

1. (a) The 91st Infantry Brigade Group will move by tactical trains to-morrow, 29th instant to area in vicinity of ST.HUBERTUSHOEK.
   (b) Personnel will entrain at ARQUES and TRANSPORT less 2nd Line and proportion of 1st Line detailed in para.5(a) at WIZERNES in accordance with accompanying Entraining Table.

2. March to Entraining Stations will be in accordance with accompanying March Table.

3. (a) Spaces as laid down in Brigade Routine Order No.274 para.3., dated 17th September, 1917, will be maintained throughout the march.
   (b) All Units will halt for the last 10 minutes of each hour.

4. (a) Baggage wagons will proceed with transport to WIZERNES Station, where they will be taken over by No.3.Company, 7th Divisional Train.
   (b) Rations for consumption on 30th September, will be dumped at WIZERNES Station and will be taken over by Units at 5.a.m. on 29th September. 21st Field Ambulance will detail 1 N.C.O. and 3 men for this purpose who will travel in the transport train.
   (c) Lorries will report as follows at 5-30.a.m. :-

   1 to each Battalion.
   1 to Brigade Headquarters and 91st T.M.Battery.
   1 to 528th (Durham) Field Coy.R.E.
   (d) Refilling Point on 30th September, will be notified later.

5. (a) No.3.Company Train and all transport not accommodated in trains will proceed by Road and will stage night of 29/30th September in WALLON CAPPEL Area.
   (b) Billeting parties will report to Area Commandant, STAPLE in advance. Each Unit will send by these parties a statement of Officers, Other Ranks and horses to be accommodated.
   (c) Rations for consumption on 30th September for men and horses will be carried.

6. The destination to which No.3.Company, Divisional Train, and above transport will march on 30th September will be notified by Area Commandant, STAPLE. Each Unit will make its own arrangements for receipt of same.

7. 2nd Bn.Queen's Regt., will detail 2nd Lieut.S.PERRY and a party of 2 Officers and 50 Other Ranks to be at WIZERNES Station at 5-45.a.m. They will load transport trains, travelling to the New Area in the train leaving WIZERNES at 12-40.p.m., 29th September.

8. Brigade Headquarters will close at ELNES at 12.midnight, 28th September.

9. ACKNOWLEDGE.

                                                    Captain,
                                    Brigade Major, 91st Infantry Brigade.

Issued at 9/45.p.m. to :-
   Copy No. 1 2nd Queen's R   9 Bde. Transport Officer.
          2 1st S.Staffs.R   10 21st Field Ambulance.
          3 21st Manch.R   11 528th (Durham) Fd.Coy.
          4 22nd Manch.R   12 Supply Officer.
          5 91st M.G.Coy.   13 No.3.Coy.Div.Train.
          6 91st L.T.M.Bty.   14 7th Division.
          7 No.3.Sec.Div.Sig.Coy.   15 File.
          8 Staff Captain.   16&17 War Diary.

ENTRAINING TABLE.

Personnel.

ARQUES.

No. of Train.	Start Entraining.	Departs.	Accommodation for -
1	10.a.m.	10-40.a.m.	Brigade Headquarters. 2nd Queen's Regt.(less 2 Officers & 50 O.R.) 1st S.Staffs.Regt. 91st Machine Gun Coy. 91st Trench Mortar Bty.
2	11.a.m.	11-50.a.m.	21st Manch.Regt. 22nd Manch.Regt. 21st Field Ambulance. 528th (Durham) Fd.Coy.R.E.

Transport.

No. of Train.	Start Entraining.	Departs.	Accommodation for -
1	6.a.m.	8-24.a.m.	Brigade Headquarters. 2nd Bn.Queen's Regt.(less 3 limbers and Cooks wagons). 1st S.Staffs.Regt.(less 3 limbers and Cooks wagons). 91st Machine Gun Coy.(less 9 limbers).
2	9-30.a.m.	12-40.p.m.	9 limbers, 91st Machine Gun Coy. 21st Manch.Regt.(less 3 limbers and Cooks wagons). 22nd Manch.Regt.(less 3 limbers and Cooks wagons).

TRANSPORT not accommodated in above will move by Road as in para.5(a).

MARCH TABLE - PERSONNEL.

Unit.	Destination.	Starting Point.	Time.	Route.
91st Inf.Bde.H.Q. (less transport).	ARQUES.	Road junction immediately S. of A of WAVRANS HALTE.	5.a.m.	HALTE - HALLINES - WIZERNES - WESTOVE - ARQUES.
2nd Queen's Regt. (less transport).	-do-	-do-	5-5.a.m.	-do-
1st S.Staffs.Regt. (less transport).	-do-	Road junction ½ mile S.W. of R of CREHEM.	6.a.m.	CREHEM - NOIR CORNET - BLENDECQUES - ARQUES.
91st L.T.M.Bty.	-do-	-do-	6-10.a.m.	-do-
91st Machine Gun Coy.	-do-	Road junction S. of O in GONBARDENNE.	8.a.m.	WESTOVE - ARQUES.
22nd Manch.Regt. (less transport).	-do-	Road junction immediately S. of A in WAVRANS HALTE	6.a.m.	HALTE - HALLINES - WIZERNES - WESTOVE - ARQUES.
21st Manch.Regt. (less transport).	-do-	-do-	6-7.a.m.	-do-
21st Field Amb.	-do-	Road junction ½ mile S.W. of R in CREHEM	7.a.m.	CREHEM - NOIR CORNET - BLENDECQUES - ARQUES.
528th (Durham) Fd. Coy.R.E.	-do-	-do-	7-4.a.m.	-do-

MARCH TABLE - TRANSPORT.

Unit.	Destination.	Starting Point.	Time.	Route.	Remarks.
91st Inf.Bde.H.Q.	WIZERNES.	Junction of Road & track ½ mile N. of 2nd E in ELNES.	3.a.m.	LUMBRES - SETQUES - WIZERNES.	
2nd Queen's Regt.	-do-	-do-	3-5.a.m.	-do-	
1st S.Staffs.Regt.	-do-	Road junction ½ mile S.W. of R in CREHEM.	4-30.a.m.	CREHEM - NOIR CORNET.	
91st Machine Gun Coy.	-do-	"			To be at WIZERNES Station at 5-45.a.m.
22nd March.Regt.	-do-	Junction of Road & track ½ mile N. of 2nd E in ELNES.	6-20.a.m.	LUMBRES - SETQUES - WIZERNES.	
21st March.Regt.	-do-	-do-	6-30.a.m.	-do-	
528th (Durham) Fd. Coy.R.E.	STAPLE.	Road junction ½ mile S.W. of R in CREHEM.	To be clear CREHEM - of starting BLENDECQUES - point by 9.a.m.	CREHEM - NOIRCCORNET - ARQUES - LE NIEPPE - STAPLE.	
21st Field Amb.	-do-	-do-	-do-	-do-	

Transport other than 21st Field Ambulance and 528th.(Durham) Field Coy.R.E.,not accommodated in train will continue the march to STAPLE via ARQUES and LE NIEPPE.

7th DIVISION.

B. H. Q.

91st INFANTRY BRIGADE.

OCTOBER 1917.

WAR DIARY

INTELLIGENCE SUMMARY

of Headquarters 6th Infantry Brigade

OCTOBER 1917

Place	Date	Hour	Summary of Events and Information	Remarks and references to Appendices
ST HUBERTUS - MOEN	1/10/17		Fine and sunny. During the night E.A. dropped several bombs in vicinity of Bde area, causing casualties to all units. Parties of officers from all units reconnoitred line in morning. In afternoon 1st S. Staffords moved forward to CHATEAU SEGARD area.	B/B
do.	2/10/17		B.Gs and B.M attended conference at Div H.Q at 7 p.m. Geo. 2nd Queen W. 2 or 1st S.S. K. 3 or W. 26 or (2 at duty) 2 1st Bn w 3 or 22nd hdn W 2 or (1 attach) Refs 2 Queens 6 or 1.S.S. 20 (1 off) 21st Bn 1 or (non probtd) Fine and Sunny. In accordance with B.O. No 21, Bde Group ler 1st S. Staffords moved to ZILLEBEKE area. B.O.S.W. called at Bde at 10.30 am. B.G. & 9 B.M. visited Div H.Q. 1st S. Staffords during the morning. Orders were issued Bo 22 re relief of Bde in forthcoming offensive of 2nd Army. In the evening Bde H.Q. moved to dugouts in HOOGE Crater and the 1st S. Staffords relieved 1st R.W.F in front line in accordance with arrangement made between CO's concerned. B.G.C. assumed command of Right Brigade Sector at 9 p.m. Casualties and Reinforcements Nil.	B.O.21 att. App.1. B.O.22 att. App.2
HOOGE	3/10/17		Dull and cold. Some showers after a fairly quiet day. Bosches moved to positions of assembly for the attack via B.O. 23. 9 concd. The 2nd Queens and 21st R.W. suffered considerable casualties from shell fire whilst known up, by Bn Q.M. Stores M.C Carts & Lumbers upon K. Wed. and in the tramway casualties 1st S. Staffords 1 or R.I.W. off 1 or 65 m 5. Reinforcements Nil.	UB
do	4/10/17	6 AM.	Still and cold. Some showers during the night. 1st South Staffords and 22nd B.R.L Regt passed up on top line suffering very few casualties. Zero Hour. Enemy Reply to our barrage was very feeble and at 7.50 am the 1st S.S Staffords reported the capture of the Red Line. about 11 am 22nd White Regt informed the capture of the Blue Line owing to the failure of the 21st Div in order to reach the Blue Line	UB

x This occurred 12 noon O.4 45 see Att 5.a.

Army Form C. 2118.

WAR DIARY
or
INTELLIGENCE SUMMARY
(Erase heading not required.)

Instructions regarding War Diaries and Intelligence Summaries are contained in F. S. Regs., Part II. and the Staff Manual respectively. Title Pages will be prepared in manuscript.

Place	Date	Hour	Summary of Events and Information	Remarks and references to Appendices
HOOGE	5/10/17		Lt Col AB Beauman formed a defensive flank facing South by moving up three companies of the Reserve Bn (2nd Queens). During the day several S.O.S. signals were sent up but no enemy attack developed. At 3.30 p.m. the B.M. arrived at the Bn where he stayed until the following morning. During the night the Bde suffered considerable shelling. Few casualties but considerable losses were sustained (for subsequent shelling casualties see unit diaries 8/10/17). Reinforcements. Nil.	OAB
do	6/10/17		Dull and cold. Showery. The enemy was very quiet but consolidation proceeded. S.O.S barrage was called for several times during the day but no counter attack developed. Lt Col Moore DSO Lt Col 9th Devons visited forward Bn HQ a reorg relief with Lt Col ____ Cdr. 9th S. Staff. Rfts. 2 S. Staff Inchen 2nd Lt.O.R. around Cav. Seconds ratt 8/10/17 Rfts. 2 S. Staff Inchen 21 OR	OAB
do	6/10/17		Cold. Rain in afternoon. B.G.O and B.M. visited forward Bn HQ. The Bde was relieved in evening by 20 R.I.Bde. The 2nd Queen and 2nd Inchen 9 R.S.R M.G.C was relieved in evening by 20 R.I.Bde. The 2nd Queen and 2nd Inchen stayed in the HOOGE area, whilst Bde HQ. 1st S. Staffs, 22nd Inchen however moved to the ZILLEBEKE area. The relief was carried out with very few casualties (see unit diaries date 8/10/17). Rfts. Nil. (Narrative of operations & further Oct. attch) Very wet all day. Bde Group moved to CHATEAU SEGARD area with exception 22nd Inchen who proceeded to camp in vicinity of HALLEBAST area. Bde HQ must camp near	W.I.d Tel B.M. Sf gdd appx g. OAB
CHATEAU SEGARD	7/10/17		CHATEAU SEGARD occupation Room. In the evening half the 1st & 2nd Ly were relieved Lt Col RM Birkett RSussex Regt assumed cmd of 2nd Bn Queen Regt. Major Kemp 2nd Lt 21st inch advised comd of 2nd R Sussex Regt. C22, 1.13, 14 non-commnd invalided and subsequent died of wounds.	OAB

WAR DIARY or INTELLIGENCE SUMMARY

Army Form C. 2118.

Place	Date	Hour	Summary of Events and Information	Remarks and references to Appendices
CHÂTEAU SEGARD	8/10/17		Bright morning. Rain afternoon and evening. Corps Commander called at Bde H.Q. in morning to congratulate Bde. R.S.O. went forward. Bns. in evening 50 or from old 4 Bns went forward by Bus to act as stretcher bearers in the afternoon on evening day. Remainder of 9th S. MG Coy were relieved from line. Casualties (Suffering from gas) Oct 3rd - noon Oct 8th incl. 2nd Queens K. off 1. OR 38. W. off 7. OR 105. M. 25 OR. 1st S. Staffords. K. off. 3. OR 36. W. off 8 (1 at duty) OR 214 (2 at duty) M. 17 OR. 2nd Inch Regt. K. off. 4. OR 37. W. off 10 (1st duty) OR 157. M. 11. 22nd Inch Regt. K. B. 1. OR 44. W. off 8 (11 at duty) OR 206. M. 2. 8. 9th M.G. Coy. K. — OR 4. W. off 1 OR 22 (1 at duty). 9th T.M. Batty W. OR 12.	EHB
do.	9/10/17		9th T.M. Batty Reinforcements Nil received in morning for 2nd Queens and 2nd Inch Regt. Sunny. High Wind. Orders received in morning to move forward to ZILLEBEKE area, so as to be available, should the tactical situation require them. Casualties Nil. Rnfts 2nd Queens 9 OR. 1st S.Staffords 60 OR 2nd Inch Regt. 4 OR. 22nd Inch Regt 2 offs 28 OR.	EHB
do.	10/10/17		Rain in morning. Sunny afternoon. Bde group were withdrawn to ST HUBERTIJHOEK area. Units occupying same camps as on previous occasion. Casualties Nil. Rnfts. 1st South Staffords 5 OR.	#A.O.23 attached EHB

Army Form C. 2118.

WAR DIARY
or
INTELLIGENCE SUMMARY
(Erase heading not required.)

Instructions regarding War Diaries and Intelligence Summaries are contained in F.S. Regs., Part II. and the Staff Manual respectively. Title Pages will be prepared in manuscript.

Place	Date	Hour	Summary of Events and Information	Remarks and references to Appendices
ST HUBERTUS-HOEK	11/10/17		Sunny but cold. High Wind. B.G.C. visited units delivering congratulation addresses on subject of recent successful operations. Casualties. 2nd Queen. W.1.O.R. 1st S.Staffords. K.1.O.R. W.3.O.R. M.1.O.R. 2/5th Durham W.3.O.R. Drafts 91 37 M.G. 10ff.	EAB
THIEUSHOUK	12/10/17		Fine morning. Wet afternoon and evening. Corps Comm. undercalled at Bde H.Q. in [?]. On afternoon Bde Group moved by march route to THIEUSHOUK area. Billets very scattered but good. Bde H.Q THIEUSHOUK. Casualties 2nd Queen W/O.R 2nd S.Staff. W [?] (8/10/17) 2.O.R. 22nd Mchn W.3.O.R. Reinforcements. Nil.	R.O.20 App.5
do.	13/10/17		Showery. Very high wind. G.O.C. called at Bde in morning. The 91st T.M. Batty was temporarily split up, two guns with proportion of personnel being attached to each Bn. for purposes of Employment, training, discipline & administration, all personnel to remain as such, available this reformed at short notice if required. Casualties Nil. Reinforcements 2nd Queen 1 off.	EAB
do	14/10/17		Bright and sunny. B.G.C. visited Bns in morning. Casualties Nil. Reinforcements 1st South Staffords. 3.O.R. (for hosp.) 2 nd S.Staff. 3.O.R (for hosp.) 22nd Mchn 200 91st M.G. Coy. 1 off.	EAB
do	15/10/17		Bright and sunny. B.G.C. and B.M. visited Bns in morning. Casualties Nil. Reinforcements. 2nd Queen 4 O.R. 2/1st Durham 50 O.R. 22nd Mchn 10ff. 40 O.R. Fine Rain in evening. B.G.C. & B.M. attended conference at Div. H.Q. at 10 a.m.	App. 6. W.D.
do	16/10/17		Motored to CALAIS to find reinforcement Camp C.o. Nil Rufts 1st S.Staffords, Suff[?] 2 nd Lt of Queen 2.P. 3.2 Lt of Durham 2 Lt M/chn 16. Heavy Rain in evening. B.G.C. R.M. S.O off Int. off went forward by car to reconnoitre trucks 2 nd M/chns H.Q. at 3.p.m. Cas. Nil. Rufts 2nd Queen 2 2.O.R.	EAB
do	17/10/17		forward area. Carefull.	EAB

WAR DIARY
or
INTELLIGENCE SUMMARY

(Erase heading not required.)

Army Form C. 2118.

Place	Date	Hour	Summary of Events and Information	Remarks and references to Appendices
THIEUSHOUK	18/10/17		Fine and Sunny. B.M. and C.O's 7, 2." Queen, 2.1.st Arehn, 1.st Stafford, 9.15 m.g. cy. went forward to reconnoitre. G.O.C Div called at Bde H.Q in afternoon. Lt. Col. Vansboy. C.O. 7." Div. (from instructed troops) and of units in afternoon. Cas. Nil. Rufts 2.1.st Arch. 40 O.R from Inf. 0.School Thursday in afternoon. S.E. Int. off. and off.s from 2." Queen, 20." Archn, 9.15 m.g. cy. went forward by lorry to reconnoitre. Brig. Gen Steele Pres. J. G.C.M. at Bde H.Q. B.S.C. watched practice attack carried out by 1.st Stafford 9.21.st Arehn. Lt. Col Hammond 9.5.0.1. called at Bde H.Q in afternoon. Cas. Nil. Rufts 2.1.st Queen 25 O.R 1." S. Stafford 1.off. 164 O.R. 21.st Arehn 2 off. 22." Arehn 1 off.	CHB
do	19/10/17			CHB.
do	20/10/17		Fine and sunny. B.G.C round Battns in morning. Reconnoitring parties from 2." Archn, 9.1.st and 9.m.g cy. went forward in the early morning to reconnoitre. G.O.C Div called at Bde in afternoon. Casualties Nil Reinforcements 2.1.st Archn 3 O.R.	CHB
do	21/10/17		Fine and Sunny. O/30 and parties from 2." Queen 22." Arehn 9.15 m.g cy. went forward early to reconnoitre. C.R.E called at Bde in afternoon. B.T.O went forward to reconnoitre transport lines. Casualties Nil. Reinforcements 1.st S. Stafford. 6 OR 2.1.st Archn 1 OR. Rein in early morning. Fine later. Bde moved by march route to No 9 Area (in vicinity of WEST OUTRE according to B.O 26.) Bde H.Q CARNARVON CAMP.	CHB.
CARNARVON CAMP	22/10/17		Bde H.Q 26.) Bde H.Q CARNARVON CAMP B.M. went forward by car with O.C 9.15 M.G. Cy & adjt 2." Queen to arrange forthcoming relief. Reconnoitring parties from 2." Queen 22." Arehn 9.15 m.g cy went forward to reconnoitre. G.O.C Div called at Bde H.Q in afternoon. Orders issued in evening for move of Brigade in forthcoming operations. Casualties Nil Reinforcements 2." Queen 4 off 46 O R 21.st Archn 1 off.	※ B.O 26 ※ B.O.27 with app.7 CHB

WAR DIARY
or
INTELLIGENCE SUMMARY
(Erase heading not required.)

Army Form C. 2118.

Place	Date	Hour	Summary of Events and Information	Remarks and references to Appendices
FAIRY HOUSE	23/10/17		Rain nearly all day. Bde moved to "C" area in vicinity of KEMMEL) Bde H.Q. FAIRY FARM. O/C's 2nd Queens, 1st S. Staffords 21st 2nd Bns went forward to arrange reliefs with C.O's concerned. Reconnoitring parties went forward early from all units. During the night 1st S. M.G. Coy. relieved the 4 guns at present in the line on Bde Battle front. Casualties Nil. Reinforcements 1st South Staffords 40 OR. 22nd 2nd Bchrs 660 R.	※ B.O. 28 attd. app 7 ☆ NB
do	24/10/17		Fine morning. Rain evening. B.M. toured Bns in morning. at 1 PM. SC. superintended the embussing of 2nd Queens and 2nd 2nd Bchrs. Bgt in accordance with app. II ※ B.O. 29. G.O.C. Div & G.S.O.I called at Bde H.Q. in afternoon. B.M. went to Corps 8 at 4.30 pm to watch Bn'l start forward march. During the night Bde relieved 117th Bde (39th Div) in line ni accordance with app. 1 B.O. 29, all arrangements being made between C.O's concerned. Casualties Nil. Reinforcements 2nd Queens 2 O/Rs, 1st South Staffords 1 OR 21st 2nd Bchrs. 9 O/Rs 22nd 2nd Bchrs 33 OR	※ app. II attd app 8 ※ app 1 attd app 9 ☆ NB
CANADA STREET	25/10/17		Fine Day. Rain ends evening. Bde H.Q moved to tunnelled dugout at CANADA ST Crew. MT SORREL) the B.G.C. taking over command of the Bde Battle front at 7 AM. Rations were sent forward to all units in evening with few casualties. Casualties see refs 28/10/17. Ref/S Nil.	☆ NB
do	26/10/17		Rain nearly all day. Zero hour 5.40 am after an advance of about 200x our attack was brought to a standstill. There was considerable fighting all day but in the evening all three Bns were holding their original line. The condition of the ground was appalling and all units suffered very severe casualties. The 3 reserves coys 22nd 2nd Bchrs were sent up during the day to reinforce the left flank. Order was received in evening for withdrawing 2nd Queen 1st South Staffords, 21st 2nd Bchrs. Accordingly the 2.0 2nd Bchrs took over the front of 1st S.C. Staffords & 21st 2nd Bchrs. And the 2/17 H.B.C. took (over)	

WAR DIARY or INTELLIGENCE SUMMARY

Army Form C. 2118.

Place	Date	Hour	Summary of Events and Information	Remarks and references to Appendices
CANADA ST.	26/10/17 cont.		over the front of the 2nd Queens. The 22nd Bns. were withdrawn into reserve in dugouts at CANADA ST. and HEDGE ST. when relieved Bns. proceeded to camps in the Neighbourhood of VORMEZEELE. Cas. under 28/10/17. Rafts Nil.	e.b.
RENINGHELST	27/10/17		Fine Sunny. Bde H.Q. relieved at 9 A.M. by 22nd Inf. Bde. and proceeded by lorry to RENINGHELST. In accordance with orders sent direct to them by Division 2nd Queens & 21st Bns. moved by lorry thence the afternoon to BLARINGHEM area. Off. column (Sig. Off.) went on by car to arrange billets. In the evening 22nd Bns. were relieved by 2nd R. W. R. Rgt. and proceeded to camp near VIERSTRAAT. Cas. under 28/10/17. Rafts Nil.	e.b.
do.	28/10/17		Fine. Frosty. Corps Commander called at Bde H.Q. in morning. B.M. visited 1st S.S.922nd Bns. Those 1st S. Staffords moved to VIERSTRAAT during the afternoon. 9th M.G. Coy relieved by 8th Bde. during the night and proceeded to camp near VIERSTRAAT. Casualties Summary from 25/10/17 - 27/10/17 in divine.	e.b.

2nd Queens.   K. off - OR 22.   W. off 8. OR 76.   M. off 2. OR 192
1st S. Staffords K. off 6 OR 38   W. off 1. OR 119. M. off 1. OR 111.
21st Bns.   K. off 6 OR 29   W. off 5 OR 118   M. off 2 OR 155.
22nd Bns.   K. off 2 OR 7   W. off 1 OR 31   M. off - OR 11.
9th M.G. Coy.   K. off 2 OR 5   W. off - OR 13   M. off 1 OR 6
9th T.M. Batty   K. off 1 OR 1.   W. off 1. OR -   M. off. - OR 1.
Reinforcements 1st S. Staffords 2 off. 2nd Bns. 1 off.

Army Form C. 2118.

WAR DIARY
or
INTELLIGENCE SUMMARY

(Erase heading not required.)

Instructions regarding War Diaries and Intelligence Summaries are contained in F. S. Regs., Part II. and the Staff Manual respectively. Title Pages will be prepared in manuscript.

Place	Date	Hour	Summary of Events and Information	Remarks and references to Appendices
EBBLINGHEM	29/10/17		Fine. Cold. Bde. H.Q. 1st S. Staffords 22nd Entus moved by train to EBBLINGHEM. 1st Entrains arrived out by S.C. at DICKEBUSCH. Detraining at 1.15 pm supervised by B.M. Bde marched to billets in vicinity of LYNDE. R&L HQ EBBLINGHEM. B.G.C. 22nd R.Welsh Fus. Capt. wiv Rnfts 22nd R.Welsh. Fus.	B.O. 29 App. CMA. S&S E&S
do.	30/10/17		Showery. B.M. went on leave in morning. S.C. became a/B.M. to at Lampon a/S.C. B.G.C. visited Bns in morning. 9th S. M.G. Coy and 2nd S. Field Amb arrived by train at 8.15 pm and proceeded to billets as allotted in area. Capt. M.I. RWF. 2nd Queens 3 OR. 1st S. Staff. 10 R.	E&S
do.	31/10/17		Fine. B.G.C. & a/B.M. visited 2nd Queens 9 O. 1st S. M. G. Coy. G.O.C. Div. called at Bde H.Q. in afternoon. Casualties. aid Rnfts 2nd Queens 7 OR. 1st S. Staff. 1 off. 47 OR. 2nd S. R. Welsh 1 off 11 OR. 40 R. 22nd R Welsh 8 off. 108 OR. 9th S. M.G. Coy 29 OR.	E&S

O.T. Pelly Brig Gen
Cmdg 91st Bde.
1/11/17

SECRET.

Copy No. 17

App 1

91st Infantry Brigade Order No. 21

Reference Map - Sheet 28 Edition 3.

2nd October, 1917.

The following moves and reliefs will take place -

1. On 2nd October and night of 2/3 October.

   (a) 1st Bn. S. Staffs Regt will relieve 1st Bn. R. Welsh Fusiliers in the line. All arrangements will be made between Battalion Commanders. Transport and details of 1st Bn. S. Staffs Regt. will move to H.31.d.4.9.

   (b) 91st Machine Gun Co. will relieve those guns of 22nd Machine Gun Co. on the frontage allotted to 91st Infantry Brigade. All arrangements will be made between Officers Commanding 91st and 22nd Machine Gun Coys.

   (c) On Completion of these reliefs command of the Right Brigade Sector will pass to B.G. Commanding 91st Infantry Brigade. The dividing line between 20th and 91st Inf.Bdes. will be J.10.b.35.85.

   (d) 21st Manchester Regt. less transport will move into dugouts on WEST side of ZILLEBEKE LAKE from point I.21.b.2.8. to I.21.b.2.3.

   (e) 22nd Manchester Regt. less transport and 91st Machine Gun Co. less transport and those guns going into the line to dugouts in Railway Embankment from point I.20.a.7.4. to I.20.d.8.8.

   (f) 2nd Queen's Regt less transport and 91st Light Trench Mortar Battery to Bivouac Camp to be pitched at I.19.d.5.4. Bivouacs for this Camp will be taken from Camp at present occupied by 1st Bn. S. Staffs Regt at H.30.c.1.6. under arrangements to be made by 2nd Queen's Regt.

   1 officer, 2nd Queen's Regt will report to "Q" Office, 7th Division (CHATEAU SEGARD) at 10-30 a.m. on 2nd October to be shewn the site of this Camp.

   On this camp being vacated 2nd Queen's Regt will provide a guard over shelters out of Details until bivouacs are collected by 7th Division.

   (g) Moves detailed in (d) (e) and (f) will be made in Battalion's own time. Officers Commanding will arrange mutually so as not to clash on road.

2. On night of 3/4 October 2nd Bn. Queen's Regt., and 21st and 22nd Bns. Manchester Regt., will move into forward area in accordance with assembly march table to be issued later.

3. ACKNOWLEDGE.

Captain,
Brigade Major, 91st Infantry Bde.

Issued at 2-45 a.m. to

Copy No.		
1	2nd Queen's R.	11 Supply Officer.
2	1st S.Staffs R.	12 No.3 Co., Div. Tra
3	21st Manch.Regt.	13 7th Division.
4	22nd Manch.Regt.	14 20th Inf.Bde.
5	91st M.G.Coy.	15 22nd Inf.Bde.
6	91st L.T.M.Batty.	16 File.
7	No.3 Sec., Div.Sig.Co.	17 War Diary.
8	Staff Captain.	18 War Diary.
9	Bde. Transport Officer.	
10	21st Field Ambulance.	

SECRET.

App 2

Copy No. 29.

91st Infantry Brigade Order No. 22.

2nd October, 1917.

Reference Maps – BECELAERE, Edn.1a, Scale 1/10,000.
HOOGE, Edn.3, Scale 1/10,000.

-:-:-:-:-:-:-:-

1. The Second Army is to resume the offensive at a date and hour to be notified later.

2. (a) The 7th Division will be the left attacking Division of the X Corps; the 21st Division will be attacking on the Right, and the 1st Australian Division on the left of the 7th Division.
(b) The role of the 7th and 1st Australian Divisions is to seize the high ground in the vicinity of NOORDEMDHOEK and MOLEMAARELSTHOEK and so obtain observation on the HEUTEBEEK Valley to the East.
The role of the 21st Division is to occupy REUTEL and the high ground in J.12.a, and thus cover the right flank of the 7th Division.

3. (a) The attack of the 7th Division is to be carried out by 91st Infantry Brigade on the right and 20th Infantry Brigade on the left. The 62nd Infantry Brigade will be attacking on the Right of the 91st Infantry Brigade.
Objectives and Boundaries are shown on attached map.
(b) The attack of the 91st Infantry Brigade will be carried out by 1st Bn.South Staffordshire Regt.(RED LINE) and 22nd Bn.Manchester Regt.(BLUE LINE). The 21st Bn.Manchester Regt.(less one Company) will be in support to the attack and 2nd Bn.Queen's Regt., will be in Brigade Reserve.
One Company of 21st Bn.Manchester Regt., will be attached to 22nd Bn.Manchester Regt., for mopping up purposes.

4. (a) The artillery barrage programme is attached.
(b) The Artillery barrage will be put down in depth by guns of all calibres,150 yards in advance of our front line.
It will remain for 3 minutes and then move forward for 200 yards at the rate of 100 yards in 4 minutes. From that point it will move to the red protective barrage, 200 yards in front of the red line, at the rate of 100 yards in 6 minutes.
From the red protective line to the final protective barrage (200 yards in front of blue line) it moves at the rate of 100 yards in 8 minutes. The protective barrage then remains stationary while a creeping barrage searches to a depth of 1,000 yards beyond the blue protective line.
(c) The protective barrage to the Red and Blue lines will, for the first 4 minutes, include a proportion of smoke shell to indicate to the Infantry that they have reached the Red and Blue Lines respectively.
(d) If the wind is from South-west to North-west a smoke screen is going to be placed on GHELUVELT and BECELAERE.
(e) During the advance of the 7th and 21st Divisions from the 1st to 2nd objective the barrage of the 5th Division is going to creep towards GHELUVELT in order to simulate an advance on that place.

5. (a) (i) By Zero minus one hour the 1st Bn.South Staffordshire Regt., will be formed up in normal attack formation with the leading line on a tape line from J.10.b.1.8. to J.10.b.1.0. The Battalion will be closed up to a depth of 120 yards from front to rear.
The forming up will be carried out gradually and in silence, under cover of advanced posts and patrols.
(ii) At Zero hour the line will creep up as close as possible to the barrage, and the advance will conform to the barrage programme.
(iii) After the 22nd Bn.Manchester Regt., have passed through, the RED LINE will be consolidated in depth, special attention being paid to the following points :-
J.10.b.9.6.
JOLTING HOUSES.
J.11.a.7.5.
(iv) The 8th Bn.Devonshire Regt.(Headquarters – The BUTT) will be attacking on the left, and 3/4th Bn. The Queen's (R.W.Surrey Regt) on the Right. Special parties will be detailed to effect a meeting with a similar party of the former at Road Fork J.11.a.8.9., and with the latter at J.11.a.8.3.

[illegible] the 22nd Bn. Manchester Regt. (plus
[illegible] Company, 22nd Bn. Manchester Regt.) will be formed up in
Artillery formation of sections on a tape line from J.10.a.75.75,
closed up to a total depth of 120 yards from front to rear.

(ii) At Zero hour the battalion will advance in conjunction with
the rear battalions on either flank for 400 yards, when it will halt.
At Zero plus 110 minutes, the advance will be continued through 1st
Bn. South Staffordshire Regt., as close to the protective barrage as
possible. At Zero plus 130 minutes, the barrage will lift, and the
advance will be carried out in accordance with the artillery
programme.

(iii) The BLUE LINE on capture will be consolidated in depth,
special attention being paid to the following localities:-
            J.12.a.15.80.
Trench at - J.11.b. 8. 4.
Strong Point at J.11.b.15.80.
            J.11.b.30.45.

(iv) The 2nd Bn. Border Regt., will be attacking on the Left, and
the 10th Bn. Yorkshire Regt., will be attacking on the Right.
Special parties will be detailed to effect a meeting with similar
parties of the former at J.6.c.15.00., and of the latter at
J.12.a.2.5.

(c) (i) The 21st Bn. Manchester Regt.(less one Company) will be
established in a position of assembly West of POLYGON WOOD in the
vicinity of J.9.c.4.1., by Zero minus 4 hours. An issue of 30%
shovels will be made to enable shelter to be dug before operations
commence.

(ii) As the attack progresses, The Officer Commanding 21st Bn.
Manchester Regt., will move forward by Companies to the vicinity
of the present front line. This will be carried out as the hostile
barrage subsides, Brigade Headquarters being kept informed as to the
progress of the operation.

(iii) The Officer Commanding, 21st Bn. Manchester Regt., will be
prepared to support Officer Commanding, 22nd Bn. Manchester Regt., on
demand from the latter should the tactical situation require it,
without reference to Brigade Headquarters. Brigade Headquarters
will however be informed at once if this is done.

(iv) The subsequent role of the 21st Bn. Manchester Regt., will
depend on the development of events.

(d) The 2nd Bn. Queen's Regt., will be established in the vicinity of
J.13.b.Central. Their role will depend on the development of events.
The Officer Commanding, 2nd Bn. Queen's Regt., will be prepared to
undertake the task of 1st Bn. South Staffordshire Regt., should the
situation demand it.

6. (a) The Officer Commanding, 91st Machine Gun Coy., will arrange to send
4 Vickers guns with the rear wave of 22nd Bn. Manchester Regt., to take
up positions in the neighbourhood of the following points :-
            J.11.b. 8. 4.
            J.12.a. 2. 5.
            J.11.b.85.80.
            J.12.a.15.85.

These guns will cover the consolidation of the BLUE LINE, and will
be so placed as to command the E. and S.E. slopes of the ridge to the
best advantage.
They will be under the tactical control of 22nd Bn. Manchester Regt.

(b) Two guns will similarly be detailed to accompany the rear wave of
1st Bn. South Staffordshire Regt., and to take up positions in the
vicinity of JOLTING HOUSES and J.11.a.9.7., whence the defence of the
RED LINE can best be carried out.
These guns will be under the tactical control of The Officer
Commanding, 1st Bn. South Staffordshire Regt.

(c) Two further guns will occupy defensive positions on the present
front line, South of JETTY WOOD, and will be prepared to assist in
repelling a hostile counter-attack from the S.E.

(d) The remaining 8 guns will be placed at the disposal of the
Divisional Machine Gun Officer for Machine Gun barrage purposes.

7. (a) The Officer Commanding, 91st Trench Mortar Battery will place one
gun and team each at the disposal of 1st Bn. South Staffordshire Regt.,
and 22nd Bn. Manchester Regt., to accompany the rear wave and deal with
any strong point if required.

-3-

(b) The remainder of the Battery will be in reserve in the vicinity of OLD CABLE HEAD, J.14.a.3.3.

8. (a) Two Sections of R.E., and one Company of Pioneers have been allotted to the Brigade for the operation. The former will wire the BLUE LINE at dusk if the tactical situation admits and if the three Companies, 21st Bn. Manchester Regt., are still available for carrying purposes. Failing this they will work on the Strong Points referred to in paras. 5(a)(iii) and 5(b)(iii) above.
The latter will probably be employed in making and improving tracks in the forward area. A Liaison Officer, representing both of above parties, will report to Brigade Headquarters by Zero plus 2 hours.
(b) The Officer Commanding, 528th (Durham) Field Coy. R.E. will arrange for the laying out of the tapes referred to in paras. 5(a)(i) and 5(b)(i) above. Separate instructions will be issued for this.

9. (a) (i) A Brigade Advanced Report Centre will be established at the BUTT (J.10.a.7.8.), and all messages handed in there will be delivered by the Brigade Signal Section.
 (ii) A buried cable exists between Brigade Headquarters and G.W. and will probably be available as far forward as P.G. by Zero day.
 (iii) Brigade Relay Runner Posts (marked by a Red Flag with white Cross) will be established along the buried cable route as under :-

> The BUTT (T.B.)
> J.9.a.4.5. (P.G.)
> J.8.d.3.8. (N.B.)
> J.14.a.4.5. (G.W.)
> Brigade Headquarters. (B.H.)

Messages will be accepted at any of these stations.
The assaulting Battalions will establish a system of Runner Posts forward.
 (iv) A Brigade Visual Receiving Station will be established on the BUTT. Lucas Lamps should be taken forward and communication opened with this point.
 (v) There are Power Buzzer sets at T.B., P.G. and G.W.
 (vi) Three pairs of pigeons per Assaulting Battalion will be issued on "Y" Day, and should be sent forward with the leading Companies. Empty baskets will as far as possible be returned.
 (vii) Telephone communication will probably be of little use. Should the situation admit, Battalions will, on moving their Headquarters, lay a line forward from The BUTT.

(b) (i) Red Flares will be lit by the leading troops on reaching the first objective, on reaching the second objective, and when the contact aeroplane fires a white light or sounds a horn.
 (ii) Contact aeroplanes will carry a black board on the left lower plane and 3 broad white bands on the body.

(c) (i) The S.O.S. Signal by day or night will be the Rifle Grenade Parachute Signal (Red over Green over Yellow).
 (ii) By day only, the Daylight Mortar Signal (Red smoke). The supplies of this are not large, and its use should be reserved for grave emergencies.
 (iii) In the forward area, Lewis or Vickers Guns firing batches of five rounds at regular intervals will be recognised as the S.O.S. Signal should a rocket or mortar not be available.

10. Liaison will be carried out as under :-
(a) A Junior Liaison Officer and a Forward Liaison Officer will be attached by the Artillery to each assaulting Battalion. The Forward Liaison Officer will advance with the infantry and send back reports to the Junior Liaison Officer who will remain at Battalion Headqtrs.
(b) The Officer Commanding, 1st Bn. South Staffordshire Regt., will arrange to attach a Liaison Officer to 3/4th Queen's (R.W.Surrey Regt) (Headquarters to be notified later).
(c) The Officer Commanding, 22nd Bn. Manchester Regt., will arrange to attach a Liaison Officer with two orderlies to 2nd Bn. Border Regt. and 10th Bn. Yorkshire Regt. (Headquarters to be notified later).
(d) ALL Battalions are responsible for keeping themselves in touch with the situation in front by means of patrols, O.Ps., and by means liaison with leading Battalions.

11. (a) Headquarters will be established as follows:-

  Brigade Headquarters.   HOOGE CRATER. I.18.b.2.6.
               (Adv. Report Centre - The BUTT).
  2nd Bn. Queen's Regt.   Vicinity of J.13.b.Central.
  1st Bn. South Staffs. Regt.   The BUTT. J.10.a.7.6.
  21st Bn. Manchester Regt.   In close proximity to 22nd Bn.
               Manchester Regt.
  22nd Bn. Manchester Regt,   In vicinity of The BUTT.
  91st Machine Gun Coy.   OLD GABLE HEAD. (J.14.a.3.3.)
  91st Trench Mortar Bty.   -do-

(b) All Units will send a runner to the nearest Brigade Relay Post on first establishing their Headquarters, and will also report their location to Brigade Headquarters.
  Brigade Posts will be informed of any subsequent changes of locations.

(c) 50 small coloured flags have been issued to each Battalion for marking a track to Battalion Headquarters.

12. (a) Arrangements, Machine Gun barrage scheme, etc., will be issued later as Appendices.

(b) Administrative arrangements and situation maps will be issued separately.

13.   ACKNOWLEDGE.

                 Moorshead

                 Captain,
              Brigade Major, 91st Infantry Brigade.

Issued at......a.m. to

  Copy No 1 2nd Queen's R   △
     2 1st S.Staffs.R   △
     3 21st Manch.R   △
     4 22nd Manch.R   △
     5 91st M.G.Coy.   X
     6 91st T.M.Bty.   X
     7 No.3.Sec.Div.Sig.Coy. X O
     8 Staff Captain. X O
     9 Bde. Bombing Officer. X O
    10 Bde. Transport Officer. X O
    11 Bde. Intelligence Officer. X O
    12 21st Field Ambulance. X O
    13)
    14) Lt. Col. M.turin, D.S.O. X
    15)   R.E.
    16)
    17 528th (Durham) Fd.Coy.R.E. X
    18 Supply Officer. X O
    19 7th Division. X O
    20 20th Inf.Bde. X O
    21)
    22)
    23) 22nd Inf.Bde. X
    24)
    25)
    26)
    27 62nd Inf.Bde. X
    28 File.
    29 War Diary. X
    30 War Diary. X O

  △ Objective Map already sent.
  O No objective map attached.
  X No Barrage Map attached.

SECRET.

Copy No. ....

APPENDIX 1.
to
91st Infantry Brigade Order No. 22.

2nd October, 1917.

1. (a) Units will stage in the ZILLEBEKE Area under arrangements already notified. While in this Area the utmost care will be taken to screen all movement against aerial observation.
   (b) The time-table for the assembly march is attached.
   (c) Every precaution will be taken to prevent the assembly being betrayed by the moonlight. Bayonets will not be fixed before Zero.
   (d) All Units will signify the completion of their assembly by the code:- "Rations have arrived".

2. During the attack, the Lewis Gun detachments of "mopping up" platoons should be detailed to deal with low-flying aeroplanes in addition to rifle fire from all available bodies of troops.

3. 3 Tanks will be in Divisional Reserve, available to clear up any strong point if required.

4. All Units except 1st Bn. South Staffordshire Regt. (to whom a watch will be sent by 11.p.m.) will take synchronised time from Brigade Headquarters on their way up to the assembly positions on "Y" night.

5. (a) The first Identification established will be reported immediately. Only fresh identifications will subsequently be reported.
   (b) All captured documents will be sent to the BUFF for immediate despatch to Brigade Headquarters.

AMENDMENTS to
91st Infantry Brigade Order No. 22.

(a) Delete sub-para. 6(c) and substitute:- "Two further guns will be held in Brigade Reserve at OLD CABLE HEAD."
(b) Sub-para. 5(b)(i) should read:- " a tape line from J.10.a.75.75. to J.10.a.45.00."
(c) Sub-para. 5(b)(ii), line 3. - For "110 minutes" read "100 minutes".

Captain;

Brigade Major, 91st Infantry Brigade.

Issued at ..... a.m.
to All recipients of Brigade Order No. 22.

SECRET.

TIME TABLE OF ASSEMBLY MARCH TO ACCOMPANY APPENDIX 1.
—:—:—:—:—:—:—:—:—

1. On 2nd October.-
   (a) 1st Bn. South Staffordshire Regt., to be clear of present billets by 5.p.m. Route – via SHRAPNEL CORNER and WARRINGTON ROAD (I.20.a.6.9 to I.17.c.8.7.)
   (b) At dusk, 1st Bn. South Staffordshire Regt., to relieve 1st Bn. Royal Welsh Fusiliers as already arranged between Commanding Officers concerned. Route – via Track junction I.17.c.75.70. – disused Light Railway Track running to I.18.b.0.3. – MENIN ROAD.
   (c) 22nd Bn. Manchester Regt., will pass SHRAPNEL CORNER at 5-45.p.m., moving via WARRINGTON ROAD.
   (d) 21st Bn. Manchester Regt., will pass SHRAPNEL CORNER at 6-45.p.m.
   (e) 2nd Bn. Queen's Regt., will reach Camp at I.19.d.5.4. at 7-30.p.m.

2. From 8-30.p.m., on October 2nd, WARRINGTON ROAD is reserved for 1st Australian Division.

3. All movement up to 6.p.m., will be by platoons at 100 yards interval.

4. On 3rd October, the following route only is available – TRACK JUNCTION I.17.c.75.70. – disused light Railway track running to I.18.b.0.3. – track running to MENIN ROAD – J.13.a.6.3. – Thence via track being made and clearly labelled 91ST INFANTRY BRIGADE TRACK, through GLENCORSE WOOD to POLYGON WOOD.

5. The assembly will be carried out as under :-

   22nd Bn. Manchester Regt., to pass track junction
		I.17.c.75.70.	at	8-30.p.m.
21st Bn. Manchester Regt.	" "	" "	at	9-15.p.m.
2nd Bn. Queen's Regt.	" "	" "	at	10-0 p.m.
91st Machine Gun Coy.	" "	" "	at	10-45.p.m.
91st Trench Mortar Bty.	" "	" "	at	11-0 p.m.

6. The route as far as HOOGE is to be picquetted by the A.P.M. Units will however arrange for the whole route to POLYGON WOOD to be thoroughly reconnoitred on "Y" Day.

7. Brigade Headquarters will close at ST. HUBERTSHOAK at 5.p.m., October 2nd, and will open at HOOGE CRATER AT 9.p.m. The Command of the 91st Infantry Brigade Sector will pass to G.O.C., 91st Infantry Brigade on completion of relief.

—:—:—:—:—:—:—:—:—

SECRET.

Copy No.....

APPENDIX 2.
to
91st Infantry Brigade Order No. 22.

2nd October, 1917.

1. (a) A map shewing the Machine Gun barrages is attached (to Battalions and Machine Gun Coy., only).
   (b) The barrage will consist of 48 Machine Guns organised in 3 groups which will move forward in turn to the advanced battery positions.
   (c) Group Headquarters will be at J.9.a.9.4. and The BUTT.
   (d) No.6. Barrage will be the S.O.S. Barrage.

2. A diagram shewing tapes to be laid out is attached (To Battalions and 528th (Durham) Fd. Coy. R.E., only). These tapes will be laid out under Brigade arrangements on night Y/Z, in conjunction with representatives of 1st Bn. South Staffordshire Regt., and 22nd Bn. Manchester Regt.

AMENDMENTS
to
91st Infantry Brigade Order No. 22.

1. Para. 5.(c)(iii) add - "In the event of the 21st Division line being held up by opposition of so serious a nature that the right support Company of 1st Bn. South Staffordshire Regt., becomes involved, The Officer Commanding, 1st Bn. South Staffordshire Regt., is authorised to call upon The Officer Commanding, 21st Bn. Manchester Regt., for a Company to replace the same.

2. Amendments (b) and (c), published with Appendix 1 are cancelled and the following substituted :-

    (b) Sub-para. 5(b)(i) should read - "A tape line from J.10.a.45.45. to J.10.c.45.85."
    (c) Sub-para. 5(b)(ii), line 3. For "10 minutes" read "90 minutes".

Captain,
Brigade Major, 91st Infantry Brigade.

Issued at ... p.m.
to
All recipients of B.O. 22.

SECRET

BM. 22/1

To all recipients of BO 22.

1. Reference 91st Infantry Brigade Order No 22. ZERO hour will be 6 am on October 4th 1917.

2. The time table for assembly issued with Appendix 1 will be amended to read as follows:—

9th Devon Regt	to pass track June I.17.c.45.70 at	9.15 pm
2nd Gordon Highrs	do	10 pm
22nd Manch. Regt	do	10.45 pm
2nd Border Regt	do	11.30 pm
21st Manch. Regt	do	12.15 am
2nd Queens Regt	do	1 am

O.C. 91st Machine Gun Coy will arrange for such guns and personnel as are operating under the Brigade Orders to take their place in the Column in rear of 22nd Bn. Manch. Regt. Remainder will assemble under the orders of the Divisional Machine Gun Officer.

Acknowledge.

H. Horsland
Captain.
Brigade Major, 91st Infantry B.

3/10/17.

SECRET

ADMINISTRATIVE INSTRUCTIONS in connection with
with 91st Infantry Bde. Order No. 22.

1. Dress and Equipment.

   (a)   (i)   Rifle and equipment less pack.
         (ii)   220 rounds S.A.A.
         (iii) Haversack on back containing Iron Rations and
                one day's rations.
         (iv)   Ground sheet rolled, with Cardigan Jacket inside,
                fixed to the back of waistbelt by supporting
                straps of pack.
         (v)   Box respirator and P.H. Helmet.
         (vi)   Two sandbags under flap of haversack.
         (vii) All waterbottles will be filled and troops warned
                to preserve their water against emergency.

   (b)   Lewis Gunners (except Nos. 1 and 2) signallers and runners
   will carry 100 rounds S.A.A.

   (c)   Rifle Grenadiers will carry 50 rounds S.A.A. and 8
   rifle grenades (Mills No. 23 where cups available, No. 24
   otherwise).

   (d)   Aeroplane flares on a scale of 300 per battalion will be
   issued under Battalion arrangements.

   (e)   Smoke Candles on a scale of 50 per battalion will be
   provided.

   (f)   Shovels on the scale of 50% of reserve companies of 1st
   Assaulting Battalions and 30% of whole of support and reserve
   Battalions, will be issued. In event of Support and Reserve
   Battalions going forward shovels will be stacked in some
   recognisable position.

   (g)   Moppers up will carry 100 rounds S.A.A., 1 "P" Bomb, 2 Mills
   No. 23 and 4 other rifle grenades (No. 23 if available).

   (h)   S.O.S. Signal Grenades at the rate of 25 per battalion will
   be issued. They will be husbanded as they are very scarce.

2. Rations and Water.

   (a)   Rations will be delivered by Train at transport lines so that
   units will always have two days rations on hand. They will be
   made up in pack loads in transport lines and can be sent up,
   if desired, by limbers (using Heavy Draught or other available
   horses) to HELL FIRE CORNER - ZILLEBEKE road whence they will
   be packed forward.

   (b)   A reserve supply of 2000 rations and 500 tins of water will be
   established at HOOGE Crater. They will only be consumed in
   emergency and on the sanction of the Brigadier being obtained.

   (c)   600 oz. of Solidified Paraffin per battalion and 160 per
   Machine Gun Co. with full rum and pea soup ration will be
   issued daily while the Brigade is in the line.

3. S.A.A., Bombs, R.E. material.

   A forward dump of S.A.A., Bombs and R.E. material will be
   established at BUTTE J.10.a.8.8.

   After commencement of operations units will draw from this dump
   as necessity arises advising Brigade Headquarters as soon as
   possible in order that dump may be maintained at sufficient
   establishment.

   (continued).

Brigade Bombing Officer will arrange direct with units for 6 YUKON packs to be placed in advanced dump at the BUTTE J.10.a.8.8. All other YUKON packs with the exception of those of the Machine Gun Co. will be placed in the dump at HOOGE Crater.

4. Transport.

"A" Echelon of the Brigade Pack Transport (less animals from Machine Gun Co.) will assemble 12 noon on 3rd October under the command of 2/Lieut. S. PERRY at a position to be notified later.

The Pack Train will be made up of the normal 3 subsections of 6 animals each from each Battalion and 8 from Brigade Hd.Qtrs. and will be ready to move at short notice loaded in accordance with Schedule A attached.

Echelon "B" of the Brigade Pack Transport will be under regimental control and will remain at present transport lines with exception of that of 1st S. Staffs Regt which will move back to former transport lines at H.31.d.4.9.

The pack transport of 91st Machine Gun Co. (less 5 animals of Echelon "B" which will report to Brigade Transport Officer at Brigade Transport Lines at 12 noon 3rd October) will be at the disposal of O.C., 91st Machine Gun Co.

"A" Echelon Machine Gun Co. will assemble under Company arrangements at a position to be notified later.

5. Prisoners of War.

(a) Units will report by the quickest means available the first identification established. Only fresh identifications will subsequently be reported.

(b) Prisoners will be handed over to M.M.P. post at HOOGE Crater under an escort not exceeding 10% of their strength.
Receipts will be taken and escorts will then rejoin their units.

6. Medical.

The Main Dressing Station will be at ECOLE de BIENFAISANCE on ~~Menin~~ MENIN Road.
Walking wounded should be directed to WOOD COTE HOUSE I.20.c.
There will be R.A.M.C. relay posts at HOOGE CRATER, HOOGE TUNNEL, TANK GUN POST, J.14.b.4.6. and J.9l.c.4.6.
Battalions will select their own Aid Posts and notify Brigade.

7. Veterinary.

An Advanced Veterinary Aid Post will be established and Battalions notified later.

8. Casualties.

All units will render estimated casualty returns to Brigade Hd.Qtrs. by 3 p.m. daily giving officers and other ranks separately.
Accurate officer casualties will be reported as soon as verified, giving name, initials and date of casualty.

9. Water in Captured Territory.

Water in captured territory will not be consumed until it has been examined by a Medical Officer and passed fit for drinking.

(continued).

10. **Personnel.**

Not more than 20 officers, excluding the Medical Officer and Pack Train Officer, will accompany each Battalion into action. Details will remain in camps in vicinity of H.31.d.4.9. and may be called on by Division for working parties.

11. Before moving on 2nd October all packs and surplus kits will be stored in one of the huts in present camp of 2nd Queen's Regt, H.31.d.4.9. 2nd Queen's Regt will provide a guard out of details.

12. All indents to replace Lewis Guns and spares will be wired priority to Brigade Headquarters.

Bde. Hd. Qtrs.
1st October, 1917.

Staff Captain, 91st Infantry Brigade.
Captain,

Copies to -

7th Division.
2nd Queen's Regt.
1st S. Staffs Regt.
21st Manchester Regt.
22nd Manchester Regt.
91st Machine Gun Co.
91st T.M. Battery.
No. 3 Sec., 7th Div. Sig. Co.
No. 3 Coy., Div. Train.
Supply Officer.
20th Inf. Bde.
22nd Inf. Bde.
Brigade Major.
Bde. Transport Officer.
2/Lieut. S. Perry.
Bde. Bombing Officer.
Bde. Q.M. Sgt.
File.
War Diary (2).

Schedule A.

SCHEDULE A.

Unit.	No.1 Subsection.	No.2 Subsection.	No.3 Subsection.
2nd Queen's Regt.	2 animals S.A.A. 2 " Wire. 2 " Picks & Shovels. x	2 animals Mills No.23 2 " Stakes. 2 " L.G.Magazines.	2 animals Picks & Shovels. x 2 " Sandbags. 2 " Hales No.24.
1st S.Stokes Regt.	4 animals Stokes Ammunition. 2 " S.A.A.	2 animals Stokes Ammunition. 2 " L.G.Magazines. 2 " Mills No.23.	2 animals Stokes Ammunition. 2 " Mills No.5. 2 " Stakes.
21st Manchester Regt.	2 animals S.A.A. 2 " Wire. 2 " Picks & Shovels. x	2 animals Mills No.23. 2 " Stakes. 2 " L.G.Magazines.	2 animals Stakes. 1 " Very Lights & Pistols 2 " Wire. 1 " Sandbags.
22nd Manchester Regt.	-ditto-	-ditto-	2 animals L.G.Magazines. 2 " Wire. 2 " Hales No.24.
Brigade Headquarters	8 animals S.A.A.		

x proportion 2 shovels to 1 pick.

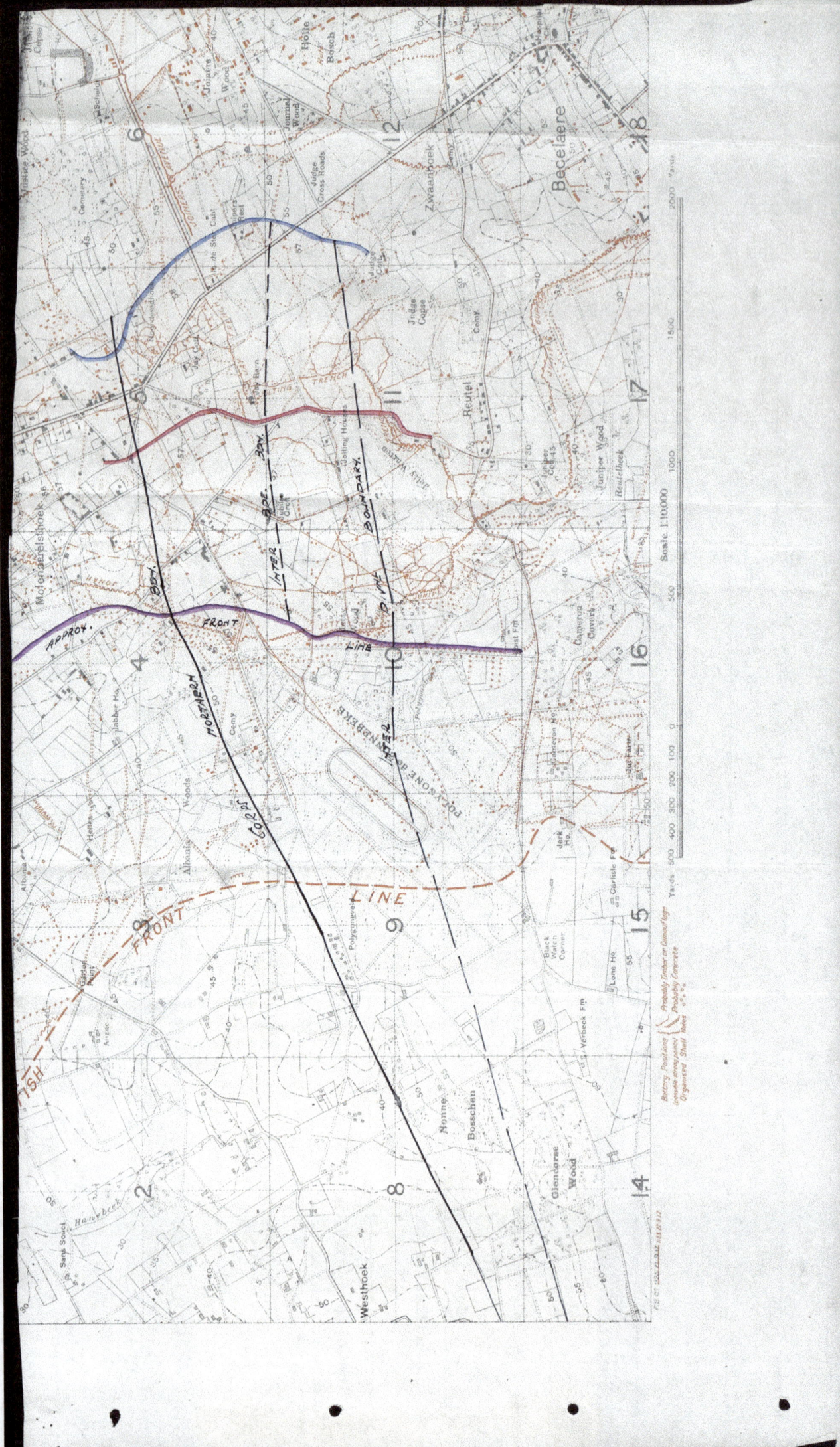

	To.........	(Signature of "Franking Officer.")	From.........
TO	2nd Bn 11BCoy K.R.R		

Sender's Number.	Day of Month.	In reply to Number.	AAA
BM 57	6		

Ref Warning Order of yesterday aaa Relief of Brigade tonight will be carried out on already arranged lines aaa considering. LRO relieve UMX aaa LRP relieve hole of UMW and UMV and that portion of UMY east of [ ] TRENCH aaa One Company LRR relieves 2 Companies UMY west of RED LINE aaa Reserve Company UMX will remain in present positions until relieved by [ ] of LRP aaa UMV will be moved to [ ] tonight [ ] arrangement to be made by DADOS and UNIT will be

From
Place
Time

The above may be forwarded as now corrected. (Z)

Censor. Signature of Addressor or person authorised to telegraph in his name.

* This line should be erased if not required.

SECRET.   Copy No. 15

91st Infantry Brigade Order No.23.

9th October, 1917.

Reference Map -
HAZEBROUCK 5A, - Scale 1/100,000.

1. The 91st Infantry Brigade will be withdrawn to No.4.Area, (vicinity of ST.HUBERTSHOEK) to-morrow, October 10th, 1917.

2. (a) Units will pass the Starting Point, HALLEBAST CORNER, as under :-

    22nd Bn. Manchester Regt.   1-0 p.m.
    1st Bn. South Staffs. Regt.   1-15.p.m.
    91st Light Trench Mortar Bty.   1-30.p.m.
    91st Machine Gun Coy.   1-35.p.m.
    Brigade Headquarters.   1-45.p.m.

   (b) (i) 2nd Bn. Queen's Regt., and 21st Bn. Manchester Regt., will march off on relief by two Battalions of 23rd Division.
       (ii) Leading Battalion of latter Division is due to arrive in ZILLEBEKE Area at 12.noon.
       (iii) 2nd Bn. Queen's Regt., and 21st Bn. Manchester Regt., will not pass the Starting Point before 1-50.p.m.

3. Intervals of 100 yards in Rear of Companies and 500 yards in rear of Battalions will be maintained.

4. Lorries at the rate of 1 per Battalion, 1 per Machine Gun Coy., and 1 for Brigade Headquarters and 91st L.T.M.Battery, are due to arrive at Brigade Headquarters at 8.a.m., whence they will be re-directed to Units.

5. Billetting parties furnished with squared maps will report to the Staff Captain at HALLEBAST CORNER at 10-30.a.m.

6. (a) The stretcher parties of 50 per Battalion will remain in the forward area until relieved.
   (b) The burial party of 91st Light Trench Mortar Bty., is being returned to-morrow night under Divisional arrangements.

7. Brigade Headquarters will close at CHATEAU SEGARD at 1.p.m., and will open at the same hour at ST.HUBERTSHOEK.

8. ACKNOWLEDGE.

                                                    Captain,
                                    Brigade Major, 91st Infantry Brigade.

Issued at 11/50 p.m. to
    Copy No 1 2nd Queen's R   11 528th (Durham) Fd.Coy.RE
            2 1st S.Staffs.R   12 Supply Officer.
            3 21st Manch.R   13 7th Division.
            4 22nd Manch.R   14 File.
            5 91st M.G.Coy.   15 War Diary.
            6 91st T.M.Bty.   16 War Diary.
            7 No.3.Sec.Div.Sig.Coy.
            8 Staff Captain.
            9 Bde.Transport Officer.
           10 21st Field Ambulance.

9. No tents or shelters issued in this Area or belonging to this Area will be removed. Unless otherwise ordered all camps will be left standing under a guard and handed over to incoming units, receipts being taken for tents, shelters and other Area stores.

SECRET.   app. 5   Copy No...16..

91st Infantry Brigade Order No.24.

12th October, 1917.

Reference Map - HAZEBROUCK 5A.
   Edition 2. Scale 1/100,000.

1. The 91st Infantry Brigade will move to the THIEUSHOUK Area this afternoon via HALLEBAST CORNER, LA CLYTTE, MONT ROUGE, MONT NOIR and BERTHEN.

2. Units will pass the starting point, HALLEBAST CORNER at the undermentioned times :-

Brigade H.Q. & 91st Light T.M.Bty.	1-0 p.m.
2nd Bn. Queen's Regt.	1-5 p.m.
1st Bn. South Staffordshire Regt.	1-20 p.m.
21st Bn. Manchester Regt.	1-35 p.m.
22nd Bn. Manchester Regt.	1-50 p.m.
91st Machine Gun Coy.	2-15 p.m.
No.3. Company, 7th Div. Train.	2-25 p.m.

3. Intervals of 100 yards in rear of Companies and 500 yards in rear of Battalions will be maintained throughout the march.

4. Arrangements for Lorries and Billetting parties have been notified separately.

5. The Officer Commanding, 21st Field Ambulance will detail two ambulances to sweep the road in rear of the column after the rear of No.3. Company, Divisional Train has passed through LA CLYTTE.

6. Brigade Headquarters will close at ST HUBERTUSHOEK at 1.p.m., and will open at THIEUSHOUK at 4.p.m.

7. ACKNOWLEDGE.

                                              Captain,
                            Brigade Major, 91st Infantry Brigade.

Issued at...a.m. to

   Copy No 1 2nd Queen's R
         2 1st S.Staffs.R
         3 21st Manch.R
         4 22nd Manch.R
         5 91st M.G.Coy.
         6 91st L.T.M.Bty.
         7 No.3.Sec.Div.Sig.Coy.
         8 Staff Captain.
         9 Bde. Transport Officer.
        10 21st Field Ambulance.
        11 528th (Durham) Fd.Coy.R.E.
        12 Supply Officer.
        13 No.3.Coy.Div.Train.
        14 7th Division.
        15 File.
        16 War Diary.
        17 War Diary.

SECRET

B.M./1210.

To all recipients of B.O.24.

1. Reference B.O.24 of to-day, Brigade will march this afternoon via RENINGHELST – HAKKEN CORNER – CROSS ROADS ¾ mile N. of B of BERTHEN – BERTHEN, where further instructions will be given to Units.

2. Starting point – Entrance to Brigade Headquarters on OUDERDOM – HALLEBAST CORNER Road.

3. Times remain as before.

4. Ambulances to join rear of Column at RENINGHELST.

5. B.O.24 will be amended accordingly.

Bde.Hd.Qtrs.

12th Oct.1917.

Captain,

Brigade Major, 91st Infantry Brigade.

SECRET.

App. 5a

Narrative of Operations of 91st Infantry Brigade

October 4th-6th, 1917.

Reference Maps - BECELAERE, 1a - Scale 1/10,000.
HOOGE, Edn. 3. - Scale 1/10,000.

-:-:-:-:-:-:-:-:-

1. **OUTLINE OF EVENTS.**

   On Saturday September 29th, 1917, the Brigade arrived in the ST. HUBERTUSHOEK Area from the Second Army Training Area. On September 28th, 29th, 30th and October 1st and 2nd, preliminary reconnaissances of the POLYGON WOOD position were carried out by Brigade and Battalion Staffs and Company Commanders. On October 2nd, the Battalions moved forward to the ZILLEBEKE Area. On the night October 2nd/3rd the Brigade front was taken over by 1st Battalion, South Staffordshire Regt., the leading Battalion in the attack, and Brigade Headquarters moved to HOOGE CRATER. On the following night the assembly took place for the attack, which was carried out at dawn on October 4th. The Brigade was relieved on night 6/7th October.

2. **GENERAL PLAN.**

   (a) In conjunction with a large operation along the fronts of the Second and Fifth Armies, the 7th Division was to capture the Southern end of the BROODSEINDE RIDGE, due East of POLYGON WOOD, the 21st Division on its right being ordered to form a defensive flank running South of REUTEL to protect its Southern flank.
   (b) The Divisional attack was to be carried out by two Brigades, the 20th Infantry Brigade on the Left, and the 91st Infantry Brigade on the Right, with objectives as under:-

   (i) RED LINE:- A line from J.5.a.6.0. to J.5.c.9.4., thence the line of the road passing West of JAY BARN and East of JOLTING HOUSES to J.11.a.85.25. (to be continued thence by 21st Division Southwards along the road passing West of REUTEL).

   (ii) BLUE LINE:- A line of observation running from J.5.b.3.2. East of NOORDHOEK and JOINERS REST to J.12.a.2.5. (to be continued thence by 21st Division S.W. through JUDGE COTTAGE and COPSE to the RED LINE South of REUTEL.

3. **BRIGADE SCHEME.**

   (a) The Northern boundary of this Brigade ran from the existing Front Line at J.10.b.3.8. to J.3.c.8.0., thence to the BLUE LINE at J.12.a.30.95. The Southern boundary ran from the Front Line at J.10.b.1.0. to the BLUE LINE at J.12.a.2.5.
   (b) The first objective (RED LINE) was allotted to the 1st Battalion, South Staffordshire Regt., who were formed up in Normal Attack Formation on a tape line from J.10.b.1.0. to J.10.b.1.8.

   The second objective (BLUE LINE) was allotted to the 22nd Battalion, The Manchester Regiment, (with one company 21st Bn. Manchester Regt., attached for "mopping-up" purposes) who were to be formed up in Normal Attack Formation on a tape line from J.10.c.45.85. - J.10.a.45.45.

   In order to avoid the probable enemy barrage line, each assaulting Battalion was closed up to a depth of 120 yards from front to rear, an interval of 200 yards being left between the rear of the first and the leading wave of the second Battalion. Two tapes 60 yards apart were laid out for each Battalion, in addition to 3 guide tapes to indicate the centre and flanks. These tape lines were reconnoitred by Officers of 528th (Durham) Field Coy. R.E., in liaison with representative Officers of both assaulting Battalions and of neighbouring Brigades, on night October 2nd/3rd, and laid at dusk on October 3rd.

(c) At Zero hour the Artillery Barrage was to open on a line 150 yards in advance of the tape line, whence, after a 3 minute pause it was to commence creeping forward at the rate of 100 yards in 4 minutes for 200 yards, after which the rate decreased to 100 yards every 6 minutes until the Infantry reached the RED LINE, (At Zero plus 40 minutes) when it remained 200 yards in advance of the RED LINE until Zero plus 2 hours and 10 minutes.

At Zero hour both assaulting Battalions were to advance behind the barrage, the leading Battalion going through to the RED LINE, the rear Battalion halting on a line 400 yards into NO MAN'S LAND until Zero plus 90 minutes, when it was to resume the advance, pass through the leading Battalion on the RED LINE and await the lifting of the barrage. At Zero plus 2 hours and 10 minutes it was to advance behind the barrage, at the rate of 100 yards in 8 minutes until reaching the BLUE LINE (at Zero plus 3 hours).

Each objective, on capture, was to be organised in depth as a defensive zone; the consolidation of the RED LINE was not to be commenced before the 22nd Bn. Manchester Regt., had passed through.

(d) The 21st Bn. Manchester Regt. (less one company) was to be in support dug in between POLYGON and NONNE BOSSCHEN Woods. At about Zero plus 2 hours. The Officer Commanding, 21st Bn. Manchester Regt., was to commence moving forward as the hostile barrage allowed to a position of assembly in the vicinity of the Old Front Line, and to establish his Headquarters with those of the 1st Bn. South Staffordshire Regt., at the BUTTE.

The 2nd Bn. "The Queen's" (Royal West Surrey Regt.) were to be dug in in the vicinity of SURBITON VILLAS (J.13.b. central), and remain in Brigade Reserve until called upon.

(e) Two Vickers Guns were to accompany the rear wave of the leading Battalion to take up positions in pre-arranged localities whence the RED LINE could be covered and the Right Flank commanded should the necessity arise. Four Vickers Guns were to proceed with the rear wave of the 22nd Bn. Manchester Regt., to take up positions for the defence of the BLUE LINE. Two of these guns were to be echelonned on the right flank of the advance to guard against trouble from that quarter.

Two guns were in Brigade Reserve at CABLE HEAD (J.14.a.3.4.). The remaining 8 guns were employed on barrage work under the Divisional Machine Gun Officer.

(f) One Stokes Gun and team was allotted to each assaulting Battalion to proceed with the rear wave and deal with any situation during or after the advance, as required.

(g) Brigade Headquarters were to be at HOOGE CRATER (I.18.b.2.6.) with an Advanced Report Centre at the BUTTE (J.10.a.7.8.). The Headquarters of both assaulting Battalions were to be at the BUTT, of 21st Bn. Manchester Regt. at J.9.c.1.5., of 2nd Bn. Queen's Regt. at J.13.b.5.5., and of 91st Machine Gun Company and Trench Mortar Battery at CABLE HEAD, which was also to form the Brigade Observation Post.

(h) Liaison Officers were exchanged with Brigades and Battalions on either flank.

4. NARRATIVE.

The assembly on night 3rd/4th October was carried out in accordance with a Divisional time-table and passed off without incident and with few casualties. The night was cloudy but dry until the early morning, with just sufficient light to be able to follow the track, which was also picketted throughout its length. There was a considerable amount of hostile shelling in and in rear of POLYGON WOOD but the forward area containing the attacking troops was almost completely immune.

The attack commenced at 6 a.m. (Summer time) at which hour a heavy drizzle had been in progress for some hours, making the going heavy and slippery. The enemy put down his barrage some five minutes after our barrage had commenced, and the bulk of it fell clear of the assaulting Battalions. The attack from the start progressed steadily according to time-table, comparatively little opposition being met with. The right flank of the advance came under

Machine Gun fire and suffered considerably, otherwise casualties were light. The leading Battalion of the Division on the right fell somewhat behind in the course of the advance, but this was observed by the Machine Gun Officer accompanying the rear wave of the 1st Bn. South Staffordshire Regt., who thereupon placed two Vickers Guns on the extreme right flank and engaged with effect several parties of the enemy until the arrival of the 3/4th Queen's, when the guns were moved to their defensive posts on the RED LINE. A large number of Germans were shot and bayonetted chiefly in small pits camauflaged with brushwood.

The 22nd Bn. Manchester Regt., advanced according to plan shaking out into Normal Attack Formation in so doing. Considerable difficulty was experienced in stopping the line when on the move under battle conditions. This was however done and formations remained intact. The line of skirmishers was found to be of little value, and the front line was closed into section groups during the course of the advance. Touch with the 10th Bn. Yorkshire Regt., was lacking from the start, the latter Battalion, failing to reach the assembly position in time to take part in the attack. The right flank was consequently exposed throughout the advance, and it was necessary to send up another Company of the 21st Bn. Manchester Regt., to reinforce the front line. In the course of the afternoon a third company was put in to strengthen the front line which, owing to lateral expansion to the right, had become thin. Throughout the day much trouble was experienced from Machine Guns and Snipers on the right flank, especially from the direction of JUDGE COPSE and from across the valley towards POLDERHOEK RIDGE. Throughout the advance close touch was kept with the 8th Bn. Devonshire Regt., and 2nd Bn. Border Regt., on the left.

As soon as it became apparent that the 21st Division on the right had failed to secure the BLUE LINE, the 2nd Bn. Queen's Regt, was ordered to move forward to take up a position in the eastern end of POLYGON WOOD. By an unfortunate chance, the Commanding Officer was fatally wounded at the moment of receiving orders for the advance, the Company Commander who succeeded him being hit immediately after. The Brigade Major was consequently sent forward to the BUTTE at 1-50.p.m., with orders to clear up the situation which was then obscure (little information having come through as to the location of the 22nd Bn. Manchester Regt., or the situation on the right flank) and to place the 2nd Bn. Queen's Regt., under the orders of Lieut-Colonel A.B. Beauman, D.S.O., Commanding 1st Bn. South Staffordshire Regt. A further supply of pigeons was taken forward at the same time, and communication through this means was found to be of the greatest value.

At 4-30.p.m., in consequence of information received from several sources that the Brigade on the right was in an instable condition, the disposition of troops on the RED LINE was readjusted in such a way as to have the greatest strength in men and Lewis Guns on the right flank, with a field of fire southwards. At the same time the 2nd Bn. Queen's Regt., were disposed as follows:- 2 Companies to form a defensive flank facing South along the JOLTING HOUSES Road, One Company in JETTY TRENCH and one Company in reserve near the BUTTE. This latter Company was subsequently allotted to The Officer Commanding, 22nd Bn. Manchester Regt., and was guided by his Right Company Commander into position (in five posts) to fill the gap between the RED and BLUE LINES on the right flank, where the 21st Division had failed to accomplish their task.

The situation at dusk on October the 4th was as follows:-
The 22nd Bn. Manchester Regt. (with 3 Companies, 21st Bn. Manchester Regt.) held from J.6.d.1.2. to J.12.a.2.6., thence back to J.12.a.0.5. A gap of about 350 yards still existed between this point and the 1st Bn. South Staffordshire Regt., occupying JOLTING TRENCH. This gap contained scattered elements of 21st Division, and was well covered by day from the JOLTING TRENCH Line. (This gap was filled before dawn by re-organising the elements of LANCASHIRE and LINCOLNS and by the Company of 2nd Bn. Queen's Regt., above referred to). Two Vickers Guns were in position at J.12.a.05.85.

and 15.75.) covering the Eastern slopes of the hill, and two (at J.11.b.75. and 8.6.) covering the defensive flank between the RED and BLUE LINES. In rear of the above system, two zones had been put in a state of defence by the 1st Bn. South Staffordshire Regt.,- JOLTING HOUSE TRENCH and the trench running from J.5.c.65.10. to J.11.a.5.4.; both of these lines gave an excellent field of fire eastwards. A Strong Point for 2 Lewis Guns and 20 Rifles had been formed at J.11.b.3.2., which proved an invaluable pivot for the right flank, having a wide field of fire in all directions. Two companies of 2nd Bn. Queen's Regt. were in position from J.11.a.20.10. to 55.30. - 80.30. whence the defensive flank was carried on by half a company of the 1st Bn. South Staffordshire Regt., to the Strong Point above referred to. Two Vickers Guns were in position at J.11.a.85.75. and on the right rear at J.11.a.5.2. The remaining Company of 21st Bn. Manchester Regt., was employed on carrying. One Company of 2nd Bn. Queen's Regt., remained in reserve in JETTY TRENCH.

The Brigade continued to hold the line throughout the 5th and 6th October, being relieved by the 20th Infantry Brigade on night 6/7th October (with the exception of the 91st Machine Gun Company, who remained in until nights 7/8th and 8/9th October). The relief passed off without incident, and was complete by 6.a.m., October 7th. All stretcher cases were evacuated from the BUTTE before relief.

With the exception of certain marked periods of quiet, such as the mornings of October 5th and 6th, the enemy kept up a continuous barrage of varying intensity on the area between CLAPHAM JUNCTION and POLYGON WOOD. The whole area was searched with guns of all calibres. POLYGON WOOD itself was subjected to stiff barrages of Light guns at frequent intervals, special attention being paid to the BUTTE and the Northern corner generally. The area between the Wood and the RED LINE was intermittently shelled with light guns from midday on October 4th. The whole RED LINE system was kept under a fairly lively shelling from the evening of the 5th October onwards. Forward of the RED LINE very little shelling was experienced.

The bulk of the casualties were caused during the afternoon of the 4th and successive days, by :-
    (a) sniping and machine gun fire from the direction of JUDGE COPSE and POLDERHOEK RIDGE.
    (b) Shelling of the RED LINE system.

On four occasions during the operations S.O.S. Signals were put up at some point on the front of the Xth and I ANZAC Corps. At no time however did a counter-attack of any magnitude develop.

5. COMMUNICATIONS.

Owing to the enforced distance between Brigade and Battalion Headquarters, communications were a matter of considerable difficulty throughout. Telephones were of little use, though they were in use from Battalion Headquarters at the BUTTE to Battalion forward command posts. Visual signalling was established from the BUTTE to CABLE HEAD, but became obscured by shelling. The power buzzer proved unreliable owing to the number of relay stations needed back to Brigade Headquarters. One of the sensitive amplifiers was commonly out of order, however the loosened soil of the crater area is reported to have militated against their efficiency. Runner Posts were slow and owing to the heavy shelling not altogether reliable. Pigeons proved by far the most effective means of communication, had the messages not taken so long to reach Brigade Headquarters. The average time taken was 55 minutes from the time of liberation. The wireless installation at the BUTTE proved of no service.

Each assaulting battalion maintained an advanced report centre, connected by telephone to Battalion Headquarters, which proved invaluable.

6. ARTILLERY.

The Artillery arrangements were throughout admirable. Both the creeping and the protective barrages earned unstinted praise from all who participated in the assault, and a large measure of the success achieved must be attributed to the excellence of the artillery programme.

7. ADMINISTRATIVE ARRANGEMENTS.

Rations were sent up by carrying parties nightly. The Brigade Pack Train made successful journeys with ammunition etc., to the BUTTE on nights October 2nd/3rd, 3rd/4th and 4/5th. The only route available for the use of this Brigade was however almost impassable across the two valleys in GLENCORSE WOOD, especially after the rain of October 3rd and 4th, and many casualties in pack animals were sustained.

8. MEDICAL.

A separate report is being forwarded on the Medical arrangements which proved inadequate throughout.

9. CAPTURES.

It is estimated that 200 prisoners were taken by the Brigade. Prisoners of the 2,4,72(Fusiliers),73,78,92,93, 212,229 and 230th Regiments, and the 5th (Augusta) Guards passed through HOOGE CRATER. These were however not all taken by this Division.

War material captured included the following:-

7 Machine Guns.
6 Medium Trench Mortars.

10. CASUALTIES.

The casualties of the Brigade were 1007, made up as under :-

Unit.	Officers.			Other Ranks.		
	Killed.	Wounded.	Missing.	Killed.	Wounded.	Missing.
2nd Queen's	1	6	-	38	107	25
1st S. Staffs.	3	6	-	36	215	23
21st Manch.	5	8	1	37	162	11
22nd Manch.	1	7	-	44	209	28
91st M.G. Coy.	-	1	-	4	22	-
91st T.M. Bty.	-	-	-	-	7	-
Total	10	28	1	159	722	87

11.

A list of recommendations for Immediate Awards has already been forwarded. A report on points of special interest for future operations will be forwarded shortly.

Bde. Hd. Qtrs.

14th October, 1917.

R.T. Pelly, Brigadier General,
Commanding, 91st Infantry Brigade.

SECRET.   Copy No. 18

app 6

91st Infantry Brigade Order No.26.

Sunday, 21st October, 1917.

Reference Maps –
BELGIUM & FRANCE, Sheet 27. – Scale 1/40,000.
   "   "   Sheet 28. –   "   1/40,000.

Moves and reliefs will take place as under :-

1.   On October 22nd.
   (a) The 91st Infantry Brigade will move to No.9.Area
       (M.9,10,11 and 12) via BERTHEN, ST. KOKERULLE and
       WESTOUTRE. Exact destination of Units will be
       notified later. Units will pass the starting point
       (Road Junction R.25.b.2.8.) as under :-

           1st Bn.South Staffs.Regt.   9–0   a.m.
           22nd Bn.Manch.Regt.   9–20 a.m.
           21st Bn.Manch.Regt.   9–40 a.m.
           2nd Bn.Queen's Regt.   10–10 a.m.
           91st Machine Gun Coy.   10–30 a.m.
           No.3.Coy.7th Div.Train.   10–35 a.m.
           Brigade Headquarters.   11–0   a.m.

   (b) Brigade Headquarters will close at THIEUSHOUK at
       10.a.m.,and open at the same hour at M.10.d.7.8.

2.   On October 23rd.
   (a) 91st Infantry Brigade will relieve the Reserve Brigade
       of 39th Division in "C" Area (M.18.a. and b.,N.7.c. and d.
       N.8.c.,N.13.and 14.) coming under the orders of 39th
       Division. Head of column will pass LA CLYTTE at 12.noon;
       March Table and destinations will be notified later.
   (b) On night 23rd/24th October,91st Machine Gun Coy.,will
       relieve the guns at present in the line on the Brigade
       Battle Front, under arrangements to be made between
       Commanding Officers concerned. Separate arrangements are
       being made for the moves and accommodation of these guns
       on 22nd and 23rd October.

3.   On night October 23rd/24th.
       91st Infantry Brigade will relieve the 117th Infantry
   Brigade,39th Division, on the Brigade Battle Front.
       Further Instructions regarding the relief and the
   move forward from "C" Area will be issued later.

4. (a) In all of the above marches intervals of 500 yards in
       rear of Battalions and 200 yards in rear of Companies
       will be maintained.
   (b) All Units will halt for the last 10 minutes of each
       hour.

5.   A watch will be circulated to all concerned with the
   early delivery on 22nd and 23rd October.

6.   The Officer Commanding, 21st Field Ambulance will
   detail an ambulance to proceed in rear of the column on
   22nd October.

7.   ACKNOWLEDGE.

                                            Captain,
                         Brigade Major, 91st Infantry Brigade.

Distribution over-leaf.

Issued at...1/15...p.m. to -

Copy No 1 2nd Queen's R.
2 1st S. Staffs. R
3 21st Manch. R.
4 22nd Manch. R.
5 91st M.G. Coy.
6 No.3. Sec. 7th Div. Sigs.
7 Staff Captain.
8 Bde. Transport Officer.
9 21st Field Ambulance.
10 528th (Durham) Fd. Coy. R.E.
11 Supply Officer.
12 No.3. Coy. Div. Train.
13 7th Division.
14 20th Manch. R.
15 20th Inf. Bde.
16 117th Inf. Bde.
17 File.
18 War Diary.
19 War Diary.

SECRET.   Copy No...18.

Amendment to 91st Infantry Brigade Order No.26.

22nd October, 1917.

-:-:-:-:-:-:-:-:-:-:-:-

Reference Brigade Order No.26., para.3., for "night October 23rd/24th" read "night October 24th/25th"

ACKNOWLEDGE.

Captain,
Brigade Major, 91st Infantry Brigade.

Copies to all recipients of B.O.26.

SECRET.

Copy No. 18

91st Infantry Brigade Order No.28.

Monday, 22nd October, 1917.

Reference Map - BELGIUM and Part of FRANCE,
Sheet 28. - Scale 1/40,000.
-:-:-:-:-:-:-:-:-:-

1. The 91st Infantry Brigade will relieve the Reserve Brigade of 39th Division in accordance with accompanying March Table.

2. (a) Intervals of 500 yards in rear of Battalions and 200 yards in rear of Companies will be maintained.
(b) All Units will halt for the last ten minutes of each hour.

3. A watch will be circulated to all concerned with the early delivery.

4. Brigade Headquarters will close at CARNARVON CAMP at 10-30.a.m., and open at the same hour at FAIRY HOUSE.

5. Transport will move with Units.

6. Lorries will report as under and be available for single journey:-

   2 to each Battalion Headquarters at 9.a.m.
   1 to 91st Machine Gun Coy.   " 9.a.m.
   1 to Brigade Headquarters.   " 9.a.m.

7. Billeting parties will be sent on two hours in advance to take over from outgoing Units.

8. ACKNOWLEDGE.

Captain,

Brigade Major, 91st Infantry Brigade.

Issued at......p.m. to

Copy No 1 2nd Queen's R   11 20th Manch.R
       2 1st S.Staffs.R   12 Supply Officer.
       3 21st Manch.R   13 No13.Coy.Div.Train.
       4 22nd Manch.R   14 7th Division.
       5 91st M.G.Coy.   15 20th Inf.Bde.
       6 No.3.Sec. Div.Sigs.   16 22nd Inf.Bde.
       7 Staff Captain.   17 116th Inf.Bde.
       8 Bde.Transport Officer.   18 File.
       9 21st Field Ambulance.   19 War Diary.
      10.528th (Durham) Fd.Coy.   20 War Diary.

MARCH TABLE.

(to accompany Brigade Order No.28.)

Unit.	Destination.	Starting Point.	Time.	Route.	Take over Camps from
91st Inf.Bde.H.Q.	FAIRY HOUSE I.18.d.7.5. VOORMEZEELE.	CANADIAN CORNER.	11-15.a.m.	BRULOOZE Cross Roads.	-
1st Bn.3.Staffs.Regt.	-do-	-do-	11-25.a.m.	LA CLYTTE-KEMMEL-VIERSTRAAT Cross Roads-BRASSERIE.	Billeting Parties to meet guides at CONFUSION CORNER at 11.a.m.
22nd Bn.Manch.Regt.	Camp at N.5.a.4.5.	-do-	11-45.a.m.	LA CLYTTE-KEMMEL-VIERSTRAAT Cross Roads.	1st Herts.Regt.
91st Machine Gun Coy. (less guns to line).	-do-	-do-	12-15.p.m.	-do-	-
21st Bn.Manch.Regt.	LITTLE KEMMEL CAMP. N.20.c.9.5.	-do-	12-30.p.m.	BRULOOZE Cross Roads.	1/6th Cheshire Regt.
2nd Bn.Queen's Regt.	FERMOY FARM N.13.c.2.0.	-do-	12-50.p.m.	-do-	4/5th Black Watch.

SECRET.   Copy No. 10

91st Infantry Brigade Order No.29.

Sunday, 28th October, 1917.

1. Brigade Headquarters, 1st Bn. S. Staffs Regt., and 22nd Bn. Manchester Regt. will move to EBBLINGHEM area to-morrow, 29th October.

2. (a) Personnel will be moved by train.
   (b) Transport will move by road and will rendezvous at EBBLINGHEM Station.
   (c) Each man will carry 1 blanket and 1 day's rations.

3. Billeting parties will proceed on bicycles to EBBLINGHEM Station where they will be met by a representative of Brigade at 12 noon.

4. Lorries will report as follows at 10 a.m. :-

   1 Brigade Headquarters.
   6 at BARDENBRUG Dump (3 for 1st Bn. S. Staffs Regt. and 3 for 22nd Bn. Manchester Regt.)

   Battalions will send guides to conduct lorries to camps.

5. Baggage wagons will report to units to-night and will rejoin the Train to-morrow. O.C., No.3 Coy., Div. Train will notify units the time at which these wagons must rejoin.

6. Time of departure of trains and station will be notified later.

7. Battalions will -
   (a) Withdraw all stragglers posts and other outlying detachments who will proceed to new area with units.
   (b) Ensure that all blankets, kits, etc. of casualties not yet disposed of are taken to the new area. Lorries may be used for two journeys for this purpose provided they rejoin their Park by night.

                                                        Captain,
                                    for Brigade Major, 91st Infantry Brigade.

Issued at 8-0 p.m. to

   Copy No. 1 1st S. Staffs Regt.
         2 22nd Manchester Regt.
         3 No.3 Sec., 7th Div. Sig. Co.
         4 Staff Captain.
         5 Bde. Transport Officer.
         6 Supply Officer.
         7 No.3 Coy., 7th Div. Train.
         8 7th Division.
         9 File.
        10 War Diary.
        11 War Diary.

S E C R E T.

Reference 91st Infantry Brigade Order No.29.

1. 91st Inf.Bde.Headquarters, 1st South Staffs Regt. and 22nd Manchester Regt. will travel to EBBLINGHEM by train leaving DICKEBUSCH at 9-50 a.m.

2. All personnel will arrive at the entraining point at 8-50 a.m.

3. The usual intervals will be maintained on the march.

4. Battalions will send on officers in advance to ascertain the location of the entraining point, which is understood to be about H.33.a.9.9., and guide Battalions in.

5. Brigade Headquarters will close at RENINGHELST at 5 a.m.

LLCohen

28th October, 1917.   Staff Captain, 91st Infantry Brigade.

Captain,

Copies to all recipients of Brigade Order No.29.

SECRET

App. 7

Copy No. 25

91st Infantry Brigade Order No. 27.

Monday, 22nd October, 1917.

Reference Map – ZILLEBEKE, Edition 6a,
Scale 1/10,000.

1. (a) The Xth Corps is to co-operate with a main attack further North by attacking GHELUVELT and POLDERHOEK WOOD. Zero date and hour will be notified later.
   (b) The role of the 7th Division is to capture GHELUVELT and some ground along the ZANDVOORDE SPUR and so render secure the TOWER HAMLETS RIDGE.
   (c) The role of the 5th Division is to capture POLDERHOEK CHATEAU and WOOD.

2. (a) The attack by the 7th Division is to be carried out by the 91st Infantry Brigade (with 20th Bn. The Manchester Regt. in reserve) on the right, and 20th Infantry Brigade (with 1st Bn. Royal Welsh Fusiliers in reserve) on the left. The dividing line between Brigades runs from J.21.c.5.8. – 22.c.0.1. – 28.a.95.65.
   (b) The attack of the 91st Infantry Brigade will be carried out by 1st Bn. South Staffordshire Regt.(Right), 21st Bn. The Manchester Regt.(Centre) and 2nd Bn. Queen's Regt.(Left). One Company of 22nd Bn. The Manchester Regt., will be attached as battalion reserve to 2nd Bn. Queen's Regt., and one Company and two Stokes Guns to 1st Bn. South Staffordshire Regt. The remaining two Companies 22nd Bn. The Manchester Regt., under Major B.G.ATKIN, M.C., will remain in Reserve at Brigade Headquarters.
   The 20th Bn. The Manchester Regt., will be in Brigade Reserve at Lock 8 (I.32.a.7.5.) with one company in LARCH WOOD. A Liaison Officer from this Battalion will report to Brigade Headquarters by 9.a.m., on Zero day.

3. (a) The artillery barrage programme is attached.
   (b) The barrage will be put down by guns of all calibres 150 yards in advance of our forming up line, where it will remain for 4 minutes. It will then advance for 200 yards at the rate of 100 yards in 6 minutes, then for a further 200 yards at 100 yards in 8 minutes, thereafter at 100 yards in 12 minutes to the RED protective barrage, 150 yards in advance of the RED LINE. After a halt of 30 minutes on this line, it will resume its advance at the rate of 100 yards in 12 minutes to the BLUE protective barrage, 200 yards in advance of the BLUE LINE. A secondary barrage will then search backwards and forwards periodically throughout the day.
   (c) The protective barrage to the RED and BLUE LINES will, for the first 4 minutes, include a proportion of smoke shell to shew the infantry that they have reached the objectives.
   As a signal to the Infantry, the rate of fire will be increased to a rapid rate for the 4 minutes immediately preceeding the resumption of the advance from the RED LINE.

4. (a) By Zero minus one hour the 1st Bn. South Staffordshire Regt., 21st Bn. Manchester Regt., and 2nd Bn. Queen's Regt., will be formed up on a tape line from J.26.b.45.00. – J.26.b.60.25. – J.20.d.85.10. – J.21.c.8.7., whence the line is being continued by 20th Infantry Brigade. This line will be reconnoitred by representatives of each assaulting Battalion on night 24/25th October, and the tape laid under battalion arrangements at dusk on 25th October. Separate Instructions on this subject will be issued later.

Battalions will/

Battalions will be closed up on the tape line to a total depth of 120 yards from front to rear. The greatest care will be taken to avoid betraying the assembly by movement or noise. Bayonets will not be fixed before Zero.
(b) At Zero hour the line will advance to as close as possible to the barrage, and the attack will conform to the barrage programme. The companies detailed for the assault on the RED LINE will advance in rear of the front line companies at Zero hour, and will halt on a line 200 yards in advance of TOWER TRENCH where they will remain for 15 minutes. They will then resume the advance (at an increased distance from the front line troops), pass through the first objective to a position close under the RED protective barrage and await the lifting of the barrage.
(c) The consolidation of all objectives will be carried out in depth, and will be based on the general principle of selecting the best permanent line of defence, special attention being paid to the following localities :-

1st Bn. South Staffordshire Regt.	Bank at J.26.b.8.0. BERRY COTTS. Spur J.27.a.7.5.
21st Bn. Manchester Regt.	Dugout J.27.a.9.6. Dugouts J.27.b.4.5. Spur. J.27.a.7.5.
2nd Bn. Queen's Regt.	Dugout J.21.d.65.20. LEWIS HOUSE. Spurs. J.28.a.2.9. and 6.6.

Special precautions will be taken to deal with low flying enemy aircraft.

5. (a) On the left of 2nd Bn. Queen's Regt., the 2nd Bn. Border Regt. (Headquarters, J.21.a.50.05.) will be attacking the RED LINE and the 2nd Bn. Gordon Highlanders (Headquarters, J.20.b.65.05.) will be attacking the BLUE LINE.
(b) No advance will be carried out by the 19th Division on the Right flank. The name and Headquarters of the Battalion on the left of 19th Division will be notified later to Officer Commanding, 1st Bn. South Staffordshire Regt.

6. (a) The Officer Commanding, 91st Machine Gun Coy., will detail four guns to accompany 1st Bn. South Staffordshire Regt. to take up positions in the neighbourhood of BERRY COTTS and JUTE COTTS, two guns to accompany 21st Bn. The Manchester Regt. to take up positions in the vicinity of J.27.a.8.5. and 7.9., and two guns to accompany 2nd Bn. Queen's Regt., to take up positions in the vicinity of LEWIS HOUSE.
(b) The remaining 8 guns will be placed at the disposal of the Divisional Machine Gun Officer for barrage purposes until Zero plus 136 minutes, when they will revert to Officer Commanding, 91st Machine Gun Coy., and will be held in Brigade Reserve.
(c) The Machine Gun barrage programme is attached. The barrage will be formed by 76 Machine Guns in addition to 18 guns of the 19th Division.

7. (a) Two Sections of R.E. have been allotted to this Brigade and will be employed on the construction of strong points in J.27.a. at dusk on Zero day if the situation permits. A Liaison Officer will report to Brigade Headquarters for instructions at 2.p.m., on Zero day.
(b) The Officer Commanding, 528th (Durham) Field Coy. R.E. will detail an Officer to assist in reconnoitring the tape line (in accordance with para.4(a) above) on night 24/25th October.

8. (a) A Junior/

-3-

8. (a) A Junior R.A. Liaison Officer will be attached to 2nd Bn. Queen's Regt., and one to 1st Bn. South Staffordshire Regt. and 21st Bn. Manchester Regt.
(b) No Liaison Officers will be exchanged between neighbouring battalions, but the closest liaison will nevertheless be maintained throughout the operations.

9. (a)(1) A buried cable will run from Brigade Headquarters to Headquarters, 2nd Bn. The Gordon Highlanders (J.20.b.65.05.) where representatives of Brigade Signal Section will accept messages for transmission to Brigade Headquarters. All Units in the forward area will ensure that runners are familiar with this point.
(2) There is also a buried cable from Brigade Headquarters to CLONMEL COPSE (J.19.c.5.2.)
(b) Brigade Relay Posts will be established as under:-

H.Q., 2nd Bn. Queen's Regt.   J.20.d.2.8.   (B.W.)
BODMIN COPSE.   J.19.d.6.5.   (B.C.)
CLONMEL COPSE.   J.19.c.5.2.   (C.O.)
Brigade Headquarters.   I.30.a.7.1.   (C.S.)

(c) 3 pairs of pigeons per assaulting Battalion and 2 pairs to 91st Machine Gun Coy., will be issued under arrangements to be made by the Brigade Signal Officer. These birds should be released singly, and all messages so sent must not contain the name of any unit in clear. Empty baskets will be returned.
(d) Visual will be established by Brigade Signal Section between K.C. (Headquarters, 2nd Bn. Gordon Highlanders) and C.O. (CLONMEL COPSE), between B.W. (Headquarters, 2nd Bn. Queen's Regt.) and B.C. (Runner Post in BODMIN COPSE), and between A.C. (Headquarters, 1st Bn. South Staffordshire Regt. and 21st Bn. Manchester Regt.) and C.O. (CLONMEL COPSE).
As soon as possible after the assault, the facilities for lamp signalling in the forward area will be reconnoitred and lamps sent forward.
(e) Power buzzer sending and receiving sets will be installed at both Battle Headquarters (B.W. and A.F.) which will communicate with K.C., whence messages will be transmitted to Brigade Headquarters by telephone.
(f) Wireless will be established from B.W. to Brigade Headquarters.
(g) The Brigade Signal Section will endeavour to maintain a laddered telephone line from K.C. to B.W. and A.F.
(h) Message Rockets should be directed on K.C.
(i) Each assaulting Battalion will endeavour to maintain a telephone line forward to an advanced report centre on the forward slope of the hill. Not more than one line per Battalion will be laid out.
(k) On reaching the RED and BLUE LINES, red and green Very Lights (respectively) will be fired as a success signal to shew that objectives have been reached.
(l) Red and White flares will be lit only when called for by the contact aeroplane, which will sound a Klaxon Horn or fire a white light.
(m)(1) The S.O.S. Signal by day or night will be the Rifle Grenade Parachute Signal (Red over Green over Yellow).
(2) By day only, the Daylight Mortar Signal may be used.
(3) In the forward area, Lewis or Vickers Guns firing batches of five rounds at regular intervals will be recognised as the S.O.S. Signal should a rocket or Mortar not be available.

10. Watches of all Battalions and Machine Gun Coy., will be synchronised by 6 p.m. on "Y" Day under arrangements to be made by Brigade Signal Officer.

11. (a) Each Battalion/

-4-

11. (a) Each battalion will detail two men to collect enemy documents in sandbags for despatch to Brigade Headquarters.
(b) The first and any subsequent identifications established will be reported by the quickest means available.

12. Headquarters will be established as follows:-

    Brigade Headquarters.   CANADA STREET (I.30.a.7.1.)
    2nd Bn.Queen's Regt.   J.20.d.2.8.
    21st Bn.Manchester Regt.   J.20.d.2.8. night Oct.24/25th.
        J.20.d.7.1. from night Oct.25/26th.
    1st Bn.South Staffs.Regt.   J.26.a.2.5. night Oct.24/25th.
        J.20.d.7.1. from night Oct.25/26th.
    22nd Bn.Manchester Regt.   Brigade Headquarters.
    20th Bn.Manchester Regt.   Lock 8 (I.32.a.7.5.)
    91st Machine Gun Coy.   J.19.c.5.2.

13. Separate instructions will be issued for the relief and assembly on nights 24/25th and 25/26th October.

14. ACKNOWLEDGE.

                Captain,
                Brigade Major, 91st Infantry Brigade.

Issued at 7.a.m. to -

    Copy No 1 2nd Queen's R *
        2 1st S.Staffs.R *
        3 21st Manch.R *
        4 22nd Manch.R *
        5 91st M.G.Coy. *
        6 No.3.Secn.7th Div.Sig.Coy.
        7 Staff Captain.
        8 Bde.Bombing Officer.
        9 Bde.Transport Officer.
       10 Bde.Intelligence Officer.
       11 21st Field Ambulance.
       12 20th Manch.R *
    13-16 C.R.A.
       17 528th (Durham) Fd.Coy.R.E.
       18 Supply Officer.
       19 7th Division.
       20 20th Inf.Bde.
       21 22nd Inf.Bde.
       22 117th Inf.Bde.
       23 Left Bde.19th Div.
       24 File.
    25-26 War Diary.

    * Artillery and Machine Gun Barrage Maps attached.
      Objective Maps have already been issued to those concerned.

S E C R E T.

Copy No....

Appendix 3 to 91st Infantry Brigade Order No.27.

23rd October, 1917.

-:-:-:-:-:-:-:-:-:-

The following additions and amendments will be made to Brigade Order No.27 :-

1. Para.3.(b) is cancelled and the following substituted:-
"The barrage will be put down by guns of all calibres 150 yards in advance of our forming up line, where it will remain for 6 minutes. It will then advance by 50 yard bounds for 200 yards at the rate of 100 yards in 8 minutes, then for a further 200 yards at the rate of 100 yards in 10 minutes, thereafter at 100 yards in 14 minutes to the RED protective barrage,150 yards in advance of the RED LINE. After a halt of an hour on this line,it will resume its advance at the rate of 100 yards in 14 minutes to the BLUE protective barrage,200 yards in advance of the BLUE LINE. A secondary barrage will then search backwards and forwards periodically throughout the day."

2. Add Para.3.(d). -
At Zero hour counter-battery work will be intense, and will continue throughout the operations that day. Arrangements are also being made to deal with any mobile groups of hostile artillery brought up to cover counter-attacks or harass our consolidation.

3. Add Para.3.(e) -
On Zero plus one day an Army barrage will be put down along the whole front commencing at 5-20.a.m.

4. Para.4(a) Add:-
"Completion of Assembly will be reported to Brigade Headquarters by the Code -

"123"

ACKNOWLEDGE.

Captain,

Brigade Major, 91st Infantry Brigade.

Issued at 11/5.p.m. to all recipients of B.O.27.

SECRET.   Copy No......

Appendix 4 to 91st Infantry Brigade Order No.27.
                                25th October, 1917.

-:-:-:-:-:-:-:-:-

Reference Para.1.(a) of Brigade Order No.27., Zero hour will be 5-40.a.m., October 26th, 1917.

[signature]
Captain,
Brigade Major, 91st Infantry Brigade.

Issued at....p.m. to all recipients of B.O.27.

SECRET.

ADMINISTRATIVE INSTRUCTIONS in connection with
91st Infantry Brigade Order No. 27

1. DRESS & EQUIPMENT.

   (a)   (i)   Rifle and equipment less pack.
         (ii) 220 rounds S.A.A.
         (iii) Haversack on back containing Iron Ration
               and two days rations.
               (Note - if the two days rations will not go
                in the haversack Battalions will make their
                own arrangements to carry this additional
                day's ration on the man).
         (iv) Ground Sheet rolled with Cardigan Jacket
               inside fixed to the back of the waistbelt
               by supporting straps of pack.
         (v)   Box Respirator and P.H. Helmet.
         (vi) Two sandbags under flap of haversack.
         (vii) All water-bottles will be filled and troops
               warned to preserve water against emergency.

   (b)   Lewis Gunners (except Nos. 1 & 2), Signallers and
         Runners will carry 100 rounds S.A.A.

   (c)   Rifle Grenadiers will carry 50 rounds S.A.A. and
         8 rifle grenades (Mills No. 23 where cups available,
         No. 24 otherwise.)

   (d)   Aeroplane flares on a scale of 200 White and 200
         Red per battalion will be distributed under battalion
         arrangements.

   (e)   Smoke Candles or No. 27 Rifle Grenades will be provided
         on a scale of 50 per battalion.

   (f)   Shovels on a scale of 25 per Company will be carried.

   (g)   Moppers-up will carry 100 rounds S.A.A., 1 "P" Bomb,
         2 Mills No. 23 and 4 other Rifle Grenades (No. 23 if cups
         available).

   (h)   S.O.S. Signal Grenades at the rate of 24 per battalion
         will be carried. They will be carefully husbanded as they
         are very scarce.

   (i)   4 Daylight Mortar S.O.S. Signals will be issued to
         each of the three assaulting battalions.

   (j)   N⁶ Message Carrying Rockets will be issued to each
         battalion (except 20th Bn. Manchester Regt.)

2. RATIONS & WATER.

   (a)   Two days rations will be carried on the man in
         addition to the Iron Ration.

         700 Preserved Meat and Biscuit rations and 88 filled
         tins of water will be dumped in vicinity of Battalion H.Q.
         at J.20.d.8.1. and J.20.d.2.8. These rations will be
         consumed on Zero plus 1 day.
         The 91st M.G. Coy. will draw their rations from the
         Dump at J.20.d.2.8.

                                                    (continued)

(b)　　On 23rd October 2 days rations will be issued and on 24th Oct. 1 day's rations will be issued with the exception of 91st Machine Gun Co. who will be issued with 2 days rations on 22nd October and O.C., 91st Machine Gun Co. will arrange for one day's rations and water to be sent up on night of 26th. He will notify Brigade Headquarters of any assistance in carrying is required stating time and place that the party is required to report and the number of men necessary.

(c)　　The tea and sugar belonging to the Reserve Rations in forward dumps may be distributed to the men prior to the attack at the discretion of Commanding Officers.

(d)　　Solidified paraffin on the scale of 100 tins per battalion and 20 tins per Machine Gun Company will be issued by the Train prior to the commencement of operations. This will not be consumed prior to the attack but will be carried on the man.
　　Further supplies of solidified paraffin will be established at forward dumps.

(e)　　Rum will be issued daily for consumption on Zero - 2 day and until the Division comes out of line. The rum ration will be sent up to the troops daily under arrangements to be made by Brigade with O.C., Detail Camps.

(f)　　100 Yukon Packs will be placed in the Brigade Dump at CANADA STREET and will be available for carrying parties.

3.　S.A.A., BOMBS, R.E. MATERIAL.

　　Two forward dumps of S.A.A., Bombs, and R.E. material will be established in vicinity of Battalion Hd.Qrs. J.20.d.8.1. and J.20.d.2.8. After commencement of operations units will draw from these dumps as necessity arises advising Brigade Headquarters when the supply of any commodity requires to be replenished.

4.　TRANSPORT.

　　"A" Echelon of Brigade Pack Transport (less animals from Machine Gun Company) will assemble at 12 noon on 25th October under the command of Brigade Transport Officer at a position to be notified later.
　　The pack train will be made up of the normal 3 subsections of 6 animals from each battalion and 8 from Brigade Headquarters and will be ready to move at short notice. Pack animals will not be loaded.
　　Echelon "B" of Brigade Transport will be under regimental control and will assemble at 11 a.m. on 25th October at a place to be notified later.
　　The pack animals of 91st Machine Gun Company will be at disposal of Machine Gun Co. They will assemble under Company arrangements at a position to be notified later.
　　Brigade Transport Officer will utilize the 8 animals of "A" Echelon to bring up Bde.Hd.Qrs. rations when necessary.

5.　PRISONERS OF WAR.

(a)　　Units will report by the quickest means available the first identification established. Only fresh identifications will subsequently be reported.

(continued).

(b) Prisoners will be sent back to Brigade Headquarters at CANADA STREET under an escort not exceeding 10% of their strength. They will be handed over at CANADA STREET to M.M.P. and receipts taken. Escorts will then rejoin their units.

The fullest possible use must be made of unwounded prisoners for carrying back of our own wounded (stretcher cases).

6. **MEDICAL.**

The line of evacuation of wounded is as follows :-

Right Aid Post	- J.25.b.2.8.
Left " "	- J.20.d.9.8.
Relay Posts support	- J.19.d.6.6.
CANADA STREET	- I.30.a.4.2.
Advanced Dressing Station	- LARCH WOOD I.29.c.3.7.
Car rendezvous	- VERBRANDEN POST I.28.b.8.4.
Main Dressing Station	- VOORMEZEELE.

7. **VETERINARY.**

An advanced veterinary aid post will be established. Location will be notified later.

8. **CASUALTIES.**

All units will render estimated casualties to reach Brigade Headquarters at 4 p.m. daily. Attention is drawn to S.C/2129 (Second Army Instructions on casualties etc.) The method of reporting casualties there laid down will be carefully followed.

9. **WATER IN CAPTURED TERRITORY.**

Water in captured territory will not be consumed until it has been examined by a Medical Officer.

10. **PERSONNEL.**

Not more than 20 Officers, excluding Medical Officer and Pack Train Officer, will accompany each battalion into action. Details will be accommodated in camps location of which will be notified later.

11. **SURPLUS KITS, ETC.**

Before moving on 24th October all packs, blankets, and surplus kits will be stored under battalion arrangements in camps and a guard provided out of details.

12. A reserve of 5 Lewis Guns will be kept at Brigade Headquarters to replace battle casualties.
All indents to replace Lewis Guns and spares will be wired "Priority" to Brigade Headquarters.

Bde.Hd.Qtrs.
21st October, 1917.

Staff Captain, 91st Infantry Brigade.
Captain,

S E C R E T.

AMENDMENTS and ADDITIONS to ADMINISTRATIVE INSTRUCTIONS
in connection with 91st Infantry Brigade Order No.27.

Ref. Map - BELGIUM & Part of France, Sheet 28, 1/40,000
-:-

1. (a) Para. 4 of Administrative Instructions is cancelled.
All transport and details of units will be accommodated in BEAVER Camp N.15.a.6.0.
(Note - The road from CONFUSION CORNER (N.10.b.9.5.) to BEAVER CORNER N.15.c.2.4. is impassable for Motor Traffic. Lorries must be unloaded at these two corners and baggage etc. transported by horse transport.)

(b) Move of transport and details will be complete by a time to be notified later.

(c) Brigade Transport Officer will arrange to meet representatives of Units at BEAVER CORNER to allot accommodation.

(d) Transport of all units of Brigade,(other than that of 91st Machine Gun Co.), will be Brigaded under the Brigade Transport Officer.

x and 20"
Manchester Rgt

(e) Personnel at Detail Camps will be under the command of Lieut.Col.F.W.WOODWARD, D.S.O.,22nd Manchester Regt.

(f) Communication by telephone between Brigade Headquarters and Detail Camp is being arranged. O.C.,Details, will arrange for a signal station at Detail Camp.

2. Divisional S.A.A. and Grenade Dump is at BARDENBRUG N.5.c.1.5. As many grenades as possible will be detonated before issue. Grenades which have to be issued undetonated will be detonated under Battalion arrangements.

3. Ordnance Stores will be at ZEVECOTEN.

4. Advanced Veterinary Aid Post will be at I.20.a.3.4.

5. Para. 11 of Administrative Instructions is amended to read as follows :-
"Before moving into the line all packs, blankets, and surplus kits will be stored under unit arrangements in Detail Camp, guards being provided out of Details. To facilitate re-distribution stores should be situated as near as possible to roads."

6. WATER POINTS.

I.30.b.4.8.	Well only.
I.30.a.8.3.	-do.-
I.29.c.6.3.	-do.-
I.29.a.3.0.	-do.-
N.6.a.3.9.	Tap (not for carts).
I.31.d.3.6.	Water Carts.
N.6.a.2.2.	-do.-
N.14.a.0.5.	-do.-
N.13.a.4.4.	-do.-
N.13.a.6.6.	-do.-
M.12.d.2.3.	-do.-
M.9.a.4.1.	-do.-
H.30.d.2.0.	-do.-
H.36.c.4.4.	-do.-

(continued).

7. **SALVAGE DUMPS.**

        I.30.b.5.7. ... ... Forward.
        I.30.a.8.3. ... ... -do.-
        I.29.c.2.8. ... ... -do.-
        I.32.a.6.2. ... ... -do.-
        N.5.d.9.8. ... ... Main.

8. **R.E. DUMPS** have been established by C.R.E. as follows :-

        I.31.a.4.4. ... ... (small)
        N.5.b.9.0. ... ... (main).

9. **MEDICAL.**

    All regimental aid posts for 20th and 91st Brigades will be situated in 5 Mebus at J.20.b.55.25.

    Owing to the congestion and lack of accommodation only two Regimental Medical Officers will be sent forward to this Aid Post.

    O.C., 1st S.Staffs Regt. and 21st Manchester Regt. will detail their Medical Officer for this duty. Should it be necessary they will be relieved during October 27th under Brigade arrangements.

Bde.Hd.Qtrs.
23rd October,1917.
                                      Captain,
                          Staff Captain, 91st Infantry Brigade.

SECRET.

FURTHER AMENDMENTS AND ADDITIONS TO ADMINISTRATIVE INSTRUCTIONS
in connection with 91st Infantry Brigade Order No.27.

Ref. Map - BELGIUM & Part of France, Sheet 28, 1/40,000.
-:-:-:-:-:-:-:-:-:-:-:-:-:-:-

1. (a) Para. 1(a) of Amendments and Additions to 91st Infantry Brigade Order No.27 is cancelled.
Transport and Q.M.Stores of units only will be accommodated in BEAVER CAMP N.15.a.6.0.

   (b) Transport of each unit will take over accommodation allotted by the Brigade Transport Officer to-day.

2. (a) All Details of the Brigade (including Details of 20th Manchester Regt.) will be accommodated in a Camp situate at H.36.a.1.1.

   (b) An Advance Party from each unit will meet an officer to be detailed by Lieut.Col.F.W.WOODWARD, D.S.O. at the Office of the Area Commandant at ANZAC CAMP H.30.c.6.6. at 6 p.m. to-night. This Officer will allot the accommodation in the Camp.

   (c) Advanced parties will take with them full details of billeting strength of their unit.

3. The moves of Transport and Details to be completed by 10 p.m. to-night.

4. ACKNOWLEDGE.

Bde.Hd.Qtrs.
24th October,1917.

Captain,
Staff Captain, 91st Infantry Brigade.

SECRET.   Copy No. 19

                91st Infantry Brigade Order No.28.

                                      Monday, 22nd October, 1917.
Reference Map - BELGIUM and Part of FRANCE,
        Sheet 28. - Scale 1/40,000.

1.   The 91st Infantry Brigade will relieve the Reserve Brigade
        of 39th Division in accordance with accompanying March Table.

2.   (a) Intervals of 500 yards in rear of Battalions and 200
        yards in rear of Companies will be maintained.
        (b) All Units will halt for the last ten minutes of each
        hour.

3.   A watch will be circulated to all concerned with the
        early delivery.

4.   Brigade Headquarters will close at CARNARVON CAMP at
        10-30.a.m., and open at the same hour at FAIRY HOUSE.

5.   Transport will move with Units.

6.   Lorries will report as under and be available for single
        journey:-

                2 to each Battalion Headquarters at 9.a.m.
                1 to 91st Machine Gun Coy.   " 9.a.m.
                1 to Brigade Headquarters.   " 9.a.m.

7.   Billeting parties will be sent on two hours in advance
        to take over from outgoing Units.

8.   ACKNOWLEDGE.

                                                        Captain,

                                Brigade Major, 91st Infantry Brigade.
        Issued at....p.m. to

                Copy No 1 2nd Queen's R   11 20th Manch.R
                     2 1st S.Staffs.R   12 Supply Officer.
                     3 21st Manch.R   13 No.13.Coy.Div.Train.
                     4 22nd Manch.R   14 7th Division.
                     5 91st M.G.Coy.   15 20th Inf.Bde.
                     6 No.3.Sec. Div.Sigs.   16 22nd Inf.Bde.
                     7 Staff Captain.   17 116th Inf.Bde.
                     8 Bde.Transport Officer.   18 File.
                     9 21st Field Ambulance.   19 War Diary.
                    10.528th (Durham) Fd.Coy.   20 War Diary.

MARCH TABLE.

(to accompany Brigade Order No.28.)

Unit.	Destination.	Starting Point.	Time.	Route.	Taken over Camps from
91st Inf.Bde.H.Q.	FAIRY HOUSE H.18.d.7.5.	CANADIAN CORNER.	11-15.a.m.	BRULOOZE Cross Roads.	-
1st Bn.S.Staffs.Regt.	VOORMEZEELE.	-do-	11-25.a.m.	LA CLYTTE-KEMMEL-VIERSTRAAT Cross Roads-BRASSERIE.	Billeting parties to meet guides at CONFUSION CORNER at 11.a.m.
22nd Bn.Manch.Regt.	Camp at N.5.d.4.5.	-do-	11-45.a.m.	LA CLYTTE-KEMMEL-VIERSTRAAT Cross Roads.	1st Herts.Regt.
91st Machine Gun Coy. (less guns to line).	-do-	-do-	12-15.p.m.	-do-	-
21st Bn.Manch.Regt.	LITTLE KEMMEL Camp. N.20.c.9.5.	-do-	12-30.p.m.	BRULOOZE Cross Roads.	1/6th Cheshire Regt.
2nd Bn.Queen's Regt.	FERMOY FARM. N.13.a.2.0.	-do-	12-50.p.m.	-do-	4/5th Black Watch.

SECRET.   COPY   Copy No. 25

Appendix 2 to 91st Infantry Brigade Order No.27.

23rd October, 1917.

1. The move of the 2nd Bn. Queen's Regt., and 21st Bn. Manchester Regt., on 24th October will be carried out as under :-

   42 busses will be on the KEMMEL - LA CLYTTE Road, head of the column at N.7.d.4.5. at 1.p.m. The loading 21 of these busses are allotted to 21st Bn. Manchester Regt., and will start at 2.p.m. The remaining 21 are allotted to 2nd Bn. Queen's Regt., and will start at 2.45.p.m. On arrival at LOCK 8 teas will be served under Battalion arrangements. Battalions will not halt within 400 yards of each other, the exact sites being arranged between O.C., 21st Bn. Manchester Regt., and O.C., 2nd Bn. Queen's Regt. O.C., 21st Bn. Manchester Regt., is responsible for ascertaining when the rear of 1st Bn. South Staffordshire Regt., is clear of junction of MONMOUTH ROAD and YPRES-WYTSCHAETE ROAD (I.32.d.0.2.) and leading on 300 yards in rear. O.C., 2nd Bn. Queen's Regt., will similarly follow 21st Bn. Manchester Regt.

   O.C., 22nd Bn. Manchester Regt., will not pass Road junction I.32.d.0.2. until 2nd Bn. Queen's Regt., is clear, halting if necessary in I.31.d.

2. (a) The 20th Bn. Manchester Regt., will move from Camp at M.5.a.1.8. to LOCK 8. on October 25th, arriving at 6.p.m. Route via OUDERDOM - HALLEBAST CORNER - VIERSTRAAT - VOORMEZEELE - MONMOUTH ROAD (via track junction I.31.d.6.2.).
   (b) On arrival at LOCK 8 a billeting party for the Company to be in LARCH WOOD will be sent on to report to Staff Captain, 58th Infantry Brigade at SPOIL BANK (I.33.c.9.7.). This Company will pass track junction I.32.d.0.2. at 9.p.m.
   (c) The accommodation at LOCK 8 consists of shelters in the vicinity of I.32.a.0.0.,   . South of Light Railway from VOORMEZEELE - LOCK 8. Battalion Headquarters are in LOCK 8.
   (d) Transport and details will proceed to BEAVER CAMP, N.15.a.6.0.

3. A representative Officer and 3 other ranks from each assaulting Battalion will report to Headquarters, 528th (Durham) Field Coy. R.E. at ZILLEBEKE BUND, I.21.b.1.5. at 3-30.p.m. on October 24th and will proceed with an Officer of that Company to reconnoitre the tape line. Each Battalion will be responsible for picketting its own line on night 24/25th October and for laying its tape on night 25/26th October.

-----oOo-----

Amendments to 91st Infantry Brigade Order No.27.

The following amendments to Brigade Order No.27. will be made :-

   (a) para.4(b), line 4. For "RED LINE" read "BLUE LINE".

   (b) Para.7(a) is cancelled.

ACKNOWLEDGE.

Morshead
Captain,
Brigade Major, 91st Infantry Brigade.

Issued at 7.p.m. to -
Copies to all recipients of B.O.27.

SECRET.   Copy No......

app. 9

Appendix No.1. to 91st Infantry Brigade Order No.27.

23rd October, 1917.

-:-:-:-:-:-:-:-:-

1.   The Brigade Battle Front will be taken over from the 117th Infantry Brigade on night October 24/25th as under:-

(a) 1st Bn. South Staffordshire Regt., will relieve the Right, Centre and Support Companies of 17th Bn. K.R.R. (Headquarters J.20.d.2.8.) each with one Company. The remaining Company of 1st Bn. South Staffordshire Regt., will be in JAVA DRIVE in the vicinity of J.26.a.2.5., where Battalion Headquarters will also be established.

(b) The 21st Bn. Manchester Regt., will relieve the Left Company of 17th Bn. K.R.R. (Headquarters J.20.d.2.8.), putting three Companies in the Area forward of the BASSEVILLEBEEK. The remaining Company of 21st Bn. Manchester Regt., will relieve the southern Company of 17th Bn. Sherwood Foresters (Headquarters J.19.d.5.8.) in support in the vicinity of J.19.d.7.7.

Battalion Headquarters, 21st Bn. Manchester Regt., will be established at J.20.d.2.8.

(c) The 2nd Bn. Queen's Regt., will relieve the Right Company of 16th Bn. Sherwood Foresters (Headquarters J.20.b.6.3.) with two companies. A third Company of 2nd Bn. Queen's Regt., will dig in in the Area forward of the BASSEVILLEBEEK. The remaining Company will relieve the Northern Company of 17th Bn. Sherwood Foresters (Headquarters J.19.d.5.8.) in the vicinity of J.19.b.5.1.

Battalion Headquarters, 2nd Bn. Queen's Regt., will be established at J.20.d.2.8.

(d) Two Companies and Battalion Headquarters of 22nd Bn. The Manchester Regt., will relieve one Company and Battalion Headquarters of 16th Bn. Rifle Brigade (Headquarters, CANADA STREET, I.30.a.7.1.). These two companies will be those to be attached to 2nd Bn. Queen's Regt., and 1st Bn. South Staffordshire Regt.

& in CANADA STREET TUNNELS

The remaining two Companies of 22nd Bn. Manchester Regt., will move to LARCH COPSE taking over accommodation vacated on afternoon of 24th October by a reserve Battalion of 19th Division.

2. (a) 117th Infantry Brigade are having Platoon guides at Brigade Headquarters, HEDGE STREET (I.30.b.4.7.) from 6-30 p.m., October 24th for all companies of 2nd Bn. Queen's Regt., 1st Bn. South Staffordshire Regt., and 21st Bn. Manchester Regt. The guides for 2nd Bn. Queen's Regt., and 21st Bn. Manchester Regt., will conduct troops to Battalion Headquarters J.20.d.2.8. along Track "A". The guides for 1st Bn. South Staffordshire Regt., will conduct troops to Company Headquarters at J.20.d.7.1. along Route B

(b) The Officer Commanding, 22nd Bn. Manchester Regt., is responsible for reconnoitring in advance the accommodation to be occupied by the Battalion in LARCH WOOD and CANADA STREET. In each case outgoing troops will move out in the course of the afternoon of October 24th without waiting for relief.

3. (a) All further details of relief will be arranged between Commanding Officers concerned.

(b) By dawn on October 25th, Battalions will be occupying their Battle Fronts. Any necessary adjustments will be made between Battalion Commanders concerned after the relief of 117th Infantry Brigade is complete.

4.(a) 2nd Bn. Queen's/

-2-

4. (a) 2nd Bn. Queen's Regt., and 21st Bn. Manchester Regt., will be conveyed to LOCK 8 by bus on afternoon of October 24th under arrangements to be notified later.
(b) The route from LOCK 8 will be as follows:- MIDDLESEX ROAD to I.28.a.9.5. - I.29.a.4.9. - I.29.a.6.5. - MORLAND AVENUE - CANADA STREET - Junction of Tracks "A" and "B" J.19.d.0.0.
(c) All movement of troops forward of LOCK 8 will be by Platoons at 100 yards interval.
(d) In order to avoid delay in front care will be taken that troops march in in the order of posts to be taken over, according to a pre-arranged plan.

5. The loading Platoons of Battalions will pass the junction of MIDDLESEX AVENUE - VERBRANDENMOLEN ROAD at the undermentioned times:-

        1st Bn. South Staffordshire Regt.   6.p.m.
        21st Bn. Manchester Regt.   6-45.p.m.
        2nd Bn. Queen's Regt.   7-30.p.m.
        22nd Bn. Manchester Regt.   8-15.p.m.

6. The guns of 91st Machine Gun Coy., to be attached to Battalions during the operations will assemble with their respective Battalions on night October 24/25th under arrangements to be made by The Officer Commanding, 91st Machine Gun Coy., direct with Battalion Commanders concerned.

7. Throughout the day of October 25th troops will be warned to avoid unnecessary movement.

8. The assembly of 2 companies 22nd Bn. Manchester Regt attached to 2nd Bn. Queen's Regt., and 1st Bn. South Staffordshire Regt., on night 25/26th October will be carried out under Battalion arrangements. The remaining two companies will move into CANADA STREET tunnels by 12.midnight, night 25/26th October.

9. Completion of relief will be reported to 117th Infantry Brigade (Headquarters HEDGE STREET, I.30.b.4.7.).

10. G.O.C., 91st Infantry Brigade will assume command of the Brigade Battle Front at 7.a.m., on 25th October, at which hour Brigade Headquarters will close at FAIRY HOUSE and open at CANADA STREET (I.30.a.7.1.)

11. ACKNOWLEDGE.

                                      Captain,

                  Brigade Major, 91st Infantry Brigade.

Issued at 1.45.a.m. -
    to all recipients of Brigade Order No.27.

7th DIVISION.

B. H. Q.

91st INFANTRY BRIGADE.

NOVEMBER 1917.

WAR DIARY
or
INTELLIGENCE SUMMARY

Army Form C. 2118.

(Erase heading not required.)

Instructions regarding War Diaries and Intelligence Summaries are contained in F. S. Regs., Part II. and the Staff Manual respectively. Title Pages will be prepared in manuscript.

[Stamp: HEADQUARTERS 9th INFANTRY BRIGADE]

1st 9th Suffolk Bn NOVEMBER 1917

Place	Date	Hour	Summary of Events and Information	Remarks and references to Appendices
EBBLINGHAM	1/11/17		Dull, wet afternoon. B.G.C. and all the remaining officers in having received casualties in recent operations. 2nd received 1st S. Staffords proceeded to 21st and 22nd Br Inchon respectively for attachment. Casualties 1st S. Staffords 10 OR. (Self-inflicted) Rufles 1st S. Staffords 3 OR.	App 5
do	2/11/17		2nd 1st S. Indian 13 OR. 22nd Indian 1 Off. Bull. Drizzle all day. B.G.C. and a/B.M visited Bars Divl Commdr called at Bde H.Qrs. Casualties Wel Rufles 2nd Queens 3 OR. 9th 1st M.S. Coy 2 Off. 20 OR.	App 5
do	3/11/17		Dull. wet afternoon. B.G.C. and a/B.M. in day having in advising. Cas. Wel. Rufts 1st S. Staffords 2 OR.	App 5
do	4/11/17		Dull morn. Sunny afternoon. a/B.M. visited 22nd Indian 9 recovered green. Manyeo. Lt. E.A. Lumford a/S.C. went to 22nd Indian Bn to hat at Staff cap. att'd 7 9th 29 Bde as S+B cap to until further orders. Maj R Miles N.Z.F.A. came to Bde as S+B cap. Lt. Col Lowan M.C. Comdg 2nd S.R. Rebels Regt. went on leave. Cas. Wel. Rufts 2nd Queen 2 OR.	App 5
do	5/11/17		Fine. Sunny. B.G.C. and a /BM congrab. trains in advising Drill. Comms. settled at. Rebels K.Q. in advising. Cas. Wel. Rufts. 2nd Queen 1 Off. 4 OR. 1st S. Staffords 8 OR. 9th M.S. Coy 1 Off.	App 5

Army Form C. 2118.

WAR DIARY
or
INTELLIGENCE SUMMARY
(Erase heading not required.)

Instructions regarding War Diaries and Intelligence Summaries are contained in F. S. Regs., Part II. and the Staff Manual respectively. Title Pages will be prepared in manuscript.

Place	Date	Hour	Summary of Events and Information	Remarks and references to Appendices
EBBLINGHEM	6.11.17		Drill Elementary Platoon - allotted to all Officers and Sergeants - by Company. 1 Platoon each Coy. men supervise 1 Bryden in morning. Brigadier + A/Bde Major visits units in afternoon. Dull and cold weather.	W.C.
"	7.11.17		Rehearsal for Divisional Inspection morning and afternoon. Dull & cold weather	W.C.
"	8.11.17		Division inspected by H.M. the King of the Belgians in morning. Divisional Commander Conference in afternoon attended by Brigadier + A/Bde Major, CO's and all Company Commanders. Dull and cold weather. Rain later in afternoon	W.C. Appx 7.
"	9.11.17		Morning - unit Company Training. Afternoon Brigadier + A/Bde Major visits units. Order No 31 issued. Wet weather - cold	W.C.
"	10.11.17		Brigade moved to BLEQUIN by bus. Wet weather	W.C. Appx III
BLEQUIN	11.11.17		Commanding Officers Conference morning. Cos and Inst. B.O.32 issued	W.C. Appx III
CAMPAGNE	12.11.17		Brigade moved to CAMPAGNE and FAUQUEMBERGUES area in accordance with B.O.32 B.O.33 issued weather fine	W.C. Appx N
FRUGES	13.11.17		Brigade moved to FRUGES area in accordance with B.O. 833. weather fine. G.O.C. proceeds on leave. Lt Col Hunter Kingston. Brigade Major returned from leave B.O. 34 issued	Appx V
TANGRY	14.11.17		Brigade moved to TANGRY in accordance with Brigade order B.O. Fine	W.M Appx VI
"	15.11.17		Rept 10: S.O.P. R.E. 500.P Newcastle of Observation in TANGRY Fine Brigade Group inspected in afternoon. Casualties nil Reinforcements: Brigade Major evacuated 21st Field Ambulance Order No 5.25 Field Coy Major Oakcroft B.O. 35 issued. Casualties Nil Reinforcement 3rd Northampton. 113.	Appx VII

2449 Wt. W14957/Mgo 750,000 1/16 J.B.C. & A. Forms/C.2118/12.

Army Form C. 2118.

WAR DIARY
or
INTELLIGENCE SUMMARY

(Erase heading not required.)

Instructions regarding War Diaries and Intelligence Summaries are contained in F.S. Regs., Part II. and the Staff Manual respectively. Title Pages will be prepared in manuscript.

Place	Date	Hour	Summary of Events and Information	Remarks and references to Appendices
TANGRY	16.11.17		The Brigade Major attended Divisional Conference at H.Q. 22nd Brigade at WAMIN at 10.30 A.M. S.D.C. returned in evening from short leave in England. Brigade Signal Officer proceeded on ordinary sick D.R.A. 6. to ITALY. Casualties NIL Reinforcements NIL	NIL
TANGRY and TRAIN	17.11.17		1st C. Sept. Riff — 122. O.R. 2nd Detached Rifles 8. Off. 146 O.R. 22nd Manchester Regt. 12. Off. 287 O.R. Brigade Major briefed 22nd Manchesters on morning Conference of Commanding Officers at 2.30 P.M. at Brigade H.Q. Entrainment commenced via Intermediate Instructions entrained at ANVIN at 10.30 P.M. Staff Captain and Major Miles remained behind to supervise entrainment and follow by last train. Casualties NIL Reinforcements NIL	NIL
TRAIN	18.11.17		2nd Headquarter train passed through ETAPLES and ABVILLE during night 17/18. Train CHANTILLY (7.25 A.M.) PARIS (9.10 A.M.) VERNEUIL (1 P.M.) FLAMBOIN (3 P.M.) RONELLE (4.30 P.M.) and TROY (6.35 P.M.) Stopping at MESSAGNY for an hour (5-6 P.M.) for hot coffee. Train to ST. FLORENTIN (9.35 P.M. – 10.15 P.M.) Casualties NIL Reinforcements NIL	NIL
TRAIN	19.11.17		Train arrived DIJON (6.15 A.M.) LEANS BEAUNE (8 A.M.) CHALONS SUR SAONE (8.40 P.M.) & MACON (10.05 – 12 noon) Trains VILLEFRANCE (1 P.M.) LYONS (3 P.M.) VALANCE (6.15 P.M.) to PIERLATTE (9.45 – 10.30 P.M.) where troops got hot coffee. Casualties NIL Reinforcements NIL	NIL
"	20.11.17		Train arrived ARLES (5.45 A.M.) to 7 A.M. Train through MIRAMAS (9 A.M.) to MARSEILLES (12 noon to 2.45 P.M.) between MARSEILLES and TOULONS two very congested and progress very slow. Casualties NIL Reinforcements NIL	NIL
"	21.11.17		Train arrived TOULONS (10.35 P.M.) and to ARES (7.15 – 8.30 P.M.) Halted for hot coffee. Casualties NIL Reinforcements NIL — Nice being reached at 12 midnight	NIL
"	22.11.17		Train arrived VINTIMILLE on FRENCH ITALIAN frontier (2 A.M.) Went through ALBENGO (5 A.M.) and SAVONA (11 – 12.15 A.M.) to GENOA (2.45 P.M.) Scene of great enthusiasm through station and. Very warm reception at GENOA where B.D.C. and officers were shown round large munition factory and treated with great hospitality. Train reached VOGHARA (9.30 P.M.) Casualties NIL Reinforcements NIL	NIL
"	23.11.17		Train arrived SUZZARA (6.30 – 9.45 A.M.) and MANTOVA (10 – 11.20 A.M.) Memo to MONTAGNANA (3.30 P.M.) where attachment was carried out and completed at 8 P.M. Brigade H.Q. at ROVEREDO. Major A. Macfarlane Q.O.R. Seaforth Germany arrived and took over 2nd Division attached at MONTAGNANA a.m. Maj. Captain Corsetti NIL Reinforcements NIL	NIL
ROVEREDO	24.11.17		Much rest. 2nd Division detained at MONTAGNANA 6.3rd M. 1st Sth Staffords Reg. Battalion and other half of WAR Order (7th Division Infantry) received but incomplete. Casualties NIL of Artillery being incomplete Reinforcements NIL	NIL

Army Form C. 2118.

WAR DIARY
or
INTELLIGENCE SUMMARY
(Erase heading not required.)

Instructions regarding War Diaries and Intelligence Summaries are contained in F. S. Regs., Part II and the Staff Manual respectively. Title Pages will be prepared in manuscript.

Place	Date	Hour	Summary of Events and Information	Remarks and references to Appendices
ROVEREDO	25.11.17		Misty day. Thick. S.O.C. units 2nd Battalion Leccio in morning at POTANA. B.M. joined after completing retirement of 1st S. Staffords. 21st Field ambulance detrained at LEGNAGO. Divisional orders No. received. 1st South Staffords arrived at ROVEREDO at 12 midday. Casualties nil. Reinforcement 2nd Leccio Regt. S.O.R. 1st S. Staffords 7.O.R. Rain.	60 mf
"	26.11.17		S.O.C. units bivouaced H.2. in morning. 7th Battalion Leccio and 22nd Battalion Manchester move in accordance with Brigade Order. Authority to hire & local carts received. Transport Commandant S.S.O.1. called at Brigade H.2. in morning. Arrangements for local transport park above own lines. Casualties Nil. Reinforcement Nil.	60 mf
ACUCLIARO	27.11.17	2.30 p.m.	Fair. Brigade Group less 7th and 22nd Manchester arrived in ACUCLIARO area at 12.30 p.m. S.O.C. went to Divisional H.2. at 1 P.M. Difficulty in billeting owing to number of Italian Officers occupying billets in some of allotted villages. Italian Brigade attached to Bde. H.2. S.O.C. and B.M. busy. Bivouaced H.2. at 9 P.M. and returned at 11.15 P.M. Casualties Nil. Reinforcement 1st S. Stafford Regt. 10.O.R.	60 mf VIII
PONTE DI BARBARANO	28.11.17		This Brigade Group moved in accordance with B.O.36 and arrived in PONTE DI BARBARANO area and vicinity. 2nd and 22nd Manchester Regts. found Brigade Group billeting at MOSSANO and BARBARANO respectively. 1st S. Stafford Regt. S.O.R. Divisional Division H.2. in morning and the billets of the 1st S. Stafford Regiment and 2nd Leccio Regiment. T.2.13.M. tested each in the two formed. First day of Italian rations received. Great formal reap. coffee and rouge – no another than hay. Hard task but not first rate. The midday Menu. Casualties Nil. Reinforcements.	60 mf
PONTE DI BARBARANO CRISIGNANA	29.11.17		Fair. Brigade S.O.C. inspected 22nd Manchester Regt. on route to PONT DI NANTO in accordance with B.O. 37. In afternoon S.O.C. visited 9nd M. E. Officers 21st Manchester Regt. The B.M. visited the Leccio. Authority received to requisition local transport if arrangements cannot be made for hire. British motor transport is having difficulty owing to state of roads and inferior of lorries of Italian Army. Supply of rations received but local are any interrupted. Casualties Nil. Reinforcements. Reinforcements 2nd Leccio Regt. 2.O.R. 2nd Manchester Regt. 11.O.R.	60 mf IX
CRISIGNANA	30.11.17		Fair. Brigade Group moved to area CRISIGNANA – CAMPODORO – VILLA FRANCA in accordance with B.O. S.O.C. inspected Battalions passing on column of route. British rations again available. Casualties Nil. Reinforcements Nil.	60 mf

R.T. Pelly Brig. Gen.
Cmdg. 91st Bde.

SECRET Appx I.

Copy No. 9

91st Infantry Brigade Order No. 30.

Wednesday, 7th November, 1917.

Reference Map. — Flanders Sheet No. 28.N.6.
— Scale 1/20,000.

—:—:—:—:—:—:—:—:—:—

1. His Majesty The King of the Belgians will inspect the 7th Division (less Artillery, Two Field Companies R.E. and Pioneers) at 11-X.a.m., 8th November, 1917.

2. Units will march on to the selected parade ground in accordance with accompanying March Table, and will be formed up in mass.

3. 91st Machine Gun Company on arrival at the parade ground will come under the orders of the Divisional Machine Gun Offr.

4. Battalions will be in position by 10-45 a.m.

5. Details of the parade have already been made known.

6. A watch will be sent to Units with the early morning R.R.

7. ACKNOWLEDGE.

Captain,
A/Brigade Major, 91st Infantry Brigade.

Issued at 8.p.m. to

Copy No 1 2nd Queen's R
        2 1st S.Staffs.R
        3 21st Manch.R
        4 22nd Manch.R
        5 91st M.G.Coy.
        6 Hd.Q.Res.7th Div.Sigs.
        7 Brigade Major.
        8 File.
        9 War Diary.
       10 War Diary.

MARCH TABLE.

(Issued with 91st Infantry Brigade Order No. ...)

Unit.	Route.	Remarks.
2nd Bn. Queen's Regt.	Move independently direct to Forced Crossroads from Frensham.	To be in position by 10-0.a.m.
22nd Bn. Manchester Regt.	Via Cross Roads B.C.D.E.F.	To pass Cross Roads at 10-2.a.m.
1st Bn. South Staffs. Regt.	do.	To pass Cross Roads at 10-10.a.m. Will be clear of Cross Roads by 10-15.a.m.
21st Bn. Manchester Regt.	Via Guildford Station.	Not to pass Guildford Station before 10.a.m. To be clear of Guildford Station by 10-5.a.m.
91st Machine Gun Coy.	do.	Not to pass Guildford Station before 10-5.a.m. To be clear of Guildford Station by 10-10.a.m.

SECRET

Addendum to 91st Infantry Brigade Order No. 30.
────────────────────────────────

The Brigadier hopes that in spite of the limited time available all men will make a special effort to be as smart as possible and that special attention will be paid to polishing cap badges, buttons and the brass work of equipment.

Breech covers will not be carried.

Bde.Hd.Qtrs.
7th November, 1917.

M Cohen
Captain.
A/Brigade Major, 91st Infantry Brigade.

SECRET. Appx II

Copy No. 14

91st Infantry Brigade Order No. 31.

9th November, 1917.

Reference Map - FRANCE, Sheet 27.S.W.
- Edition 2. Scale 1/20,000.

1. The 91st Infantry Brigade will move to the BLEQUIN Area by Bus on 10th November, 1917.

2. Busses will be on the EBBLINGHEM - RENESCURE Road - head of column T.23.a.0.3. - at 7.a.m.

3. Units will march to the positions allotted to them in the column in accordance with attached march table.
   Each Unit will send an Officer and 2 Other Ranks to report to the Brigade Major at T.23.a.0.3. at 6-15.a.m.

4. Troops will be told off in groups of 25 or 20 (20 for seated lorries - 25 for busses) and will be distributed along the road from T.23.a.0.3. eastwards. Six groups will be told off to each 80 yards.

5. Transports of Units will move independently by Road and complete the journey to the new area in one day. They must be clear of the embussing point T.23.a.0.3. by 6-15.a.m., or will follow in rear of the Bus column.

6. Baggage wagons will march with the Train Company. They will report to Units by 6.p.m., 9th November, and will return to No.3. Company, Divisional Train loaded by 7.a.m., 10th November.

7. Rations for 10th November will be carried on the man.
   Rations for 11th November will be issued on arrival in the new area. Refilling Point will be notified later.

8. In addition to the Busses for personnel, lorries for baggage will be available for the move as under :-

   Two to each Battalion.   6.a.m.
   One to Machine Gun Coy.   6.a.m.
   One for Brigade H.Q.   5-30.a.m.

   One guide from each Unit will be at Brigade Headquarters at 5-30.a.m., to guide lorries to their Headquarters.
   No baggage will on any account be carried on the busses for personnel.
   Baggage lorries will follow in rear of the Bus Column.

9. One blanket will be carried on the man.

10. Destination of Units and number of busses available for each will be notified later.

11. No.3. Company, Divisional Train will move by Road in rear of the Bus Column.

12. A certificate that Area Stores, billets and tents are left intact and clean on vacation will be rendered to this office by all Units by 6.p.m., 10th November.
    Receipts will be taken for any tents handed over.

13. Brigade Headquarters/

-2-

3. Brigade Headquarters will close at EBBLINGHEM at 6.a.m., and will open at BLEQUIN at the same hour.

4. ACKNOWLEDGE.

                                                                  Captain,

            A/Brigade Major, 91st Infantry Brigade.

Issued at 1.p.m. to -

        Copy No 1 2nd Queen's R
               2 1st S.Staffs.R
               3 21st Manch.R
               4 22nd Manch.R
               5 91st M.G.Coy.
               6 No.3.Coy.Div.Sigs.
               7 Brigade Transport Officer.
               8 21st Field Ambulance.
               9 528th (Durham) Fd.Coy.R.E.
             10 Supply Officer.
             11 No.3.Coy.Div.Train.
             12 7th Division.
             13 File.
             14 War Diary.
             15 War Diary.

MARCH TABLE.
(Issued with 91st Infantry Brigade Order No.31.)

Unit.	Position in Bus Column.	Route.	To be in position by-	Remarks.
91st Machine Gun Coy.	1*	Via Cross Roads T.22.b.9.3.	6-30.a.m.	—
21st Bn.Manch.Regt.	2		6-30.a.m.	—
1st Bn.S.Staffs.Regt.	3	Via EBBLINGHEM Station.	6-35.a.m.	To pass Station at 6-25.a.m.
22nd Bn.Manch.Regt.	4	-do-	6-40.a.m.	" " " 6-30.a.m.
2nd Bn.Queen's Regt.	5	-do-	6-45.a.m.	" " " 6-40.a.m.
91st Inf.Bde.H.Q.	6	-do-	6-50.a.m.	" " " 6-45.a.m.

* Numbers represent position in Bus Column from West to East.

NOTE:- On arrival in position in the Column troops will be drawn up as far as possible off the Roadway on the right hand side. Embussing will be superintended by Brigade Major who will inform each Unit when to commence.

S E C R E T.

Copy No. 14

AMENDMENTS AND ADDITIONS
to
91st Infantry Brigade Order No.31.

9th November, 1917.

1. March Table issued with 91st Infantry Brigade Order No.31. is cancelled and the attached substituted.

2. The Column will be composed of 50 Busses and 60 Lorries - All Busses in front. These are allotted as follows:-

    CONVOY 1.

    91st Machine Gun Coy.   6 Busses. - 7 men in 7th Bus.
    22nd Bn.Manchester Regt. {28   "   including 7th Bus.
                              {10 men in 35th Bus.
    1st Bn.S.Staffs.Regt.   {16 Busses including 35th Bus.
                              { 7 Lorries.

    CONVOY 2.

    21st Bn.Manchester Regt. 26 Lorries.
    2nd Bn.Queen's Regt.   23 Lorries.
    91st Inf.Bde.Headqtrs.   4 Lorries.

    Convoy 1 will debus at SENLECQUES.
       "   2   "   "   " BERGNEUILLE.

3. Units will be billetted in the New Area as follows:-

    Brigade Headquarters. BLEQUIN.) Guides to be at
    2nd Bn.Queen's Regt.   "   ) Church BLEQUIN.

    1st Bn.S.Staffs.Regt. BECOURT. Guides at Church
                                   BECOURT.
    21st Bn.Manch.Regt. SENLECQUES. Guides at debussing
                                    Point of Convoy 2.
    22nd Bn.Manch.Regt. ZOTEUX.   Guides at Cross Roads
                                   FAUCHELLES.
    91st Machine Gun Coy. MIEURLES. Guides at Cross Roads
                                    MIEURLES.
    No.3.Company,Div.Train. RIPPEMONT,with Refilling
                                      Point BLEQUIN.

4. ACKNOWLEDGE.

                                              Captain,
                        A/Brigade Major,91st Infantry Brigade.

Issued at 7/45 p.m. to all recipients of B.O.31.

MARCH TABLE.

(Issued with Amendments & Additions to 91st Inf.Bde.Order No.31.)

Unit.	Position in Bus Column.	Route.	To be in position by :-	Remarks.
91st Machine Gun Coy.	ẋ 1	Via Cross Roads T.22.b.9.3.	6-30.a.m.	-
22nd Bn.Manch.Regt.	2	Via EBBLINGHEM STATION.	6-35.a.m.	To pass Station at 6-30.a.m.
1st Bn.S.Staffs.Regt.	3	-do-	6-35.a.m.	" " " 6-25.a.m.
21st Bn.Manch.Regt.	4	-	6-25.a.m.	-
2nd Bn.Queen's Regt.	5	Via EBBLINGHEM STATION.	6-45.a.m.	To pass Station at 6-40.a.m.
91st Inf.Bde.H.Q.	6	-do-	6-50.a.m.	" " " 6-45.a.m.

ẋ Numbers represent position in Bus Column from West to East.

NOTE:- On arrival in position in the Column, troops will be drawn up as far as possible off the Roadway on the Right hand side. Embussing will be superintended by Brigade Major who will inform each Unit when to commence.

SECRET.   appx III   Copy No. 15

91st Infantry Brigade Order No.32.

11th November, 1917.

Reference Map – CALAIS, Sheet 13 – HAZEBROUCK 5A
Scale 1/100,000.

1. The 91st Infantry Brigade Group will move to the CAMPAGNE and FAUQUEMBERGUES Areas on 12th November, 1917, in accordance with attached March Table.

2. (a) Spaces as laid down in Brigade Routine Order No.274, para. 3, dated 17th September, 1917, will be maintained throughout the march.
(b) All Units will halt for the last 10 minutes of each hour.

3. Billeting parties will proceed in advance to reach destination not later than 6.a.m. They will take over billets from present occupiers.

4. Baggage wagons will march with Units and remain attached to them until further orders.

5. Number of lorries available for Battalions, Machine Gun Coy., and 21st Field Ambulance will be notified later.
Guides from these Units will report at Brigade Headquarters at 7.a.m., to conduct lorries to the Headquarters of their Unit.

6. Refilling Point on 12th November will be LE MESNIL.

7. A certificate that Area Stores, Billets and Tents are left intact and clean on vacation will be rendered by all units by 7.p.m., 12th November.

8. Brigade Headquarters will close at BLEQUIN at 12.noon., and open at CAMPAGNE at the same hour.

9. ACKNOWLEDGE.

Captain,
A/Brigade Major, 91st Infantry Brigade.

Issued at 7.p.m. to –

Copy No 1 2nd Queen's R   9. 21st Field Ambulance.
         2 1st S.Staffs.R   10. 528th (Durham) Fd.Coy.
         3 21st Manch.R   11. Supply Officer.
         4 22nd Manch.R   12. No.3.Coy.Div.Train.
         5 91st M.G.Coy.   13. 7th Division.
         6 No.3.Coy.Div.Sigs.   14. File.
         7 Staff Captain.   15. War Diary.
         8 Bde.Transport Officer. 16. War Diary.

MARCH TABLE.

(Issued with 91st Infantry Brigade Order No.32.)

Unit.	Destination.	Starting Point.	Time.	Route.	Take over billets of -	Remarks.
2nd Queen's Regt.	THIEMBRONNE.	Cross Roads ½ mile N of M in LEDINGHAM.	10-0 a.m.	LEDINGHAM - ECUIRE.	24th Manch. Regt. (Pioneers).	
1st S.Staffs.Regt.	WISMES and DROINVILLE.	Cross Roads immediately S.W. of 1st S in SENLECQUES.	8-30 a.m.	Via SENLECQUES.	1st R. Welsh Fhslrs.	
21st Manch.Regt.	LEDINGHEM.	Cross Roads S. of 1st N of NEUF MANOIR.	10-0 a.m.	Via NEUF MANOIR.	2/1st H.A.C.	
22nd Manch. Regt.	CAMPAGNE.	Road junction S. of T in LES MORTIERS.	11-0 a.m.	Via BOURTHES.	2nd R. Warwick. Regt.	
91st M.G.Coy.	LE FAY.	Road junction ½ mile S. of M in MEURLES.	11-0 a.m.	Via CAMPAGNE.	22nd M.G.Coy.	
21st Field Amblce.	ECUIRE.	Cross Roads S.E. of 2nd S in SENLECQUES.	9-55.a.m.	-	Field Amb.et present in Billets.	Not to be on main DESVRES-OUVE-WIRQUIN Road until 1st S. Staffs.I. has passed.
No.3.Coy.Div. Train.	LE MESNIL.	Cross Roads ½ mile N of M in LEDINGHAM.	10-10.a.m.	Via LEDINGHAM.	No.2.Coy. Div.Train.	
528th (Durham) Fd.Coy.R.E.	HAPPE.	Cross Roads at M in BEAUMONT.	11-30.a.m.	Via CAMPAGNE.	54th Field Coy.R.E.	
91st Inf.Bde.H.Q.	CAMPAGNE.	Cross Roads N of M in LEDINGHAM.	1-0 p.m.	Via LEDINGHAM.	-	-

SECRET.   Appx IV   Copy No. 15

91st Infantry Brigade Order No. 33.

12th November, 1917.

Reference Maps - CALAIS, Sheet 13 &
                 HAZEBROUCK, Sheet 5a. - Scale 1/100,000.

1. The 91st Infantry Brigade Group will move to the FRUGES Area on 13th November, 1917, in accordance with the attached March Table.

2. (a) Spaces as laid down in Brigade Routine Order No. 274, para. 3, dated 17th September, 1917, will be maintained throughout the march.
   (b) All Units will halt for the last ten minutes of each hour.

3. Billeting parties will proceed in advance to reach destination not later than 5.a.m. They will take over billets from present occupiers, except in the case of 528th (Durham) Field Coy. R.E., whose Area will be vacant.

4. Baggage wagons will march with Units and remain attached to them until further orders.

5. Number of lorries available for Units will be notified later. Guides from all Units will report at Brigade Headquarters at 6.a.m., to conduct lorries to their respective Headquarters.

6. Refilling Point on 13th November, will be FRUGES.

7. A certificate that Area Stores, Billets and Tents are left intact and clean on vacation will be rendered by all Units by 7.p.m., 13th November.

8. Brigade Headquarters will close at CAMPAGNE at 8-30.a.m., and open at FRUGES.

9. ACKNOWLEDGE

                                                    Captain,
                                    A/Brigade Major, 91st Infantry Brigade.

Issued at. 10.p.m. to

Copy No 1 2nd Queen's R   9 21st Field Ambulance.
       2 1st S. Staffs R   10 528th (Durham) Fd. Coy.
       3 21st Manch. R   11 Supply Officer.
       4 22nd Manch. R   12 No. 3. Coy. Div. Train.
       5 91st M.G. Coy.   13 7th Division.
       6 No. 3. Sec. Div. Sigs.   14 File.
       7 Staff Captain.   15 War Diary.
       8 Bde. Transport Officer. 16 War Diary.

MARCH TABLE.

(Issued with 91st Infantry Brigade Order No. 3.)

Unit.	Destination.	Starting Point.	Time.	Route.	Take over billets of
2nd Queen's Regt.	FRUGES.	Road junction N of Z in WILLAMETZ.	9-0 a.m.	Via FAUQUEMBERGUES and MONTEVILLE.	1st R.Welsh Fus.
1st S.Staffs.Regt.	VERCHOCQ.	Cross Roads, DROIEVILLE.	8-30.a.m.	Via THIEMBRONNE and RUMILLY.	2nd R.Warwick.Regt.
21st Manch.Regt.	RIMEUX & ASSONVAL. ✻	Cross Roads N of M in BEAUMONT.	7-30.a.m.	CAMPAGNE-ERGNY-RUMILLY and VERCHOCQ.	2/1st H.A.C.
22nd Manch.Regt.	COUPELLE -VIEILLE.	Cross Roads ¼ mile S.E. of Church in CAMPAGNE.	8-0 a.m.	ERGNY - RUMILLY - VERCHOCQ.	20th Manch.Regt.
91st M.G.Coy.	COUPELLE-NEUVE	Road junction S. of I in THIEMBRONNE.	9-0 a.m.	FAUQUEMBERGUES - FRUGES.	22nd M.G.Coy. & 22nd T.M.Bty.
21st Field Amb.	FRUGES.	Road junction ½ mile S.E.of 2nd E in EQUIRE.	9-0 a.m.	THIEMBRONNE - FAUQUEMBERGUES.	22nd Field Amb.
No.3.Coy.Div.Train.	FRUGES.	Road junction ½mile E. of 2nd L in LE MESNIL.	6-30.a.m.	DROINVILLE-CLOQUANT-HERVAREC CHAU. - FAUQUEMBERGUES.	No.4.Coy.Div.Train.
528th (Durham) Wd. Coy.R.E. ⊙	VANDONNE.	Cross Road HAPPE.	8-0 a.m.	THIEMBRONNE- FAUQUEMBERGUES- AUDINCTHUN.	Billets vacant.
91st Inf.Bde. H.Q.	FRUGES.	Cross Roads S of E in LES BOULONNAIS.	9-30.a.m.	FAUQUEMBERGUES.	22nd Inf.Bde.H.Q.

✻ GOURNAY also available if required.   ⊙ Will pick up transport at FAUQUEMBERGUES en route.

SECRET.   Copy No.... 16

91st Infantry Brigade Order No.34.

                                              13th November, 1917.

Reference Maps – CALAIS, Sheet 13.)
                HAZEBROUCK, Sheet 5a.) – Scale 1/100,000.
                LENS, Sheet 11.   )
                -:-:-:-:-:-:-:-:-:-

1.   The 91st Infantry Brigade Group will move to the 1st ARMY Area No.1. on 14th November, 1917, in accordance with the attached March Table.

2.   (a) The usual spaces will be maintained on the march.
     (b) All Units will halt for the last ten minutes of each hour.

3.   Billeting parties will proceed direct to destinations under Unit orders, to arrive not later than 9.a.m.

4.   Baggage wagons will march with Units and remain attached to them until further orders.

5.   Lorries will be available for the move. Each Battalion, 91st Machine Gun Coy., and 21st Field Ambulance will send guides to Brigade Headquarters at 5-30.a.m., to guide lorries to their Headquarters.

6.   Refilling Point on 14th November, will be at BOYAVAL.

7.   A certificate that Area Stores, Billets and Tents are left intact and clean on vacation will be rendered by all Units by 10.p.m., 14th November.

8.   The 12th Mobile Veterinary Section will join the 91st Infantry Brigade Group on the 14th November, and will be billetted in BOYAVAL.

9.   Brigade Headquarters will close at FRUGES at 5.a.m., and will open at TANGRY on arrival.

10.   ACKNOWLEDGE.

                                                    Captain,
                                     A/Brigade Major, 91st Infantry Brigade.

Issued at 7/30.p.m. to

    Copy No.1 2nd Queen's R   9 21st Field Ambulance.
         2 1st S.Staffs.R   10 528th (Durham) Fd.Coy.
         3 21st Manch.R   11 Supply Officer.
         4 22nd Manch.R   12 No.3.Coy.Div.Train.
         5 91st M.G.Coy.   13 No.12.Mobile Vet.Section.
         6 No.3.Sec.Div.Sigs.   14   7th Division.
         7 Staff Captain.   15 File.
         8 Bde.Transport Off.   16 &17 War Diary.

MARCH TABLE.

(Issued with 91st Infantry Brigade Order No.34.)

Unit.	Destination.	Starting Point.	Time.	Route.	Remarks.
91st Inf.Bde.H.Q.	TANGRY.	Road junction ¼ mile W of 1st P in PETIT St.POL.	7-0 a.m.	CREPY - PETIT ANVIN - EPS - SAINS LES PERNES.	
2nd Queen's Regt.	HUCLIER and CONTEVILLE.	-do-	7-5.a.m.	CREPY -ANVIN-MONCHY CAYEUX-Cross Roads S.of 2nd T in SAUTRECOURT.	
21st Field Ambulance.	BOYAVAL.	-do-	7-15.a.m.	CREPY-Cross Roads S of 1st U in BERGUENEUSE-HEUCHIN.	
No.3. Coy.Div.Train.	BOYAVAL.	-do-	7-20.a.m.	-do-	
91st Machine Gun Coy.	SAINS LEZ PERNES.	-do-	7-25.a.m.	-do-	
22nd Manch.Regt.	FLEFS	Church FAUGES.	7-30.a.m.	VERCHIN-LISBOURG-PREDEFIN - FONTAINE-lez-BEULAHS.	Not to pass Road junction ½ mile S of FRUGES till 91st M.G.Coy.is clear.
21st Manch.Regt.	EPS and HESTRUS.	Road junction ¼ mile W of 1st P in PETIT St.POL.	8-10.a.m.	COUPELLE-VIELLE - FRUGES - CREPY - PETIT ANVIN.	
1st S.Staffs.Regt.	HEUCHIN.	-do-	8-20.a.m.	COUPELLE-VIELLE - FRUGES - CREPY - Cross Roads S of 1st U in BERGUENEUSE.	
528th (Durham) Fd. Coy.R.E.	SAINS LEZ PERNES.	Road junction VANDONNE.	7-35.a.m.	MATRINGHEM-BEAUMETZ-lez-AIRE - LAIRES - FLEFS.	

SECRET.

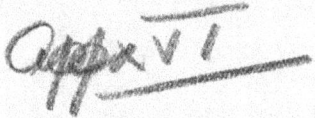

NARRATIVE OF OPERATIONS OF 91ST INFANTRY BRIGADE.
----oOo----

26th October, 1917.

Reference Map - GHELUVELT, 28 N.E.3. Edn.7a. Scale 1/10,000.
BELGIUM & FRANCE, Sheet 28.   "   1/40,000.

1. **OUTLINE OF EVENTS.**

   On Tuesday October 23rd, 1917, the Brigade arrived in the VIERSTRAAT Area after ten days rest in the NIEUSHOUCK area. Reconnaissances of the battle area were carried out by the Brigade and Battalion Staffs and Company Commanders daily from October 17th inclusive. On the night October 24/25th the Brigade Battle front on the TOWER HAMLETS RIDGE was taken over from 117th Infantry Brigade, 39th Division, by the three attacking Battalions, the command of the Sector being assumed at 8.a.m., October 25th. On the following night the tape line was laid and battle positions were assumed. The attack took place at dawn on October 26th, and the Brigade was relieved the same night by 22nd Infantry Brigade, the Command passing at 8-30.a.m., October 27th. The Brigade was subsequently withdrawn by rail and bus to the EBBLINGHEM area by October 29th.

2. **GENERAL PLAN.**

   (a) Simultaneously with a larger attack opposite PASSCHENDAEL, the 7th Division was to capture GHELUVELT and complete the capture of TOWER HAMLETS RIDGE, the 5th Division on the left being ordered to capture POLDERHOEK CHATEAU and WOOD. The 19th Division on the right were not operating.
   (b) The Divisional attack was to be carried out by two Brigades, the 91st Infantry Brigade on the right and the 20th Infantry Brigade on the left, with objectives as under:-

   (1) RED LINE:- A line from the BANK at J.26.d.7.9., South of HAMP FARM and BERRY COTTS to Strong Point at J.27.b.0.5. (inclusive) thence to GHELUVELT CHURCH and the East edge of POLDERHOEK WOOD.
   (2) BLUE LINE:- A line from J.27.b.05.55. - Strong Point at J.27.b.central - Road junction J.28.b.15.60. - MENIN ROAD at J.22.d.45.10. - the SCHERRIABEEK at J.22.a.45.60.

3. **BRIGADE SCHEME.**

   (a) The Northern Boundary of the Brigade ran from J.21.c.5.8. - J.28.b.0.6., and the attack was to pivot on the bank at J.26.b.85.10., which was said to be in our possession. This frontage was subdivided into 3 Battalion Sectors by a line from J.21.c.1.5. - J.27.b.8.5., and a line from J.20.d.75.35. - J.27.a.6.5.

   The 2nd Bn. Queen's Regt. (with one Company, 22nd Bn. Manchester Regt., attached) was to attack on the left, the 21st Bn. Manchester Regt., in the centre, and the 1st Bn. South Staffordshire Regt. (with one Company, 22nd Bn. Manchester Regt. attached) on the right. Two Vickers Guns and two Stokes Mortars each were attached to 2nd Bn. Queen's Regt., and to 21st Bn. Manchester Regt., and four Vickers Guns and four Stokes Mortars to 1st Bn. South Staffordshire Regt. The 22nd Bn. Manchester Regt., less two companies was in Brigade Reserve in CANADA STREET TUNNELS. In addition to this, the 20th Bn. Manchester Regt., was placed at the disposal of this Brigade and was established at LOCK 8 with one Company in LARCH WOOD.

(b) By Zero/

(b) By Zero minus one hour the attacking Battalions were to be formed up on a tape line from J.26.b.45.00. - J.26.b.60.25. - J.20.d.85.10. - J.21.c.8.7., whence the line was to be continued by the 20th Infantry Brigade. This line was reconnoitred by representatives of all assaulting Battalions with the assistance of an Officer of the 528th (Durham) Field Coy.R.E., at dusk on October 24th and laid on the following evening under Battalion arrangements. Each Battalion was closed up to a depth of 120 yards from front to rear.

(c) At Zero hour the Artillery barrage was to be put down on a line 150 yards in advance of the tape line. After a pause of six minutes it was to advance by 50 yard lifts at the rate of 100 yards in 8 minutes, decreasing to 100 yards in 14 minutes after the first 400 yards until reaching a line 150 yards in advance of the RED LINE where it was to remain for an hour, subsequently continuing its advance at the same rate to the BLUE protective barrage 200 yards in advance of the final objective. At Zero the Infantry were to advance to as close as possible to the barrage, and carry out the attack in conformity with the above programme. The companies detailed for the assault of the BLUE LINE were to advance in rear of the front line troops, halt and re-organise on a line 200 yards in advance of TOWER TRENCH, and resume the advance after a 15 minutes pause, passing through the first objective to a position close under the protective barrage and await the lifting of the barrage.

(d) The consolidation of the position was to be carried out in depth, the best permanent line of defence being selected irrespective of its position with regard to the objectives allotted.

(e) Brigade Headquarters were to be at CANADA STREET (I.30.a.7.1.) those of 2nd Bn.Queen's Regt., at J.20.d.2.8., and of 21st Bn.Manchester Regt., and 1st Bn.South Staffordshire Regt. at J.20.d.7.1. The Headquarters of 91st Machine Gun Coy., was to be at CABLE HEAD (J.19.c.5.2.) which was also the Brigade Observation Post.

4. NARRATIVE.

The main portion of the assembly (i.e. the relief on night 24/25th October) passed off without incident and with very few casualties. Hostile artillery was active throughout the 25th, four company commanders becoming casualties before the commencement of operations.

The withdrawal on to the tape line was carried out with great skill by Battalion Commanders, in spite of the proximity and vigilance of the enemy and the bright moonlight during the earlier part of the night. As was anticipated, the enemy shelling was directed throughout the night on the rear communications and the DUMBARTON LAKES Area, the forward area being comparatively quiet. Shortly before Zero hour the weather became overcast and cloudy and rain fell throughout the forming up period.

At 5-40.a.m., the attack was launched. On the right, heavy machine gun fire was immediately opened and a medium barrage came down along the whole ridge almost at once. The Right Company of the 1st Bn.South Staffordshire Regt., being to some extent protected by the lie of the ground was able to carry out a determined attack on the Bank at J.26.b.9.0., a prominent feature of considerable tactical importance which had been erroneously reported as being in our possession. This proved to be strongly held by the enemy, and heavy fighting ensued. After a prolonged and desperate struggle during which both Officers and all the Senior N.C.Os were killed, the position was carried, and the enemy retired, leaving many dead

and a heavy/

and a heavy machine gun behind. The position was consolidated, but no information to this effect reached Battalion Headquarters owing to heavy casualties in runners. During the afternoon our artillery persistently shelled the position, and owing to their isolation the remnants of the garrison were compelled to fall back at dusk, after destroying the captured machine gun. On the left, the attack appears to have proceeded steadily for some 200 yards, when very heavy cross fire was opened at close quarters from machine guns in LEWIS HOUSE, BERRY COTTS and HAMP FARM, causing heavy casualties. Several organised attempts were made to outflank these obstructions by pressing on, in the course of which almost all the Officers and senior N.C.Os became casualties. At about this time a large body of men of the Brigade on the left, having lost direction, crossed the front of this Brigade in a disorganised state, introducing considerable confusion and a retrograde tendency into the operations. Elements of 2nd Bn. Gordon Highlanders and 2nd Bn. Border Regt., were subsequently found to be inextricably mixed with Units of this Brigade South of STOUT WOOD. The line was however eventually reorganised and gaps filled, a third company of the 22nd Bn. Manchester Regt., and a further two Vickers Guns being sent forward to 2nd Bn. Queen's Regt., at 8.a.m., to assist in this task.

By dusk on the 26th all troops were back on their original line of posts.

5. CAUSES OF FAILURE.

In my opinion the failure of the operations is directly attributable to three causes in equal degree.
   (a) The state of the ground which, in spite of the fair wind of October 25th, was very soft. In this connection the rain immediately before Zero hour was most unfortunate. In consequence of this a very large percentage of rifles and Lewis Guns were rendered useless early in the operations.
      (It is worthy of note that the enemy made extensive use of bombs throughout the operations, in addition to machine guns and snipers).
   (b) The artillery barrage, a separate report on which has already been forwarded.
   (c) The loss of direction of the troops on the left, which quickly infected all troops in the vicinity at a time when LEWIS HOUSES, the key to the position, might have been outflanked by troops pressing on.

6. COMMUNICATION.

This proved exceptionally difficult in the forward area owing to exceedingly heavy sniping and machine gun fire throughout the hours of daylight. Once over the crest of the ridge, as all troops who had effected any advance found themselves, any movement by day proved impossible.

Communications in rear of Battalion Headquarters were of very much the same nature as in the operations on October 4th. The pigeon service proved slow.

7. CASUALTIES/

CASUALTIES.

The casualties were as follows :-

Unit.	Officers.			Other Ranks.		
	Killed.	Wounded.	Missing.	Killed.	Wounded.	Missing.
2nd Queen's	—	0	2	22	76	192
1st S. Staffs.	6	1	1	38	119	111
21st Manch.	6	5	2	29	118	155
22nd Manch.	2	1	—	7	31	11
91st M.G.Coy.	2	—	1	5	13	6
91st T.M.Bty.	1	1	—	1	—	1
TOTAL.	17	16	6	102	357	476

Bdc.Hd.Qtrs. R.T. Pelly   Brigadier General,

14th Nov.1917. Commanding, 91st Infantry Brigade.

SECRET.

Appx VII

Copy No. 19

91st Infantry Brigade Order No. 35.

15th November, 1917.

-:-:-:-:-:-:-:-:-:-

1. The Brigade Group will move by train in accordance with Administrative Instructions already issued.

2. Times and dates of trains will be notified later.

3. (a) Orders for the entrainment of 12th Mobile Veterinary Section are being issued by 20th Infantry Brigade.
   (b) The detachment of 24th (Pioneer) Bn. The Manchester Regt., proceeding by train No. 7., will conform to the Instructions issued herewith.

4. Brigade Headquarters will close at TANGRY five hours before the departure of the first train. Subsequent communications from Units remaining in this area will be addressed to the Staff Captain at ANVIN STATION.

5. ACKNOWLEDGE.

Moorshead
Captain,
Brigade Major, 91st Infantry Brigade.

Issued at 3.30 p.m. to

Copy No 1 2nd Queen's R
2 1st S. Staffs. R
3 21st Manch. R
4 22nd Manch. R
5 91st M.G. Coy.
6 No. 3. Sec. 7th Div. Sig. Coy.
7 Staff Captain.
8 Bde. Transport Officer,
9 21st Field Ambulance.
10 528th (Durham) Fd. Coy. R.E.
11 Supply Officer.
12 No. 3. Coy. Div. Train.
13 12th Mobile Vet. Section.
14 24th Bn. Manch. R
15 7th Division.
16 20th Inf. Bde.
17 File.
18 War Diary.
19 War Diary.

3.0/1002/17.

Instructions for Entraining of 91st Infantry Brigade commencing 17th November, 1917.

1. The entraining will be carried out in accordance with Instructions issued by 7th Division which have already been issued to units.

2. Battalion H.Q., with M.O., Quartermaster and Transport Officer will proceed with the first train allotted to them, the Second-in-Command and Transport Sergeant in the second train.

3. Major R. MILES, R.F.A., will proceed to ANVIN Station by 9 a.m. 16th November, 1917, and will perform the duties of acting R.T.O. until entrainment is complete. He will report to the R.T.O. (if any) from whom he will receive his instructions.

4. O.C., 22nd Bn. Manchester Regt. will detail
   (a) an entraining party of 2 officers and 100 O.R. to report to Major MILES at 9 a.m. on November 16th at ANVIN Station.
   (b) A C.Q.M.S. and guard of 1 N.C.O. and 3 men and an unloading party of 20 O.R. as required by para. 36 of Divisional Administrative Instructions.

   Arrangements are being made to billet these parties in the vicinity of the station. They will proceed by the last train, and will be rationed under Battalion arrangements up to the day following their entrainment (inclusive).

   Party (a) will also perform the duties laid down in para. 34(3) of Divisional Administrative Instructions.

5. Eight days rations and forage to be taken in the trains are being dumped at ANVIN Station. Four hours before each train is due to depart, the Quartermaster (or his representative in the case of the second train of any unit) will hand an A.B.55 for 8 days train rations and forage to the Supply Officer, and will proceed to transfer the rations to the train with a carrying party to be detailed under unit arrangements.

6. (a) On arrival of the 1st train at its destination the personnel of 91st Machine Gun Company will be at the disposal of the Brigade Transport Officer for unloading duties.

   (b) The unloading of all subsequent trains will be carried out by a party of 2 Officers and 100 O.R. to be previously detailed by O.C., 2nd Bn. The Queen's Regt. This party will report to the Brigade Major on the arrival of the 2nd train at the detraining station, and will be billetted in the vicinity of the station until the completion of the detrainment. O.C., 2nd Bn. The Queen's Regt. will arrange that this party has a days rations in hand (in addition to the Iron Ration) on detraining.

7. Where units are divided between two trains and vehicles and animals are similarly divided the division of vehicles will be arranged so that the number of axles in each half will be the same.

8. O.C., 91st Machine Gun Company will provide the sanitary squad, with the necessary appliances, referred to in para. 6 of Divisional Medical Arrangements, for Train No.1. O.C., 21st Field Ambulance will provide that for Train No.6.

Bde. Hd. Qtrs.
15th November, 1917.

Captain,
Staff Captain, 91st Infantry Brigade.

S.G/3002/A.

Instructions for Entraining of 91st Infantry Brigade
on 16th November,1917.
:-:-:-:-:-:-:-:-:-:

1. The operation will be carried out in accordance with Instructions issued by 7th Division, which have been issued to units.

2. Battalion Commanders, Quartermasters and Transport Officer will proceed with the advance parties of Units to them, the Second-in-Command and Transport Sergeant with the train.

3. Major A.D.McNaughton will proceed to ARVEN Station by 8 a.m. 16th November, where he will take up the duties of acting R.S.O. until instructions to cease do so are received from the R.T.O. (if any) from whom he will receive his instructions.

4. O.C. 22nd Manchester Regt. will detail
   (a) an entraining party of 2 officers and 100 O.R. to report to Major HELME at 9 a.m. on November 16th at ARVEN Station.
   (b) a C.S.M. and guard of 1 N.C.O. and 3 men and an embarking party of 80 O.R. as required by para. 35 of Divisional Administrative Instructions.

5. Arrangements are being made to billet these parties in the vicinity of the station. They will proceed by the last train, and will be rationed under Battalion arrangements up to the day following their entrainment (inclusive).

   Major (a) also perform the duties laid down in para.36(d) of Divisional Administrative Instructions.

6. Eight days rations and forage to be taken in the trains are being dumped at ARVEN Station. Four hours before each train is due to depart, the Quartermaster (or his representative in the case of the second train if any will) will hand at ARVEN 8 days train rations and forage to the Supply Officer, and will proceed to transfer the rations to the train with a carrying party to be detailed under unit arrangements.

7. (a) On arrival of the 1st train at its destination the personnel of 91st Machine Gun Company will be at the disposal of the Brigade Transport Officer for unloading duties.

   (b) The unloading of all subsequent trains will be carried out by a party of 2 Officers and 100 O.R. to be previously detailed by O.C.,2nd in the Queen's Regt. This party will report to the Brigade in for on the arrival of the 2nd train at the detraining station, and will be billetted in the vicinity of the station until the completion of the detachment. O.C., 2nd Bn. The Queen's Regt. will arrange that this party has 2 days rations in hand (in addition to the Iron Ration) on detraining.

8. Where units are divided between two trains and vehicles and animals are similarly divided the division of vehicles will be arranged so that the number of units in each half will be the same.

9. O.C. 91st Machine Gun Company will provide the sanitary squad, with the necessary appliances,referred to in para.6 of Divisional medical arrangements for Train No.1. O.C. 21st Field Ambulance will provide that for Train No.2.

Copies to -
2nd Queen's Regt.
1st S.Staffs Regt.
21st Manchester Regt.
22nd Manchester Regt.
91st Machine Gun Co.
No.3 Coy., Div. Train.
528 (Durham) Fld.Co.,R.E.
21st Field Ambulance.
24th Manchester Regt.
7th Division "Q".
Brigade Major.
Major R.Miles, R.N.Z.A.
Supply Officer
Bde.Transport Officer.
Bde.Qr.Mr.Sgt.

A.J.Captain,
Staff Captain,91st Infantry Brigade.
15th November,1917.

SECRET.   Appx VIII   Copy No. 19

91st Infantry Brigade Order No.36.

Reference Maps – VERONA-PADOVA – Scale 1/200,000.
                 FERRARA – Scale 1/200,000.

27th November, 1917.
-:-:-:-:-:-:-:-:-:-

91st Inf.   1.   The 91st Infantry Brigade Group, consisting of the
Bde.H.Q.   marginally named units, will move to the BARBARANO
2nd Queen's R   area to-morrow, November 28th, 1917 as under. The march
1st S.Staffs.R   will probably be continued on the following day.
21st Manch.R
22nd Manch.R   2.   (a) 1st Bn. South Staffordshire Regt., to MOSSANO. To
91st M.G.Coy.   be clear of CAMPIGLIA by 9.a.m.
No.3.Coy.   (b) 21st Bn. Manchester Regt., to BARBARANO. To be
Div.Train.   clear of POJANA by 9.a.m. Route via SOSSANO.
528th Field Coy.   (c) 22nd Bn. Manchester Regt., to BARBARANO. To be
54th Field Coy.   clear of POJANA by 8-45.a.m. Route via SOSSANO.
22nd T.M.Bty.   (d) 91st Machine Gun Coy., to PONTE di BARBARANO. To
21st Field Amb   be clear of AGUGLIARO by 9-15.a.m.
                      (e) No.3.Company, 7th Divisional Train to PONTE di
                      BARBARANO. To be clear of AGUGLIARO by 9-25.a.m.
                      (f) 91st Infantry Brigade Headquarters to PONTE di
                      BARBARANO. To be clear of AGUGLIARO by 9-30.a.m.
                      (g) 528th (Durham) Field Coy. R.E., to VILLAGA via
                      SOSSANO. To enter POJANA at 9-5.a.m.
                      (h) 21st Field Ambulance to VILLAGA via SOSSANO. To
                      enter POJANA at 9-15.a.m.
*   (i) 54th Field Coy. R.E., to VILLAGA via SOSSANO.*
54th Field Coy.
& 22nd L.T.M.Bty.   (k) 22nd Light Trench Mortar Battery to VILLAGA via
to be clear of   SOSSANO.*
line CAMPIGLIA
- ORGIANO by   3.   Units will march closed up, and will halt for
9-30.a.m.   the last ten minutes of each hour.

                4.   The Officer Commanding, 21st Field Ambulance will
                      arrange to patrol the road with a motor ambulance in
                      rear of the column passing through POJANA.

                5.   (a) Billetting parties from 21st Field Ambulance,
                      54th and 528th Field Coys. R.E., and 22nd Light Trench
                      Mortar Battery, will meet the Staff Captain at the
                      Church VILLAGA at 9.a.m.
                      (b) 22nd Bn. Manchester Regt., will take over billets
                      vacated by 20th Bn. Manchester Regt., in BARBARANO.
                      (c) 21st Bn. Manchester Regt., will similarly take
                      over billets of 2nd Bn. Border Regt.
                      (d) 91st Machine Gun Coy., and No.3.Coy., 7th Div.
                      Train will take over billets vacated by corresponding
                      Units of 20th Infantry Brigade.
                      (e) Brigades concerned have been requested to leave
                      rear parties to facilitate (b) (c) and (d) above.

                6.   (a) One lorry will be sent to Headquarters 1st Bn.
                      South Staffordshire Regt., at 8-30.a.m., to convey
                      blankets to MOSSANO. It will then return to
                      Headquarters 22nd Bn. Manchester Regt., POJANA to
                      convey blankets of that Battalion to BARBARANO,
                      returning to Brigade Headquarters by 8-30.p.m.
                      (b) One lorry will report to Headquarters, 21st Bn.
                      Manchester Regt., at 8-30.a.m., to be at disposal of
                      that Battalion throughout the day, returning to
                      Brigade Headquarters by 8-30.p.m.
                                              (c) O.C., 54th Field/

-2-

(c) The Officer Commanding, 34th Field Coy.R.E., is responsible for providing transport for that portion of the stores of 22nd Light Trench Mortar Battery which cannot be carried on the handcarts of that Unit.

7. Brigade Headquarters will close at AGUGLIANO at 9.a.m., and open at PONTE di BARBARANO at 12.noon.

8. ACKNOWLEDGE.

Morshead

Captain,

Brigade Major, 91st Infantry Brigade.

Issued at 7/30.p.m. to

Copy No 1 2nd Queen's R
2 1st S.Staffs.R
3 21st Manch.R
4 22nd Manch.R
5 91st M.G.Coy.
6 No.3.Sec.7th Div.Sig.Coy.
7 Staff Captain.
8 Bde.Transport Officer.
9 21st Field Ambulance.
10 528th (Durham) Field Coy.
11 Supply Officer.
12 No.3.Coy.Div.Train.
13 54th Field Coy,R.E.
14 22nd L.T.M.Bty.
15 20th Inf.Bde.
16 22nd Inf.Bde.
17 7th Division.
18 File.
19 War Diary.
20 War Diary.

SECRET.

Appx IX

Copy No. 16

91st Infantry Brigade Order No.37.

Reference Map - PADOVA - Scale 1/100,000.

29th November, 1917.

-:-:-:-:-:-:-:-:-:-

1. The 91st Infantry Brigade Group, composed as under, will move to the VILLAFRANCA Area to-morrow, November 30th, 1917.

2. (a) The following table gives the destination of Units and times of reaching the starting point (Cross Roads 3 kilometres E. of PONTE di NANTO):-

Unit.	Destination.	Time.
22nd Bn.Manchester Regt.	VILLAFRANCA.	10-30.a.m.
1st Bn.S.Staffs.Regt.	PIAZZOLA.	10-40.a.m.
2nd Bn.Queen's Regt.	PIAZZOLA.	10-50.a.m.
21st Bn.Manchester Regt.	VILLAFRANCA.	11-10.a.m.
No.3.Coy. 7th Div.Train.	VILLAFRANCA.	11-20.a.m.
91st Machine Gun Coy.	CAMISANO.	11-25.a.m.
91st Inf.Bde.Headquarters.	CAMISANO.	11-30.a.m.
24th Bn.Manchester Regt.	CAMISANO.	11-35.a.m.
528th (Durham) Field Coy.R.E.	CAMPODORO.	11-45.a.m.
21st Field Ambulance.	CAMPODORO.	11-50.a.m.

(b) All Units will march to the starting point via PONTE di NANTO.

3. In addition to the hourly halt, a halt for dinners will be observed by all Units from 12-30.p.m., to 2.p.m.

4. Battalion Commanders (less Officer Commanding, 24th Bn. Manchester Regt.) and Officer Commanding, 91st Machine Gun Coy. will meet the Brigadier at the starting point at 10-25.a.m.

5. Lorries will report as under :-
(a) One to Headquarters, 1st Bn.South Staffordshire Regt., at 8.a.m., to proceed to PIAZZOLA and return to Headquarters, 22nd Bn.Manchester Regt.
(b) One to Headquarters, 21st Bn.Manchester Regt., at 8.a.m., to proceed to VILLAFRANCA and return to Headquarters, 2nd Bn. Queen's Regt.
(c) One journey only will be made per Battalion, on completion of which lorries will return to Brigade Headquarters, CAMISANO.

6. Billetting parties will report as under :-
(a) From 24th Bn.Manchester Regt., and 91st Machine Gun Coy., to Staff Captain at the Church CAMISANO at 10-30.a.m.
(b) From 2nd Bn.Queen's Regt., and 1st Bn.South Staffordshire Regt., to Brigade Signal Officer at the Church PIAZZOLA at 10-30.a.m.
(c) From 21st and 22nd Bns.The Manchester Regt., and No.3.Coy. Div.Train, to Major MACFARLANE, Brigade Headquarters, at the Church VILLAFRANCA at 10.a.m.
(d) Officers Commanding, 21st Field Ambulance and 528th (Durham) Field Coy.R.E., will arrange mutually regarding billetting in CAMPODORO.

7. The Officer Commanding, 21st Field Ambulance will arrange to patrol the road in rear of the column.

8. A watch is circulated herewith to Units concerned.

9. Brigade Headquarters/

9.   Brigade Headquarters will close at PONTE di BARBARINO at 9-30.a.m., and open at CAMISANO at 4-30.p.m.

10. ACKNOWLEDGE.

—:—:—:—:—:—:—:—:—

Captain,
Brigade Major, 91st Infantry Brigade.

Issued at .. p.m. to

Copy No 1 2nd Queen's R
         2 1st S.Staffs.R
         3 21st Manch.R
         4 22nd Manch.R
         5 91st M.G.Coy.
         6 No.3.Sec. 7th Div. Sig.Coy.
         7 Staff Captain.
         8 Bde. Transport Officer.
         9 21st Field Ambulance.
        10 528th (Durham) Fd.Coy.R.E.
        11 Supply Officer.
        12 No.3. Coy. Div. Train.
        13 24th Manch.R
        14 7th Division.
        15 File.
        16 War Diary.
        17 War Diary.

www.ingramcontent.com/pod-product-compliance
Lightning Source LLC
Chambersburg PA
CBHW081434300426
44108CB00016BA/2365